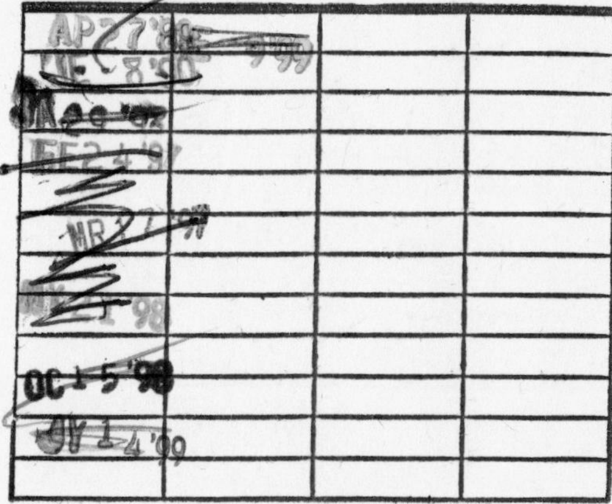

An Introduction to

TWENTIETH CENTURY MUSIC

Fourth Edition

The twentieth century is more splendid than the nineteenth century, certainly it is much more splendid. The twentieth century has much less reasonableness in its existence than the nineteenth century but reasonableness does not make for splendor. The seventeenth century had less reason in its existence than the sixteenth century and in consequence it has more splendor. So the twentieth century is that, it is a time when everything cracks, where everything is destroyed, everything isolates itself, it is a more splendid thing than a period where everything follows itself. So then the twentieth century is a splendid period, not a reasonable one in the scientific sense, but splendid. The phenomena of nature are more splendid than the daily events of nature, certainly, so then the twentieth century is splendid.

Gertrude Stein

An Introduction to

Twentieth Century Music

Fourth Edition

Peter S. Hansen

Newcomb College, Tulane University

Allyn and Bacon, Inc.
Boston/London/Sydney/Toronto

Library of Congress Cataloging in Publication Data

Hansen, Peter S

An introduction to twentieth century music.

1. Music — History and criticism — 20th century.
2. Music — Analysis, appreciation. I. Title.

ML197.H25 1977 780'.904 77–9296

ISBN 0–205–05921–X

Sources of photographs appearing in chapter openings:

Page 10 Permission S.P.A.D.E.M. 1971 by French Reproduction Rights, Inc.

34 Compix/United Press International, New York.

56 Copyright 1953 Richard Fish, Encino, Calif.

78 La Galleria Nazionale d'Arte Moderna, Rome.

84 Broadcast Music, Inc. (B.M.I.) Archives.

98 Archive of New Orleans Jazz, Tulane University Library—from *New Orleans Jazz: A Family Album* (Louisiana State University Press, 1967).

108 Photo by Roger-Voillet, Paris. (Shown are: from left, standing, Milhaud, Auric, Honegger, Tailleferre, Poulenc, and Durey. Cocteau is at the piano.)

124 Wide World Photos, Inc., New York.

148 Columbia Records Photo.

170 Bettmann Archive, Inc.

192 Bettmann Archive, Inc.

230 Boosey and Hawkes.

246 Broadcast Music, Inc. (B.M.I.) Archives.

256 Bettmann Archive, Inc.

274 Oxford University Press.

288 Bettmann Archive, Inc. (Shown are: at left, Virgil Thomson; at right, standing, Herbert Elwell; sitting, Walter Piston and Aaron Copland.)

316 Photo by Susanna Schapowalow, Hamburg.

322 Nordisk, from Pictorial Parade, Inc., New York.

328 Courtesy of Boosey and Hawkes.

370 Courtesy of Boosey and Hawkes.

408 News release, public domain.

412 Courtesy of SESAC, Inc., New York.

Contents

Part Two: 1920–1950

Preface

THE PURPOSE OF THIS BOOK is to present the main lines of development of twentieth-century music through a study of selected compositions by its most influential composers. The author assumes that the reader has some knowledge of the mainstream of music and an understanding of its underlying principles (such as tonality, harmony, form, etc.), since the new style traits are outgrowths of this more familiar music. On the other hand, extensive technical knowledge is not necessary in using this book.

In surveying the era and attempting to evaluate its musical achievements, one finds that the first half of the twentieth century has as many shifting patterns and designs as a kaleidoscope. To impose a definitive pattern is impossible at this time, and the different books devoted to the subject reflect various points of view. Some books supply us with a year-by-year recording of events, while others describe musical activities within geographical boundaries. Still others discuss the period by writing biographies of composers, analyzing significant compositions, or by defining certain aspects of music theory. All of these approaches are valid and helpful.

This book seeks to treat the principal factors involved — personalities, chronology, style — in a manner that shows various interrelations as well as fundamental trends in the development of the art. The special problem in writing contemporary cultural history is the necessity of making judgments about persons, events, and works of art that have not yet stood the test of time — the only true criterion of aesthetic value. As a result it is inevitable that there will be differences of opinion concerning emphasis and proportion in a book such as this and that the final decisions will be more personal than if one were making a survey, say, of the music of the first half of the sixteenth century. The author has been guided by his experiences with, and predilections for, twentieth-century music and by the decision to limit his discussion to those composers who have been most influential in this period.

The underlying organization is chronological, as evidenced by the three main divisions: 1900–1920; 1920–1950; and 1950–1975. As the first World War lasted from 1914 to 1918 and the second from 1941 to 1945, these divisions correspond roughly to the pre-World War I period, the period between the two world wars, and the post-World War II period. Within these large divisions, the contributions of individual composers are described against a background of their particular cultural environments. This is not the neatest possible plan, since some of the composers who have lived through all three periods are encountered in more than one chapter; yet it has the advantage of serving the author's broad purpose of showing large trends and period styles, as well as introducing important compositions in their period settings. The chronological charts spaced throughout the book will aid the reader in associating simultaneous events sometimes described in widely separated chapters, and the chronological list of composers will show still other relationships to composers mentioned in no other place in the book.

The various approaches employed — chronological, cultural-historical, biographical, analytical — have but one aim: to give the reader insights, understanding, and increased enjoyment of twentieth-century music. All of the compositions discussed have been recorded. These recordings should be available and should be carefully listened to, for nothing is more futile than to read about music unheard in performance.

Preface to the Fourth Edition

IN THE SEVENTEEN YEARS SINCE this book first appeared much has happened in the world of music. New composers and movements have become important, while some of the older composers and movements have lost ground. This fourth edition reflects these changes. Part II (1920–1950) has been abridged somewhat, while Part III (1950–1975) has been expanded. Biographies and chronological charts have been brought up to date and bibliographies have been expanded to include recent important books and articles. As in earlier editions, generalities have been avoided as much as possible by giving attention to specific compositions that are especially important.

The author is indebted to his students and colleagues in the Music Department at Newcomb College, Tulane University, for many helpful suggestions. Special acknowledgments are made to the following individuals:

Mr. Lehman Engel, New York, for permission to quote from a letter written to him by Charles Ives.

Mrs. Frederick W. Knize, New York, for permission to include a reproduction of the portrait of Schoenberg painted by Kokoschka.

Mr. Rollo Myers, London, for permission to make citations from his translation of Cocteau's *Coq et Harlequin*.

Mrs. Gertrud Schoenberg, Los Angeles, for permission to make citations from Arnold Schoenberg's works.

The late Igor Stravinsky, for permission to make citations from his published writings and for the revisions and clarifications of passages of his *Conversations* made for this book.

Acknowledgment is also made to the various music publishers for permission to make citations from scores.

P.S.H.

An Introduction to

Twentieth Century Music

Fourth Edition

1900 · 1920

Part One

Wagner

1

Richard Wagner stands before my eyes suffering and great as that nineteenth century whose complete expression he is.

Thomas Mann

Nineteenth Century Background

MOST OF THE PEOPLE WHO heard the first performances of *Pelléas et Mélisande* (1902), *Pierrot Lunaire* (1912), and *Le Sacre du printemps* (1913) believed they were witnessing a brutal assault on musical sensitivity, intelligence, and morality. It seemed as if the continuum of music history had been broken and that the rich beauties of the past had been replaced by willful and capricious ugliness. Impressed by what they considered a complete change in style, critics spoke of *neue Musik*, new music, just as their predecessors of 1600 and 1300, also times of style change, had spoken of *nuove musiche* and *ars nova*.

Now that three quarters of the twentieth century have passed, we hear this music with different ears. What seemed to be unplanned cacophony we now accept without a shudder, and the various idioms that were so shocking have been analyzed and systematized in textbooks. Furthermore, we now realize that the continuum of history was not broken: Debussy, Stravinsky, and Schoenberg each developed in a particular musical environment, and their music is as much a result of their having been born at a certain time and place as is Beethoven's or Palestrina's.

Because of this close connection with the immediate past, the discussions of the composers and styles of twentieth-century music will be preceded by a short survey of the music of the nineteenth. Because a comprehensive discussion of the nineteenth century is obviously inappropriate to this book, the purpose of this survey is only to reacquaint the reader with the musical environment into which composers of twentieth-century music were born and in which they developed.

Nineteenth-century music extends from Beethoven to Wagner. This period was, of course, the century of romanticism, and music, the most romantic of all the arts, assumed a dominating position and acquired a listening public far surpassing that which it had enjoyed in earlier times. Instead of being associated almost entirely with church or court, music became one of the most prized possessions of the new middle class. People of the day performed music for their own pleasure as never before, whether as amateur pianists playing the *Songs Without Words* or four-hand arrangements of Mozart symphonies, or as parlor singers rendering one of the hundreds of love songs that were published at the time, or as members of a municipal chorus. For listeners, too, an opportunity to hear symphonies and operas as well as glamorous virtuosos was provided by the public concerts that, for the first time, were given in large numbers.

The Position of Beethoven

Beethoven is the great figure towering over all nineteenth-century music, and his influence was so enormous that it was felt by the most distant of his followers. Both Wagner and Brahms, for instance, no matter how different their ideals, could claim to be his heir. The composer of music dramas looked to the last movement of the Ninth Symphony as evidence that instrumental music needed words in order to be truly expressive, while Brahms, who had actually been hailed as the third "B," found it natural to write most of his works in Beethoven's favorite modes of organization, the sonata and variation forms.

Beethoven's technical contributions to the art of music can be summarized in the word *expansion*, for he pushed open all of the dimensions of music. He exploited extremes of pitch, both high and low, and extremes of dynamics, both loud and soft. His compositions are longer, his rhythms are stronger and more complex, and his palette of orchestral color is more varied than that of any composer of the eighteenth century.

As a result of this expansion, his music became a powerful expression of individual, personal feeling, and it is the development and exploitation of this function of music which is perhaps Beethoven's greatest legacy. We commonly speak of his music as being *noble, tragic, boisterous, dramatic,* and although the words are not the exact equivalents of the expression of the music, they continue to be used with meaning. Much of Beethoven's music is *serious,* and both he and Wagner censured Mozart for having written an opera based on so trivial and immoral a story as *Don Giovanni.* They believed that music was an art that should elevate and ennoble its listeners and therefore should not be used for lesser purposes.

Wagner, for instance, did not write his music dramas to provide an evening's casual entertainment. He insisted that the *Ring* should be performed not in a traditional opera house, but in a shrine of its own away from any commercial atmosphere, to which pilgrims would come for spiritual elevation, following the pattern of the ancient Greeks attending their annual rites. After the Festspielhaus was built in Bayreuth, for several years he restricted the performances of *Parsifal* to this sacred auditorium. It is significant that an enthusiastic audience that accepted Wagner's terms attended the opening performances in 1876. Many of those present had prepared themselves for the experience by memorizing the leitmotifs (the musical themes associated with characters and situations in the operas), and it is said that some devotees went so far as to fast before the performances in order to be in a sufficiently elevated mood.

Importance of Wagnerian Music Drama

The fact that it was opera that demanded such respect (opera of the particular kind that Wagner wrote) points up another strong tendency of nineteenth-century music—its growing ties with literature. Here the line of Beethoven (of the Ninth Symphony)-Berlioz-Liszt-Wagner is clear, for each added to the notion that music is somehow better if it tells a story, paints a picture, or describes a character. Although the symphonic poem, the character piece for piano, and the lied accomplished this very well, it was opera that provided the perfect setting for bringing together all the arts. The ideal of the *Gesamtkunstwerk* (collective art work) was to combine poetry, gesture, movement, and color with music in order to make a product greater than the sum of the parts. This breaking down of the boundaries of the arts was a typically romantic obsession.

Other Trends

In the preceding résumé of nineteenth-century music, only the more spectacular and progressive tendencies have been mentioned. Since the state of music is never entirely consistent at any time, it should not be forgotten that the ideals of absolute (nonprogrammatic) music persisted in the chamber works and symphonies of Schumann, Brahms, and Bruckner.

Toward the end of the century, another group of composers, called the nationalists—such men as Smetana, Dvořák, Grieg, and the Russian "Five" (Balakirev, Borodin, Moussorgsky, Cui, and Rimsky-Korsakov)—made strong contributions to music with their folk-inspired melodies, rhythms, and colorful orchestrations.

Style Characteristics

ORCHESTRATION

Because of technical advances in the art, music became expressive in a new way. However, the converse of the statement is equally true; that is, the powerful feelings experienced by the composers demanded new sounds and technical advances for their expression. Among these was the vastly expanded and more richly colorful orchestra. Again the line is Beethoven-Berlioz-Liszt-Wagner, with some important side contributions from von Weber and Mendelssohn.

The change in sound from the orchestra of Haydn and Mozart is to be accounted for by the addition of new instruments—trombones, English horns, harps, bass clarinets—and by the greater number of instruments. For example, Wagner wrote for eight horns compared with Haydn's two, and Berlioz's dream orchestra consisted of 467 performers, compared with the 30-odd performers in Haydn's orchestra.

To think of nineteenth-century music is to think of expressive tone color —the oboe and clarinet duets in the second movement of Schubert's *Unfinished,* the horn call at the beginning of his Seventh Symphony, the same instruments in the overture to *Oberon,* the trio of horns in the "Nocturne" of the *Midsummer Night's Dream* music, the English horn solo in the third movement of the *Fantastic Symphony* and its duet with the oboe, the timpani in the "March to the Scaffold"—the list is endless. Wagner above all is particularly rich in moments of magical tone color—the cellos at the beginning of *Tristan,* the horns in Act II, the mournful English horn in Act III, the brilliance of the "Ride of the Valkyries," the ebullience of Siegfried's horn call—again the list is endless.

CHROMATIC HARMONY

Music became more colorful in another sense, too, with the growing complexity of its chords and chordal relationships. Here practically every composer of the nineteenth century made a contribution: Schubert, with his alternating and mixing of major and minor modes; Chopin, with his splashes of nonharmonic chromatic tones, sometimes unresolved; or Liszt, with his use of augmented chords and exploitations of augmented fourth relationships.

Once again, it was Wagner who developed this enriched harmony to the limits of possibility. *Tristan und Isolde* is generally accepted as being the apex of chromatic harmony; from its first measure to its last, the freely altered chords make a shimmering, amorphous, ever-changing tissue of sound, ideally suited to the expression of the surging passions of the drama. Freedom in modulation is also fully developed here, and in great sections of the opera there is no clear establishment of key. Fluctuation from key to key is the normal state of affairs, and final cadences usually occur only at the ends of acts.

PSYCHOLOGICAL FORM

Through the process of evading cadences, Wagner was able to write music of unheard-of breadth, continuous for long periods. In these extended, continuous forms, which were used in the symphonic poem and romantic piano music as well, virtually no respect was paid to the forms of organization that had shaped so much of the music of the preceding century. Instead of sonata forms, rondos, or minuets and trios, a type of organization best described as *psychological form* came into being. By this is meant that the musical composition—be it a symphonic poem, a sonata by Liszt, or an act of an opera—is shaped by dramatic, rather than by strictly musical considerations. Unity was often achieved through the use of theme transformation. Whether it was called the *idée fixe*, a leitmotif, or a characteristic phrase, the theme that had special significance and was transformed as the composition progressed became the means by which many musical compositions were held together.

Romantic Composers in Society

The composers in the Beethoven-Wagner line played a role in society that was vastly different from the role played by their predecessors. As "free" artists, i.e. unemployed, they wrote as their inspirations dictated and not in fulfillment of contractual obligations. Bach, Haydn, and Mozart wrote most of their compositions to order; but Beethoven wrote nine symphonies and thirty-two piano sonatas, along with many other works, because he was inclined to do so. Bach's cantatas were written because he needed new music to perform, but Wagner's operas were written when there was little probability that they would ever be staged. As a result of this freedom from external conditioning, the romantic composer gave full rein to his musical imagination. Not stopping to ask if his compositions were playable or not, he immeasurably enriched the vocabulary and dimensions of music.

Moreover, the "free" artist of the nineteenth century was able to indulge in personal idiosyncrasies. Beethoven could live in disorder and confusion; Schubert could live in a state of unashamed irresponsibility; Liszt could theatrically flout middle-class morality; Wagner, as the *grand seigneur*, could ride over everyone in egomania; these were prerogatives of romantic composers.

The Relation of the Nineteenth Century to the Twentieth

Subsequent events have proven that the composers of the late nineteenth century were the culminating figures of romantic music because their fulfillment of romantic ideals was so complete that a change in ideal and style would inevitably follow them.

To find the direction of this change was the task of the next generation whose leaders were Debussy, Stravinsky, and Schoenberg—all of whom were born between 1862 and 1882. These men were Janus-faced. Each had deep roots in his respective national heritage and each grew up in the heyday of Wagner and colorful nationalism, a heritage evident in their early works. As they matured in the new century they developed their own highly original and influential styles, partly as a continuation of romanticism, and partly as a reaction against it. Their contributions will be described in the chapters immediately following.

Suggested Readings

An excellent study of nineteenth-century music is Alfred Einstein's *Music in the Romantic Era* (New York, 1947). Two later books are Rey Longyear's *Nineteenth-Century Romanticism in Music* (Englewood Cliffs, 1969) and "The Romantic Period," from the eight-volume *Oxford History of Music* (New York, 1973). Three books showing the continuity of nineteenth and twentieth-century music are *A Hundred Years of Music* by Gerald Abraham (New York, 1938), *A Century of Music* by John Culshaw (London, 1952), and *Romanticism and the 20th Century* by Wilfred Mellers (London, 1957).

Debussy

2

Music should humbly seek to please: within these limits great beauty may well be found. Extreme complication is contrary to art. Beauty must appeal to the senses, must provide us with immediate enjoyment, must impress us or insinuate itself into us without any effort on our part.

Claude Debussy

Paris

PARIS HAS ALWAYS BEEN MORE than a settlement of people living on the banks of the Seine, for throughout the ages it has symbolized many things—the vigor of the Middle Ages, the elegance of the Renaissance, the splendor of the Baroque, the enthusiasm of the Romantic Period, the *dernier cri* of our day. In period after period the artistic creators of the world have found Paris a congenial place in which to work, and since the days of Abelard it has been a mecca for students.

In the early years of the twentieth century Paris was in a very mellow mood. It was a time of peace—the scars of 1870 were forgotten and new friendship with Russia augured well for the future. It was a time of prosperity in general, and prosperity in particular for those who had stock in the Suez Canal Company or Russian railroads. Paris became a new symbol, this time one of luxury and sophisticated sensuality—a place where enjoyment of life, food, and the fine arts was of prime concern.

Fin de Siècle—Symbolism and Impressionism

The expression *fin de siècle,* originally applied to the 1890s, not only names a decade but also describes a mood or attitude toward life which prevailed until the outbreak of the First World War in 1914, when the nineteenth-century way of life finally came to an end. The term connotes an attitude of decadence and overrefinement, and suggests a time when youthful enthusiasm and striving to improve had been supplanted by exquisite sensitivity and self-indulgence. It implies ripeness rather than vigor, and pagan rather than puritan attitudes. Des Esseintes, the hero of Huysman's novel *Against the Grain*, is an exaggerated portrait, to be sure, but nevertheless he is the typical man of the time who lives only for the stimulation and gratification of his senses. He has no regard for his fellow man and no moral sense. Life for him is a matter of feeling textures, smelling fragrances, and hearing sounds. He is a superlatively refined animal.

Symbolist poets—especially Verlaine, Mallarmé, and Jules Laforgue—and impressionist painters such as Monet, Pissaro, Sisley, and Renoir helped to sharpen the senses of their contemporaries. The poets became increasingly sensitive to the sound of words, often at the expense of clarity of statement. They aimed primarily at establishing vague and evanescent moods through the sheer sound and rhythm of their verses and avoided all attempts to tell a story or underline a moral. The painters also avoided anecdotal or historically realistic subjects in order to concentrate on the effects of light in nature. Subject matter became unimportant, while color, broken up into small patches to achieve a vibrant quality, became the chief interest. Monet's successive paintings of a haystack and the portico of the cathedral of Rouen at different hours of the day, revealing the subtle changes of color, show wherein his interest lay. Formal composition in painting became as unimportant as subject matter in poetry.

Debussy, 1862–1918

Debussy, the composer who best expressed the impressionist-symbolist ideal in music, was no more interested in the grand gesture and the dramatic moment than was Monet in painting scenes of crisis. Because Debussy's aim was the creation of exquisite, evocative sounds, he sought the *ton juste* (precise sound) as diligently as Flaubert sought the *mot juste* (precise word).

Debussy was born in St. Germain-en-Laye, a suburb of Paris, to the wife of a shopkeeper. As a young child he took lessons from a neighborhood piano teacher who had been a pupil of Chopin. Debussy's talent and aptitude were so pronounced that, following the long-established route of the musically gifted in France, he entered the Conservatoire in 1873. Here he was known as a brilliant pianist and also as a disturbing element in the theory classes, because he was more interested in playing shocking chords than he was in writing conventional harmony exercises.

When nineteen years old, he was engaged by Madame von Meck, the Croesus-rich Russian widow, the patroness and "unknown beloved" of Tchaikovsky, as musical tutor for her children and as a general house-musician. He lived with the family for a short time in Italy and later in Russia and Austria. In 1884 he won the coveted Prix de Rome and spent the next year and a half in Rome composing, and counting the days until he could return to his beloved Paris. He did this in 1887 and, except for short trips to London, Vienna, and Bayreuth, remained there until his death in 1918, composing, writing music criticism, and editing piano music for Durand, the music publisher.

An intimate friend of symbolist poets and impressionist painters, he frequented the famous Thursday afternoon symposia at the home of Mallarmé, the poet. He collected Oriental *objets d'art* and was unusually fond of the color green. In his early years he showed his disdain for middle-class conformity by wearing outlandish clothes (including a western-style Stetson) and by his stormy personal life. He became more conservative, however, after his election to the Institut de France, the ultimate honor his country pays to her most distinguished citizens, and after his growing recognition as a composer. His last years were plagued by ill health, and he died as the Germans were cannonading Paris in 1918. Not only did his life span two eras, but also his music served as one of the most significant bridges between the nineteenth and twentieth centuries.

Musical Background

What was the musical environment of a composer growing up in *fin-de-siècle* Paris? At the Conservatoire, Debussy received a thorough, academic training based on eighteenth- and early nineteenth-century music. He was well grounded in Bach, Mozart, and Beethoven, and as a pianist he played Chopin, Liszt, and Schumann.

The successful French composers of the day were those who wrote operas. Gounod, Massenet, Delibes, and Thomas were the men who enjoyed acclaim and official recognition. Their operas were predominantly lyrical, tuneful, sentimental, and carefully scored so that the orchestra would not overpower the typically small French voices. The librettos of these works were frequently sophisticated and daring (*Manon* and *Hérodiade*, for example), which added to their popular appeal. They were written to provide an evening's entertainment, and because the music was lovely and unobtrusive their success was inevitable. Although Debussy did not write any operas in this vein, he was too much of a Frenchman not to be aware of the charm, grace, and elegance embodied in these scores.

Another of the sources strongly influencing Debussy's style was the music of the Russian nationalists that he heard at a series of concerts conducted by Rimsky-Korsakov at the Paris Exposition in 1889. This exotic, brilliantly orchestrated music was a revelation to the young French composer. The Exposition provided another sound world that stimulated him—the music of the Gamelan orchestra which played in the Far East pavilion. The intricate rhythms, the hypnotic web of sound, and the pentatonic scales left their mark on his compositions.

The music of Moussorgsky also had a powerful effect on the formation of Debussy's style. He had a score of *Boris Godounov,* a rather famous copy that had been brought back from Russia by Saint-Saëns. It passed from hand to hand among a small circle in Paris, making a deep impression on Debussy and others because of its great originality. Here he found rhythmic and harmonic freedom unlike anything he had seen before. Unresolved dissonances, modal melodies, frequent meter changes, pedal points, ostinatos, and bell sonorities in the orchestra—all of these made *Boris* a magic garden of fascinating, seductive sound.

Perhaps the strongest influence was "that old sorcerer" Richard Wagner, whose conquest of France began in 1887 with the first performance of *Lohengrin* in Paris. In 1893 *Die Walküre* was given and a group of enthusiasts, including Baudelaire, became active propagandists; the Wagnerian ideal of combining the arts into a new synthesis was close to their aim of bringing words, music, and color into new intimacies. Many French aesthetes traveled to Vienna, Munich, or Bayreuth to hear the music dramas, and the scores were studied intensely by others who stayed at home.

Young Debussy shared this enthusiasm. He made his Bayreuth pilgrimages and many of his early works, such as the songs *Cinq poèmes de Baudelaire,* show unmistakable traces of Wagner's harmonic style. Later, as he developed a more personal idiom, he became increasingly critical of Wagner and held up the French ideal of *clarté et concision* (clarity and conciseness) against the opulence of the German's music. Nevertheless, the fact that he continued to write about Wagner in his critical essays shows that he was always aware of his adversary. In a letter written during the time he was working on *Pelléas et Mélisande,* he complained of his difficulties: "And worst of all, the ghost of old Klingsor, alias R. Wagner, appeared at a turning of one of the bars so I tore up the whole thing and set off in search of some more characteristic compound of phrases."[1]

This, then, was the background of the composer who opened the door to the new century. Firmly rooted in the tradition of French music, and building from the style of his immediate environment, he created a musical language of the highest originality and beauty, a language that was to leave its mark on many of the composers who were to follow.

Debussy's Compositions

This language was not achieved all at once. The style of a composer is not fixed and static; it develops and changes gradually, much as a human personality passes erratically and imperceptibly from childhood through adolescence to maturity. Style periods are not rigid, watertight compartments sealed off from one another, containing strongly contrasting material. They are simply a convenience in discussing a composer's works. For the sake of convenience, therefore, Debussy's compositions will be discussed in three periods.

PERIOD 1: 1884–1900

The most important of the early works are:

CANTATAS

L'Enfant prodigue (*The Prodigal Son*; 1884)
La Damoiselle élue (*The Blessed Damozel*; 1888)

ORCHESTRAL

Prélude à l'après-midi d'un faune (*Prelude to the Afternoon of a Faun*; 1894)
Nocturnes. I. Nuages. II. Fêtes. III. Sirènes. (1893–99)

PIANO

Deux Arabesques (1888)
Suite bergamasque. I. Prélude. II. Menuet. III. Claire de Lune. IV. Passepied. (1890–1905)
Pour le piano. I. Prélude. II. Sarabande. III. Toccata. (1896–1901)

SONGS

Cinq poèmes de Baudelaire (1889)
Ariettes oubliées (1888)
Fêtes galantes (1892)
Chansons de Bilitis (1899)

CHAMBER MUSIC

String Quartet (1893)

In these well-known compositions one can trace Debussy's transition from a talented young composer of salon pieces to his emergence as a composer with a highly personal and original style. The influence of Massenet is strong in the two cantatas and the *Suite bergamasque* for piano, which includes "*Clair de lune*." As this well-known piece testifies, Debussy's music at this time was delicate, charming, and occasionally sentimental.

The String Quartet is more sharply chiselled. Organized in cyclic form, which attracted so many composers of this period, it is unified by a motto theme that undergoes numerous transformations. Of note are the pert syncopations in this theme, the flowing figurations, the pizzicatos and rhythmic complexities

Debussy and Stravinsky, 1911
The Bettmann Archive

of the second movement, the muted sonorities of the third, and the dissonances and excitement of the last. It is a composition of strongly personal imprint.

Perhaps the most important piece of this early period is *L'après-midi d'un faune,* which is flawlessly executed. Many of the sounds of the impressionist orchestra are revealed here in the languid flute solos, the swirl of the harp, the pianissimo chords of the four horns, and the poignant oboe solos. The over-all form of the piece is ternary, with the melodic D-flat portion forming the middle section. The two outer sections are dominated by the opening flute melody which appears ten times altogether, each time with a different harmonization and rhythm. Here is the original melody and one of the variants, showing that Debussy, along with other composers of his time, was interested in theme transformation.

EXAMPLE 1

The suite *Pour le piano* is more courageous in its harmonic vocabulary. In the *"Prélude"* there are striking passages of parallel augmented chords and whole-tone scales, and in the modal *"Sarabande"* chords are "blurred" by the addition of unresolved seconds.

The songs that Debussy wrote before 1900 should not be overlooked, for they established a new type of art song as different from the dramatic and highly charged lieder of German composers as it is from the simple melodies of the earlier French composers. Debussy usually set the verses of the decadent poets, and like the poems, the songs are often fragmentary, elusive, erotic, and atmospheric. There are no melodies in the sense of tunes-to-remember, for the vocal lines rise and fall subtly with the words.

Chansons de Bilitis, a setting of three poems by Pierre Louÿs, a friend of the composer, will be described to show some of the characteristic features of his songs. The first and last, *"La Flûte de Pan"* and *"Le Tombeau des Naïades,"* have a pseudo-antique flavor reminiscent of the subdued murals painted by Puvis de Chavannes in the Sorbonne and the Pantheon. The strictly syllabic setting of the words and conjunct melodies immediately proclaim the style (see Example 2). The first song is unified by the Lydian scale, suggesting the syrinx of the poem, heard in the introduction and again in the middle and in the postlude. Arpeggio figurations, reflecting the words, appear from time to time. The harmonies are very rich, particularly in the middle section where chains of parallel ninth and thirteenth chords fluctuate beneath the voice line. The third song of the set is similar in style, although here the solemnity of the poem is reflected in the constant sixteenth-note figure of the accompaniment. The second song, *"La Chevelure,"* is more personal and dramatic in its depiction of an erotic dream. Its haunting, inconclusive ending has a more powerful effect than the usual high climactic note.

EXAMPLE 2*

* Permission for reprint granted by Editions Jean Jobert, Paris, copyright owners; Elkan-Vogel Co., Inc., Philadelphia, agents.

These are songs that demand a particular kind of artistry on the part of the singer, and a particular kind of sympathy on the part of the audience. An understanding of French is necessary to appreciate them because of the close association of words and music. Furthermore, the poems are virtually untranslatable. Only in French can one say so little and imply so much.

PERIOD 2: 1900–1910

The more important works of this period are the masterpieces of impressionist music which established Debussy as a major composer.

OPERA

Pelléas et Mélisande (1902)

PIANO

Estampes (1903)
Images (1905 and 1907)
Préludes (Book I, 1910; Book II, 1913; 12 compositions in each book)

ORCHESTRAL

La Mer: I. De l'aube à midi sur la mer. II. Jeu de vagues. III. Dialogue du vent et de la mer. (1903–05)
Images: I. Gigues. II. Ibéria. III. Rondes de printemps. (1909)

Debussy's single opera *Pelléas et Mélisande* startled Paris with its originality and caused one of those scandals which would greet so many premières in the years to come. It is a marvelously subtle work, but it has never become popular because of its great restraint and constant understatement. The elusive characters move in a dream world, perfectly reflected in the quiet vocal lines and unresolved harmonies of the orchestra.

There are interesting, ambivalent relationships between this opera and the music dramas of Wagner. On the one hand, there are similarities in the musical structure. Debussy followed Wagner's lead in writing a continuous, recitativelike voice line, in treating the words in his libretto with great respect, and in avoiding arias and ensembles. Furthermore, he associated musical themes with characters and situations, and in choosing Maeterlinck's play as his libretto he chose a story very similar to that of *Tristan und Isolde;* both operas are concerned with the betrayal of an old king by his wife and a younger man.

But here the similarities end, for in other respects we see that the two operas are actually worlds apart. Their differences are epitomized in a comparison of the earth-shaking love scene in the second act of *Tristan* with Mélisande's timid declaration of love:

EXAMPLE 3a

EXAMPLE 3b*

Every element of *Tristan*'s drama is expressed at length and with overpowering insistence, while in *Pelléas* everything is merely suggested or hinted. Isolde tells all; Mélisande, nothing.

In *Pelléas* and in the orchestral and piano music of this time a vocabulary of musical impressionism is established. Debussy is the most important composer of piano music since Chopin and Liszt, for he discovered new sonorities,

* Permission for reprint granted by Durand et Cie., Paris, copyright owners; Elkan-Vogel Co., Inc., Philadelphia, agents.

pedal effects, and timbres in the instrument. His two books of *Préludes,* each containing twelve pieces, are important landmarks of twentieth-century music. Each piece has a poetic or descriptive title such as *"La Cathédrale engloutie"* ("The Submerged Cathedral"), *"Minstrels,"* or *"Bruyères"* ("Heather").

"Feux d'artifice" ("Fireworks"), the last composition of the second book, is typical and some of its salient features will be described here. It starts with the alternation of a three-note fragment suggesting the key of F with another suggesting G-flat.

EXAMPLE 4*

Above this complex, tonally ambiguous sound, tones a diminished fifth apart are sounded. Everything is pianissimo until a sudden crescendo leads to a descending glissando on the black keys to the bottom of the keyboard. The motion starts again with a cluster of alternating minor seconds that lead to sweeping arpeggios under which a trumpetlike call is heard. One figure is heard from time to time in rhythmic variants. It is the nearest approach to a theme in a piece that otherwise is a succession of pianistic figures of greatest diversity.

* *"Feux d'artifice,"* Copyright 1913, Durand et Cie. Used by permission of the publisher. Elkan-Vogel, Inc., sole representative, United States.

EXAMPLE 5

One particularly happy invention exploits the augmented fourth (C–F-sharp). With its ambiguous tonal relationship, this interval fascinated the progressive composers of the first decades of the century. Example 6 also shows the juxtaposition of chords unrelated by key.

EXAMPLE 6

The music becomes more frenzied until a shattering, two-handed glissando in minor seconds again drops to the bottom of the keyboard. Next there is a low background on the notes D-flat and A-flat. Above it, in C, a few notes of the *Marseillaise* are heard. The succession of these highly original, fragmentary effects marvelously evokes a celebration of the French national holiday, the fourteenth of July (Bastille Day).

The compositions for orchestra written in these years are worthy of close study, for the sound and syntax of large-scale impressionist music were established through them. Among the unforgettable moments are the fragmentary English horn melody at the beginning of *"Nuages,"* the muted trumpets in *"Fêtes,"* and the transition between the second and third movements of *"Ibéria"* in which dance rhythms of a "Festival Morning" gradually supersede the exotic sounds of "Perfumes of the Night."

La Mer will be discussed in more detail. It consists of three sections, each having its own title. The first is called *"De l'aube à midi sur la mer,"* and starts with a scarcely heard, low rumble, indistinct and fragmentary, a characteristic beginning for music of the 1900 period—so different from the clear-cut statements which mark the beginnings of earlier music. Timpani, harp, and low strings sound the background against which the oboes sing a plaintive fragment. Soon a theme is announced by the trumpet and English horn in octaves, an unusual combination of timbres, but one which shows Debussy's characteristic feeling for fresh and interesting colors.

EXAMPLE 7

This is used as a source theme from which much of the musical material of the entire piece is derived. It is tonally ambiguous, because of the bitonal relationship between the melody and the bass. The supple rhythm of triplet divisions of the beat against a duple background is also characteristic.

There is a change in tempo and key as the movement proper starts. Figurations are heard in the strings and woodwinds along with a new melody in the horns, which shows relationships with the source theme. The texture becomes richer and richer, until there are seven different simultaneous rhythmic patterns.

EXAMPLE 8*

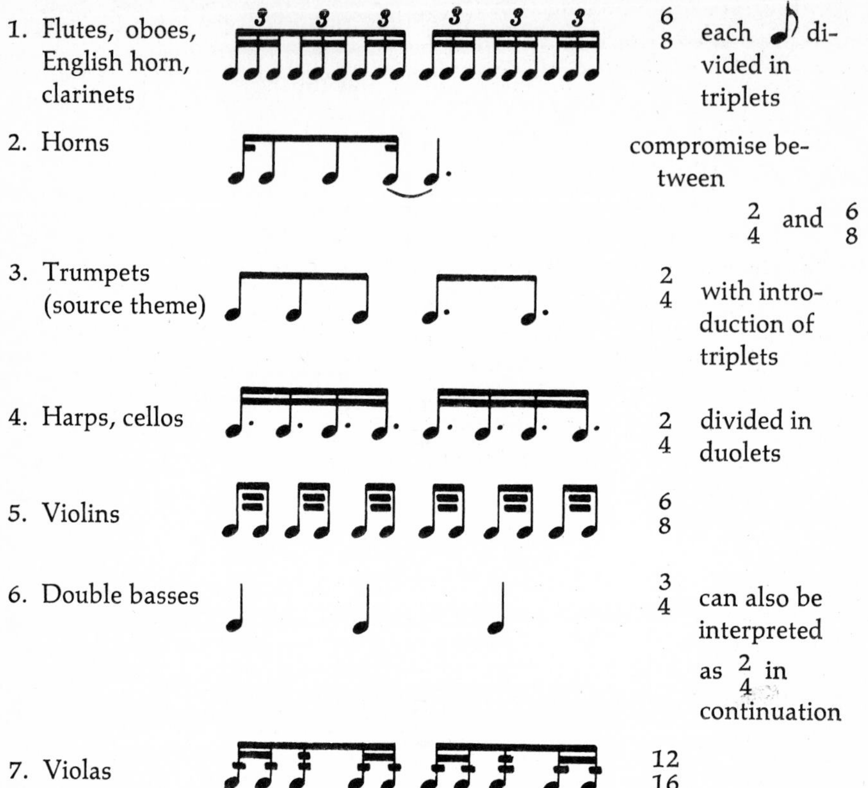

When this section comes to a close, a more rhythmic, more definitely tonal section begins with the following motive:

EXAMPLE 9

* From *Debussy*, by Jean Barraqué (Paris, Éditions du Seuil, 1962), by permission.

The timbre is distinctive here, since the composer calls for sixteen cellos divided into four groups. This section works up to a climax with sequences of ninth and augmented chords underlying the rhythmic figurations. When the motion quiets, the theme shown in Example 7 is again heard. There is a coda, and the last three notes of the movement refer once more to the source theme.

Paradoxically, there is interesting evidence of Wagner within this movement. The second measure of Example 7 is identical with the important Tristan motive of the opera, and the frenzied figuration of the middle section reminds one of the second act duet, with its diatonic ninth chords. Wagner was so powerful that many who denounced him could not entirely avoid his influence.

The second movement, *"Jeu de vagues,"* is a marvelous example of impressionist, sensuous music. It is a catalog and textbook of orchestral devices, with its muted trumpets, harp glissandos, horns playing soft, close-voiced augmented triads, the celesta, and subtle cymbal sounds. As in the first movement, fragmentary melodies and ear-tickling effects alternate with a dancelike section in triple meter. The principal theme also has a relationship to the source theme of the whole work:

EXAMPLE 10

The last movement, *"Dialogue du vent et de la mer,"* again starts with a low rumble, built on a prominent augmented fourth. The source theme is heard in the muted trumpet playing *forte,* another unusual color effect. A new, warmly sentimental theme is heard in the oboe, and this, alternating with transformations of the source theme, forms the thematic content of the movement. In the final measures the references to the source theme cannot be missed.

EXAMPLE 11

La Mer is an important achievement in twentieth-century music. The richness of its orchestral sound, the freedom and complexity of the harmony, and its firm structural devices make it a masterpiece.

PERIOD 3: 1911–1917

Because of his failing health, the rich flow of Debussy's compositions slackened in the last years of his life. The principal works are:

Jeux (*Games*, ballet; 1912)
Twelve Études for piano (1915)
Sonatas for: Cello and Piano (1915)
Flute, Viola, and Harp (1916)
Violin and Piano (1916–17)

A definite change in style is to be noted in these compositions, in which the lush, evocative sounds of impressionism give way to a new simplicity. A comparison of the titles of some of these piano pieces (e.g., "For the Five Fingers" and "For Double Notes" with "Gardens in the Rain" and "Pagodas") shows the change in orientation.

The ballet *Jeux* is a very interesting work. The orchestral writing is entirely different from earlier compositions such as *La Mer* in that the elaborate background figurations have largely disappeared and a much more transparent texture prevails. Rich timbre combinations likewise have given way to melodies that pass from one solo instrument to another. All traces of symphonic structure, of theme statement, development and return have also disappeared and the composition progresses from one phrase to another connected by a kind of free association. For these reasons, *Jeux* has gained the interest and attention of composers and theorists of the 1960s, who see it as the precursor of style elements more characteristic of their time than of 1912. It is certainly one of Debussy's more forward-looking compositions.

In the last set of sonatas Debussy returns to the formal types of organization he had neglected since the String Quartet. The third, for violin and piano, has a minimum of atmosphere. The harmonies are diatonic for the most part and concise themes are developed in the service of over-all design. In this, his last composition, he recalls the music-hall mood of "*Minstrels*" in the second movement, and at the end of the last, in his final final cadence, the bright key of G major is affirmed fortissimo. The enveloping fogs of impressionism have blown away.

Style Characteristics

Debussy was one of the great innovators in the development of music. While he was not the sole inventor of some of the devices he used, as we have noted, he was the first to exploit them to such a degree that they became part of the vocabulary of music. Perhaps the most striking of his style traits was his preference for scales other than the familiar major and minor forms. Among these, the whole-tone scale is important, although he actually used it rarely. Two examples are to be found in *"Voiles"* and *"Le Tombeau des Naïades."*

EXAMPLE 12*

Whole-tone passages such as this, and those found in the following example, have become so associated with Debussy that when other composers employ the scale they inevitably, and unfortunately, sound "like Debussy."

EXAMPLE 13

* *"Voiles,"* Copyright 1910, Durand et Cie. Used by permission of the publisher. Elkan-Vogel, Inc., sole representative, United States.

Far more frequent are the modal scales. These are sometimes used programmatically to suggest medieval times, as in *"La Cathédrale engloutie"* and in *Pelléas,* but more often they are used for purely musical reasons. Debussy's interest in Oriental scales is well known. A pentatonic melody is to be found in *"Pagodes."*

EXAMPLE 14

Debussy's melodies frequently consist of fragmentary motives joined asymmetrically; the repetitions, extensions, and developments found in romantic music are generally avoided. He once said:

I should like to see the creation—I, myself, shall achieve it—of a kind of music free from themes, motives, and formed on a single continuous theme, which nothing interrupts and which never returns upon itself. Then there

> will be a logical, compact, deductive development. There will not be, between two restatements of the same characteristic theme, a hasty and superfluous "filling in." The development will no longer be that amplification of material, that professional rhetoric which is the badge of excellent training, but it will be given a more universal and essential psychic conception.[2]

Debussy's vocal melodies are remarkably close to the spoken word in both rhythm and inflection, and in general his instrumental melodies consist of short motives rather than extended lines. Some compositions, such as *"Poissons d'or,"* are without melody at all (in the usual sense) while others have but momentary allusion to tunes, as in *"Les Collines d'Anacapri"* or *"La Sérénade interrompue."*

In matters of rhythm and meter, Debussy along with other French composers is fond of establishing compound meters ($\frac{6}{8}$ or $\frac{9}{8}$) and contrasting duple subdivisions of the beats. *"Clair de lune"* contains many examples of this practice. Spanish rhythms, especially those of the tango and the habanera, are frequently found. *"La Soirée dans Grenade," "La Sérénade interrompue,"* and *"Ibéria"* are examples. Syncopated rhythms associated with music halls and vaudeville are also found, inspired by the American minstrel shows which were touring Europe at the time. For examples see *"Golliwog's Cakewalk," "General Lavine—Eccentric,"* and *"Minstrels."* In general, Debussy uses no strongly accented rhythmic patterns, but smooth, unaccented passages in which the rhythmic life flows gently in the background.

Debussy made his strongest contributions in the realm of harmony. Not only did he exploit new combinations of tones, but also he freed dissonant chords from the musical obligations they had carried for centuries. The principle that dissonance must be prepared and resolved, that moments of harmonic tension must be followed by moments of relaxation, was challenged by Debussy. The impact of this step upon music history was tremendous, for it attacked the foundations of tonality. In effect it was an attack on the morality of music, for the behavior of chords, established through the practice of hundreds of years, was suddenly freed from restraint. As in other matters, steps toward this freedom had been taken by certain composers who preceded Debussy, but they merely hinted at the newer practices.

If Debussy did not resolve his chords in the "proper" way, where did he lead them? Most often, to a similar dissonance on another level. Examples of this parallel treatment of chords can be found in *"Ce qu'a vu le vent d'ouest"* (illustrated in Example 15), *"En sourdine," "Le Tombeau des Naïades,"* and *"La Soirée dans Grenade."*

Another example is found in *Pelléas et Mélisande,* when Mélisande, leaning out of her tower window, is speaking to Pelléas, who stands below. Her

EXAMPLE 15

Ce qu'a vu le vent d'ouest*

long hair becomes untied and envelops him. The chords that accompany the scene are shown in Example 16.

Besides the parallel treatment of dissonance, the combination of two planes of chord progressions sometimes gives rise to very complex combinations. An example can be found in "*Les Sons et les parfums tournent dans l'air du soir.*" Debussy is also fond of deep pedal tones that add to the complexity of the harmonic moment.

In single chords there is also a special vocabulary. Augmented chords are frequent. The dominant ninth chord is also used very often, usually in parallel chains. (See Example 13.)

* "Ce qu'a vu le vent d'ouest," Copyright 1910, Durand et Cie. Used by permission of the publisher. Elkan-Vogel, Inc., sole representative, United States.

EXAMPLE 16*

The "added tone" technique produces other combinations. Most frequent is the adding of seconds which makes for a blurred effect. Examples may be found in *"La Danse de Puck"* and *"Minstrels."* Chords without thirds are used sometimes to give an archaic impression. *"La Cathédrale engloutie"* offers many examples.

Debussy's treatment of dissonance changed its function. Heretofore dissonance had been used for its dramatic, expressive effect; that is, the intensity of the emotion was matched by the complexity of the chord. Now, however, very complex combinations were used not to create tension but simply to add color.

Another field in which Debussy made major contributions was that of timbre. Perhaps this is the outstanding characteristic of his music, since all of the other elements, including harmony, can be considered subservient to it. Debussy's piano writing follows the overtone displacement so beautifully exploited by Chopin—low pedal tones and dispersed chord tones spread over the entire piano with the more dissonant tones appearing near the top. Sometimes he leaves the middle area empty and combines extreme high tones with low tones, as for example in *"La Terrasse des audiences du clair de lune."*

In writing for voice he often exploits the lower reaches of the soprano or tenor range. This is a region that is not rich dramatically or strong in volume, but completely right for whispering intimacies.

In general, he shows great sensitivity to the individuality of the woodwinds, as the melancholy English horn in *"Nuages,"* the warm clarinet in *"Fêtes,"* and the limpid flute in *L'après-midi* demonstrate.

Closely connected with timbre is the element of dynamics. Debussy is

**Pelléas et Mélisande,* Copyright 1911, Durand et Cie. Used by permission of the publisher. Elkan-Vogel, Inc., sole representative, United States.

the great master of the whisper, and his scores abound in *pianos* and *pianissimos.* Seven of the *Préludes* of the first volume start *pp* and the other five are marked *p*. Stunning dynamic climaxes occur, but they are momentary flashes, soon to be replaced by quiet. Debussy's music is suggestive and insinuating. One cannot gain such effects by shouting.

From everything that has been said, it will be clear that the forms of classical music are rarely found in his music. He wrote sonatas only at the beginning and end of his life, and it has been already pointed out that the three last compositions are sonatas in name only. Debussy's innovations have been described at length because it was he more than any other composer who broke with the conventions that had governed music for the past three hundred years. Although some earlier composers had taken tentative steps in this direction, his loosening of the bonds of tonality and free treatment of dissonance, as well as his disregard for logical, formal processes of musical development, opened vistas for composers as disparate as Bartók, Schoenberg, and Stravinsky. The disintegration of the harmonic syntax of music, which was to characterize twentieth-century music, received its strongest impetus from Debussy.

Suggested Readings

The bibliography on Debussy is wide. Martin Cooper's *French Music from the Death of Berlioz to the Death of Fauré* (London, 1951) is an excellent survey of French music of the period. The authoritative biography and study of the compositions is Edward Lockspeiser's *Debussy: His Life and Mind* (New York, 1962; Vol. II, 1965). An older but still valuable book is Leon Vallas' *Claude Debussy, His Life and Works* (London, 1933), which contains a thematic index of all the works. An article by Marcel Dietschy, "The Family and Childhood of Debussy," *Musical Quarterly*, Vol. XLVI, No. 3 (July 1960), reveals some new facts about the composer's early years. Specialized studies are: *Piano Works of Claude Debussy* by E. Robert Schmitz (New York, 1950); Alfred Cortot's *French Piano Music* (London, 1932); and Lawrence Gilman's *Debussy's Pelléas et Mélisande* (New York, 1907). An important analysis of *Jeux* by Herbert Eimert is found in *die Reihe*, Vol. 5 (Bryn Mawr, 1961). Two excellent "BBC Music Guides" are: *Debussy Piano Music* by Frank Dawes (Seattle, 1971), and *Debussy Orchestral Music* by David Cox (Seattle, 1975). The critical writings of Debussy can be found translated in his *Monsieur Croche, The Dilettante Hater* (New York, 1928), and in Vallas' *The Theories of Claude Debussy* (London, 1929). Christopher Palmer's *Impressionism in Music* (New York, 1973) traces impressionist traits in later composers.

Ravel

3

Don't try to be a genius in every measure.

*Gabriel Fauré**

* Fauré's advice to a composition student.

Paris: Other Composers

DEBUSSY WAS BY NO MEANS the only composer of importance in France during the period 1900–1920. Gabriel Fauré (1845–1924), the chief representative of a more conservative French tradition that existed side by side with impressionist music, was restrained, elegant, and economical in his compositions. He wrote many songs, music for piano, and chamber music. His setting of the *Requiem Mass* is noteworthy among the larger works. Never tempted by the "free floating" parallel dissonance of the impressionists, he developed instead a conservative, but at the same time highly original, harmonic syntax. Fauré's chords are chromatic and his modulations are frequently to remote keys, but because of his fondness for modal scales (with their lack of leading tones) the effect is one of serenity rather than one of feverish intensity that characterizes so much chromatic music.

A great deal can be learned about the styles of Fauré and Debussy by comparing the songs that they wrote to the same poems. For instance, in the two settings of Verlaine's poem "C'est l'extase," Fauré uses only the tonic chord in the two-bar introduction while Debussy starts his song with a melodic motive built on the dominant thirteenth and uses rich chords throughout, with new accompaniment figures reflecting the changing thoughts of the verse. Fauré, on the other hand, does not vary his accompaniment figure from start to finish; although he modulates freely to remote keys, his harmonies are rarely more complex than seventh chords of various types. Because they are not so completely conditioned by the words with which they are associated, Fauré's melodies have a wider curve and a more regular profile than Debussy's.

EXAMPLE 17 (FAURÉ)*

EXAMPLE 18 (DEBUSSY)*

Fauré's contributions to the music of the early twentieth century are more important than these few paragraphs would indicate. However, since

* "C'est l'extase langoureuse," Copyright 1913, Jean Jobert. Used by permission of the publisher. Theodore Presser Company, sole representative, United States, Canada, and Mexico.

he was a conservative rather than forward-looking composer, we shall turn now to Maurice Ravel, his most distinguished pupil, who played a more significant role in establishing the new idioms.

Ravel, 1875–1937

Complex, but not complicated.
Ralph Vaughan Williams on Ravel's Music

Ravel was born in Ciboure in the French Basque country near the border of Spain. His father was a French engineer, and his mother was presumably of Basque origin. The family moved to Paris soon after the birth of Maurice and settled in Montmartre, at that time the habitat of many of the painters who were to revolutionize twentieth-century art. Ravel followed the path of most French musicians by entering the Conservatoire and receiving all his musical education there. His general education he received from Paris itself, and from the artists and writers who were his friends.

His life was outwardly uneventful. The controversy caused by his failure to receive the Prix de Rome and the newspaper debate as to whether he or Debussy was the first to write music of authentic Spanish flavor brought some prominence to his name, but it was not until 1911 and the production of his one-act comic opera *L'Heure espagnole* that he first achieved fame as a composer. He held no teaching posts and for the most part lived a quiet bachelor's life, enjoying the companionship of a small circle of friends. However, with the composition of *Boléro* in 1927 he did achieve world recognition suddenly. He found himself in great demand to conduct concerts of his music, and he made a tour of the United States. His health failed soon after, however, and he died after brain surgery in 1937.

Ravel's Compositions

Ravel was a meticulous composer—a "Swiss watchmaker," his friend Stravinsky called him—and the list of his compositions is not long. Since there are fewer style changes in them than in other composers' works, division into style periods is somewhat arbitrary. However, a distinction can be made between earlier and later works. For the most part, the former group of compositions embodies impressionist, *fin-de-siècle* ideals as shown by their titles and their evocative sounds. It is interesting to note the similarity of genres found in the following list to those employed by Debussy at the same time. Both composers wrote a string quartet, an opera, songs, a ballet, orchestral music of strong Spanish flavor, and much piano music.

PERIOD 1: 1900–1911

OPERA

L'Heure espagnole (1907)

ORCHESTRAL

Rapsodie espagnole (1907)
Daphnis et Chloé (1909–12)

CHAMBER MUSIC

String Quartet (1902–03)
Introduction et allegro (for harp, flute, clarinet, and string quartet; 1906)

PIANO

Jeux d'eau (*Play of the Water*; 1901)
Miroirs (1905). I. Noctuelles. II. Oiseaux tristes. III. Une Barque sur l'océan. IV. Alborada del Gracioso. V. La Vallée des Cloches.
Sonatine (1903–05)
Gaspard de la nuit (1908). I. Ondine. II. Le Gibet. III. Scarbo.
Ma Mère l'Oye (Mother Goose), duet (1908). I. Pavanne de la Belle au Bois Dormant. II. Petit Poucet. III. Laideronette, imperatrice des pagodes. IV. Le Jardin féerique.

SONGS

Shéhérazade (1903)
Cinq mélodies populaires grecques (1907)
Histoires naturelles (1906)

As a composer of piano music, Ravel not only rivals Debussy but also actually anticipates him in certain areas. *Jeux d'eau* is an example. Written in 1901 long before Debussy published the first book of *Préludes*, it exploits the treble region of the piano which was to be used so much by the older composer. It is very interesting harmonically, from its opening on a tonic ninth chord to its closing on a tonic seventh (Examples 19a and 19b).

EXAMPLE 19a

EXAMPLE 19b

These chords are typical of Ravel's music, for he preferred diatonic dissonances to more tonally ambiguous chromatic combinations. The cadenza, built on superimposed triads of C and F-sharp, is an intriguing swirl of sound. *Jeux d'eau* was the first in a long series of "water" pieces to be written by impressionist composers. His sets of pieces, *Miroirs* and *Gaspard de la nuit,* are more involved and are among the finest piano works of the period. The lovely *Sonatine* might be cited as evidence of Ravel's interest in classical forms at a time when such an interest must have seemed reactionary.

One of Ravel's most popular early orchestral compositions is the suite arranged from the ballet *Daphnis e Chloé,* a key work of impressionist music that should be known by all students of the period. It starts in a characteristics manner, with a scarcely audible chromatic figure in the lowest strings while divided flutes and clarinets play murmuring figures. The horns sustain pianissimo chords behind the harp glissandos. "The Break of Day" (the title of the first section) is suggested by the flowing figure that starts in the double basses and eventually rises through the orchestra.

EXAMPLE 20*

A pastoral section follows, featuring the oboe and English horn.

EXAMPLE 21

The flute, the most favored instrument of the impressionists, is heard in the next section which consists of two dances, one slow and the other fast. The celesta and piccolo add to the color. After a pause, an exciting bacchanal starts and works up to a glittering climax. The meter is $\frac{5}{4}$ and continuing triplets suggest the vigorous dance movement of the *corps de ballet.* The

* *Daphnis et Chloé,* Copyright 1913, Durand et Cie. Used by permission of the publisher. Elkan-Vogel, Inc., sole representative, United States.

main theme shows an indebtedness to certain sections of Rimsky-Korsakov's *Scheherazade.*

EXAMPLE 22

The motive d-e-b (d#-e#-b in Example 22), bracketed in Examples 20, 21, and 22, unifies the whole ballet.

PERIOD 2: 1911–1931

OPERA

L'Enfant et les sortilèges (*The Bewitched Child;* 1925)

ORCHESTRAL

La Valse (1920)
Boléro (1927)

CONCERTOS

Concerto for Piano (1931)
Concerto for Piano, left hand (1931)

CHAMBER MUSIC

Trio in A minor (1914)
Sonata for Violin and Cello (1922)
Chansons madécasses (*Songs of Madagascar;* for voice, flute, cello, piano; 1925–26)

PIANO

Valses nobles et sentimentales (1911)
Le Tombeau de Couperin (*The Tomb of Couperin,* i.e., In memory of C.; 1917)

The later works of Ravel become more austere in manner, and the warm, subjective expression of *Daphnis et Chloé* is not encountered again. The two large compositions for piano illustrate this trend. There is no elaborate figuration in the set of waltzes inscribed to the "eternally new and delicious pleasure of a useless occupation." In its place there is acrid, biting dissonance. This is the opening:

EXAMPLE 23*

Le Tombeau de Couperin, a suite of eighteenth-century dances preceded by a prelude and fugue and followed by a toccata, employs a harpsichord style in which complex pedal effects are entirely absent. Each detail is sharply outlined in these tributes to the past. The same tendencies can be noted in other works—notably in the song cycles with instruments and in the piano concerto, although *La Valse* reverts to the rich sonorities of the earlier period.

Style Characteristics

Ravel's fondness for modal scales, particularly the Dorian and Phrygian, is affirmed in many of his compositions from *Pavane* (1899) to the Piano Concerto (1931). He also uses pentatonic and six-tone scales.

Although he occasionally writes in $\frac{5}{4}$ meter (*Daphnis* and the Trio), he more frequently uses the familiar ones. He is fond of dance rhythms, whether they be Spanish (*Boléro, Habanera, Malaguena*), baroque (*Forlane, Rigaudon, Pavane*), or jazz (Violin Sonata, certain scenes of *L'Enfant et les sortilèges,* and the Piano Concerto).

He developed a distinctive vocabulary of chords, preferring complex diatonic structures on tones other than the dominant to Debussy's "juicy" ninth chords. He frequently adds to the pungency of a chord by sounding a

* *Valses nobles et sentimentales,* Copyright 1911, Durand et Cie. Used by permission of the publisher. Elkan-Vogel, Inc., sole representative, United States.

chromatic appoggiatura along with its note of resolution. The following is one of his favorite chords:

EXAMPLE 24

The *Valses nobles* are a rich mine of such complex chords.

Ralph Vaughan Williams, the English composer, studied with Ravel for a short time in 1908. In his autobiographical sketch he reports:

> He [Ravel] was horrified that I had no pianoforte in the little hotel where I worked. 'Sans le piano on ne peut pas inventer de nouvelles harmonies,' he said [Without a piano one cannot invent new chords.] [1]

Obviously Ravel regarded the invention of new chords as an important phase of composition. That he is one of the master orchestrators is evidenced by *Boléro* and by his transcriptions of his piano works and Moussorgsky's *Pictures at an Exhibition.* In common with Debussy, he favored the smaller forms and wrote sonatas only at the beginning and end of his career.

Although Ravel is sometimes thought of as merely a minor impressionist, this notion is far from true, for his impressionist works are of great importance. However, when he deserted impressionist ideals for a more precise language he returned to an older and more genuinely French tradition. Never reactionary, his original vocabulary of chords and his fine sense of orchestral color added much to French music of the time.

Diaghilev and the Young Stravinsky

Ravel's ballets were written at the instigation of Serge Diaghilev, the famous director of the Russian Ballet and one of the key figures in twentieth-century art. In 1909 Diaghilev arranged a concert of Russian music in Paris, including the first performance there of *Boris Godounov,* with Chaliapin singing the title role. The next year he dazzled Paris by presenting the Imperial Russian Ballet, with such superb dancers as Pavlova, Karsavina, and Nijinsky in the company. The enterprise was so successful that he returned each year thereafter and, with a wonderful combination of flawless taste and inspired showmanship, made these seasonal affairs the focus of Parisian social and artistic life. At first the repertoire consisted of such classical ballets as *Les Sylphides* and *Giselle,* as well as works of a strong Russian-Oriental flavor, such as the *Polovetzian Dances* of Borodin, *Cleopatra* by Arensky, and Rimsky-Korsakov's *Scheherazade.* However, with the European success of the Russian Ballet assured, Diaghilev began to commission new works so that he would have fresh and spectacular ballets to present each season. It was in this area that he showed particular genius, for he brought together the most prominent composers, choreographers, and painters to create the music, dances, settings, and costumes for the ballets he conceived. Until his death in 1929 he was without rival in presenting to the public what was new in the arts.

For the season of 1910 he brought together a new team—Fokine for the choreography, Bakst for the *décor,* and a 25-year-old Russian, Igor Stravinsky, for the music. This young composer, the son of an opera singer in St. Petersburg, was just beginning his career in music. After graduating from the University in law he studied for a short time with Rimsky-Korsakov. The only composition of his that Diaghilev had heard was a promising student piece, *Fireworks.* But Diaghilev made few mistakes, and the new ballet, *The Firebird,* was enormously successful and launched the career of one of the most distinguished composers of the century.

The Firebird is based on a fairy tale and follows the tradition of colorful, quasi-oriental ballets of the time. Musically it shows the heritage of the young composer—Rimsky-Korsakov, Borodin, Scriabin, and Moussorgsky. However, it is by no means entirely derivative, for it contains more than one hint of his mature style.

The suite that is most often performed at concerts consists of six sections. The introduction starts with mysterious sounds in the lowest strings. The interval of the diminished 5th which is outlined by the melody is prominent throughout this work:

EXAMPLE 25*

* Permission for reprint granted by J. W. Chester, London.

Stravinsky, Drawing by Picasso in Neoclassic Style
The Bettmann Archive

Gradually the melody ascends to higher regions of the orchestra, interrupted from time to time by fantastic birdlike sounds from the violins, playing harmonics, and by chirping sounds in clarinets and bassoons. Muted horns and low flutes add to the impressionist effect.

The "Dance" that follows, suggesting whirling wings, is also full of magically evocative sounds. In the quiet section, "Dance of the Princesses,"

Stravinsky harks back to his Russian heritage. The melody is an adaptation of a Russian folksong, and the atmosphere is very close to that of the "Young Prince" in *Scheherazade.*

EXAMPLE 26

In the "Dance of Kastchei" the real Stravinsky appears. In its brusque rudeness and in the vigor of its syncopation, a new voice is heard. Once again the tritone is prominent.

EXAMPLE 27

The brilliance of the trumpet and lower brasses, the strident xylophone, and the glissandos in the trombones give it an excitement that is still powerfully felt.

The "Berceuse" shows Stravinsky's fondness for the bassoon in the high, poignant range, and the tritone is outlined in the main melody. The double ostinato in the harp and strings should also be noted, for pedal figures become a characteristic feature of the composer's mature style. Moussorgsky's sound-world is heard in the "Finale" where changes are rung on a recurring bell-like theme with constant variations of color.

This score is important historically in two ways. In the first place, it shows many of the influences that the sensitive young composer had experienced up to that time; secondly, it has been a source of inspiration to many later composers.

With the success of *The Firebird,* Diaghilev lost no time in using his new composer again. The next year saw the production of *Petrouchka,* also a "Russian" work, but one far removed from the fairy-tale atmosphere of the first ballet. In this, the setting is a folk fair and the mood is earthy. The sound of the music is different also, for there are few impressionistic colors here, since a more objective style prevails. Instead of concealing the sound of individual instruments in order to achieve striking new combinations, Stravinsky, in this score, exploits the individuality of the instruments. Chromaticism is abandoned and subtle melodies are replaced by vulgar street tunes. There is little mystery, and one can be sure that the stage lighting was much brighter for this work than for *The Firebird.*

The initial musical kernel for *Petrouchka* was a complex chord which attracted the composer—a C–major chord with a superimposed F-sharp–major chord. Here we meet again that tritonal relationship which colored so much of the music of the time. Stravinsky first planned to exploit this effect in a piano piece but Diaghilev persuaded him to use it in the new ballet. This accounts for the prominence of the piano in the score.

In listening to this music and to the other ballet music, one should not forget that it was written for dancers and that the demands of the stage conditioned the form of the music. The lack of continuity in the opening scene, for instance, reflects the wandering of the crowd at the fair. The "Russian Dance," with its striking parallel chords, has become one of the best known of Stravinsky's compositions. (Example 28.) The prevalent peasant flavor is gained through imitations of accordions and hurdy-gurdies and parodies of street tunes.

EXAMPLE 28*

The frequent meter changes reflect the variety of movement and the activity of the crowd but they also show the composer's interest in complex, irregular rhythmic patterns. This had already become one of his outstanding characteristics.

If *Petrouchka* showed many signs of increasing individuality over *The Firebird,* the next Diaghilev-inspired ballet, *The Rite of Spring* (*Le Sacre du printemps;* 1913), startled the musical world with the certain knowledge that a new and disturbing composer had come of age. Few compositions have ever caused such a stir. *The Rite* had the same effect for Stravinsky as the publication of *Childe Harold* had for Byron—on the morning after the première he awoke to find himself famous.

This landmark of contemporary music was conceived and established by Diaghilev, in a characteristic blending of artistic sensitivity and calculated showmanship. Faced with the necessity of presenting a new and sensational ballet each year, and ever sensitive to what was new and "smart," he decided to capitalize on the current interest in primitive art. While Japanese prints had inspired the painters in the 1880s, African sculpture and masks had now captured the attention of the artistic world. The rude distortions and simplifications of the masks deeply stimulated German painters such as Kirchner and Marc, as well as Picasso and Braque, then young cubists in Paris. In addition, the publication of Frazer's *Golden Bough* pointed up an interest in a past far older than the Greco-Roman world which had been the source of so much art since the Renaissance.

The time was right, then, to exploit this dim past in the theater, and Diaghilev was the man to do it. He chose a new team, this time with Stravinsky for the music, Nijinsky for the choreography, and Roerich for the settings and costumes. The theme was the religious rites of prehistoric man in propitiation of Spring, culminating in a human sacrifice.

The reaction of the opening-night audience has been recounted by several eye-witnesses and participants. The audience soon took sides, those who were shocked at the ballet opposing those who were in favor of it. Soon duchesses were attacking their neighbors with their evening bags, and dignified, bearded Frenchmen were having fist fights. Those who were not physically engaged were screaming, either to show their disapproval of the ballet or to show their disapproval of those who were vocal in *their* disapproval. A few moments after the opening curtain, pandemonium reigned, and no one, not even the dancers on the stage, could hear the music. Nijinsky stood in the wings shrieking out the rhythmic pattern so that the dancers could have something to dance to.

What stirred this audience to such violence? They were repelled by the utter lack of charm and prettiness of the production. Ballet had been traditionally colorful and gorgeous, with beautiful dancers in magnificent costumes portraying characters in a fairy tale, all to the sound of charming music. There was none of this in *The Rite of Spring.* The dancers were dressed in dark brown burlap sacks and their gestures were rough and angular. The music was shatteringly dissonant and the rhythmic life of the score was brutal. It seemed as if the very foundations of music and all of the cultured refinements of ages were being attacked.

The Rite of Spring is in two acts, each preceded by an orchestral introduction. It is masterfully planned from the point of view of the theater, with its changes of pace and well-placed moments of climax. The first act, "The Adoration of the Earth," is concerned with the youth of prehistoric Russia reveling in games and dances honoring Spring. They pay homage to the Earth and the Sage, who reminds them of the ancient rites. In the orchestral "Introduction" there is an evocation of the primitive forest. The composer has written of this passage: "My idea was that the Prelude should represent the awakening of nature, the scratching, gnawing, wiggling of birds and beasts." [2] Stravinsky achieves this effect by depending almost entirely on reedy woodwind instruments. The opening notes, for instance, so poignant in their brutish sorrow, are played on the bassoon, but in a range far higher than that normally attempted by this usually jovial instrument. The effect is strange, pinched, dreamlike (Example 29).

EXAMPLE 29*

In these opening notes many of Stravinsky's characteristics are to be heard—the narrow range of the melody, the meter changes, and the treatment of a melodic figure in such a way that when it is repeated its notes fall on different parts of the measure. The melodies are made up of little fragments, stopping and starting, with insistent repetitions, although the repetitions are never precisely the same. The buzzings and twitterings increase in volume and speed and then break off suddenly. Once again the lament of the bassoon is heard.

The "Dance of the Adolescents" follows. This is one of the most sensational pieces of music ever written, for while the "Introduction" exploited strange and original timbres, this section calls upon rhythmic resources hitherto unused in Western music. Its opening has become one of the classic passages of twentieth-century music. It begins with what sounds like a savage beating of drums (actually it is the strings repeating a very complex chord). Eight horns suddenly bark, and over the tom-tom of the strings this horn complex is repeated. The interval of time between the repetitions is not regular, however, and the jointed, rough effect is partially due to the fact that there are one,

EXAMPLE 30

five, two, three, and four beats between the horn chords. Rhythms like this are called *additive* because they are formed by *adding* varying-length groups of the smallest unit (in this case the eighth note). This is different from conventional rhythms that are divisive because the basic unit (usually a quarter or half note) is *divided*. Conventional rhythms result in regular meters, expressed by the familiar time signatures. Additive rhythms tax rhythmic notation and result in Stravinsky's changing time signatures. These sections of great rhythmic complexity vary with others of almost mechanical regularity in which sing-song primitive tunes are heard.

EXAMPLE 31a

EXAMPLE 31b

EXAMPLE 31c

The second of these melodies is typical in its narrow range and its continual rearrangement in ever-changing patterns as though the notes were being played on a primitive flute that contained just a few tones, and the only variations possible were gained by changing the order in which they were played.

The next section, "Dance of Abduction," is the wildest yet encountered. There are several ideas—a dashing tune played first by the high wind instruments, and an answering horn call. Toward the end there is a great deal of additive rhythm expressed in the frequently changing meter signatures, which sometimes vary every measure. Here is a typical sequence:

$$\frac{7}{8}\ \frac{3}{4}\ \frac{6}{8}\ \frac{2}{4}\ \frac{6}{8}\ \frac{3}{4}$$

There are also examples of polyrhythm in which two or more rhythmic patterns are superimposed. The effect is deeply stirring.

"Spring Rounds," which follows, is a welcome relief after all this excitement. It moves at a slower tempo and opens with a clear woodwind color, obviously introducing another set of dancers. There is a halting, syncopated string accompaniment and a primitive hymn in the flutes. It is a solemn, sweet melody, and when repeated later by the whole orchestra, it is duplicated at the interval of a fifth and sixth.

EXAMPLE 32

Vigorous action returns in the "Game of the Rival Cities," in which there are violent clashes of chords and keys and constant variety in meter. The idea of the competing cities is expressed through antiphonal writing (each city having its own music) and through a particularly astringent use of polytonality.

The same blatant tune is used as the main thematic material for the "Entrance of the Sage." The pages of the score become blacker with notes as more instruments are added.

"The Dance of the Earth," which concludes Act I, is even more violent. Over an ostinato in the bass the instruments are used rhythmically, for individual timbre and individual melodic lines tend to be lost in the density of the sound. This section really needs the stage action to be convincing, for only as the accompaniment to a wildly rushing dance does it justify itself.

The second act is concerned with the sacrifice of a young girl, the Chosen One, to propitiate the God of Spring. The "Introduction" is a placid section, describing the pagan night. Here all flows quietly and another primitive, few-note melody is heard. The sound of the orchestra is reminiscent of

Debussy and Ravel, with the prominent flutes, violin harmonics, and the three muted horns that close the section.

The same melody is used as the main thematic material of the first dance of the act, "The Circle of the Adolescents." A characteristic doubling is heard at Number 94 in the score:

EXAMPLE 33

"The Glorification of the Chosen One," the next dance, is another wildly shrieking piece. The principal idea is a rush of sound upwards, followed by a resounding blow on the kettledrums and then a three-note figure descending. The whole theme expresses a choreographic idea, suggesting violent upward arm thrusts and spasmodic gestures.

In the short dance that follows, the "Evocation of the Ancestors," the texture is simplified somewhat and the tom-tom rhythms take over, calling the elders to participate in the ritual. They do so in the slow "Ritual Action of the Ancestors." Here the English horn and flute carry on an acrid dialogue over the driving beat of the rest of the orchestra until the horns take over in a proud theme.

The whole ballet comes to a climax in the final "Dance of the Chosen One," and Stravinsky's task of writing a climax to a work so extremely sensational must have been challenging indeed. It is another cataclysm of sound in which everything is at the service of rhythm, and with little individuality of instrument or of melody. Once again the irregularity of the phrase lengths is reflected in the numerous meter changes but what seemed chaotic to one generation is now seen instead as a very complex and novel pattern. In the following diagram, the time signatures of the first 34 bars of the "Danse Sacrale" are given, arranged so that the underlying pattern of the meter changes is revealed.

The sound effects are also carefully selected by the composer and he gives precise directions in the score for achieving each one. He tells the timpanist when to change from a hard, felt stick to a wooden one, and directs the gong player to describe an arc on the surface of the gong with the triangle stick. He instructs the horn players to play with the bells of their instruments pointing upward so that a particularly robust tone is achieved. For the last tone-cluster of the entire piece, the cellists are instructed to retune their A-string to G so that they can play their final chord savagely on open strings, a subtlety which might not be heard when at the same time four horns, tubas, four timpani, bass drum, and cymbals are playing fortissimo. Nevertheless, Stravinsky calls for precisely this sound and gives directions for obtaining it.

It is little wonder that the first performance of this piece ended in a riot. The audience apparently felt that violence had been done to the noble art of music. While Debussy had been puzzling and bizarre, at least his compositions were most often delicate in sound and almost precious in expression. But this was another matter. This was music of brutality and ugliness, not unlike the savage canvases being painted at the same time by artists of the Fauve—or "wild beast"—school. To condone this kind of expression was to attack the very basis of art.

DANSE SACRALE

1	2	3	4	5					
3/16	2/16	3/16	3/16	2/8					
	6	7	8	9					
	2/16	3/16	3/16	2/8					
		10	11	12	13				
		3/16	3/16	5/16	2/8				
			14	15	16				
			3/16	2/8	5/16				
				17	18	19			
				5/16	2/8	3/16			
					20	21			
					2/8	3/16			
						22	23	24	
						2/16	3/16	2/8	
						25	26	27	
					(notated 3/8 in the score)	2/16	2/8	3/16	
						28	29	30	
						2/16	3/16	2/8	
						31	32	33	34
						2/16	3/16	3/16	2/8

While *The Rite of Spring* seemed like the last word in modernity to its first audiences, to one evaluating the work six decades later, knowing the course pursued by twentieth-century music since 1913, it seems rather to belong to the past—a product of late romanticism. In Chapter 1 it was pointed out that an important tendency of nineteenth-century music was its growing complexity and intensity in its role as collaborator with literature and drama in symphonic poems and operas. *The Rite of Spring* belongs to this tradition, since its novel and startling musical vocabulary was conceived to express the primitivism of Diaghilev's ballet.

Subsequent events have proved it to be an end point. After *The Rite* (and a few futile imitations by other composers) Stravinsky and many of the young composers around him turned to quite different ideals of composition. However, the powerful, irregular rhythms can be found in innumerable compositions of the following years.

The date of *The Rite of Spring*—1913—is significant. It was written just before the outbreak of World War I, and perhaps the violence of the music foreshadowed the destruction and carnage that were about to begin. This war was the real end of the nineteenth century, for after it, the political, economic, and social life of Europe changed drastically. Not until the 1920s was the "brave new world" born.

Stravinsky's later compositions will be discussed in Chapters 10 and 20.

Suggested Readings

A standard study of Ravel's life and music is Roland Manuel's *Maurice Ravel* (London, 1947). Other recommended books are *Ravel* by Norman Demuth ("The Master Musicians, New Series," London, 1947), Victor Seroff's *Maurice Ravel* (New York, 1953), Vladimar Jankélévitch's *Ravel* (New York, 1959), Hans Stuckenschmidt's *Maurice Ravel* (Philadelphia, 1968), and Arbie Orenstein's *Maurice Ravel, Man and Musician* (New York, 1975). The orchestral music is treated in *Ravel Orchestral Music* by Lawrence Davis (Seattle, 1971).

Two fascinating books devoted to Diaghilev are Arnold Haskell's *Diaghileff, His Artistic and Private Life* (New York, 1935) and Serge Lifar's *Serge Diaghilev, His Life, His Work, His Legend* (New York, 1940). There are many books written by people who were connected with Diaghilev's ballet. Among them, *Nijinsky* by Romola Nijinsky (New York, 1934) is recommended for its pictures of backstage intrigue and insights into the complicated personalities of the important people involved in these crucial productions.

Schoenberg

4

The situation in Germany is serious but not hopeless; the situation in Austria is hopeless but not serious.

Viennese Saying

Germany and Austria

IN THESE RICH YEARS BEFORE World War I a musical tradition very different from that in France flourished in the German-speaking countries on the other side of the Rhine. Whereas France could boast of but one cultural center—Paris—scores of German, Austrian, Polish, and Bohemian cities enjoyed their own opera houses, orchestras, and conservatories. The Brahms-Wagner controversy, debated in Germany and Austria with the vehemence usually reserved for political discussions in France, shows how important such artistic matters were to these people. The Germans were immensely proud of the long line of composers they could claim, and when Paris capitulated to the music dramas of Wagner in the 1880s they were as proud as they had been of Bismarck's victory over the French in 1870.

The turn of the century witnessed the complete victory of Wagnerian ideals, which were carried forward in the works of Richard Strauss (1864–1949) and in those of a host of lesser talents. Strauss's tone poems, from *Don Juan* (1888) to *Ein Heldenleben* (1898), are extremely vital works that are still regularly performed. Around 1900 he turned to opera, and *Salome* (1905) and *Elektra* (1909) fascinated and repelled the musical world with their violence. These are overpowering works, completely devoid of "prettiness" or charm in the usual sense. Scenes such as the decapitation of John the Baptist were so sensationally neurotic that the performance of *Salome* was banned by several opera houses for some years. Musically, they are characterized by the use of rich dissonance (one thinks, for example, of the famous *Salome* chord heard at the climax of the opera), by an enlarged orchestra that continually threatens to engulf the singers, by leitmotifs that permeate the texture, and by cadence-avoiding continuity. In order to maintain dramatic and musical tension these operas are not divided into acts. Great demands are made upon the singers in the expression of their tortured emotions.

All of these traits are enlargements of Wagnerian principles, but *Salome* and *Elektra* are nevertheless far removed from the emotional world of such a work as *Tristan.* In the latter, the leading characters are highly moral court personages and the depiction of their fate is kept within conventional bounds. In *Salome* and *Elektra* restraint is cast aside and unrelieved starkness reigns.

Strauss himself went no further in this direction and his later operas reveal entirely different characteristics. *Der Rosenkavalier* (1909–10), *Ariadne auf Naxos* (1911–12), and *Arabella* (1930–32) are typical of his later works. They return to an atmosphere of warm sentiment and charm, and their musical vocabulary has little to do with the progressive tendencies of the twentieth century. For that reason they will not be discussed in this book—a fact that has nothing to do with their enduring value.

Expressionism

The depiction of hysterical, larger-than-life emotion in *Elektra* was characteristic of much of the art produced in Europe in the early years of the century. Not only in music but also in painting, in the novel, and in drama, subjects heretofore considered off-limits were now exhaustively explored. In one sense, this development was actually no reversal from the art of high romanticism for that, too, was subjective, free in form, and relatively unrestrained. Rather, this new art enlarged these romantic traits to a higher degree in the service of a lower, or at any rate, different, order of subject matter.

This kind of art came to be called *expressionist* and embodied an artistic ideal that in one form or another became one of the poles of twentieth-century art. The term was apparently used for the first time to describe a group of paintings shown in the Paris Salon of 1901, as an antonym of the then popular term *impressionism.* Where the ideal of the latter was a fleeting impression of the outer world, expressionist painting emphasized the subjective emotions of the artist. Van Gogh's troubled canvases soon defined the style, and other painters, such as the Norwegian Edvard Munch, made important contributions. These men were followed in Germany by such painters as E. L. Kirchner and Schmitt-Rottluff of the group known as *die Brücke,* and by Marc and Kandinsky of the group called *der Blaue Reiter.* Expressionism came to the theater in the later plays of Strindberg and Wedekind, and in the next generation, in those of Georg Kaiser and Ernst Toller. These plays were antirealistic and dreamlike, and were rich in symbols. James Joyce's *Ulysses* and *Finnegans Wake* are the archetypes of the expressionist novel.

One of the best and most succinct definitions of expressionist art came from the German critic Hermann Bahr, when he called it the "shriek of the soul."

Vienna and Expressionism

Vienna, one of Europe's music centers since the beginning of the eighteenth century, developed its own variety of *fin-de-siècle* atmosphere. In contrast to the sensuous hedonism of the French, and the sometimes shocking brutality of the Germans, the Viennese enjoyed a curious and unique mood of carefree fatalism. Ernst Krenek has described it in these words:

> The feeling of the approaching decay was growing throughout the late 19th century, when the inability of coping with the increasing political difficulties on the part of the representatives of the imperial idea became more and more evident. A most particular attitude of hedonistic pessimism, joyful skepticism touching on morbid sophistication, became the dominant trait in Vienna's intellectual climate.[1]

Of particular significance to the overall picture was the fact that Sigmund Freud lived and practiced in Vienna at this time. His discoveries in the realm of the heretofore hidden aspects of human personality greatly increased interest in the expression of subjective states—the main province of the expressionists.

Vienna quite complacently regarded herself as the capital of the music world. Her noble tradition of Haydn, Mozart, Beethoven, and Schubert was undoubtedly something to be proud of, but in their veneration of the past the Viennese had very little interest in newer trends. In the mid-nineteenth century they had been skeptical of such progressive composers as Schumann and Liszt, and their opposition to Wagner, crystallized in the writings of Eduard Hanslick, their foremost critic, was diametrically opposed to the enthusiastic reception given the music dramas by the Parisian intelligentsia.

The most important composers active in Vienna at the end of the century were Brahms (died 1897), Bruckner (1896), and Mahler (1911). Among these Brahms held a special place. He was the composer who, without being reactionary, was firm in his allegiance to the ideals of absolute, nonprogrammatic music. His rich harmonic style and subtle rhythmic sense were employed not in operas and symphonic poems, but in symphonies, concertos, chamber-music, pieces for the piano, and in songs.

Bruckner, although "tainted" by his affinity with the large orchestral sonorities and the time-scale of Wagner, nevertheless held a position of dignity as professor of composition at the Vienna Conservatory. His most important compositions were his symphonies and religious choral works. He wrote no subversive, "modern" tone poems.

Because he was a conductor as well as a composer, Gustav Mahler did a great deal to make and disturb the musical atmosphere of Vienna. As music director of the Royal Opera he established new levels of perfection in his performances of Mozart and Wagner. As a composer he is remembered principally for his ten symphonies (1888–1910, the tenth unfinished) and his works for voice and orchestra, of which the most frequently performed are *Lieder eines fahrenden Gesellen* (*Songs of a Wayfarer*, 1883); *Kindertotenlieder* (*Songs on the Death of Children*, 1904); and *Das Lied von der Erde* (*The Song of the Earth*, 1908).

Mahler's compositions have always caused controversies; critical reaction to them seems to be either highly enthusiastic or unfavorable. His is an all-embracing style, typically late romantic in its joining of opposing elements. Heroic proportions and epic "messages" contrast with intimate genre pieces; massive forces (the Eighth Symphony, the "Symphony of a Thousand," calls for a large orchestra, two choruses, eight solo voices, and a boys' chorus) contrast with delicate combinations of solo instruments; and wide-intervalled, complex melodies contrast with folk tunes. Certain aspects of Mahler's later works —particularly the wide-spanned melodies and the use of guitar, harp, and solo instruments—left their traces in the works of Schoenberg, Berg, and Webern.

Schoenberg, 1874–1951

If a composer doesn't write from the heart, he simply can't produce good music.
Schoenberg

Arnold Schoenberg, one of the giants of twentieth-century music, was born into the cultural milieu we have just described. Even though he was in no sense a prodigy either as a performer or composer, he nevertheless began to study violin at the age of eight, taught himself to play the cello, took part in amateur chamber music groups, composed a little, and avidly attended Vienna's concerts and opera performances. In order to augment his family's income, he became a bank clerk after the death of his father. It was at this time that he met the composer Alexander Zemlinsky and studied counterpoint with him for a few months; this was the only formal instruction he ever received. In a short autobiographical sketch, *My Evolution,* Schoenberg tells of these formative years:

> I had been a "Brahmsian" when I met Zemlinsky. His love embraced both Brahms and Wagner and soon thereafter I became an equally confirmed addict. No wonder that the music I composed at that time mirrored the influence of both these masters, to which a flavor of Liszt, Bruckner and perhaps also Hugo Wolf was added. . . . True, at this time I had already become an admirer of Richard Strauss, but not yet of Gustav Mahler, whom I began to understand only much later, at a time when his symphonic style could no longer exert its influence on me.[2]

Schoenberg started to compose in earnest and before the turn of the century had decided to make music his lifework. He spent two years in Berlin (1901–1903), where he was music director in a cabaret, but then he returned to Vienna and settled as a teacher, theorist,* and composer. World War I interrupted this way of life and he spent two years in the Austrian army (1915–1917). While in the army, Schoenberg devoted himself entirely to being a soldier. His only musical activity was to sketch his *Jacobsleiter,* an oratorio that was never finished.

Schoenberg's Prewar Compositions

Because the works of Schoenberg show a gradual change in style, it will be helpful to group them into periods. It should be emphasized, however, that even when the musical vocabulary changes, the common core that runs through all his works is the musical personality of a composer who is at this time an expressionist artist—the deeply, sometimes excessively, emotional creator. This is important to emphasize, for much of Schoenberg's music has been completely misunderstood. Because of its complexity and difficulty it has been called mathematical or cerebral, but his own views on the function of art show how far this view is from his intent. He has written, "A work of art can produce no greater effect than when it transmits the emotions which raged in the creator to the listener, in such a way that they also rage and storm in him." [3] Another clear definition of his intention is found in this sentence: "In reality there is only one greatest goal towards which the artist strives: to express himself." [4] This is scarcely the credo of an "intellectual" composer.

* His book *Harmonielehre* was published in 1911; the English translation, *Theory of Harmony,* in 1948.

PERIOD 1: CHROMATIC

The first period extends from 1897 to 1908, Opus 1 through Opus 10. All of these compositions breathe the air of late romanticism.

Opus 1, 2, 3, 6, 8	Songs
4	*Verklaerte Nacht* (*Transfigured Night;* 1899)
5	*Pelleas und Melisande* (symphonic poem: 1902–03)
7	String Quartet #1 (1904–05)
9	*Chamber Symphony* (1906)
10	String Quartet #2 (1907–08)
No opus number	*Gurrelieder* (1900–01)

Verklaerte Nacht is the composer's most accessible and most frequently performed composition. Originally written for string sextet, this tone poem is usually heard today in a version for string orchestra. The poem that inspired the music describes the emotions of a couple walking through the woods. The woman confesses that she has been untrue, but on the man's assurance that he still loves her, her gratitude transfigures the night. This close association of man and nature is typically romantic; it permeates most of the art of that era.

If the "program" of *Verklaerte Nacht* is akin to that of *Die Walküre* (troubled love against a troubled landscape) the musical style is also Wagnerian. The themes, although untitled, have a leitmotif sound; furthermore, they recur constantly in rhythmic transformations and are therefore developed in the Liszt-Wagner-Strauss manner. In the essay already mentioned, Schoenberg speaks of the work:

> In *Verklaerte Nacht* the thematic construction is based on Wagnerian 'model and sequence' above a roving harmony on the one hand, and on Brahms' technique of developing variation, as I call it, on the other.[5]

This is precisely the kind of music against which Debussy was rebelling at the time. In 1899 he was a vastly more progressive composer than Schoenberg.

Other Wagnerian aspects are the texture, which is primarily homophonic, with clear melodies sounding against figuration, and the extensive use of chromatic nonharmonic tones. Only rarely does a chord occur on a strong beat without a decorating note. The form is that frequently found in symphonic poems—a long, one-movement structure of contrasting moods, unified by themes that recur from time to time.

That Schoenberg was deeply concerned with the emotional effect of the piece is proved by the numerous words of expression he wrote in the score.

These are almost always preceded by the word *sehr* (very). On a single page one finds *sehr breit* (very broad), *sehr langsam* (very slow), and *sehr ausdrucksvoll* (very expressive.) The expressionist composer always deals in large denominations of emotion.

Closely akin to *Verklaerte Nacht* in style is *Gurrelieder* (the songs of Gurre, a castle in Scandinavian mythology) written, however, for a gigantic orchestra and multiple choruses and soloists. It is a work that shows the influence of Mahler in its great length, size of the orchestra, and use of voices. The score calls for:

4 piccolos
4 flutes
3 oboes
2 English horns
3 clarinets
2 E-flat clarinets
2 bass clarinets
3 bassoons
2 contra bassoons
5 solo voices
3 four-part male choruses
eight-part mixed chorus

10 horns
6 trumpets
1 bass trumpet
1 alto trombone
4 tenor trombones
1 bass trombone
1 contra bass trombone
1 tuba

6 timpani
bass drum
cymbals
triangle
glockenspiel
side-drum
tambour
xylophone
tam-tam
an iron chain
four harps
strings

It should be pointed out, however, that although this mammoth orchestra is used, there are many passages that are delicately scored.

Following these large-scale pieces, Schoenberg turned to writing for smaller groups of instruments, as demonstrated by the first two string quartets and the *Chamber Symphony* for instruments.

The First String Quartet is also close in spirit to *Verklaerte Nacht.* Although it is without a published program it sounds as if it might have one, with its emotionally charged themes and clearly defined sections. It is a huge, one-movement work, lasting almost 45 minutes, gaining unity through transformations of the main themes. Its emotional gamut is wide, ranging from the headlong strength of the opening section, to hesitating "Viennese" charm in $\frac{3}{4}$ time, to Schumann-like syncopations. There are climaxes that tax the resources of the four instruments, and long sections of tremolos and of special effects such as *ponticello* and harmonics.

With the *Chamber Symphony* and the Second Quartet important changes in Schoenberg's style take place. Both show his growing interest in contrapuntal devices and in treating his material with great economy. In the last movement of the quartet a soprano joins the strings to sing a setting of Stefan Georg's poem, "I hear the breath of other planets," and the complex harmonies reach moments of atonality. In the *Chamber Symphony* there are also sections that go beyond conventional tonality; and the theme on which it is written, composed of a series of fourths, gives rise to a complex harmonic idiom of nontonal implications.

PERIOD 2: ATONAL

Schoenberg's second period of composition extends from 1908 to 1912, from Opus 11 through Opus 21. The most important works are:

Opus 11	*Three Pieces for Piano* (1909)
15	*Das Buch der hängenden Gärten* (*The Book of the Hanging Gardens,* 15 poems for high voices; 1908)
16	*Fives Pieces for Orchestra* (1909)
17	*Erwartung* (*Expectation,* a one-character opera; 1909)
18	*Die glückliche Hand* (*The Lucky Hand;* 1910–13)
19	*Six Little Pieces for Piano* (1911)
21	*Pierrot Lunaire* (1912)

In these compositions Schoenberg achieved a highly personal idiom, of the utmost importance to the whole of twentieth-century music, for in them he made the significant step that took him beyond major-minor tonality. Music "beyond tonality" is usually called *atonal* music, and in spite of the negative connotation of the term and the fact that the composer did not approve of it, it is generally used.

Considered from one point of view, the change between Opus 10 and Opus 11 was but a small one, for with the increasing use of chromatic tones all through the nineteenth century, the boundaries of the classical key system had already been vastly broadened. The continuously modulating, cadence-avoiding style of Wagner or Franck, for example, had definitely undermined clear tonal definition. Nevertheless, in such music, no matter how devious and adventurous the journey from opening to closing tonic chord, there was always a tonal goal toward which the composition progressed. The underlying principles were the same as those which had governed music since the time of Bach.

When a composer rejects these tonal principles he is faced with tremendous problems. The main one concerns organization, for without tonality —a tonal goal—how does one "go" anywhere and how does one "arrive" any place? When is one finished? It is not unlike the problem faced by completely nonobjective painters. When a painter frees himself from any attempt to portray objective reality he is faced with a terrifying freedom of choice. If any shape or color may be used without reference to the visible world, how does one start, organize, or complete a canvas?

This analogy to painting is especially meaningful in connection with Schoenberg, for he became very interested in the visual arts at this time and was a friend of Kandinsky, one of the founders of nonobjective, expressionist painting. In writing of these years Schoenberg said, "With great joy I read Kandinsky's book, *On the Spiritual in Art,* in which the road for painting is pointed out."[6] The composer started to paint and even had one-man shows in Vienna, Berlin, and Munich.

What takes the place of tonality as a structural principle in atonal music? The compositions of Schoenberg's second period show various answers to the question. The composer himself has described the problem:

> The first compositions in this new style were written by me around 1908 and, soon afterwards, by my pupils, Anton von Webern and Alban Berg. From the very beginning such compositions differed from all preceding music, not only harmonically, but also melodically, thematically, and motivally. But the foremost characteristics of these pieces in *statu nascendi* were their extreme expressiveness and their extraordinary brevity. At that time, neither I nor my pupils were conscious of the reasons for these features. Later I discovered that our sense of form was right when it forced us to counterbalance extreme emotionality with extraordinary shortness. Thus subconsciously, consequences were drawn from an innovation, which, like every innovation, destroys while it produces. . . . New colorful harmony was offered; but much was lost.
>
> Formerly the harmony had served not only as a source of beauty, but more important, as a means of distinguishing the features of the form. For instance, only a consonance was considered suitable for an ending. Establishing functions demanded different successions of harmonies than roving functions; a bridge, a transition, demanded other successions than a codetta; harmonic variation could be executed intelligently and logically only with due consideration of the fundamental meaning of the harmonies. Fulfillment of all these functions–comparable to the effect of punctuation in the construction of sentences, of subdivisions into paragraphs, and of fusion into chapters–could scarcely be assured with chords whose constructive values had not as yet been explored. Hence, it seemed at first impossible to compose pieces of complicated organization or of great length.[7]

The *Three Piano Pieces,* op. 11, are somewhat transitional, in that elements of tonality are still present. The first piece, so darkly expressive, is at the same time taut and economical in construction, a state of affairs often prevailing in Schoenberg's compositions. It is built on manipulations and developments of this melody heard at the beginning:

EXAMPLE 34*

The accompanying chord in the third measure consists of the same intervals (a third followed by a second) sounded together. The chord in the previous measure is similar, except that the third has been expanded to a fourth.

A traditional transposition of the material a fourth lower occurs a few bars later. After a short cadenza-flourish, motives from the theme are heard over a chord in piano "harmonics," showing Schoenberg's interest in unusual color effects. The effect is gained by depressing the notes F, A, C-sharp, and E in the central octave of the piano and then sharply striking the same notes low in the bass. The released strings sound in sympathetic vibration.

The rest of the piece consists of continuing references to the basic motive, sometimes inverted, sometimes expanded with larger intervals or with interpolated notes. But in one form or another, the theme-shape is almost always present. After a climactic fortissimo statement, the theme returns in its original form at the same pitch level as at the beginning. There is no doubt that this gives a feeling of tonality, although the final chord, a structure in fourths, is not related to any tonal center.

The second and third pieces of Opus 11 show family resemblances to the first. Thus, in the second, thirds are replaced with augmented fourths and fifths, but the descending minor second is still prominent, and there are many reappearances of the original series of intervals. The key of D minor is established by the accompaniment figure that appears at the beginning and end of the piece, which as a whole is divided into sections, defined in the traditional manner by recurrences of motives.

The third piece, the most violent, starts with an expanded version of the basic theme.

* Used by permission of Universal Edition.

EXAMPLE 35

Extremely complex chords are employed, such as that in Measure 4 which contains ten different notes.

This important opus, one of the first of Schoenberg's atonal compositions, is worthy of close analysis because of the insights it gives into his methods of composition. The tightness and economy of structure, the continuing variations and development of a basic theme-shape, and the intense expression are features that will characterize many of his later works.

Five Pieces for Orchestra is one of the most important compositions of the time, startling and beautiful in its originality. Written for a large orchestra, the instruments are used more for their individual color than for mass effects. Tuttis are rare, and when they occur are short. The first piece, *Vorgefühle* (*Premonitions*), is based on two ideas. The first is stated immediately by the muted cellos:

EXAMPLE 36*

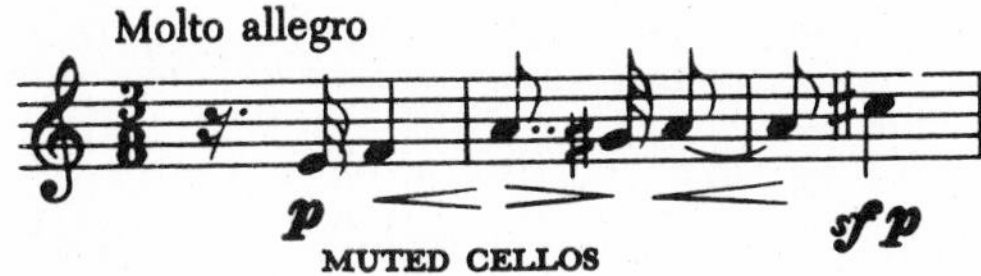

while the second is an ostinato figure:

EXAMPLE 37

* Permission for reprint granted by C. F. Peters Corp., New York.

· **Germany and Austria**

The contradiction between the length of the figure with the meter expressed by the barline shows that Stravinsky was not the only composer interested in the device at the time. The piece is violent and strident.

The second, *Vergangenes* (*Yesteryears*), is characterized by delicate color and delicious sound. It is permeated with a theme that is heard in many

EXAMPLE 38

rhythmic variants, and the shimmering sound of flutes, celesta, and the staccato bassoons give it a sheen as colorful as anything written by a French composer. Nevertheless, the third piece, *Sommermorgen an einem See* (*Summer Morning by a Lake*), surpasses it in its dependence on tone color. In this piece Schoenberg employs a concept he called *Klangfarbenmelodie* in which changes of orchestral color take the place of changes in pitch. This is one of the most static pieces ever written; much of it is merely the substitution of one instrument or group of instruments for another sounding the same note. Harmony, melody, and rhythm are sacrificed to timbre in this unusual composition. The score is loaded with dynamic indications, every note receiving its exact degree of loudness.

Music such as this, and particularly music written later by followers of Schoenberg, has been called *pointillistic*. This is a term associated with a technique of painting employed by Seurat, the French painter, and others. These men painted by putting thousands of vari-colored little dots or points on the canvas, which, when seen from a distance, seem to represent the outlines of solid shapes and objects. The term *pointillism* is used in music to describe a similar technique of avoiding solid, continuous musical lines and textures and, instead, employing a fragmentary style. The ear makes connections between the tones much in the same way as the eye constructs outlines that really do not exist in the paintings.

The fourth piece, *Peripeteia* (a term associated with Greek drama, referring to a sudden reverse of circumstances), alternates rude sonorities and wide-interval melodies with passages for muted horns, while the last, *Das Obligate Rezitativ* (*The Obbligato Recitative*), is a slow waltz, redolent of Viennese nostalgia.

These pieces for orchestra furnish further insights into Schoenberg's musical personality. They are the works not of an ascetic but of a hypersensitive colorist, and their emotional gamut is wide, from moments of terrifying force to almost immobile lassitude.

Erwartung is another fascinating work. It is a monodrama, an opera for one character, and portrays the actions, reactions, and reflections of a woman who goes in search of her lover in a forest at night. As she is in a highly emotional state, her moods range from joyful expectation to fear of the forest with its insects and animals, to anguish and hysteria when she does not find the man she seeks. Exhausted, she sinks down on a bench. Feeling something with her foot, she discovers it to be a corpse—the body of her lover. She lies beside it and kisses it. Her mood changes as she reviles her dead lover for having been untrue to her (Death being the "other woman"). She kicks the body. Later she makes love to it again, and as dawn approaches she sings her irrational farewells.

This grisly work shows Schoenberg's fascination with morbid and unhealthy emotion. It also shows him as the direct descendant of Wagner and Strauss, as they too created heroines, Isolde and Salome, who found love and death to be indivisible. However, this unhappy woman with her unhinged behavior and frequent references to the moon, which always lights such scenes, is much closer to Salome than to the noble Irish queen.

Musically, *Erwartung* is also in the Wagner-Strauss tradition, shown in the start-to-finish continuity and in the relation of the voice to the orchestra. The voice line resembles a highly charged recitation of the words and calls for musicianship and vocal range not often found. Here are two characteristic phrases:

EXAMPLE 39a*

EXAMPLE 39b

* Used by permission of Universal Edition.

The orchestra accompanies, or rather proceeds simultaneously with the voice in the timbre-rich, pointillistic manner of the *Five Pieces for Orchestra.* The brief interludes that connect the scenes are striking, and the last measures of the work, quoted here from the piano score, show the great originality of the opera (see Example 39c).

Along with these resemblances to Wagner and Strauss, there is one important difference. *Erwartung* is *athematic* in that there are virtually no themes or motives that are repeated, developed, or transformed.

EXAMPLE 39c

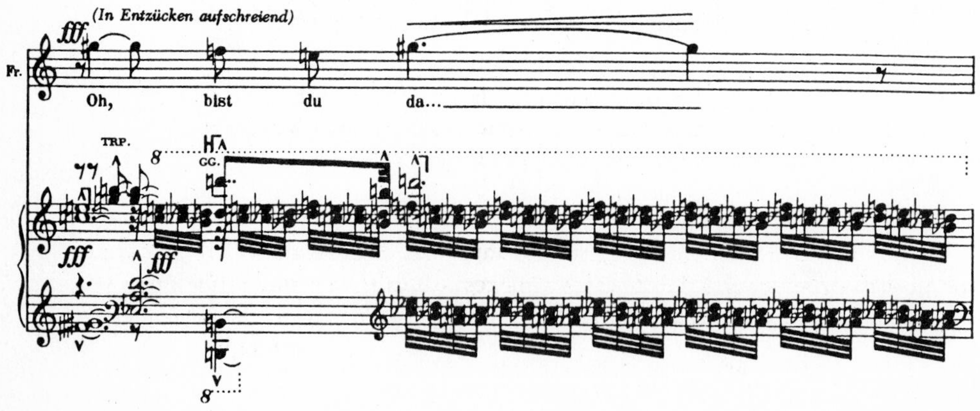

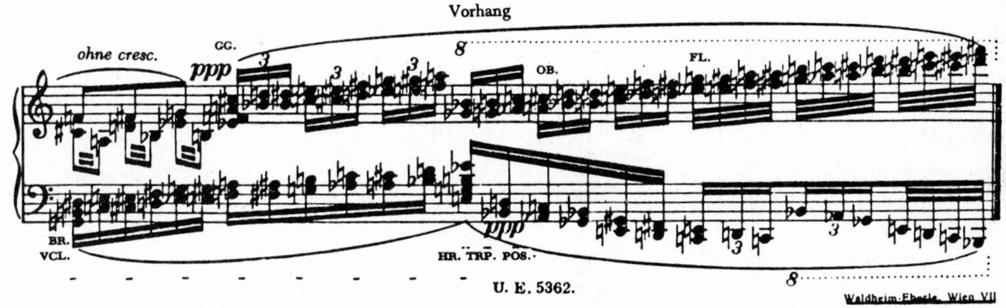

Debussy's ideal of a "music free from themes, motives . . ." is achieved in *Erwartung*.*

Die glückliche Hand is close to *Erwartung* in feeling and technique. The general atmosphere of the work can be gathered from the stage directions for the opening scene:

> The stage is almost dark. Towards the front lies the Man with his face to the floor. On his back sits a cat-like fantastic animal (Hyena with large feather wings) which apparently has bitten the man's neck.[8]

It is another "nightmare" opera.

The *Piano Pieces,* op. 19, are examples of the miniature forms mentioned by the composer. Three of the pieces are but nine measures long; the longest has seventeen measures. Each is a highly expressive statement that is

* See page 29.

neither extended nor developed. The effect is not unlike that of a Japanese *haiku*, a brief poem, of which the following is an example:

> Although it is not plainly visible to the eye
> That autumn has come,
> I am alarmed
> By the noise of the wind!
>
> *Fujiwara No Toshiyuki* [9]

Poems such as these were the models of the group of poets known as the imagists who were writing at this time. Their motivation was the same as Schoenberg's—to avoid rhetoric, preconceived patterns, and the elaborate structures of the nineteenth century, and to intimate by imagery rather than to describe concretely and directly.

Pierrot Lunaire is another important work of the prewar period. This is a composition for a speaker and a small group of instrumentalists—pianist, flutist (who also plays piccolo), clarinetist (who also plays bass clarinet), violinist (who also plays viola), and cellist. A setting of twenty-one short poems by the Belgian poet Albert Giraud, translated into German, the flavor of the poems is artificial and sophisticated, "arty" perhaps, typically *fin-de-siècle.* They are concerned with the familiar figures of Pierrot and Columbine, the moon, night, and serenades, but in contexts far removed from their usual surroundings. A translation of one of the poems will suggest the prevailing mood:

PIERROT LUNAIRE—#7—*THE SICK MOON*

> Nocturnal, deathly-sick moon,
> There on the dark pillow of the sky,
> Your look, so full of madness,
> Enchants me as a strange melody.
>
> You die of unappeasable sorrow,
> Of longing, deep within,
> You nocturnal, deathly-sick moon,
> There on the dark pillow of the sky.
>
> The lover, who in his intoxication
> impulsively goes to his love.
> Enjoys the play of your beams,
> Your pale, tormented blood,
> You nocturnal, deathly-sick moon! *

* Translated by Charles Hamm.

The most novel feature of the work is the fact that the poems are recited above the instrumental accompaniment rather than sung. The recitation, moreover, is not in a natural tone of voice, but is highly stylized with extreme variety of pitch and rigidly controlled rhythm. The part is indicated in the score in regular notation, but the composer gives directions that it is not to be sung, but to be intoned in *Sprechstimme* (speaking voice), which is neither conventional singing nor recitation. The effect, in performance, is eerie and disturbing, particularly for Americans, who as a rule have little experience with stylized recitation or acting.

The instrumental music is as strange in its way as is the manner of reciting the verse. James Huneker wrote this description of a performance in Berlin in 1912:

> What did I hear? At first the sound of delicate china shivering into a thousand luminous fragments. In the welter of tonalities that bruised each other as they passed and repassed, in the preliminary grip of enharmonics that almost made the ears bleed, the eyes water, the scalp to freeze, I could not get a central grip on myself. . . . What kind of music is this, without melody, in the ordinary sense; without themes; yet every acorn of a phrase contrapuntally developed by an adept; without a harmony that does not smite the ears, lacerate, figuratively speaking, the ear-drums; keys forced into hateful marriages that are miles asunder or else too closely related for aural matrimony. . . . [10]

While *Pierrot Lunaire* no longer calls forth such purple prose, it still impresses the listener with its originality. The small group of instruments that varies with every number sounds more bizarre than the large orchestra of *Erwartung*. The musical characteristics are much the same—an atonal idiom with a preponderance of dissonant intervals both melodic and harmonic, chords in fourths, and unusual timbres. There is a great deal of imitation between the instrumental lines, and even with the voice line where the pitches are indefinite.

Several of the pieces have a complex contrapuntal structure. For instance "Night," no. 8, is a strict passacaglia. "Parody," no. 17, is even more contrived and the viola is imitated by the spoken voice (in direction and rhythm only). Later there is a canon between the speaker and the piccolo and at the same time there is another canon progressing between the clarinet and viola. Perhaps the most complicated structural plan is found in "Moonspot," no. 18, where there is a three-part fugue in the piano and the piccolo and clarinet have a canon in diminution of the first two fugal voices. The viola and cello proceed in an independent canon. In the middle of the tenth bar these two complexes reverse themselves and play their notes in reverse order, achieving the symmetry of an ink blot. This use of contrapuntal devices as a means of organization foreshadowed the music Schoenberg was to write after World War I.

Stravinsky heard a performance of *Pierrot Lunaire* in 1912. His reactions as reported in his *Autobiography* are revealing:

> I was not at all enthusiastic over the estheticism of the work which seemed to me a reversion to the superannuated cult of Beardsley. But as an instrumental achievement, the score of *Pierrot Lunaire* is unquestionably a success.[11]

Some of the instrumental effects that probably impressed Stravinsky were the piano's "tinkling," high treble sounds; the variety of string effects—pizzicatos, harmonics, glissandos, playing on the bridge and with the back of the bow; the flute's flutter-tonguing, and the clarinet's sudden changes of register and dynamics. *Pierrot* sounds as "modern" today as it did a half century ago and its influence was still felt in later compositions.

This was Schoenberg's last composition before the outbreak of World War I. When he returned to Vienna after being released from the army, he entered his third and most important style period. These developments will be discussed in Chapter 11.

Other Composers

Closely associated with Schoenberg at this time were two student-colleagues, Alban Berg and Anton Webern. While they studied composition with the older man, theirs was more than a teacher-and-pupil relationship, for all three explored the new idioms together. For the rest of their lives the three composers held each other in the warmest personal affection and respect.

After the war, Berg and Webern achieved their own personal styles and wrote compositions that are among the most important of the twentieth century. These later works will be discussed in Chapter 12. At this point, however, the prewar compositions will be mentioned to show their close relationship to those of Schoenberg.

Berg started to study with Schoenberg in 1904. Never a prolific composer, he wrote six works before 1914. His Piano Sonata (op. 1, 1908), as well as the String Quartet (op. 3, 1910), are good examples of his youthful style: they are intensely chromatic and close to *Tristan* and *Verklaerte Nacht*. He followed Schoenberg in the atonal aphoristic style in his *Five Orchestral Songs to Postcard Texts* (op. 4, 1912) and *Four Pieces for Clarinet* (op. 5, 1913).

Webern wrote eleven compositions before the war. They are similar in idiom and type to Schoenberg's and Berg's, consisting of: songs; brief atonal pieces for violin and piano, cello and piano, and string quartet (*Five Movements for String Quartet*, 1909, and *Six Bagatelles*, 1913); and pointillistic short pieces for orchestra (*Six Pieces for Orchestra,* 1909; *Five Pieces for Orchestra,* 1913). They are works of great originality, startling in the audacity of musical ideas, in their brevity and sonority. Schoenberg described Webern's short pieces as "a whole novel condensed in a single sigh."

Webern's *Six Pieces for Orchestra,* op. 6, is dedicated to "Arnold Schoenberg, my teacher and friend, with utmost love." In dimension, they are similar to Schoenberg's Opus 19 piano pieces, for the whole set takes less than ten minutes to perform. In spite of this, a large orchestra is called for (quadruple brasses and an augmented percussion section) although the instruments are never used together. As in *Pierrot Lunaire,* each piece has its own instrumentation.

The opening of the first piece can serve as an example of Webern's pointillism. The melodic line, divided among several instruments, changes from one fleeting, ravishing timbre to another as it progresses. Since each instrument plays but a few notes, the changes succeed each other rapidly, and many listeners are at first baffled and then fascinated by the effect. Here are the first few notes:

EXAMPLE 40*

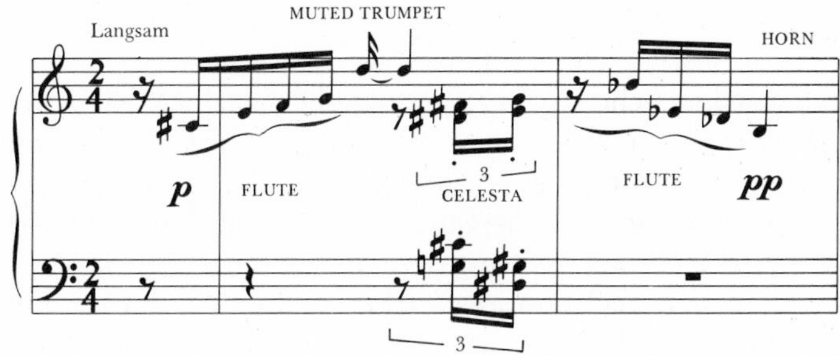

Webern uses some of his favorite timbres in these few measures—muted trumpet, flute in the low register, and celesta—sounds associated with French impressionistic music of the time. Through the unusual timbres and the original musical ideas, each of the remaining pieces evokes an immediate mood.

The emotional climate of the whole opus seems to be highly neurotic. This is particularly true of the fourth piece which is accompanied throughout by pendulumlike strokes on the bass drum, tam-tam, and a bell of undetermined pitch. It builds to a shattering climax, and although the piece is but forty measures long, its expression of the "shriek of the soul" is both masterful and complete. It would be a fitting "accompaniment" to Munch's painting *The Shriek*.

Style Characteristics

As indicated by the foregoing, there is too much variety in the prewar compositions of Schoenberg and his colleagues to make possible valid generalizations concerning their style. Starting as late-romantic Wagnerian composers, around 1908 they gradually turned to an atonal, highly dissonant idiom. Not having solved the problem of writing extended independent compositions without the structure provided by tonality, these composers wrote works that achieved their form through association with words, or they avoided the problem of form by writing one-sentence statements. They increasingly resorted to contrapuntal devices to provide structural frameworks.

All three were extremely sensitive to unusual, subtle tone color. Avoiding the mass effects of the late romantic orchestra, they sought sounds at the top and bottom of instrumental ranges and were fascinated by flutter-tonguing and mutes for the brass instruments, as well as harmonics and glissandos for the strings. Instruments such as the celesta and xylophone were raised to positions of great importance.

This extreme sensitivity to tone color as well as the fragmentary quality of their melodies and the freedom with which they treated dissonances make for interesting points of contact with the music of Debussy. The French composer is objective and cool, while these composers are subjective and burning, but the sound worlds they inhabit are not totally dissociated. Most of the composers of the time were faced with the problem of writing music without the structure provided by major-minor tonality. It is not surprising that their various solutions were sometimes similar.

Suggested Readings

The bibliography of Schoenberg will be found at the end of Chapter 11, and that of Berg and Webern in Chapter 12, but attention is called to the booklet accompanying *The Music of Arnold Schoenberg,* Vol. 1, Columbia Records M2S-679, which includes perceptive essays on *Erwartung* and *Pierrot Lunaire* by Robert Craft and George Perle. Charles Rosen has contributed valuable new insights into Schoenberg's atonal works in his *Arnold Schoenberg* (New York, 1975).

Ferruccio Busoni, Painting by Umberto Boccioni

Kill the nineteenth century dead!

Gertrude Stein

Experiments in Music

EACH OF THE COMPOSERS ALREADY discussed believed, to some extent, that the musical resources of the past were exhausted and that the twentieth century must find a new vocabulary and syntax. The compositions of Debussy, Stravinsky, and Schoenberg suggested some of the directions in which music might progress.

These recommendations were modest, however, compared to the plan of some composers who had a simple and drastic suggestion: to scrap all of the music of the past and start again with a new medium for sound—noise. This truly radical group argued that the time had come when the familiar and traditional material of music—"musical" tones produced by the human voice and instruments—was no longer capable of expressing man's feelings and emotions. "We are living in a new world," they said, "let us develop a musical style that is equally new." Their contemporaries dismissed them as being publicity-seeking lunatics, but curiously enough, time has proved that there was merit in some of their ideas. Avant-garde music of the second half of the century is once again exploring these areas. These prewar experiments will be discussed in the following pages.

Noise Music

The impulse to increase the material of music by including noises originated in Milan, Italy. It was part of the program of the

Futurists, a group of poets, painters, and musicians who felt that all art needed a new aesthetic if it were to express the modern world. The painters of the group decided that speed and motion expressed the essence of their times. Consequently they painted objects as if they were in motion, by superimposing images, much like the photographs taken by a stroboscopic camera (which had not been invented at the time). The best-known picture of this school was painted somewhat later by the French artist Duchamp, the famous *Nude Descending a Staircase.*

In a manifesto written in 1913 by Russolo, the case for futurist music is made. He says, "Life in ancient times was silent. In the nineteenth century, with the invention of machines, Noise was born." He then goes on to trace the course of contemporary music and the ways in which it reflects the complexity of modern life. However, even the most extreme modern music is too limited in expression, he feels.

> We must break out of this narrow circle of pure musical sounds, and conquer the infinite variety of noise-sounds. . . . Let us wander through a great modern city with our ears more attentive than our eyes, and distinguish the sounds of water, air, or gas in metal pipes, the purring of motors (which breathe and pulsate with an indubitable animalism), the throbbing of valves, the pounding of pistons, the screeching of gears, the clatter of streetcars on their rails, the cracking of whips, the flapping of

1	2	3	4	5	6
Booms	Whistles	Whispers	Screams	Noises obtained by percussion on metals, wood, stone, terra-cotta, etc.	Voices of animals and men:
Thunderclaps	Hisses	Murmurs	Screeches		
Explosions	Snorts	Mutterings	Rustlings		Shouts
Crashes		Bustling noises	Buzzes		Shrieks
Slashes		Gurgles	Crackling sounds obtained by friction		Groans
Roars					Howls Laughs Wheezes Sobs *

* *Music Since 1900* (1949, 3rd ed.); reproduced by permission of the publishers.

> awnings and flags. We shall amuse ourselves by orchestrating in our minds the noise of the tall shutters of store windows, the slamming of doors, the bustle and shuffle of crowds, the multitudinous uproar of railroad stations, forges, mills, printing presses, power stations, and underground railways.[1]

Finally he suggests the instrumentation of a futurist orchestra and recommends six families of noises, to be produced mechanically (as shown on page 80).

Not much came of these concepts before World War I because the manifesto was only one in a time when manifestos were everyday occurrences. However, in the twenties the works of the Franco-American composer Edgard Varèse moved in this direction, and after World War II the composers of *musique concrète* in France employed the sound medium that Russolo, the futurist, had recommended in 1913.

Microtonal Music

Another group of experimenters felt that the solution to the problem lay in scales consisting of more than twelve semitones to the octave. Of these *microtone scales,* the one that has received most attention is that involving quarter tones, but there have also been experiments with sixth tones, eighth tones, and even smaller divisions of the octave. Although they were not numerous, proponents of this program could be found throughout the world, for experimenters in Germany, Italy, Russia, Mexico, and the United States worked on the idea.

Busoni, the celebrated pianist and composer, suggested in his book *New Musical Aesthetics* that sixth tones be used in music of the future, and his ideas were followed by the Czech composer Alois Hába, who wrote many compositions, including the opera *Die Mutter,* using microtones. There was sufficient interest to warrant his appointment as a professor of microtone music at the Prague Conservatory.

Although the use of microtones appeared to be reasonable (because the natural overtone series, the basis of traditional Western music, contains intervals smaller than semitones in the higher partials), there was no immediate wide acceptance of the idiom. The fact that the usual instruments (except strings) are incapable of playing such music created an impasse, and furthermore, because a new system of notation is necessary, other problems have arisen. The most serious deterrent to microtonal music lies in the limitations of the human ear. Although it might be possible to train musicians to produce small divisions of the whole step, and although listeners could conceivably learn to discriminate among these divisions, we have not reached this point yet. Until we have, these small intervals simply will sound "out of tune."

Later Developments

After World War II, with the development of the tape recorder and electronically produced tone, all of the mechanical difficulties met by the pioneers of noise music and microtonal music disappeared, and since 1950 great interest has been shown in these areas. These later developments will be described in Chapter 20.

Suggested Readings

There are numerous books on various aspects of the Futurist Movement. Recommended is Jane Rye's *Futurism* (New York, 1972), which contains many pictures as well as the score of Russolo's *Awakening of a City*, a noise composition. Translations of many statements of aims can be found in *Futurist Manifestos* by Umbro Apollonio (New York, 1973). Other books are: *Futurism: The Story of a Modern Art Movement* by Rosa Clough (New York, 1961) and *Futurist Art and Theory* by Marianna Martin (Oxford, 1968).

Busoni's writings on music are found in his *Sketch of a New Esthetic of Music* (New York, 1911) and *The Essence of Music and Other Papers* (London, 1957).

Ives

It's a complex fate, being an American, and one of the responsibilities it entails is fighting against a superstitious veneration of Europe.

Henry James

Music in The United States

WHAT WAS HAPPENING TO MUSIC in the United States in these rich years of the early twentieth century? Was anything produced comparable to *Le Sacre* or *Pierrot Lunaire*? The answer is an unqualified *no,* for the lack of a musical environment such as that enjoyed by Berlin, Paris, or Vienna, with their great opera houses, orchestras, and well-established conservatories, made the creation of musical masterpieces in the United States virtually impossible. If a genius had been born in our Midwest in the 1870s and if he had spent all of his formative years there, think what his musical experiences would have been in comparison with Debussy's or Schoenberg's! What would he have heard of Wagner or Moussorgsky? It is not surprising that the United States did not make strong contributions to music in these years, for great works of art do not appear spontaneously in a barren atmosphere.

This is not to say, however, that there was no musical activity at all. A few of our larger communities had orchestras, conservatories, and opera houses, but in most cases these were but pale copies of European organizations. Since broadcasts and recordings had not yet appeared on the scene, "serious" musical experiences were limited to those living in one of not more than a dozen cities. When one considers the vastness of our country it is clear that most of the population lived without hearing concert music, whether old or new.

The music that was heard was in all probability written and performed by Europeans. Foreign virtuosos, conductors, opera singers, and orchestra musicians completely dominated the American musical world. Children took lessons from a German *Professor* while their parents applauded the *signore* and *signori* at the opera.

If an American aspired to enter the profession it was taken for granted that he would complete his studies in Europe, preferably in Germany. When one reads the biographies of prominent musicians of the day—such men as John Knowles Paine (1839–1906), Dudley Buck (1839–1909), George Chadwick (1854–1931), Horatio Parker (1863–1919), or Edward MacDowell (1861–1908) —the story is invariable. Each studied piano with a German-born piano teacher (or with someone who had studied in Germany). Some continued their studies at Harvard or Yale and all went to Germany for advanced study at the conservatories at Munich, Leipzig, or Berlin. Depending on where they studied, and under whose influence they came, they returned home conservative followers of Brahms or progressive followers of Liszt and Wagner. They wrote piano pieces, songs, tone poems, oratorios, and occasionally an opera. A few attempted to write "American" music by basing their compositions on Negro spirituals or on Indian themes.

It is not difficult to assess these compositions. They are sincere, honest, well written, but completely without the essential touch of genius that gives music lasting value. Nevertheless, these composers and their music were of genuine temporary value for they produced an environment in which stronger musical personalities could thrive. Without these American composers of the *fin de siècle* we would not be enjoying our present musical life, which differs so radically from that just described.

While these academic compositions and limited musical experience are characteristic of the musical life in the United States in the early years of the century, under the surface and in quiet isolation there was some indigenous musical activity that proved to have great significance and interest. During these years, American ragtime and jazz, soon to be heard around the world, was in its formative stage, and one American composer, Charles Ives, was writing compositions that were as audacious as anything being written on the continent.

Ives, 1874–1954

I feel strongly that the great fundamentals should be more discussed in all public meetings, and also in meetings of schools and colleges. Not only the students but also the faculty should get down to more thinking and action about the great problems which concern all countries and all peoples in the world today, and not let the politicians do it all and have the whole say.

I have often been told that it is not the function of music (or a concert) to concern itself with matters like these. But I do not by any means agree. I think that it is one of the things that music can do, if it happens to want to, if it comes naturally, and is not the result of superimposition—I have had some fights about this.

Charles Ives *

The solitary Charles Ives is the grand exception to this genteel tradition; he is one of the most thorny of rugged individualists in all music history.

As the son of a band director in Danbury, Connecticut, he was intimately associated with music from his earliest youth. His father, by no means the usual town band master, had a remarkable interest in novel combinations of sounds and a flair for experiments. He tried to imitate the sound of church bells on the piano and contrived musical instruments that would play quarter tones. Dividing the members of his band into small groups, he had them play different pieces in an antiphonal and overlapping manner. He encouraged his son Charles to experiment with dissonances at the piano, and often had the family sing a familiar tune in one key while he accompanied in another.

Charles attended Yale as a music student and received traditional instruction, but after graduation he went to New York, entered the insurance business, and composed music as a hobby until the mid-twenties while becoming a successful and wealthy businessman.

Because Ives made little effort to have his work performed, it was virtually unknown until the 1930s, when a small group of musicians became aware of this inspired amateur. Two movements of his Fourth Symphony were played in New York in 1927, and four years later an orchestral piece, *Holidays*, was played in Europe. In 1939 his *Concord Sonata* for piano was heard in New York. From that time the Ives legend has grown, for the imagination of the public was captured by the idea of a businessman-composer-recluse who wrote astonishingly complex and dissonant music.

* In a letter to Lehman Engel.

In 1947 he was awarded a Pulitzer Prize for the Third Symphony he had written some twenty years previously, and in 1955, a year after his death, a full-scale biography and critical study of his works was published. The Fourth Symphony finally achieved a complete performance in New York in 1965, made possible through a grant by the Rockefeller Foundation to pay for the extra rehearsals needed to play the enormously difficult score.

The centennial of Ives's birth in 1974 renewed interest in the composer. Festivals were held in various parts of the country, a large number of new recordings appeared, several book-length studies of the man and his music were published, and innumerable articles paid him homage and evaluated his contribution.

Ives's Compositions

Ives's music includes four symphonies, four sonatas for violin and piano, two piano sonatas, two string quartets, over a hundred songs, and smaller pieces for orchestra and for piano. Since much of this was written before 1918, it belongs to the pre-World War I period that witnessed so many changes in music.

The *Concord Sonata* (1909–1915) is a good example of his work. At a first hearing of this huge work one is likely to be stunned, for it is long, loud, and thick with notes. There are surprising differences in style from page to page and it is entirely unpredictable. The best way to approach the piece is through the titles and the written introductions provided by the composer.

The first movement is a portrait of Emerson, one of Ives's heroes. The composer describes him as "America's deepest explorer of the spiritual immensities," and his style of writing as "based on the large unity of a series of particular aspects of a subject, rather than on the continuity of its expression. As thoughts surge to his mind, he fills the heavens with them, crowds them in if necessary, but seldom arranges them along the ground first." [1] This applies to Ives's sonata.

EXAMPLE 41

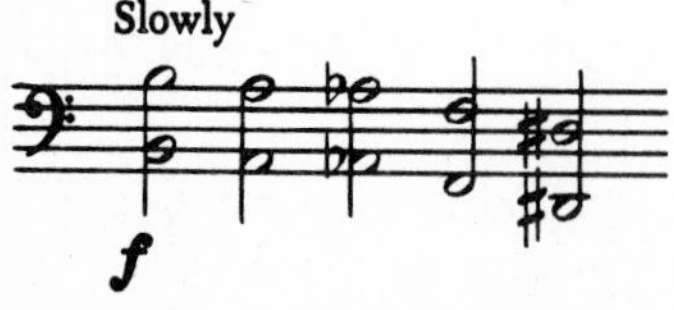

The movement starts with two lines of dissonant counterpoint in contrary motion. The notes in the left hand form a motive which is used throughout the whole sonata. A moment later the signal theme of Beethoven's Fifth Symphony is heard, somewhat disguised. The latter theme also permeates the whole work. Ives tell us that it signifies:

> . . . the spiritual message of Emerson's revelations—the Soul of humanity knocking at the door of Divine mysteries radiant in the faith that it *will* be opened—and that the human will become the Divine.

The piece progresses without barlines, meter (the omission being programmatic, in that the music relates to Emerson's prose as contrasted to his poetry), and without definite tonality. This is rambling, rhapsodic music with occasional references to the two main motives. It soon becomes violent in its dissonance and dynamics, one particularly astringent chord being explained as "but one of Emerson's sudden calls for a Transcendental Journey."

EXAMPLE 42

The structure in seconds is characteristic of the many tone clusters in the piece. A quieter section follows where the writing for several pages resembles Debussy's or Ravel's with a pedal established in the bass, and widely dispersed arpeggios in the left hand against a fragmentary melody in the right. Sections of "heaven-filling thoughts" alternate with pages of reflective music while the references to the Beethoven theme become more insistent. The end of the movement is pure impressionism, with its pedal built on a diminished fifth while intervals are sounded *pppp* above.

Another aspect of New England culture is expressed in the second movement, entitled "Hawthorne." Ives explained that he was not dwelling on the guilt-obsessed aspect of the author of *The Scarlet Letter* in this movement, but rather that he was "trying to suggest some of his [Hawthorne's] wilder, fantastical adventures into the half-childlike, half-fairylike phantasmal realms." This piece, a scherzo in mood, makes tremendous demands on the performer. The opening suggests the figuration of Ravel's "*Scarbo.*" Passages of wild syncopation, probably never notated before this time, alternate with passages to be played with a "board 14¾ inches long, and heavy enough to press the keys down without striking." In the middle of this vertiginous music there is suddenly a quotation from a simple old hymn with directions to play it "as a hymn is sometimes heard over a distant hill just after a heavy storm." A moment later a perky march-tune appears. These allusions to popular music are literal; that is, with their original chords and meter, and result in an almost surrealistic incongruity with the general climate of dissonance.

The slow third movement of the sonata is called "The Alcotts" and is an evocation of the simple, domestic life of the period. It is the most approachable movement and the allusions to additional gospel hymns, parlor songs, and "Here Comes the Bride," form a cohesive whole. The movement ends with a triumphant statement of the Beethoven theme in C major.

The last movement, "Thoreau," is a landscape with a figure. A detailed program concerned with a day in the life of the philosopher of Walden Pond accompanies the piece. The rhapsodic style of the first movement returns near the end, when a pedal figure starts, and above it are heard ever slower and more expressive versions of the basic melodic theme. At the very end, the Beethoven theme is referred to once again.

The first complete performance of Ives's Fourth Symphony in 1965 and its subsequent recordings revealed the climactic example of his unique style. Written between 1909 and 1916, when he was writing the *Concord Sonata*, its originality and performance problems have yet to be equaled.

The symphony is written for a fairly standard large orchestra, with the addition of a solo piano, celesta, organ, and four-hand orchestral piano. There is also a four-part chorus as well as a "distant choir" consisting of two to five violins, solo viola, and harps.

Throughout the thirty-minute work there are continual references to hymns and popular nineteenth-century tunes, often so distorted or covered with conflicting material that they are not perceived as such.

In the first movement, the main orchestra plays jagged, dramatic music while in the background the offstage orchestra plays the hymn "Bethany" very quietly. The chorus enters, singing a unison setting of "Watchman, tell us of the night," in a swinging $\frac{6}{8}$ meter as the orchestra progresses in $\frac{3}{4}$ and $\frac{4}{4}$ simultaneously.

The second movement is so complex that Ives recommended that two conductors lead, respectively, the sections of the orchestra proceeding in different meters and tempos. One finds directions like these in the score:

	Meter	
Conductor I	3/2	Adagio (lower orchestra)
Conductor II	4/4	Allegro, gradually faster (upper orchestra)

In another place we find:

	Meter	
Conductor I	4/4	(♩ = 126–132)
Conductor II	3/2	(𝅗𝅥 = 95–99)

In still another:

Conductor I	Andante
Conductor II	Allegro

In addition to these simultaneous meters and tempos, the individual beats are divided into "irrational" divisions, making scores such as *La Mer* and *Le Sacre du Printemps* seem relatively simple. From time to time the violins are asked to play in quarter tones. The result is frequently a mass of sound in which neither the tune-quotations nor the meter-tempo differentiations can be distinguished, but toward the end the forces coalesce for a moment into a blatant Sousa-type march. Example 43 shows a typically complex combination of tunes.

All of these complexities have programmatic explanations. According to the composer, the program depicts "an exciting, easy, and worldly progress through life, contrasted with the trials of the Pilgrims in their journey through the swamp. The occasional slow episodes—Pilgrims' hymns—are constantly crowded out and overwhelmed by the former. The dream, or fantasy, ends with an interruption of reality—the Fourth of July in Concord—brass bands, drum corps, etc."

The third movement is a total contrast. It is a slow, tonal fugue, primarily for strings, with occasional doublings by solo winds or brass, originally written as an academic exercise while Ives was still at Yale, many years before. In the composer's words, this movement is "an expression of the reaction of life into formalism and ritualism."

[Faster, up to about 138 = ♩ if possible]
40
Più allegro
Piccolo
Flutes
Clarinets in B♭
Bassoons
in octs. ad lib.
ORCHESTRA PIANO
Primo
Secondo
Cornets in C
Trumpets in C
Trpts. I & II
Trpts. III & IV
Trombones
Trbs. III & IV
Trbs. I & II
Tuba
Celesta
Triangle
High Bells
(ad lib.)
Low Bells
Tympani High Low
Indian Drum
Snare Drum
Bass Drum
○ = with Cym.
Gongs a) Light b) Heavy
Più allegro [Faster, up to about 138 = ♩ if possible]
Solo Piano
Violins I
Violins II
Violas
Violoncellos
Basses
½ pizz. ½ arco

The last movement returns to the complexity of the second, expressing an "apotheosis of the preceding content, in terms that have something to do with the reality of existence and its religious experience." [2]

In these brief descriptions of the *Concord Sonata* and the Fourth Symphony, the programmatic contents have been stressed in order to account for the music. Practically all of Ives's music is programmatic, and as his programs were complex and all-inclusive, his music has the same characteristics.

The large pieces he wrote between 1908 and 1918 are undoubtedly the most advanced, the most radical music written anywhere at that time. Other composers were more modest, or else they did not have the courage to assault all aspects of music at once. When Stravinsky exploited asymmetrical rhythmic patterns, for instance, he reduced the other elements (such as melody) to relative simplicity. When Schoenberg was writing his first atonal pieces he made them very short. Ives, however, took on all the difficulties at once.

For that reason, some of his shorter pieces and songs are more successful than the extended compositions. For instance, "The Housatonic at Stockbridge" from *Three Places in New England* (1903–1914) is a beautiful piece of impressionistic music with a shimmering, hazy atmosphere. Fragmentary melodies in the oboe, English horn, and French horn (typical impressionist timbres) are in the foreground, while the background is provided by the violins in quite another key. The early date of this piece makes it one of the first polytonal compositions. Another unqualified success is *The Unanswered Question* (1908), written for trumpet, four flutes, and string orchestra. Here the strings play simple diatonic chords in the background while the solo trumpet enters from time to time with a cryptic, wide-interval melody in a different key. At unexpected intervals the four flutes play independent flourishes. All of this is programmatic. According to the composer's directions,

> The strings play *ppp* throughout with no change in tempo. They are to represent "The Silence of the Druids—Who Know, See, and Hear Nothing." The trumpet intones "The Perennial Question of Existence," and states it in the same tone of voice each time. But the hunt for "The Invisible Answer" undertaken by the flutes and other human beings (sic), becomes gradually more active, faster and louder. . . . [3]

This composition stands the test of good program music. It is deeply expressive to the listener who has no knowledge of its program or even that a program exists. It is complete in its evocative sound.

◄ EXAMPLE 43*

* Charles Ives: Symphony No. 4.

The collection, *114 Songs*, privately printed by the composer, contains an essay in which he writes, "Some have written a book for money; I have not. Some for fame; I have not. Some for love; I have not. . . . In fact, gentle borrower, I have not written a book at all—I have merely cleaned house." Later he writes, "Some of the songs in this book, particularly among the later ones, cannot be sung." [4] A new edition of the songs was published in 1975.

Such candor on the part of a composer prevents any criticism, but the volume does show further examples of Ives's untiring imagination and range of styles. Songs burlesquing popular songs of the nineties, with all of the naïveté of the time, are printed next to songs in the advanced idiom of the *Concord Sonata*, including fourteen-note tone-clusters and unbarred measures. A few songs avoid such extremes and can be judged highly successful and worthy of performance.

Style Characteristics

Some of the outstanding characteristics of Ives's writing have already been mentioned. His style is difficult to describe because of its great originality and apparent lack of system or order.

The idioms of the composers already discussed can be talked about with reference to their musical heredity and environment. For example, we saw that there was something of Massenet in Debussy and more than a little of Wagner in Schoenberg. In creating their own languages and syntax, these composers extended and developed the aspects of music they knew best. Although Ives had a powerful connection with his musical past, it is a relationship different from those we have just seen. When he uses his heritage—American popular music, both sacred and secular—he does so blatantly in literal quotations. Such quotations, however, usually interrupt music that is startlingly new in syntax and vocabulary.

Because he was completely emancipated from the normal musical practices of the day, he had no qualms about using any type of complexity. His dissonant counterpoint, for instance, proceeds with no regard for the ensuing clashes.

His chords are chosen from a range of possibilities not limited by any preconceived notion of what a chord must be. Cluster combinations of seconds, played with the help of a piece of wood cut to a specified length, vary with accumulations of thirds, fourths, or wide, dissonant intervals.

Rhythms are often so complicated that they challenge the ingenuity and experience of highly trained performers and conductors. A decade before *The Rite of Spring* Ives wrote additive rhythms commonly associated with Stravinsky, such as $\frac{5}{8}$, $\frac{11}{8}$, $\frac{7}{4}$, and in orchestral works he sometimes wrote as many as ten different simultaneous patterns that do not coincide until the end.

Ives's formal structures are also without precedent. In his symphonies and sonatas there is little if any adherence to the conventions of sonata structure beyond the fact that they contain several contrasting movements. Within the movements there is more variety than unity as highly contrasting sections succeed each other. An overall unity is achieved more through programmatic or external concepts than through strictly musical means.

The complexity of Ives's music has several bases. First in importance is the experimental attitude he inherited from his father. Most of the composers of his generation growing up in the musical centers of Europe only gradually found musical emancipation from their immediate backgrounds; but paradoxically, Ives, growing up in a small town in New England, became familiar with dissonances that were undreamed of in other parts of the world.

Ives's freedom from such practical considerations as finding publishers or performers for his music meant that he could give full play to his original ideas. He wrote to please only himself and he chose a career in business rather than in music so that he could continue to do so. He never reorchestrated a piece as even the unyielding Schoenberg did "to make it more practical for performance," nor did he ever write music on commission with attached conditions as Stravinsky often did, nor did he write a set of piano pieces of graded difficulty as Bartók did. Ives's music was uninfluenced by external considerations.

The difficulty of Ives's music also had a philosophical origin. As a follower of the New England transcendentalists, he believed life's important matters were so complex and difficult that any attempt to simplify or reduce them to easily understood statements would be weak and dishonest. He had deep scorn for what he termed "pretty" or "nice" music. Ives knew that his music was complex and he wanted it to be that way.

While practically all of the music of his American contemporaries has been forgotten, Ives's continues to interest the musical world. Even young composers of the mid-seventies find inspiration in his achievement. Among the traits they admire are his refusal to limit his music to what was considered to be "polite" or pleasing; his interest in all kinds of music; and his courage to write extremely complex music. His simultaneous presentation of divergent musical material also seems to be a valid expression of the contemporary world. Ives's position as a typically American artist, along with Thoreau, Whitman, and George Caleb Bingham, seems assured.

Suggested Readings

The most complete study of Ives's music is *Charles Ives and His Music,* Henry and Sidney Cowell (New York, 1955). Two collections of the composer's prose writings that give insight to his thinking are: *Epilogue, with an Addendum* (New Haven, 1956) and *Essays Before a Sonata* (New York, 1962).

Several books have been published in connection with the Ives centennial, among them *Ives: Memos,* edited by John Kirkpatrick (New York, 1972). *Charles Ives Remembered* by Vivian Perlis (New Haven, 1974) is a series of transcribed interviews with people who knew Ives at various stages of his career. Rosalie Perry's *Charles Ives and the American Mind* (Kent, Ohio, 1974) and Frank Rossiter's *Charles Ives and American Culture* (New York, 1974) discuss the composer in relation to his time and place. David Wooldridge's *From the Steeples and Mountains* (New York, 1974) is still another recent study.

Books that cover the whole field of American music are *Our American Music* by John Tasker Howard (New York, 1965, 4th ed.) and *America's Music* by Gilbert Chase (New York, 1966, 2nd ed.). Wilfred Mellers's *Music in a New Found Land* (London, 1964) surveys the life and music of Ives, discusses the development of jazz, and attempts to define the essence of American music.

Buddie Petit's New Orleans Jazz Band, c. 1910

7

What contemporary observer would have guessed that the folk music of a small group would become the language of an entire people fifteen or twenty years later and in a few more years, a worldwide phenomenon, with jazz bands existing simultaneously in Melbourne, Tokyo, and Stockholm?

Andre Hodier

Jazz and Popular Music

Unquestionably, the most significant contribution made to music by the United States in the period under discussion lay in the field of jazz and popular music. From its beginnings, this uniquely American music attracted great numbers of people, and even before the advent of phonograph recordings and radio it spread throughout the world in live performances.

Much of this music was created by black musicians. Travelers' reports of the deep South in the early nineteenth century tell of the slaves' singing and dancing, of their work songs, of the religious songs derived from the hymns sung in churches, and of the rhythmic patterns they played on sticks and bones. Many of these musical practices originated in West Africa, the area from which most of the slaves first came, and many of these people were to leave a lasting mark on jazz.

Ragtime

After the Civil War and the gradual move of many blacks to cities, other kinds of popular music arose. Among these none is more important than ragtime, the creation of black pianists. Ragtime is piano music with a strongly syncopated right-hand part played over a steady, marchlike bass. This is dance music; there are no words to be sung.

Example 44 is a quotation of the beginning of the "Maple Leaf

M. L. R.

Rag" (1899) by Scott Joplin, the most famous ragtime figure, showing the syncopated right hand over the steady bass.

Ragtime swept the world, spread by the minstrel shows that regularly toured the United States and Europe even before the Civil War. Minstrel shows were produced and performed by white entertainers impersonating and caricaturing blacks. These shows started with a cakewalk, a burlesque grand entry march called the "walk-around." The cakewalk consisted of elaborate prancing and exaggerated bowing—the black takeoff of "polite" white society. This opening was followed by skits, monologues, and dances, all accompanied by banjos and bone rattlers. European composers were so fascinated by the sprightly lilt of this music that several tried their hands at the idiom. Debussy's *Golliwog's Cake-Walk* (1908), Stravinsky's *Ragtime for Eleven Instruments* (1918), several numbers of his *L'Histoire du soldat* (1918), and Satie's "Ragtime du Paquebot" from *Parade* (1917) are examples.

Early Jazz

Ragtime is distinguished from early jazz because it was played by a solo pianist, and it was written out and sold as sheet music; performers tried to play it as precisely as possible. Early jazz, on the other hand, is group music, and its essence is improvisation on a known melody. It was not written out, for most of the early musicians could not read music. As a result the early history of jazz is obscure until the first recordings were made around 1917. We can only be certain that jazz shared many of the characteristics of various kinds of popular music of the time, since the same performers played in different kinds of groups without appreciably changing their style of playing, whether in a street band, a minstrel show, or for dancing.

New Orleans was the cradle of jazz and a particular combination of instruments—the Dixieland band—consisting of one or two cornets, a clarinet, and a trombone for the melody, and a piano, banjo, and drums for the rhythm.

*Dippermouth Blues,** played by King Oliver's Band, is a typical piece. It was recorded in 1923 but it is characteristic of the earliest jazz. Because it is a blues it follows the typical AAB pattern, each phrase being four bars long, making the chorus twelve bars in all. This recording starts with an introduction followed by the first chorus played by the whole group in a polyphonic texture. In the second two choruses there is a clarinet solo in which the melody

* This recording is included in the Smithsonian *History of Jazz.*

◄ EXAMPLE 44

is freely varied. The whole group returns to play the next three choruses, while the cornet takes over in the three following. The whole group returns again in the last chorus.

Dippermouth Blues employs the blues scale, which involves a flatting of the third and seventh tones as alternates to the normal notes of the major scale, and the "bending" or playing of certain notes flat for expressive purposes.

The word "jazz" was first used in print in 1917 and the Original Dixieland Jazz Band (a white group) made the first recordings in that year. This marked the close of the New Orleans period, for with the end of World War I jazz spread all over the United States and eventually the world. It was a dynamic music that underwent many stylistic changes. These developments will be described in later chapters.

Suggested Readings and Recordings

There are many books on various aspects of jazz. Only a few of the most important are mentioned here. Gunther Schuller's *Early Jazz* (New York, 1968) is the authoritative study of jazz up to 1930. *Jazz, Hot and Hybrid* by Winthrop Sargeant (New York, 1946, 2nd ed.) is still valuable because of its analyses of musical elements. *The Story of Jazz* by Marshall Stearns (New York, 1956) is a good general survey, while *Modern Jazz, A Survey of Developments Since 1939* by Morgan and Horricks (London, 1957) surveys the later periods. *A Pictorial History of Jazz* by Keepnews and Grauer (New York, 1950) contains excellent pictures. Two books on ragtime are: *They All Played Ragtime* by Rudi Blesh and Harriet Janis (New York, 1971, 4th ed.) and *The Art of Ragtime* by William J. Schaefer and Johannes Riedel (Baton Rouge, 1973).

An excellent set of records is the *Smithsonian Collection of Classic Jazz,* distributed by W. W. Norton and Company in New York.

	FRANCE	GERMANY & AUSTRIA	OTHER COUNTRIES	OTHER ARTS, EVENTS
1900	Debussy: *Nocturnes for Orchestra*		Puccini: *La Tosca*	Freud: *The Meaning of Dreams* Exposition Universelle in Paris
1901	Ravel: *Jeux d'eau* Debussy: *Pour le piano*	Mahler: Symphony No. 4	Rachmaninoff: Piano Concerto No. 2	Picasso: Blue Period Mann: *Buddenbrooks*
1902	Debussy: *Pelléas et Mélisande*		Sibelius: Symphony No. 2 Ives: Symphony No. 2	Kandinsky opens art school in Munich
1903	Satie: *Trois morceaux en forme de poire* Debussy: *Estampes*	Strauss: *Sinfonia Domestica*	Ives: Symphony No. 3	Strindberg: *A Dream Play*
1904		Schoenberg: Quartet No. 1 Mahler: *Kindertotenlieder*	Puccini: *Madama Butterfly* Scriabin: Sonata No. 4	Wright brothers: first airplane flight
1905	Ravel: *Miroirs* Debussy: *La Mer* Ravel: *Sonatine*	Strauss: *Salome* Mahler: Symphony No. 5 Lehár: *The Merry Widow*	Falla: *La Vida Breve* Scriabin: *Divine Poem* Sibelius: Violin Concerto	Picasso: Circus Period Founding of *Die Brücke* Fauves exhibit (Rouault, Matisse, Derain, Dufy, Braque) Einstein: *Theory of Relativity*
1906		Mahler: Symphony No. 6 Schoenberg: *Kammersymphonie*		Picasso: Negro period Wedekind: *Frühlings Erwachsen*

	FRANCE	GERMANY & AUSTRIA	OTHER COUNTRIES	OTHER ARTS, EVENTS
1907	Ravel: *L'Heure espagnole* Dukas: *Ariane et Barbe-Bleue*			Picasso: *Les Demoiselles D'Avignon* Kokoschka: *Mörder, Hoffnung, der Frauen* (drama) Bergson: *Creative Evolution*
1908	Debussy: *Ibéria*	Mahler: *Das Lied von der Erde* Schoenberg: Three Pieces for Piano Webern: Passacaglia Schoenberg: String Quartet No. 2	Bartók: Quartet No. 1 Prokofiev: *Suggestion diabolique* Ives: *The Unanswered Question* Ives: Sonata No. 1, Violin-piano	Brancusi: *The Kiss* Cubism: name coined Gertrude Stein: *Three Lives*
1909		Schoenberg: *Erwartung* Strauss: *Elektra* Schoenberg: Five Pieces for Orchestra Webern: Six Pieces for Orchestra	Rachmaninoff: Piano Concerto No. 3	First season of Diaghilev's Ballet Russe in Paris Marinetti: *Futurist Manifesto*
1910	Debussy: *Préludes,* Bk. I.	Strauss: *Der Rosenkavalier* Berg: String Quartet Mahler: Symphony No. 9	Ives: Sonata No. 2, Violin-piano Puccini: *Girl of the Golden West* Stravinsky: *The Firebird* Vaughan Williams: Symphony No. 1	Exhibition of Post-Impressionist art in London

	FRANCE	GERMANY & AUSTRIA	OTHER COUNTRIES	OTHER ARTS, EVENTS
1911	Ravel: *Valses nobles et sentimentales*	Schoenberg: *Gurrelieder* (completed)	Sibelius: Symphony No. 4 Stravinsky: *Petrouchka* Bartók: *Duke Blue-beard's Castle* Bartók: *Allegro barbaro* Irving Berlin: "Alexander's Ragtime Band"	Marc: *Red Horses* First exhibit: *Der Blaue Reiter* Lehmbruck: *Kneeling Woman*
1912	Milhaud: Quartet No. 1 Ravel: *Daphnis et Chloé*	Schoenberg: *Pierrot Lunaire* Strauss: *Ariadne auf Naxos*	Cowell: First performance of tone-clusters Prokofiev: *Toccata*	Duchamp: *Nude Descending a Staircase* Kandinsky: *Art of Spiritual Harmony* Picasso: Collages Mann: *Death in Venice*
1913	Debussy: *Préludes,* Bk. II. Milhaud: *Agamemnon* Ravel: *Trois poèmes de Mallarmé* Satie: *Descriptions automatiques*	Schoenberg: *Die glückliche Hand* Berg: Four Pieces for Clarinet and Piano	Stravinsky: *Le Sacre du printemps* Scriabin: *Prometheus*	Proust: *Swann's Way* Malevitch: Suprematism New York: Armory Show
1914	Ravel: *Trio* Satie: *Sports et divertissements*		Ives: *Three Places in New England* Prokofiev: *Scythian Suite* Vaughan Williams: *London Symphony* Handy: "St. Louis Blues"	Milan: Concert of Noise Music Gertrude Stein: *Tender Buttons* Robert Frost: *Home Burial* Outbreak of World War I

1920·1950

Part Two

Les Six and Cocteau, 1951

Musicians ought to cure music of its convolutions, its dodges and its tricks, and force it as far as possible to keep in front of the listener.

Jean Cocteau

Paris After World War I

EXCEPT IN TERMS OF THE calendar, the twentieth century was not born until after the 1918 victory of the Allies, for only then was it apparent that many of the basic premises of nineteenth-century life had disappeared. Before the war much of Europe had been ruled by kings and aristocrats, but after 1918 most of the monarchs were deposed and sent into exile. The founding of democratic systems of government was not easily accomplished, and the transition period was difficult. The most drastic of these social upheavals took place in Russia; but Germany, Austria, Italy, and many of the central European countries, once a part of the Austro-Hungarian empire, were faced with the problem of learning to govern themselves. It was a time of confusion, but there was general optimism too, for everyone felt the war had not been fought in vain and the world had been saved for democracy.

France, having escaped the necessity of changing her form of government, recovered rather rapidly. Paris quickly regained its importance as an international art center, and for some years this position was uncontested while Germany and Austria were struggling to reestablish their economic lives. Darius Milhaud, twenty-seven years old at the time, has described Bastille Day, 1919:

On the night preceding July 14th, the scene in the streets was unforgettable. There was dancing at every street corner, to the strains of little Bal Musette orchestras. On the 14th at dawn, Honegger, Vaurabourg, Durey, Fauconnet and I made our way towards the Étoile. We managed to clamber up on a seat from which we had a view over the heads of the crowd. There were people everywhere; every tree, every roof, every balcony had its cluster of human faces, and from all sides the crowd continued to arrive in an uninterrupted stream. . . .

The march-past began at eight o'clock. Now at last the Victory that had been paid for so dearly was felt to be something tangible, visible, making our hearts swell with boundless hope. All the great Allied leaders, whom we only knew by their photographs or the newsreels in the cinemas were now before us in flesh and blood: Marshal Foch, Marshal Joffre, Field Marshal Lord Haig, and General Pershing preceded the French regiments each with the flag they had covered in glory, ... Everything at that time seemed to us to be big with promise for the new era of peace.[1]

The painters and sculptors of prewar Paris reopened their studios. Gertrude Stein's home became the meeting place of young writers such as Ernest Hemingway and Sinclair Lewis. James Joyce managed to find a publisher for *Ulysses,* and chapters of *Finnegans Wake* started to appear in *transition,* the publication of the avant-garde. Stravinsky became a French citizen, and Nadia Boulanger, that amazing teacher, spread the doctrine of neoclassicism among the first of hundreds of students who were to study with her. Paris was a magnet, attracting artistic young people from all over the world to sit at the feet of the great—or beside the great in the Café du Monde.

Cocteau, 1891–1963

A key figure of this exciting time was a man difficult to classify. He was the originator and propagandist of many of the new ideas in the arts and the friend and adviser of the most important creators. A poet, an artist, a playwright, he also directed and produced some of the most advanced films of the century. This was Jean Cocteau, who was to be an unpredictable and stimulating figure in the art world for the next fifty years.

In 1918 he published a little book called *Coq et Arlequin,* consisting of a number of aphorisms that succinctly expressed a new aesthetic creed for composers. This creed repudiated romanticism as an ideal, whether of the Wagnerian *Gesamtkunstwerke* variety or its French counterpart, impressionism. Its fighting words were *precision, clarity,* and *order.* Here are a few of the aphorisms from the book. The economy with which Cocteau expresses his ideas is characteristic, for by principle he avoided anything long-winded.

With us, there is a house, a lamp, a plate of soup, a fire, wine and pipes at the back of every important work of art.

A young man must not invest in safe securities.

The Nightingale sings badly.

Beethoven is irksome in his developments, but not Bach, because Beethoven develops the form and Bach the idea. Beethoven says, "This penholder contains a new pen; there is a new pen in this penholder; the pen in this penholder is new." Bach says: "This penholder contains a new pen in order that I may dip it in the ink and write, etc." There is a difference.

A poet always has too many words in his vocabulary, a painter too many colors on his palette, and a musician too many notes on his keyboard.

A dreamer is always a bad poet.

Wagner's works are long works which are long, and long drawn out, because this old sorcerer looked upon boredom as a useful drug for the stupefaction of the faithful.

Debussy missed his way because he fell from the German frying pan into the Russian fire. Once again the pedal blurs rhythm and creates a kind of fluid atmosphere congenial to *short sighted ears.* Satie remains intact. Hear his "Gymnopédies," so clear in their form and melancholy feeling. Debussy orchestrates them, confuses them, and wraps their exquisite architecture in a cloud. Debussy moves further and further away from Satie's starting point and makes everybody follow in his steps. The thick lightning-pierced fog of Bayreuth becomes a thick snowy mist flecked with impressionist sunshine. Satie speaks of Ingres; Debussy transposes Monet "à la Russe." Satie teaches what, in our age, is the greatest audacity, simplicity. Enough of hammocks, garlands and gondolas; I want some one to build me music I can live in, like a house. Enough of clouds, waves, aquariums, water-sprites, and nocturnal scents; what we need is a music of the earth, everyday music. We may soon hope for an orchestra where there will be no caressing strings. Only a rich choir of wood, brass and percussion.[2]

It was inevitable that Diaghilev, returning to Paris shortly after the war to reestablish his ballet (now the Ballet Russe de Monte Carlo), would immediately call upon the talents of Cocteau for his new creations. The two created some of the most novel ballets of the era, always staying one step ahead of the public. Diaghilev had no desire to continue producing the grand ballets of prewar days. His aim now was to shock, to startle, to amuse, and to amaze. *Pulcinella,* a ballet score based on fragments by Pergolesi, brought together Cocteau, Picasso, and Stravinsky, and the excursion into the eighteenth century by these completely modern artists set the pattern for many other forays into a pre-nineteenth-century past.

Satie, 1866–1925

While Beethoven, Wagner, and Debussy are frequently taken to task in *Coq et Arlequin,* one composer is praised—Erik Satie. Chronologically, this strange man belongs to an earlier generation of composers, the period of Debussy. However, since he was always ahead of his time in his musical style, and since it was not until the 1920s that he was widely recognized, it is proper to discuss his works here.

He was born in Honfleur on the Normandy coast, but his family moved to Paris a few years later. Because he showed musical talent he was sent to the Conservatoire, but his real interest lay in the cafés of Montmartre where he played the piano and for which he composed sentimental ballads. Even from the beginning he showed a flair for novel musical ideas and his first serious compositions reveal this originality. The *Gymnopédies,* published in 1897, avoid all of the clichés of the time and strike a note of chasteness quite different from the feverish music of the day. His *Three Sarabandes* for piano of the same year include some very interesting parallel ninth chords which were later to become an important feature of the styles of Debussy and Ravel. In some of his compositions of the next few years he used Gregorian modes as well as chords built in fourths, again anticipating musical idioms that would be extensively developed in the next twenty-five years.

In 1898 Satie "retired" to Arcueil, a suburb of Paris, and for the next twenty-seven years he earned a well-deserved reputation for eccentricity. He lived quietly, spending much of his time in cafés. He was known by a small group of musicians including Debussy, whose home he visited. Because he was unusually sensitive and erratic, friendship with him was precarious and often ended abruptly with some imagined affront.

During these years he wrote a number of piano pieces and gave them ridiculous titles, perhaps parodying the elaborately evocative titles Debussy sometimes gave to his compositions. Debussy called one of his preludes *La terrace des audiences au clair de lune,* while Satie used titles such as *Three Pieces in the Shape of a Pear,* written after someone had criticized his music for having no "form," *Three Flabby Preludes for a Dog,* and *Desiccated Embryos.*

On the scores the performer is bombarded by directions far different from those used by other composers: "Play like a nightingale with a toothache"; "with astonishment"; "sheepishly"; "from the top of the teeth." Other jokes

Satie, Drawing by Picasso
The Bettmann Archive

are found in the scores, such as a perfectly simple passage written in an extremely complicated notation, or popular tunes that are suddenly quoted.

Paradoxically, the real joke comes from the music, for it is often serious in tone. *Three Pieces in the Shape of a Pear,* for instance, are ingratiating, straightforward, and unpretentious. They suggest a mood of gentle melancholy and contain some unusual harmonic progressions. Strikingly absent are any of the usual characteristics of the time—rich Debussyan or Franckian harmonies, or sweetly sentimental tunes.

Satie would have been an interesting subject for psychoanalysis, for he was undeniably maladjusted. Perhaps his humor and his ridiculous titles were defenses for himself and his music, similar to the actions of a sensitive person who plays the clown in social situations to hide his insecurities.

This tendency to underplay the importance of his compositions reached its climax in the music he wrote in 1920 for the opening of an art gallery. Rollo Myers has described the occasion:

> The music was played by a little band of instruments consisting of a piano, three clarinets, and a trombone and was introduced . . . in the following terms: "We present for the first time, under the supervision of MM. Erik Satie and Darius Milhaud and directed by M. Delgrange, furnishing music to be played during the entr'actes. We beg you to take no notice of it and to behave during the entr'actes as if the music did not exist. This music . . . claims to make its contribution to life in the same way as a private conversation, a picture, or the chair on which you may or may not be seated. . . ." [3]

Unfortunately the audience disregarded these instructions and kept silent while the music was being played. This greatly annoyed Satie, who went around urging people to talk and make a noise, since the music, which consisted of fragments of popular refrains from *Mignon* and the *Danse macabre* and isolated phrases repeated over and over again, like the pattern of wallpaper, was meant to be nothing more than a background and was not intended to attract attention in any way.

This is a complete reversal of values when one considers the reverence with which many people listen to music. The contrast between this attitude and that of Wagner, for example, who didn't want to have his music performed except in a specially constructed temple, throws into relief the sharp differences between the nineteenth- and this early twentieth-century aesthetic. Cocteau in another of his aphorisms scorned the traditional point of view:

> *Pelléas* is another example of music to be listened to with one's hands. All music which has to be listened to through the hands is suspect. Wagner's is typically music which is listened to through the hands.[4]

Whether we like it or not, we must accept the fact that music that is "simply there," like wallpaper, is a part of the modern world. Today, in fact, we encounter such music at every turn—in supermarkets, department stores, restaurants, and factories—and millions of people "listen" to their radios while reading, doing housework, or driving. The role such music plays in modern life is not being defended here; it is merely being recognized as an unfortunate reality.

Most of Satie's pieces are short, but after World War I he wrote four extended compositions. By this time he had been "discovered" by the younger composers and he came to the attention of Diaghilev. The result of this meeting was the ballet *Parade*. It brought together four outstanding talents of the day: Cocteau, who provided the subject; Picasso, who designed the curtain, stage settings, and costumes; Massine, who created the choreography; and Satie. This was an important work in the history of the theater and ballet, for it brought cubism to the stage for the first time. The costumes and settings of Picasso were like pieces of animated sculpture in which human traits were no more evident than they were in the pictures he was painting then. The large, angular costumes made it necessary to find a whole new vocabulary of the dance. Cocteau has given a synopsis of the "action":

> The Chinaman pulls out an egg from his pigtail, eats and digests it, finds it again in the toe of his shoe, spits fire, burns himself, stamps to put out the sparks, etc.
>
> The little girl mounts a race-horse, rides a bicycle, quivers like pictures on the screen, imitates Charlie Chaplin, chases a thief with a revolver, boxes, dances a rag-time, goes to sleep, is shipwrecked, rolls on the grass on an April morning, buys a Kodak, etc.

What of the music for *Parade?* Again we quote Cocteau:

> Satie's orchestra abjures the vague and the indistinct. It yields all their grace, without pedals. It is like an inspired village band. It will open a door to those young composers who are a little wary of fine impressionist polyphonies. "I composed," said Satie modestly, "a background of certain noises which Cocteau considers indispensable in order to fix the atmosphere of his characters."
>
> Satie wanted to employ a battery of noise makers, including compressed air, a dynamo, Morse apparatus, sirens, express train, airplane and propeller, and typewriters; but he settled for a conventional dance band.[5]

There is a great deal of the "wallpaper" quality in this music, evidenced by an inordinate repetition of the simplest figures. The music accompanying the first Manager (one of the leading roles in the ballet) consists of repetitions of this figure in rhythmic variants:

EXAMPLE 45*

Later sections consist of pseudo-Chinese music, a "rag-time of the steamboat," and music-hall waltzes to accompany the acrobats.

Two later works, *Mercure* (1924) and *Relâche* (1924), again with the collaboration of Picasso and Massine, anticipate surrealism with their noticeable lack of connection between the action on the stage and the mood of the music.

In 1918 Satie wrote *Socrate*, a "symphonic drama," which many critics consider his most important work. A setting to music of fragments of three Platonic dialogues, the *Symposium*, *Phaedrus*, and *Phaedo* (the last having to do with the death of Socrates), it shows an unsuspected serious side of the composer. Four solo sopranos sing the words, accompanied by a small chamber orchestra consisting of flute, oboe, English horn, clarinet, horn, trumpet, harp, kettledrums, and strings. The work is distinguished by its atmosphere of calm and gentle repose. The words are set exclusively to eighth and quarter notes in a kind of rhythmic recitative that avoids regularity and tunefulness.

Socrate is completely nondramatic in concept, for the words of Socrates

* Permission for reprint granted by Rouart, Lerolle et Cie., Paris.

are sung by one of the sopranos. The role of the orchestra is merely to accompany; it rarely takes part in the melodic line. A few characteristically neutral figures are shown in Examples 46a and 46b.

Socrate, according to Collaer in *La Musique moderne,* is the "masterpiece of its composer, and one of the capital works of contemporary music." [6] Other critics have been equally enthusiastic, but some listeners find an undeniable monotony in the work. The unvarying rhythms, the extreme continuity of the vocal line, the unrelieved vocal timbre, the repetitiousness of the accompaniment, the absence of high and low moments—all of these elements make it less than a complete success. Of course one cannot argue with Satie for having written *Socrate* in this manner, for he wanted it to be pale, undramatic, and neutral. One can say, however, that these are qualities that are more successfully projected in shorter compositions.

EXAMPLE 46a

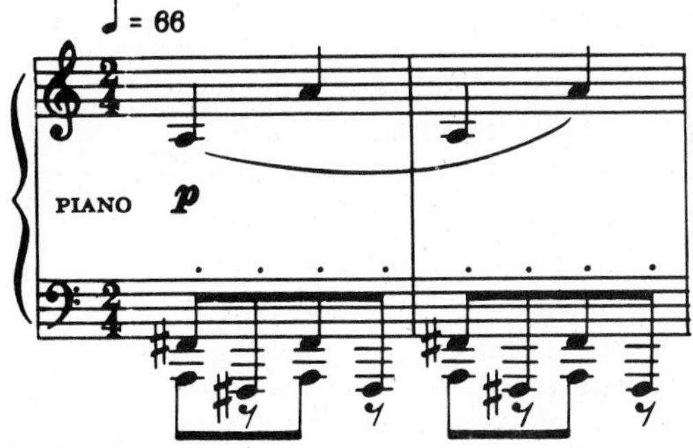

EXAMPLE 46b*

The historical, as contrasted with the artistic, importance of the work is undeniable. *Socrate* is an extreme example of music dedicated to ideals that are totally different from Wagnerian-impressionist-romantic ideals. This is a work of cool objectivity and deliberate modesty in its means and effects—the values that Cocteau had encouraged. These values were to become increasingly important in the music of the next decades and indeed even in the 1970s in the compositions of some avant-garde composers.

Les Six

Henri Collet, a French critic, published an article in 1920 entitled *The Russian Five and the French Six and Erik Satie.* In it he called attention to the music of a group of young composers who had joined together to present concerts of their compositions. The six were Darius Milhaud (b. 1892), Arthur Honegger (b. 1892), Francis Poulenc (b. 1899), Georges Auric (b. 1899), Louis Durey (b. 1888), and a young woman, Germaine Tailleferre (b. 1892). Even though they had been friends from their school days, they were not united by any group "program" or even by a similarity of style. Cocteau was their spokesman; and perhaps the only platform they shared was a negative one—to purge French music of nineteenth-century grandiloquence and impressionist fog. But each had his own idea as to how this should be done, and one rugged individualist, Arthur Honegger, was not sure that it should be done at all.

The general public, however, likes labels, and "Les Six" caught its fancy. No matter how different the composers were to become, they were never allowed to forget this youthful association, sometimes to their annoyance. Milhaud, many years later, described the creation of Les Six:

> Quite arbitrarily he (Collet) had chosen six names: Auric, Durey, Poulenc, Tailleferre, Honegger, and my own, merely because we knew one another, were good friends, and had figured on the same programmes; quite irrespective of our different temperaments and wholly dissimilar characters. Auric and Poulenc were partisans of Cocteau's ideas, Honegger derived from the German Romantics, and I from Mediterranean lyricism. I fundamentally disapproved of joint declarations of aesthetic doctrines, and felt them to be a drag, an unreasonable limitation on the artist's imagination, who must for each new work find different, often contradictory, means of expression. But it was useless to protest. Collet's article excited such world-wide interest that the "Group of Six" was launched and willy-nilly I formed part of it.[7]

For a short time the group was young and carefree together and even collaborated on a joint work written on a libretto of Jean Cocteau called *Les*

Mariés de la Tour Eiffel. Auric wrote the Overture, Milhaud the "Wedding March," Tailleferre the "Quadrille" and "Waltz of the Telegrams," Poulenc the music for a bathing-beauty scene, and Honegger the "Funeral March," the bass of which was the "Waltz" from *Faust.*

Some Typical Compositions

At the time of this common enterprise each of Les Six except Honegger went through a Cocteau-Satie phase. A few characteristic compositions will now be examined. Poulenc's *Mouvements perpétuels* is a good example. These are three unpretentious, amusing pieces for piano. The first starts with an innocent, almost folklike melody over a recurring bass. In the third bar the "shock" occurs. The right hand starts playing a melody involving an unexpected E natural. The important tritone relationship is involved and the effect is like seeing a nice little girl, dressed in her Sunday best, suddenly giving a large and sophisticated wink to her audience. All is not so innocent as appeared at first. Later these dissonances occur over the recurring bass:

EXAMPLE 47*

This use of dissonance is characteristic of Les Six, for the ninths are used not as a point of climax of emotion, but quietly, as an added color. This is, of course, a continuation of Debussy's attitude toward dissonance.

The second and third pieces of the set continue in the same mood of sophisticated play. The second is marked *indifférent* and the third has a music-hall flavor so popular at the time.

Milhaud's song cycle *Catalogue de fleurs* is also a typical Les Six conception. These are musical settings of words that might have come out of a

* Permission for reprint granted by J. W. Chester, London.

seed catalog. For instance, the words to the second song read, "Begonia Aurora, double blossom, apricot mixed with coral, very pretty, rare and unusual." There is something impertinent about setting words like these to music when one remembers the hundreds of "flower" poems set by the romantic composers, such as "*Du bist wie eine Blume*" ("Thou art like a flower"). The romantic was always personal, but the young composers in question did their best to stay away from personal involvement in their music.

Milhaud's and Cocteau's ballet *Le Boeuf sur le toit* (*The Ox on the Roof* or *The Nothing-Doing Bar*) perfectly embodies the spirit of the twenties. It was an immediate success and it "typed" the composer more than any other of his works, a fact that he later regretted. In his autobiography, he summarizes the action of the ballet:

> The setting is in a bar in America during Prohibition. The various characters were highly typical: A Boxer, a Negro Dwarf, a Lady of Fashion, a Redheaded Woman dressed as a man, a Bookmaker, a Gentleman in evening clothes. The Barman, with a face like Antinous, offers everyone cocktails. After a few incidents and various dances, a Policeman enters, whereupon the scene is immediately transformed into a milk-bar. The clients play a rustic scene and dance a pastorale as they sip glasses of milk. The Barman switches on a big fan which decapitates the Policeman. The Redheaded Woman executes a dance with the Policeman's head, ending up standing on her hands like the Salome in Rouen Cathedral. One by one the customers

EXAMPLE 48*

VERSION FOR VIOLIN AND PIANO

drift away, and the Barman presents an enormous bill to the resuscitated Policeman.[8]

As might be expected, the music of Milhaud is anything but "appropriate" to this outrageous libretto, for it consists exclusively of South American popular music he had learned to like in Brazil: tangos, rumbas, sambas, street marches, and fados. The trite tonal melodies are usually accompanied by instruments playing in other keys, but these sounds do not give the impression of a complex chord, for the ear separates the planes of the harmony. The effect is as if one's hearing were out of focus, for it is impossible to form a single, clear sound image (see Example 48). Here the top voice is in E-flat, the second, doubling the melody, in G, with the accompaniment also in these two keys.

Le Boeuf sur le toit fully embodies Cocteau's recommendations. It is full of fun and irreverence and is close to the music of cafés, music halls, and the streets.

Suggested Readings

There are many interesting memoirs that give insights into the artistic world of Paris during the twenties. Recommended to all students of the period are: *The Autobiography of Alice B. Toklas*, Gertrude Stein (New York, 1933); *Passport to Paris*, Vernon Duke (Boston, 1955); *Bad Boy of Music*, George Antheil (Garden City, N.Y., 1945), and *A Moveable Feast*, Ernest Hemingway (New York, 1963).

Two studies of Erik Satie are: *Erik Satie* by Rollo Myers (London, 1948) and *Satie* by Pierre Daniel Templier (Cambridge, 1969). *The Banquet Years* by Roger Shattuck (New York, 1958) contains an illuminating chapter on Satie. *Jean Cocteau* by Margaret Crossland (New York, 1956) surveys the life and works of this versatile artist. Continued interest is shown in the publication of Cocteau's autobiography, *Professional Secrets* (New York, 1970), and another biography, *Cocteau* by Steegmuller (Boston, 1970).

Milhaud

Half artist and half anchorite,
part siren and part Socrates.

Percy MacKaye: France

Les Trois

NO GREATER MISTAKE COULD BE made than to believe that Cocteau's ideals dominated Les Six throughout their creative lives. We have already said that Honegger did not enter this Cocteau-Satie phase at all, and for the others it was merely a passing one. Thus it would be erroneous to think of Milhaud or Poulenc as an eternal *enfant terrible.*

The group had no formal or dramatic breakup, for it was too informal an association for that. In the following years the young composers followed their individual destinies and developed their personal styles of composition, reassembling occasionally for reasons of sentiment or publicity. Durey retired to the country and from music; Mlle. Tailleferre wrote little of lasting importance; Auric became one of the most successful composers of music for motion pictures and eventually achieved international fame with his waltz "Moulin Rouge."

The remaining three—Milhaud, Honegger, and Poulenc—became France's leading composers of the second quarter of the century. Although their music was by no means similar—Milhaud's description of their essential characteristics (cited in the previous chapter) makes this clear—they carried forward the ideals of order, clarity, and charm always associated with their country. Their careers and music will be the subject of this chapter.

Milhaud, 1892–1974

Down with Wagner!
Darius Milhaud

"I am a Frenchman from Provence and of the Jewish faith." This is the opening sentence of Milhaud's autobiography *Notes Without Music.* Its directness and straightforward quality reflect the man and his music.

He was born in Aix-en-Provence, a charming old city in the south of France. His boyhood as reported in the autobiography seems to have been idyllic, for his parents were cultured, well off, and solicitous of his education and well being.

He began to study the violin at the age of seven, but it was not until he was seventeen and had completed his general education that he went to Paris to enter the Conservatory. Paris in 1909 was an exciting place for a student from the provinces. Milhaud immersed himself in the musical world, attending the ballet and opera and becoming acquainted with the new works of Debussy, Ravel, and Stravinsky. He lost no time in making allegiances. He was attracted to the music of Chabrier, Satie, and Roussel, and was repelled by Brahms and Wagner.

By 1912 he had given up the idea of becoming a violinist, in order to concentrate on composition. His teachers were Widor and Gédalge, excellent disciplinarians, who sensed that they were working with an unusually gifted student. At the outbreak of World War I in 1914, Milhaud, whose health had never been robust, was not called to serve. Instead, he went to Brazil as the secretary of the French ambassador, Paul Claudel, an extraordinary diplomat, poet, dramatist, and man of letters. The association with Claudel was to result in some of Milhaud's most significant compositions. However, the most important musical experience of this stay in South America was his exposure to the popular music there, which made a lasting impression on him.

Returning to Paris after the war by way of the United States, he discovered jazz, which was also to influence his music. Milhaud has written of his pleasure in going to nightclubs in Harlem:

> The music I heard was absolutely different from anything I had ever heard before, and was a revelation to me. Against the beat of the drums the melodic lines criss-crossed in a breathless pattern of broken and twisted rhythms . . . . Its effect on me was so overwhelming that I could not tear myself away.[1]

The jazz records he purchased in Harlem were his most precious travel souvenirs.

The role Milhaud played in the twenties as a member of Les Six has already been described. The following years were full of excitement and growing achievement. Although increasingly handicapped by arthritis, he made extensive tours of Europe and the United States to conduct his works. He usually spent summers at his home in Provence where he continued his indefatigable composing.

World War II changed the pattern of his life. Escaping the German occupation of France, he came to the United States with his wife and son and spent the war years teaching at Mills College in Oakland, California. As soon as the war was over, however, the traveling resumed; this included teaching at Mills College and the Paris Conservatory during alternate years, and teaching at the Aspen Music School in Colorado during summers.

Milhaud's Compositions

Milhaud was one of the most prolific of twentieth-century composers. In 1952, at the age of sixty, he completed his Opus 300 and during the next four years he added fifty additional titles—an average of one composition a month. The year 1963, when the composer was 71, saw Opus 404 and by that time he had written sixteen operas, fifteen ballets, twelve symphonies, incidental music to thirty-five plays and twenty films, twenty-eight choral works, thirty additional works for orchestra, thirty-five concertos for various instruments (including one for marimba and one for vibraphone), ten works for voice and orchestra, eighteen string quartets, and many sonatas for piano and various instruments, a setting of the Sacred Service for synagogues, about two hundred songs with piano, and vocal duets and quartets. By the time of his death in 1974 he had achieved Opus 426.

This stream of music shows great diversity in dimension and quality and therefore a comprehensive impression of it is difficult to obtain, not only because of its sheer quantity, but also because some of the larger compositions are rarely performed while some of the less important have become popular through recordings and frequent performances.

Most of Milhaud's compositions were commissioned and the various functions they fulfilled accounted for their dimensions and characteristics. When large, serious operas were called for he wrote *Christophe Colomb* (1928), *Maximilien* (1930), and *Bolivar* (1943). When asked to write a work commemorating the 3,000th anniversary of the founding of Jerusalem, he wrote the pageant-opera *David* (1954). The popularity of ballet in Paris during the twenties brought forth *Le Boeuf sur le toit* already discussed, and three other jaunty, irreverent scores, *Le Train bleu* (1923), *La Création du monde* (1923), and *Salade* (1924). Among the compositions written for theatrical production are *Protée* (1913), a mythological farce; *Les Euménides* (1922), an adaptation of the classical Greek tragedy; *L'Announce faite à Marie* (1932), a devout Catholic play, and incidental music for a fireworks spectacle. Many of the absolute works are the result of requests from soloists, chamber music ensembles, orchestras, or institutions that desired a commemorative piece. These multifarious works elude style-period classification, for Milhaud was not the type of composer who followed a steady line of evolution. Three contrasting compositions will now be discussed.

Les Choëphores (1915) is the incidental music written for Paul Claudel's translation of Aeschylus' play. Although written during the First World War when the composer was still in his early twenties, it must be counted among his important large-scale works. In the first section, the "Funereal Vociferation," the vocal melody is in C major. Against it, the orchestra enters with a B–major chord followed by a D-sharp–minor chord, causing sharp half-step dissonances. This is a clear-cut use of two keys simultaneously, and such *bitonality*, or *polytonality* as it is called when several keys are involved, became one of Milhaud's favorite modes of expression.

The two sections "Présages" and "Exhortation" are very exciting. Here Milhaud dispenses with musical sounds and writes rhythmic word-settings for the chorus accompanied by a large battery of percussion instruments. In the preface to the score he tells why he abandoned singing at this point:

> Two scenes are to be found which create a difficult problem for the composer: they are savage, cannibal, as it were. The lyrical element in these scenes is not musical. How was I to set to music this hurricane? I finally decided to make use of a measured speech, divided into bars, and conducted as if it were sung.[2]

The result is as striking and startling as a savage chant.

La Création du monde (1923), like *The Rite of Spring*, was based on primitive legends, but the differences in conception and production between the two ballets clearly show how the postwar aesthetic differed from that of prewar days. In order to express the savagery and mystery of the primeval forest Stravinsky wrote a score of tremendous difficulty that called for an orchestra of more than one hundred players. Milhaud, writing ten years later, used a seventeen-piece jazz band. In his autobiography he wrote:

> At last I had the opportunity I had been waiting for to use those elements of jazz to which I had devoted so much study. I adopted the same or-

chestra as used in Harlem, seventeen solo instruments, and I made wholesale use of the jazz style to convey a purely classical feeling.[3]

The settings and costumes for Stravinsky's ballet were semirealistic and aimed at giving an illusion of primitive times. Léger's colorful and childlike settings and costumes for *La Création du monde* made no more attempt to depict the African forest realistically than Milhaud's music did to sound authentically or evocatively primitive. The earlier ballet was for the theatre of illusion, the later for the theatre of stylization—another way of describing the difference between late romantic and early twentieth-century art.

The introduction starts with a neutral Satie-like figure in the piano and strings, playing an accompaniment to a mournful melody played on the E-flat saxophone. There are quiet, syncopated "breaks" by the trumpets and other instruments. The harmonic planes are often rich in contrast when various groups of instruments enter in keys other than that of the melody. The polytonality in this piece is always of this nature, for one hears a principal key against which other keys appear. There is no feeling of equality among them; the effect is of an enrichment of one basic key. The basic key is D minor, frequently colored with the major third, F-sharp.

The first dance is fuguelike with this jazz theme as subject:

EXAMPLE 49*

This shows how well Milhaud had listened to jazz in Harlem. The piano is treated as a rhythm instrument.

The second dance starts with a slow chorale, followed by a section that bears a startling resemblance to a Gershwin melody:

EXAMPLE 50

The third features a three-note figure against a background of four:

EXAMPLE 51

The "Gershwin" melody returns in strings.

The last section is very close to jazz, for the solo instruments play improvised-like flourishes over a barbershop chord progression (F#, G#^{7}, C#^{7}, F#^{7}) played by the rhythm section. The atmosphere becomes frenetic as the piece moves with convulsive rhythms. Themes from earlier sections are recalled and the work ends with a quiet coda in which Example 50 is played by the oboe with an obbligato in the horn. The final cadence is appropriate (see Example 52). This use of jazz was not unnoticed by the critics. Milhaud summarized their reaction:

> The critics decreed that my music was frivolous and more suitable for a restaurant or a dance hall than for the concert hall. Ten years later the self-same critics were discussing the philosophy of jazz and learnedly demonstrating that *La Création du monde* was the best of my works.[4]

EXAMPLE 52

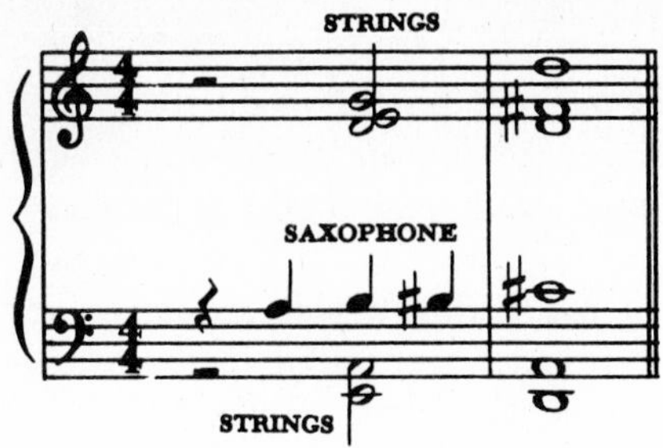

Milhaud's Symphony No. 1 was started in 1939 when the composer was forty-seven. When it is compared with his early works, however, one finds little difference in style, for it contains the elements that have always characterized his works—exuberance; folklike dance rhythms; noisy, polytonal processional sections; quiet pastorals; and sweetness and charm.

The order of the movements is not the usual one for symphonies, for it opens with a pastorale, featuring the flutes. The rhythmic "strumming" in the strings suggests a country dance. The movement is relaxed and amiable, with gracefully flowing melodic lines.

The second movement is loud and brassy with jagged melodic lines and dissonant polytonal chords. In the middle there is a *fugato.*

The third movement starts with a chorale played by wind instruments, but soon a style reminiscent of the "blues" section in *La Création du monde* is established. Two contrasting themes, a noisy and energetic polytonal march and a rhythmic folk dance, are contrasted in the last movement.

Although this symphony was written during the darkest days of World War II, it does not in any way reflect the anguish he felt on leaving France or the problems he faced in adjusting to life in a new country. Regardless of where he might be or his frame of mind, Milhaud's music usually reflected Mediterranean lyricism and exuberance.

Style Characteristics

While most of the older composers of twentieth-century music (Debussy, Schoenberg, and Stravinsky) gradually worked their way free from nineteenth-century music in a process that can be traced from work to work, Milhaud began to compose at a time when the new resources were at hand. His earliest compositions were as dissonant as his latest, and because he was never an adherent of any particular *ism* (expressionism, primitivism, neoclassicism), he moved freely from one idiom to another.

Polytonality is the style characteristic most commonly associated with Milhaud. He was not the first to write music progressing in two or more keys simultaneously, for Bartók, Stravinsky, Szymanowski (the Polish composer), and others had also used this idiom. Milhaud, however, made systematic studies of the effects of combining keys and made this device an important feature of his compositions. Examples have already been cited in the works discussed but none is as striking as that found in the fourth of his five short symphonies written during the 1920s. These are not symphonies in the usual sense, for they are one-movement pieces for various chamber-music combinations. The Fourth Symphony is for ten solo strings, and the last movement is a ten-voice canon with two subjects. Each part enters in one of five different keys.

The concept of a musical texture consisting of several planes of harmony underlies much of Milhaud's music. This manner of writing is often polytonal, for the planes may be differentiated by key, but there are many other possibilities. For instance, in *Les Euménides* Milhaud combines four *ostinatos* (each note thickened with a dissonant chord) of different overlapping lengths, with rhythmic figures and a melodic line.

The combination of so many different factors makes for an extraordinary complexity and thickness of texture, usually alleviated by clear orchestration. Such passages have tremendous vitality, but occasionally, when the individual parts cannot be differentiated, turgidity results.

Milhaud did not always use such a complex style. His many compositions inspired by folk or popular music are simple and direct. Among his best-known pieces of this type are the *Suite provençale* (1936) and the *Suite française* (1944), two compositions for orchestra. He did not limit himself to Franch folk music, as some of the following titles indicate: *Saudades do Brazil* (1920), *Le Bal martiniquais* (1944), *Carnival at New Orleans* (1947), and *Kentuckiana* (1948). In these compositions he retains the folk melodies, adding a pungent harmonization and a loud, brassy orchestration.

His rhythms are usually regular but marked with strong syncopations. One of his favorite rhythmic devices is to group a series of eighth notes in irregular patterns.

EXAMPLE 53

This is one of the rhythms Milhaud learned in Rio de Janeiro. He frequently employs this pattern and other popular dance rhythms in "abstract" (that is, nonfolkloristic) compositions.

Milhaud was a composer with an excellent technique and a practical attitude toward his art. Neither an introspective poet waiting for inspiration to move him to write profound works nor a philosopher-theorist concerned with aesthetic problems, he was like a versatile architect who designs a factory or an embassy, a church or a stadium, according to the wishes of his clients. Such an architect keeps abreast of his times, employing appropriate new materials and methods of construction. His creative personality is apparent in everything he did, not through the exploitation of personal idiosyncrasies, but through the good taste, restraint, and efficiency that mark all of his works.

Honegger, 1892–1955

My desire and my endeavor have always been to write music which would be noticed by the large masses of listeners and which would, at the same time, be sufficiently devoid of banalities to interest music lovers.

Arthur Honegger

Honegger should never have been included with Les Six, for he had little in common with the other composers of the group. He was not even French (although born in Le Havre where his Swiss father was a coffee importer) and he received his early musical training in Zurich where the training was Germanic. When he enrolled at the Paris Conservatory in 1913 his musical gods were Bach, Wagner, Strauss, and Reger—scarcely the idols of his friend Darius Milhaud, whose battle cry was, "Down with Wagner!"

Honegger's experiences as a composer were different from those of his young friends in that his compositions met with approval instead of the hisses and riots that greeted Milhaud's premieres. He continued to write program music at a time when the other members of Les Six felt that tone poems were hopelessly out of date. For example, his piece for orchestra called *Pacific 231* (1923) is a vivid description of a train starting, accelerating, and stopping. Although the subject comes from the mechanized twentieth century (as the Futurists recommended) and a very dissonant style is employed, it is still in the tradition of descriptive music. Because the piece had a firm structure, being a series of figurations over a chorale-like set of chords, it could also be easily enjoyed by the "large masses as well as by music lovers."

By the mid-twenties Honegger was recognized as one of the foremost composers of his generation. He settled in Paris and lived the life of a twentieth-century composer, writing mostly commissioned works for movies, plays, and radio productions, teaching composition, conducting his own works, and writing criticism and essays on music.

In this last role he wrote a very interesting book, *Je suis compositeur* (1951), in which he not only states his creed as a composer but also expresses his outlook for the future of music. He clearly states the differences between his attitude and that of some of his colleagues, particularly those who followed Satie and renounced the resources of romantic music in favor of a more austere language. As for himself:

> I am neither a polytonalist, atonalist, nor dodecaphonist. My great model is J. S. Bach. I do not attempt, as do certain anti-impressionists, to return to simple harmony.[5]

Honegger disappproves of composers who feel that they must adopt a different style in each new work, and remain in a state of constant revolution.

He is frankly bitter about the lack of interest in new music at the mid-century:

> The profession of composer has the peculiarity of being an activity and preoccupation of a man who strives to make a product which no one wishes.[6]

He believes that while more concerts are given now than ever before, less music is heard because only the same few classics are repeated continually. Furthermore, he accuses the audience of being more interested in virtuoso soloists and conductors than in the music:

> The most important attribute of a composer is that he be dead.

Honegger goes even further in writing:

> I sincerely believe that, in a few years, the art of music such as we know it will no longer exist. It will disappear along with the other arts, but no doubt more rapidly. Finally, I believe that we are living in the last moments of our civilization; inevitably these last moments are miserable. They will become more so.[7]

It is not often we hear such gloomy views from a widely respected, honored, and successful man. Perhaps Honegger's experiences during the war (he remained in Paris) and declining health account for them. Perhaps he came to doubt the possibility of writing for the masses as well as the connoisseur. In any event, his book reflects a pessimistic attitude rarely expressed openly, even if felt by many in this age of anxiety.

Honegger's Compositions

Honegger wrote approximately two hundred works in a great variety of forms and media. Perhaps the best known are his "big machines," written for narrator, chorus, soloists, and orchestra: *King David* (1921), *Jeanne d'Arc au bûcher* (1935), and *La Danse des morts* (1938). There is an austere opera on Cocteau's version of *Antigone* (1927). He wrote five symphonies between 1930 and 1951 and symphonic poems such as *Pastorale d'Été* (1920), *Horace Victorieux* (1920), and *Pacific 231* (1923). The charming Concertino for piano and orchestra (1924) pays its tribute to jazz. In addition, he wrote a great deal of piano music, chamber music, many songs, and background music for films and plays.

King David was Honegger's first important work and its success did much to establish his reputation as a composer. He wrote it originally as incidental music for a Biblical drama produced in Switzerland in 1921, and a few years later it was recast so that it could be performed as an oratorio with a narrator taking the place of the actors. In this form it has been very popular and continues to be performed widely.

As given now, the work is divided into three parts. The first part is concerned with David as a young shepherd, his battle with Goliath, and his conflict with Saul. It consists of fourteen musical numbers each separated by the words of the narrator. This makes for a rather fragmentary style since many of the music sections are short. Furthermore, there is a surprising change of musical style from number to number.

King David begins with an orchestral introduction in which the Jewish-Oriental setting is suggested by an oboe melody rich in augmented seconds. Immediately some of the style traits of the composer are evident, such as the dissonant pedals, chords in fourths, and the clear differentiation between the orchestral choirs. The second piece, David's shepherd song, is in folksong style with dissonant counterpart in the violins. The third section, a psalm sung by the chorus in unison, is unmistakably in Bach style with its clear diatonicism, strong rhythms, and bright trumpets.

Simple, lyrical solos alternate with theatrical, polytonal fanfares in the following sections. Battle scenes of strong dissonance flank Jewish songs of mourning. One of the most effective numbers of the first part is the "Incantation of the Witch of Endor." "The March of the Philistines" that follows shows Honegger's talent for original orchestral timbres.

The second part consists of but two extended numbers, a festive song and the "Dance before the Ark," celebrating the crowning of David as king of the Jews. The contrary motion of the outer voices in the opening chorus is characteristic of the composer. This section is a huge canvas that Honegger skillfully fills with large musical gestures, such as the unison passages between the orchestra and chorus, simple, four-square rhythmic patterns, figures rising chromatically to points of climax, and responsorial singing between men and women. The middle section, in triple meter, is the dance of King David, which reaches a strong climax through repetitions of rhythmic figures. A soprano solo, the voice of an angel, predicts the birth of Solomon. The section closes with an alleluia, one of Honegger's happiest inspirations.

EXAMPLE 54*

This chorus is somewhat Bach-like but moves freely from one key to another.

Part III is concerned with events of David's maturity and death; here one finds more large numbers alternating with quiet solos. Particularly striking are the songs of penitence (Numbers 19 and 20), the instrumental march of the Israelites, and the psalm (Number 25), in which the violence of the orchestra reminds one of *Le Sacre.* The work ends on a note of great amplitude and spaciousness. The magnificent alleluia that closed Part II reappears, this time in combination with a chorale melody. Even if the Protestant melody is anachronistic in this scene of Jewish splendor, the effect is undeniably powerful.

Honegger has written with disarming frankness about *King David,* admitting that there are too many short pieces in the first part. He comments on hearing a performance:

I find myself getting bored at Number 6, and I start thinking about Number 8 because I am curious to see if it is going to be played much too fast again this time. At the *Chorus of the Prophets* and at the *Camp of the Israelites* I doze off. I awake at the words, "The Eternal is my light." The *Dance before the Arc,* in spite of certain details, gives me a sort of satisfaction for the development contains a good progression. In the third part, my preference goes to the *Chorus of Penitence.* Naïvely and with pride, I must confess that the combination of the *Chorale* with the *Alleluia* at the end seems to me to realize something of what I hoped.[8]

Honegger's Symphony No. 5 is an example of his mature, serious style. It was written after World War II and received its first performance in 1952 by the Boston Symphony Orchestra. This work is subtitled *Di tre re* (of three D's), referring to the note D on which each movement ends.

The first movement opens immediately with a statement of the main theme played by the whole orchestra, except for the horns, moving in solemn, thickly dissonant chords. Because the passage is characteristic of the composer, it is worthy of investigation in some detail. It consists of two melodic lines in contrary motion:

EXAMPLE 55*

* Permission for reprint granted by Editions Salabert, Paris.

The relation of the two voices is a further example of Honegger's penchant for contrary motion. Each note of this two-voice theme is harmonized with a triad, built down from the upper note serving as the fifth of the chord, and up from the bass serving as a root, resulting in a richly dissonant series of polychords.

After this presentation in the full orchestra, the same material is heard in trumpets and trombones until a second, contrasting theme enters stealthily in the bass clarinet.

EXAMPLE 56

The new theme is treated contrapuntally and rises throughout the orchestra until the first theme recurs fortissimo. This time a new element is added to the polychords—shrill, protesting figures in the trumpets.

After a climax, the first theme complex returns in the strings, but *pianissimo* against gentle figuration in the woodwinds. The movement ends somberly with an occasional reference to the second theme. It ends on the note D, low in the strings.

The second movement, an allegretto, contrasts with the first in mood and tempo. It, too, has a two-voiced theme presented by the violins and clarinets.

EXAMPLE 57

The nine-measure structure of the phrase is noteworthy, for it is maintained for some time, each succeeding nine bars consisting of a contrapuntal derivative of the violin theme. Thus, in Bars 10–19 the retrograde inversion is heard in the bassoon; in Bars 20–29 the inversion is heard in the flutes, and in Bars 30–39 the retrograde version is given to the oboes and English horn. This material is interrupted by woodwind passages punctuated with chords in the strings at irregular intervals, but fragments of the main theme in its various forms are seldom absent.

A short and serious adagio interrupts the scherzo. When the allegretto resumes, the clarinet and violas present the first theme and its inversion in one-measure fragments. The adagio returns, but this time the allegretto theme appears simultaneously. A climax in volume and excitement occurs with material resembling that of the first movement, treated with the triad harmonization and in contrary motion. The movement ends quietly on a low D after further contrapuntal developments.

The third movement is bustling and busy, suggesting the energy and mechanization of the modern world. It is a type of piece not uncommon in the music of Honegger and his contemporaries. Stravinsky and Prokofiev also are fond of writing similar passages of reiterated eighth notes with unexpected and unpredictable accents.

The most prominent theme of this movement is:

EXAMPLE 58

Note the augmented fourth; it still makes its effect.

In moments of climax, polychords reminiscent of the first movement are heard. Various fragments of the basic theme appear and a tremendous amount of energy is created by the perpetual motion of the strings. Suddenly a diatonic theme is heard in dialogue between two horns. Later it appears in canon between the strings and horn, recalling the last movement of the Franck Sonata for Violin and Piano.

But the movement does not end in this positive mood. The equivocal, tonally ambiguous main theme of the movement returns, the motion slackens, and the basses sink to low D for the final notes.

This is a far cry from the "victory after difficulty" pattern that Beethoven established and so many composers of the romantic era followed. The Symphony *Di tre re* is a statement that parallels the disillusioned, pessimistic views expressed in the composer's book.

Style Characteristics

Honegger was not a revolutionary composer who ruthlessly cast aside the ideals and vocabulary of late nineteenth-century music. Neither was he a composer who exploited any single facet of the newer developments. His credo, cited earlier, defines his position. When it served his expressive purpose Honegger used polytonality, chords in fourths, dissonant counterpoint, and complex rhythms. At other times he wrote with great simplicity.

However, there are several characteristics that are often found in his music. One is his habit of changing the order of the first- and second-theme groups in the recapitulation of sonata-form movements, producing an "arch" structure:

		DEVELOPMENT		
	SECOND THEME		SECOND THEME	
FIRST THEME				FIRST THEME

He is also fond of writing outer voices in contrary motion—a characteristic found so often that it is almost a mannerism; examples have been cited from *King David* and the Symphony *Di tre re.* Along with other composers of the time, Honegger makes frequent use of ostinato figures that are in dissonant relationship to the rest of the material. This is one of his favorite ways of building a climax. Examples can be found in the opening and the "Porcus" chorus of *Jeanne d'Arc au bûcher;* and in the "Procession," "Dance before the Ark," the end of "Alleluia," and "Psalm of Mourning" from *King David.* In purely instrumental works, stirring pedal passages occur in the coda of the first movement of the First String Quartet, and in the first, second, and fourth pieces of *Sept Pièces Brèves* for piano.

Many of Honegger's scores are characterized by the expression of powerful, driving energy. *Pacific 231, Rugby,* and *Horace Victorieux* are examples of this aspect of his style. The effect is often gained by using constantly repeated eighth notes in bustling, clashing counterpoint.

Many twentieth-century composers avoid large gestures and big, stirring effects. Not Honegger. He has written some of the most rousing compositions of the time.

Poulenc, 1899–1963

I would by far prefer to write something mediocre with full consciousness and lucidity, than to give birth to a masterpiece among masterpieces in a state of trance and agitation.
Paul Valéry

Francis Poulenc was the member of Les Six who was most faithful to the ideals of Cocteau and Satie. To amuse, to charm, to be gauche in a well-mannered way, to please—these seem to have been his aims.

He was thoroughly Parisian, having been born in Paris just before the turn of the century to a family that was artistic, musical, and affluent. His mother was a fine pianist and Francis began lessons at the age of five. Eventually he became an excellent pianist after working with Ricardo Viñes, a friend of Debussy and Ravel who first performed much of their piano music. While still in his teens Poulenc met Satie, who left a permanent mark on his musical ideals. When he was eighteen he wrote *Rapsodie nègre* for baritone, string quartet, flute, and clarinet. Its lighthearted irreverence and music-hall atmosphere established his right to be a charter member of Les Six when the group was named a few years later.

Poulenc spent most of his life in Paris, except for concert tours that included several trips to the United States after World War II. Although he served briefly in both world wars, active duty was ruled out in World War I because of his youth, and in World War II because of his age. The humor and uncomplicated, direct expression of his music reflect a life that seems to have been singularly untroubled. As a result, there is little difference in style between Poulenc's early and later works, or between his religious and secular compositions.

Poulenc's Compositions

Poulenc's musical interests were primarily lyric, and of his compositions those for voice are certainly his most important. These include almost 150 songs with piano accompaniment, and many choral works both with and without accompaniment. Among the choral works are a setting of the Mass (1937), a *Stabat Mater* (1950), and secular works. He has written over twenty compositions for piano as well as a sonata for two pianos, one for violin and piano, concertos for piano, for organ, and for two pianos. Poulenc wrote no large formal works for orchestra, but the music he wrote for a Diaghilev-inspired ballet, *Les Biches* (1923), was very successful. Two operas, *Les Mamelles de Tirésias* (1944) and *Les Dialogues des Carmélites* (1957), are among his larger works.

The early set of songs, *Cocardes* (1919), written to poems by Cocteau, perfectly embodies the poet's aphorisms. These are songs that suggest Paris streets—the accompaniment, consisting of cornet, violin, bass drum, and trombone, resembles the little street bands that still play there. There is no old-fashioned sentiment here. On the contrary the words follow each other in free association in the manner of Gertrude Stein, while the music proceeds with childish simplicity, with an occasional, planned *gaucherie*. However, not all of Poulenc's songs are in this vein. The cycle *Tel Jour telle nuit* (1937), written to poems of Paul Éluard, celebrates the quiet pleasures of life with sincerity and directness. The melody of the first song, "Bonne Journée," moves in a calm and beautiful line over the simplest of accompaniment figures, reaching its climax only at the end. There are no dissonances, but there are unprepared modulations. The other songs in the cycle continue this mood of quiet simplicity.

Poulenc wrote two strongly contrasting operas. The first, *Les Mamelles de Tirésias* (1944), is a surrealistic farce, witty and clever with many quotations of old-fashioned popular music. *Les Dialogues des Carmélites* is quite different. The story concerns the spiritual development of an aristocratic girl who becomes a Carmelite nun during the French Revolution and chooses death by the guillotine rather than return to the world. Poulenc's great lyrical gifts are revealed in this work, which must be considered one of his most important pieces of music.

Suggested Readings

Milhaud's autobiography *Notes Without Music* (London, 1952) is highly recommended for the insights it gives into the musical world up to World War II. The useful *Catalogue of the Works of Milhaud* by Georges Beck was published in 1949 with a supplement in 1956 by Heugel in Paris. Humphrey Searle (op. cit.) devotes a chapter to "Milhaud and Polytonality" in *Twentieth Century Counterpoint* (New York, 1954).

Honegger's book of essays *Je suis compositeur* (Paris, 1951) has been translated (New York, 1966). There is no full-scale study in English. Landowsky's *Honegger* (Paris, n.d.) contains many interesting photographs.

An authoritative biography of Poulenc is Henri Hell's *Francis Poulenc* (London, 1959).

	FRANCE	GERMANY & AUSTRIA	OTHER COUNTRIES	OTHER ARTS, EVENTS
1915	Milhaud: *Les Choëphores* Debussy: *Études*		Falla: *El Amor brujo* Prokofiev: *Chout* Ives: *Concord Sonata*	T. S. Eliot: *The Love Song of J. Alfred Prufrock* Kafka: *Metamorphosis* Picasso: Classic Period Einstein: *General Theory of Relativity*
1916	Debussy: Sonate for Flute, Viola, Harp		Bloch: *Schelomo* Ives: Symphony No. 4 Prokofiev: *Scythian Suite* Holst: *The Planets*	Kaiser: *From Morn Til Midnight* Joyce: *A Portrait of the Artist as a Young Man* Dadaism invented
1917	Satie: *Parade* Stravinsky: *Renard* Ravel: *Le Tombeau de Couperin* Debussy: Sonata for Violin and Piano Poulenc: *Rapsodie nègre* Honegger: String Quartet No. 1		Prokofiev: *Classical Symphony*	Apollinaire: *Les Mamelles de Tirésias* Word *surrealism* invented Term *expressionism* defined Kokoschka: *Self Portrait* Bolshevik revolution in Russia U.S. enters World War I

	FRANCE	GERMANY & AUSTRIA	OTHER COUNTRIES	OTHER ARTS, EVENTS
1918	Stravinsky: *L'Histoire du soldat* Poulenc: *Mouvements perpétuelles* Stravinsky: *Ragtime*			Zurich: Dada Manifesto Cocteau: *Coq et Harlequin* Spengler: *The Decline of the West*
1919	Stravinsky: *Pulcinella* Milhaud: *Le Boeuf sur le toit* Milhaud: *Protée* Poulenc: *Cocardes* Satie: *Socrate*	Strauss: *Die Frau ohne Schatten*	Bartók: *The Miraculous Mandarin* Prokofiev: *The Love for Three Oranges* Falla: *The Three-Cornered Hat*	Gide: *La Symphonie pastorale* Kafka: *In the Penal Colony* Bauhaus founded Treaty of Versailles
1920	Ravel: *La Valse* Honegger: *Pastorale d'Été* Les Six named			Picasso: neo-classic period T. S. Eliot: *Gerontion* First commercial radio broadcast Lewis: *Main Street*

	FRANCE	GERMANY & AUSTRIA	OTHER COUNTRIES	OTHER ARTS, EVENTS
1921	Honegger: *King David* Milhaud: *Saudades do Brazil*	Berg: *Wozzeck* Hindemith: *Mörder, Hoffnung der Frauen*	Bartók: Sonata for Violin and Piano No. 1 Prokofiev: Concerto for Piano No. 3	Picasso: *Three Musicians* Pirandello: *Six Characters in Search of an Author*
1922	Stravinsky: *Mavra*	Hindemith: *Die junge Magd*	Vaughan Williams: *Folk Song Symphony* Shostakovich: *Three Fantastic Dances*	Gertrude Stein: *Geography and Plays* Joyce: *Ulysses* T. S. Eliot: *The Wasteland* Klee: *Twittering Machine*
1923	Honegger: *Pacific 231* Stravinsky: *Octet* Milhaud: *La Création du monde* Poulenc: *Les Biches*	Hindemith: *Das Marienleben* Schoenberg: Five Piano Pieces Schoenberg: *Serenade*	Sibelius: Symphony No. 6 Walton: *Façade* Prokofiev: Piano Sonata No. 5	von Stroheim: *Greed*

	FRANCE	GERMANY & AUSTRIA	OTHER COUNTRIES	OTHER ARTS, EVENTS
1924	Satie: *Mercure* Stravinsky: Concerto for Piano Stravinsky: Sonata for Piano Varèse: Hyperprisme Milhaud: *Les Malheurs d'Orphée*		Sibelius: Symphony No. 7 Gershwin: *Rhapsody in Blue* Puccini: *Turandot* Prokofiev: *Les Pas d'acier*	Breton: *Manifesto of Surrealism* Mann: *The Magic Mountain*
1925	Stravinsky: *Serenade for Piano* Ravel: *L'Enfant et les sortilèges*	Berg: *Wozzeck* (1st performance) Berg: *Chamber Concerto* Hindemith: *Kammermusik* Webern: Three Songs	Shostakovich: Symphony No. 1 Varèse: *Intégrales*	Kafka: *The Trial* Gide: *The Counterfeiters* Fitzgerald: *The Great Gatsby* T. S. Eliot: *The Hollow Men*
1926	Ravel: *Chansons madécasses* Milhaud: *Le Pauvre Matelot* Roussel: *Suite en Fa*	Berg: *Lyric Suite* Hindemith: *Cardillac*	Bartók: Piano Sonata	Hemingway: *The Sun Also Rises*

	FRANCE	GERMANY & AUSTRIA	OTHER COUNTRIES	OTHER ARTS, EVENTS
1927	Ravel: *Boléro* Honegger: *Antigone* Stravinsky: *Oedipus Rex*	Hindemith: *Hin und Zurück* Schoenberg: String Quartet No. 3	Prokofiev: *The Flaming Angel* Bartók: Quartet No. 3	
1928	Stravinsky: *Le Baiser de la Fée* Milhaud: *Christophe Colomb* Honegger: *Rugby*	Schoenberg: *Variations for Orchestra* Webern: Symphony Weill: *The Three-penny Opera*	V. Thomson: *Four Saints In Three Acts* Bartók Quartet No. 4 Prokofiev: *L'Enfant prodigue*	Huxley: *Point Counter Point* D. H. Lawrence: *Lady Chatterley's Lover*
1929	Stravinsky: *Capriccio*	Hindemith: *Neues vom Tage* Schoenberg: *Von Heute auf Morgen*	Walton: Viola Concerto	Faulkner: *The Sound and the Fury* New York Museum of Modern Art founded

Stravinsky in 1960

10

For I consider that music is, by its very nature, essentially powerless to express anything at all, whether a feeling, an attitude of mind, a psychological mood, a phenomenon of nature, etc. . . . Expression has never been an inherent property of music. That is by no means the purpose of its existence. If, as is nearly always the case, music appears to express something, this is only an illusion and not a reality. It is simply an additional attribute which, by tacit and inveterate agreement, we have lent it, thrust upon it, as a label, a convention—in short, an aspect which unconsciously or by force of habit, we have come to confuse with its essential being.

Igor Stravinsky

Stravinsky 1882-1971

At the outbreak of World War I in 1914, Stravinsky moved to neutral Switzerland, where he lived for the next five years. The war made great changes in his life, heretofore singularly free from two problems that often plague young composers—lack of money and lack of recognition. Now, the revolution in Russia cut off his income and the disbanding of the Ballet meant that his music was no longer performed. He lived quietly, recovered from a serious illness, and worked on compositions that had little in common with the prewar ballets that had brought him such quick fame.

After the armistice, he returned to France and lived for a time in several cities on the Riviera until 1925, when he settled in Paris. Several years later he became a French citizen. Paris was the right setting for Stravinsky, for he represented in music the ideal of neoclassicism that Picasso, Gide, and Valéry—also Parisians at the time—were expressing in paintings, novels, and poetry. This doctrine will be discussed later in the chapter.

Stravinsky did not restrict his activities to Paris, for he started the world tours as a conductor and pianist that continued almost until his death. His autobiography tells about his musical journeys, giving an excellent picture of the musical world in the twenties.

In 1939 Stravinsky came to the United States to give a series of lectures at Harvard University (since published as *The Poetics of Music*). When the outbreak of World War II made his return to Europe impossible, he settled in Hollywood and in 1945 became an American citizen. The change of locale and nationality did not alter the pattern of his life, for he continued composing and conducting his new works in all parts of the world. While his succeeding premieres did not cause riots, each was awaited with interest and followed by controversies. He was never a neglected composer.

For almost six decades Stravinsky was an acknowledged leader of twentieth-century music and the chief representative of an attitude toward life and the arts that underlies much of the aesthetic activity of the era. Because this attitude is so important, it will be described here.

Stravinsky's Position

It has long been recognized that there are two ideals or poles of art. Various pairs of words have been used to describe them: such words as classic and romantic; Apollonian and Dionysian; objective and subjective; of-the-head and of-the-heart. These antonyms indicate that although works of art express the feelings and emotions of their creators (romantic attitude), they are also man-made constructions created by the artist's sensitivity to the materials he uses (classic attitude). While the supreme works of art embody both attitudes, there seems to be a demonstrable shift of emphasis from one ideal to the other in different style periods. Many historians of culture have noted these shifts, but Curt Sachs has perhaps documented them most fully in his book *The Commonwealth of Art*.

There is no doubt where Stravinsky stood in this matter. Since World War I he had been the embodiment of the classical, the objective, the Apollonian ideal. This does not mean, of course, that his music is inexpressive, for sounds and rhythms by their very nature are expressive. It simply means that when Stravinsky wrote a composition he was not concerned (as Schoenberg was) about "writing from the heart" but in constructing a logical and controlled structure in sound. He has explained his position in these words:

> What is important for the clear ordering of the work, for its crystallization, is that all the Dionysiac elements which set the imagination of the creator in motion and cause the life sap to rise should be properly subjugated and finally subjected to the rule of law before they intoxicate us: for this Apollo demands.[1]

If Stravinsky, then, wrote music not to "express himself" (compare the statement of Schoenberg quoted in Chapter 4), what were his motivating forces? Tansman has described his attitude in this manner:

Each work presents for Stravinsky a certain particular problem to resolve, a problem of order for the intelligence, an obstacle to conquer, and if he doesn't have one, he creates one in order to conquer it.[2]

The chapter "The Composition of Music" in his *Poetics* further explains his attitude toward creation. As might be expected, Stravinsky gives inspiration only a small role in the process. Instead, he speaks of an "appetite" to compose:

This appetite that is aroused in me at the mere thought of putting in order musical elements that have attracted my attention is not at all a fortuitous thing like inspiration, but as habitual and periodic, if not as constant as a natural need.[3]

The actual composition, the writing down of notes, the making of a musical construction, is the activity that delights Stravinsky.

The idea of work to be done is for me so closely bound up with the idea of the arranging of materials and of the pleasure that the actual doing of the work affords us, that, should the impossible happen and my work suddenly be given to me in a perfectly completed form I should be embarrassed and nonplussed by it, as by a hoax.[4]

At the end of the chapter the most pertinent remarks are made. "The more art is controlled, limited, worked over, the more it is free," he writes. He speaks of his terror in the limitless possibilities he faces when starting a new composition:

What delivers me from the anguish into which an unrestricted freedom plunges me is the fact that I am always able to turn immediately to the concrete things that are here in question. . . . My freedom thus consists in my moving about within the narrow frame that I have assigned myself for each one of my undertakings. . . . The more constraint one imposes, the more one frees one's self of the chains that shackle the spirit.[5]

Stravinsky, then, was a controlled, anti-Bohemian, orderly man of the twentieth century. Everything about his daily life was on a regular schedule, from setting-up exercises in the morning, through hours of composition, to a relaxing game of Chinese checkers. His workroom has been described by Ramuz, a friend of the Switzerland years:

Stravinsky's writing table resembles the instrument stand of a surgeon . . . the bottles of different colored inks set out according to rank. Each has its little role in the grand affirmation of a superior order. They were ranged together with rubber erasers of various kinds and sizes, all sorts of shining steel objects, rulers, eradicators, penknives, drawing pens, not to mention a kind of instrument with wheels Stravinsky had invented for drawing staves . . . . Here was an order which did enlighten, by its reflection of an inner clarity. This clarity revealed itself too in all those large pages covered with writing made more complex, persuasive, and demanding by means of various inks, blue, green, red, black—two kinds of black, ordinary and Chinese—each having its own place, meaning, and special utility. One ink was for notes, another for the first text, a third for the second, still others for titles, and a special one for the various written indications that go into a score. The bars were drawn with a ruler and errors carefully removed with a steel eraser.[6]

The Problem of Style Changes

One of the results of this attitude led to much confusion and misunderstanding in the world of music. This was Stravinsky's penchant for stylistic changes and for composing "in the manner of" other composers. In the nineteenth century, an original musical language and manner of composing was assumed to be of prime importance; most composers strove to achieve a highly personal style. Stravinsky, on the other hand, seemed now to abandon deliberately the style that had brought him such quick success and, instead, to flit irresponsibly from one manner of composition to another.

It was pointed out earlier that *Le Sacre* was a landmark of violently expressive music. The effects of its dissonances and irregular rhythmic patterns and the brutal sound of the orchestra have already been described. When Stravinsky resumed his composition after the war, his admirers and detractors alike were confused and disappointed because his new compositions seemed completely different from earlier works. *Pulcinella,* for instance, his first postwar ballet, was based on melodies of Pergolesi, and its charm and lack of pretension baffled an audience expecting musical violence.

But this was just the beginning. Next came pieces more or less in the style of Bach or other baroque composers. Then a series of austere ballets and oratorios appeared, bathed in the atmosphere of classical Greece. Following these came compositions based on composers as different as Rossini, Tchaikovsky, and Grieg. These posed even greater problems, for everyone knew that Stravinsky was antiromantic. "What could he be doing?" "Was he serious?" the public asked. Some critics accused him of being a "time-traveler," looking over the whole past history of musical styles and choosing now this composer and now that one—whichever would be the most unlikely and startling—to serve as a model.

After World War II Stravinsky found a new love, the music of Webern and the other two composers of the second Viennese school, Schoenberg and Berg, and started to use the twelve-tone technique. This was embarrassing, for critics and scholars had pointed out that the differences between his music and Schoenberg's were utterly irreconcilable and that the two styles formed, as a matter of fact, diametrically opposed poles of twentieth-century music.

What was not commonly understood was that Stravinsky, no matter what the inspiration for a particular piece, was always true to himself and his conception of music. If a composition is primarily a construction, something made, and is not the expression of a composer's inner life, then it is immaterial if the initial impetus is something original or something given. The composition itself is the important matter, and not its revelation of the composer's unique feelings.

Stravinsky's mind and musical imagination were far-reaching, and his curiosity and appetite insatiable. His problem-solving attitude has already been described, and one can see that all styles, past and present, interested and inspired him as points of departure. His public gradually learned that every bar he wrote was imbued with his own musical personality, no matter what the particular idiom happened to be.

The public also learned that no composer, not even Stravinsky, writes an unbroken series of masterpieces. Living composers do not share the advantage that time bestows on those long dead in separating their great from their lesser works. We do not often hear the weak compositions of Beethoven or Bach, and our opinion of these masters is formed through knowledge of their masterpieces. When the total output of Stravinsky is sifted, some of the derived as well as some of the nonderived works will disappear, and in both categories a few will undoubtedly be counted among the masterpieces of all time.

Relation to Picasso

It was pointed out that Stravinsky was not alone in his attitude toward creativity. Picasso's career and works, for instance, offer many parallels. He too was the best-known creator in his field whose every work was awaited with interest and greeted with acclaim or angry confusion because of his frequent changes in style. No sooner had the public recovered from the shock of one kind of intellectual, problem-solving painting than Picasso started painting according to a whole new "set of rules." Thus, he too had his famous periods—rose, blue, cubist, neoclassic, and others—which varied from extremes of abstraction, to realistic portraits, to wildly expressionist, highly charged paintings—a bewildering variety of styles and media.

At an age when many artists would be repeating themselves, both Picasso and Stravinsky continued their tireless experimentation. They reflected the artistic atmosphere of the first half of the twentieth century, a time of searching and probing, of asking questions rather than finding answers.

Stravinsky's Compositions

Stravinsky's first style period came to an end with *Le Sacre*. Because of his constancy of purpose on the one hand and his variability from piece to piece on the other, his compositions after that elude stylistic classification. For convenience, they will be discussed here in three groups: those written during the early twenties, the compositions of the thirties and forties, and finally, the later works.

PERIOD 2: c.1914–c.1925

The main compositions of this period are:

STAGE WORKS

Le Rossignol (lyric tale; 1909–14)
L'Histoire du soldat (pantomime with narrator; 1918)
Pulcinella (ballet; 1919)
Mavra (comic opera; 1922)
Les Noces (ballet with songs; 1923)

ORCHESTRAL AND CHAMBER WORKS

Ragtime (for 11 instruments; 1918)
Symphonies of Wind Instruments (1920)
Octet for Wind Instruments (1923)
Piano Concerto (1924)

PIANO

Sonata (1924)
Serenade (1925)

L'Histoire du soldat is a stage work written for three dancer-pantomimists and a narrator. It immediately proclaims the "new" Stravinsky. Postwar

Europe could no longer afford Diaghilev's sumptuous ballets, so the composer collaborated with the poet C. F. Ramuz to create a little theatrical piece that could be presented with a minimum of expense. Limitations of this kind did not hinder Stravinsky—they simply provided him with a new "set of rules" to compose by. Instead of writing for a full ensemble he called for a skeleton orchestra of one violin and a double bass, a clarinet and a bassoon, a cornet and a trombone, and a large number of percussion instruments. This strident group, somewhat resembling a dance band, accompanies the stage action in a series of harshly dissonant, satirical pieces. There are tangos, paso dobles, marches, ragtime pieces, and chorales. The violinist has an important part, as does the percussionist who concludes the work in a cadenza of the greatest rhythmic complexity.

In 1919 Diaghilev resumed his activities. Sensing that postwar Europe would no longer be interested in fairy-tale or folk ballets, he turned to the eighteenth century for inspiration. This neoclassic trend was antiromantic in effect, for instead of large, emotionally charged works he now projected modest but highly "chic" productions.

Pulcinella, one of the first of the postwar ballets, was the product of Diaghilev, Picasso, Massine, and Stravinsky. The impresario presented the composer with some melodies purportedly by Pergolesi (1710–1736) and Stravinsky based his score on them. It is his first composition based on another composer's music, and he has described his frame of mind in approaching it:

> Before attempting a task so arduous, I had to find an answer to a question of the greatest importance by which I found myself faced. Should my line of action with regard to Pergolesi be dominated by my love or by my respect for his music? Is it love or respect that urges us to possess a woman? Is it not by love alone that we succeed in penetrating to the very essence of a being? But, then, does love diminish respect? Respect alone remains barren, and can never serve as a productive or creative factor. In order to create there must be a dynamic force, and what force is more potent than love? To me it seems that to ask the question is to answer it.[7]

What is the result of this love? *Pulcinella* resembles both mother and father. Some sections seem to be little more than Stravinsky's strongly personal orchestration of Pergolesi's melodies. The dry, staccato bassoons, the bright treble reeds, the boisterous flourishes of the trombones, and the grotesque double bass solos all proclaim Stravinsky. As Example 59 indicates, the harmonizations are also his. Polychords and dissonant pedals add a touch of salt to the bland melodies. Occasionally the regularity of Pergolesi's melodies is disturbed by contracting or elongating the measures.

EXAMPLE 59*

This novel mixture of old and new was confusing and disturbing, and the composer did not help the situation when he complained:

> What am I to do? Some say they want me to write music that is shocking and provoking like my earlier works; others say that only now do I write proper music. They think I write like Verdi—such nonsense! They don't listen right. These people always want to nail me down. But I won't let them! On the next occasion I do something different and that bewilders them.[8]

In the Octet for Wind Instruments the instruments called for are flute and clarinet, two bassoons, two trumpets, and two trombones. This combination is further evidence of Stravinsky's reaction against the large, prewar orchestra, and his avoidance of lush string quality. He now consciously limits his palette of sound, just as the early cubists restricted themselves to browns and grays, reacting against the exuberant color of the impressionists.

Stravinsky has explained why he chose this group of instruments:

> I began to write this music without knowing what its sound medium would be—that is to say, what instrumental form it would take. I only decided that point after finishing the first part, when I saw clearly what ensemble was demanded by the contrapuntal material, the character, the structure of what I had composed. . . . I remember what an effort it cost me to establish an ensemble of eight wind instruments, for they could not strike the listener's ear with a great display of tone. In order that this music should reach the ear of the public it was necessary to emphasize the entries of the several instruments, to introduce breathing spaces between the phrases (rests), to pay particular care to the intonation, the instrumental prosody, the accentuation—in short, to establish order and discipline in the purely sonorous scheme to which I always give precedence over elements of an emotional character.[9]

The first movement starts with an introduction called "Sinfonia," a title used by baroque composers designating an introductory movement. It has the characteristic dotted rhythms of the French overture. The neutral melody is given rhythmic interest as the meter changes from $\frac{2}{8}$ to $\frac{3}{16}$ to $\frac{3}{8}$ to $\frac{2}{4}$. This section closes on a complex chord that turns into a dominant seventh.

The movement proper starts with this theme:

EXAMPLE 60

Note the leap of a seventh and the "extra" eighth in the sixth measure that throws the beat off from where it is expected. This theme, the basis of much of the movement, is developed and given bustling counterpoints. Later, the trumpet has a second, contrasting theme:

EXAMPLE 61*

The constant displacement of accents, the syncopations and the somewhat banal character of this theme show Stravinsky's awareness of jazz. There is a healthy, vigorous optimism about the piece.

The second movement is a set of variations on this theme:

EXAMPLE 62

The first half is given to the flute and clarinet. While the two woodwinds sing the melody, the rest of the instruments accompany in short after-beat chords. After eight measures the melody passes to one of the trumpets and then to one of the trombones. The pace is comfortable, and the mood is one of quiet melancholy.

The first variation presents the theme without the graceful turn of the second measure. The theme is first played by the trombone, while the other instruments provide sweeping flourishes from low to high register. The second half of the theme is heard from the flute, oboes, and trumpet in after-beat fragments. This variation, along with the trombone scale at the end, is repeated several times in the course of the movement.

In the second variation, resembling a march, the trumpet is prominent. The mood is gay and the dotted-eighth figure recalls "Funiculi-Funicula." In the second half, the woodwinds have a more delicate version but the trumpet reappears at the end.

Material from the first variation is repeated as an interlude to the third, which, in its pastoral coloring and innocent, hesitating rhythms, is a marked contrast to the preceding variation. Few changes of meter occur in this section, which has the feeling of a slow waltz.

This idyll is interrupted by another "busy" variation introduced by the bassoons playing a staccato figure. The melody appears in its original form against figures in the other instruments which are as gay as ballet music of Offenbach. Once again the long scales of the first variation are heard as an introduction to the last variation, which is a *fugato*.

An unaccompanied flute solo serves as a transition to the last movement, which starts with:

EXAMPLE 63

The atmosphere is unmistakably Bach's. A little later, a jazz-inspired melody by the trumpet is heard and the rest of the movement is concerned with the development of these two themes. The ending is particularly striking as it dissolves into rhythmic fragments.

The Octet was one of the first neoclassic compositions by Stravinsky. It would be more accurate to call such pieces neobaroque, since they contain certain features that bring them close to the spirit of Bach and Vivaldi: the contrapuntal texture, the use of instruments and forms suggesting the concerto grosso, and the avoidance of chromatic harmonies and romantic shadings in dynamics.

PERIOD 3: c.1925–c.1950

There is no break in style between the pieces of Period 2 and those of Period 3. Several of the latter are neoclassic in a strict sense, in that they are inspired by subjects of ancient Greece. Others pay homage to various composers, while still others show no external models. The principal works are:

· **Stravinsky**

STAGE WORKS

Oedipus Rex (opera-oratorio; 1927)
Apollon Musagète (ballet; 1928)
Le Baiser de la Fée (ballet; 1928)
Perséphone (for speaker, tenor, chorus; 1934)
Jeu de cartes (ballet; 1936)
Orpheus (ballet; 1948)
The Rake's Progress (opera; 1951)

CHORAL WORKS

Symphony of Psalms (1930)
Mass (for mixed chorus and double wind quintet; 1948)

ORCHESTRAL, CHAMBER AND SOLO WORKS

Capriccio (for piano and orchestra; 1929)
Violin Concerto (1931)
Concerto for Two Pianos (1935)
Dumbarton Oaks (concerto for 16 strings; 1938)
Symphony in C major (1940)
Danses concertantes (for chamber orchestra; 1942)
Sonata for Two Pianos (1944)
Ebony Concerto (for Woody Herman; 1945)
Symphony in Three Movements (1945)

In his *Autobiography*, Stravinsky tells of the "rules" he set up in composing his *Symphony of Psalms*. He was invited to write a symphony for the Boston Symphony Orchestra and accepted even though he had no intention of writing a conventional symphony, "the latter being simply a succession of pieces varying in character." Deciding to write a work with "great contrapuntal development" he chose a choral and instrumental ensemble in which "the two elements should be on an equal footing." After this, he decided to set verses from the Psalms. This sequence of calculations (so different from the motivations of a romantic composer who would probably have started with an urge to write religious music, then found an appropriate text, and then chosen his medium) is characteristic of his objectivity.

Stravinsky often gives individuality to a composition by employing a unique, *ad hoc* combination of instruments chosen for their appropriateness to the work in question. The *Symphony of Psalms* has no violins or violas, and the score leans heavily on the woodwinds, a fact which adds to the stark, ancient, biblical flavor of the work. The text of the opening section is taken from Psalm 39, verses 12–13. In the King James Version it is as follows:

Hear my prayer, O Lord, and give ear unto my cry; hold not Thy peace at my tears: for I am a stranger with Thee, and sojourner, as all my fathers were. O spare me, that I may recover strength, before I go hence, and be no more.

It starts with a sharp E-minor chord spaced and orchestrated in such a manner that it sounds entirely new, both in timbre and in effect. It is an example of what Walter Piston reported from a conversation with the composer about another piece. "How happy I was when I discovered that chord," said the composer. Piston comments:

It was an ordinary D-major chord but he meant this particular setting, spacing, and dynamics . . . . When we realize that such precision marks Stravinsky's approach to every technical and esthetic problem connected with musical composition, we begin to see why his influence has been inescapable, why his music has been so great a stimulation to other composers.[10]

If the first chord alone has such precision and effect, it is not surprising to find that every detail of the movement is as carefully planned. After the opening chord, oboes and bassoons play a broken chord figure consisting of major and minor thirds. This juxtaposition of thirds gives unity to the entire movement; there is scarcely a measure in which they do not appear. When the chorus enters with its supplication

EXAMPLE 64

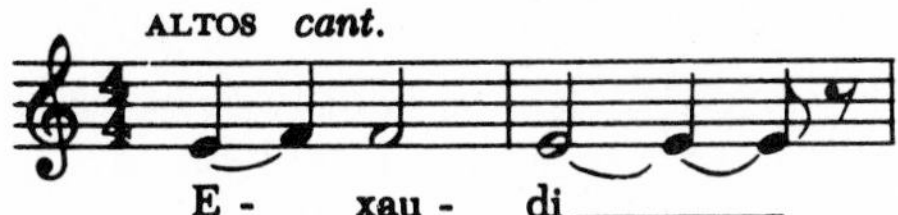

the accompanying thirds appear in this form:

EXAMPLE 65*

The second movement is a large double fugue. A translation of the text follows:

I waited patiently for the Lord: and he inclined to me, and heard my cry. He brought me up also out of an horrible pit, out of the miry clay, and set my feet upon a rock, and established my goings. And He hath put a new song in my mouth, even praise unto our God: and many shall see it, and fear, and shall trust in the Lord.

The first subject starts in the orchestra, stated by the oboe in a high register. Although it outlines a major seventh, the relationship to the basic theme of the whole work is obvious:

EXAMPLE 66

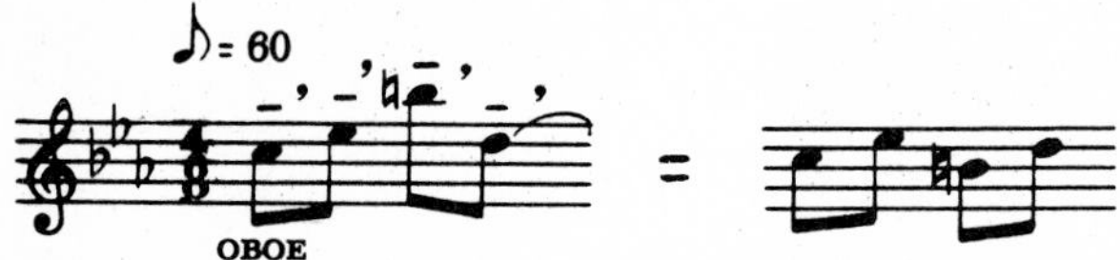

Here is an example of a favorite device of the composer, that of transferring a note an octave away from its original position. In this case the octave displacement results in the diminished fourth becoming an augmented fifth.

The chorus enters with the second subject of the fugue, while the orchestra continues with the first. There is a short section for the chorus *a cappella* including a *stretto*. It ends with a beautifully quiet cadence reminding one of sixteenth-century voice leading. The ending is particularly lovely in its seraphic calm. The chorus sings E-flats spread over two octaves while the basses continue the basic theme. Simultaneously, the theme is played by the soprano trumpet and by the flutes as a cluster.

The third and longest movement is a setting of Psalm 150, a song of praise and thanksgiving, a translation of which follows:

Praise ye the Lord. Praise God in His Sanctuary: praise Him in the firmament of His power. Praise Him for His mighty acts: praise Him according to His excellent Greatness. Praise Him with the sound of the trumpet: praise Him with the psaltery and the harp. Praise Him with the timbrel and dance: praise Him with stringed instruments and organs. Praise Him upon the loud cymbals: praise Him upon the high sounding cymbals. Let everyone that hath breath, praise the Lord. Praise ye the Lord.

This is one of Stravinsky's noblest achievements. It begins with the words *alleluia laudate*, set with the simplicity and directness of truly great statements; even on first hearing these measures are memorable:

EXAMPLE 67

The two ideas shown above recur in the middle and at the end of the movement. After this solemn opening an orchestral interlude introduces the main body of the movement. Here again is the familiar Stravinsky atmosphere of strong, irregular rhythms, reiterated chords in the horns and bassoons, brilliant flashes of sound, and strong dissonances. Throughout the section prominent use is made of the basic interlocking third motive. The chorus enters into this new milieu giving words to the horn's repeated-note motive:

EXAMPLE 68

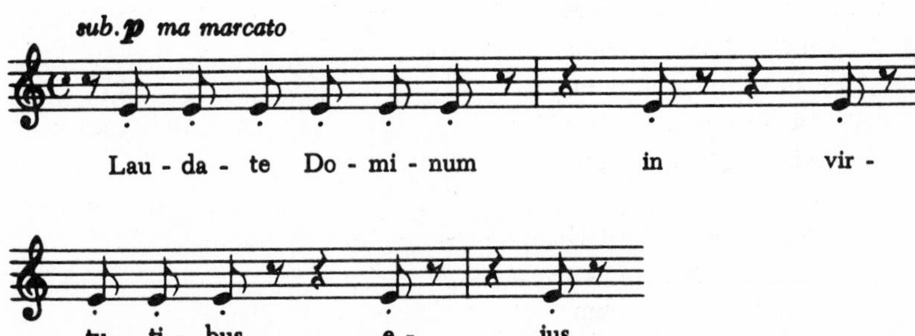

The mood of almost barbaric exultation is interrupted by another statement of the alleluia phrase, and then much of the early material reappears in a free recapitulation. The coda starts with a diatonic D-major canon of great simplicity leading into a section in E-flat of the utmost calm. One is reminded of tolling bells by the constant reiteration of E-flat, D, C, D over an ostinato moving in fourths. The *alleluia laudate* is heard for the last time and the work ends on a seraphic C-major chord. The *Symphony of Psalms* is one of Stravinsky's masterworks and it may well enter into the small group of twentieth-century masterpieces.

The opera *The Rake's Progress* (1951) is another of Stravinsky's major compositions. Its first performance in Venice, followed by the production at the Metropolitan Opera in New York, aroused great interest.

Given his predilections, it is not surprising that Stravinsky wrote *The Rake's Progress* on an eighteenth-century, Mozartian model, with the result that it is a "number" opera consisting of arias, duets, and occasional choruses. The numbers are separated by *recitativo secco*, accompanied on a harpsichord. It is a singer's (as opposed to a singing actor's) opera, with high notes at the expected places and opportunities for bravura display. The orchestra part, although rich in unusual instrumental effects, does not compete with the vocal line.

Written by W. H. Auden and Chester Kallman, the libretto is a dramatization of Hogarth's series of well-known engravings depicting realistic scenes in the "progress" of a dissipated young man who finds corruption and death in eighteenth-century London. As is usual in earlier operas, the story is developed during the recitatives while the resulting emotional states are expressed in the arias.

The third scene of Act I is typical. It is sung entirely by Ann, the sweetheart Tom has abandoned when he goes to London with the evil Nick Shadow. After expressing her concern over Tom's safety in a recitative, she sings a beautiful aria invoking the night and the moon to watch over him. It starts out as shown in Example 69. The throbbing accompaniment figure is used throughout. Note the characteristic "blurring" of the otherwise consonant harmony.

In the short recitative that follows, Ann decides to leave her father and go to London to find Tom. The succeeding brilliant C-major *cabaletta* in which she expresses her joy and excitement is an aria as demanding as Mozart's "Martern aller arten," and ends, as might be expected, on a sustained high C.

There is great variety in the opera, from scenes of ribald humor to scenes of pathos. One of the latter is the moving scene in Bedlam, where Tom is confined after he loses his sanity. It is interesting to compare this scene with the close of *Erwartung*, which is also concerned with insanity. Schoenberg expresses madness through the accumulation of atonal dissonance and wide leaps in the melody. The music itself, in other words, is irrational. On

EXAMPLE 69*

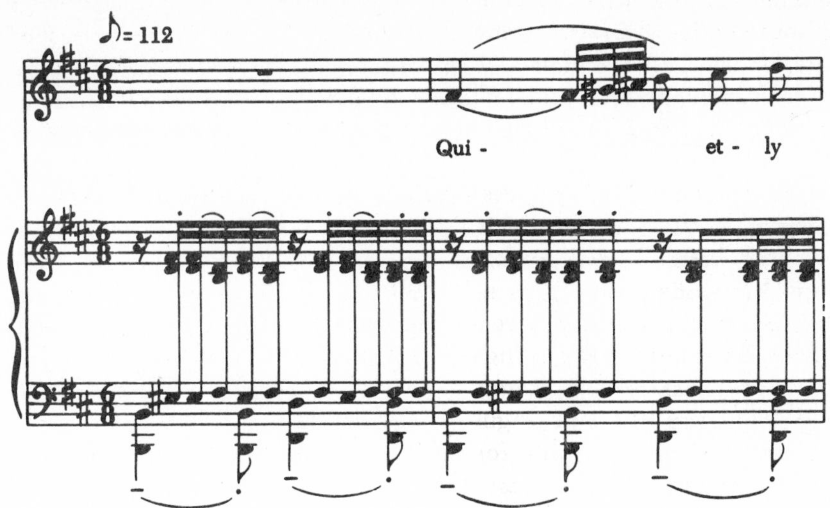

the other hand, Stravinsky expresses the pathos of Tom's madness, instead of the madness itself, in a quiet song in A major.

The Rake's Progress, like *Don Giovanni,* concludes with an epilogue in which a homely moral is brought home to the audience. This conventional ending underlines Stravinsky's intentions. He never thought of his characters as real people whose fate would move his audience to tears. They are simply characters in a fable providing the excuse for a series of beautifully written, contrasting songs.

This opera was Stravinsky's last neoclassic work. His later compositions will be discussed in Part III.

Style Characteristics

Stravinsky's melodies are often built on short fragments of diatonic scales. They frequently have a narrow range and a sing-song quality as they revolve around a central axis and turn back on themselves, gaining directional power from the interplay of the irregular rhythmic patterns. Sometimes this conjunct motion is interrupted by octave transposition, resulting in a jagged line.

Another type of melody frequently found is based on the notes of a broken chord. One of many examples can be found at the opening of the third movement of the *Danses concertantes.* Stravinsky has been accused by some critics of being a poor melodist, and it is true that when one thinks of any of his compositions one usually recalls a complex of rhythm, harmony, and tone color rather than a melody. He will not be remembered as the great melodist of the age.

On the other hand, no one ever called Stravinsky's rhythms weak, for his loosening of the shackles of metrical consistency by his irregular groupings is possibly his greatest technical contribution to music. Attention has been called to specific examples in the compositions already discussed. Almost any passage chosen at random from any of his works reveals striking rhythmic devices—from the polyrhythms of *Petrouchka* to the Webern-inspired silences of *Agon.* Throughout his scores the rests take on great importance, giving an effect like the drop into an unexpected airpocket when one is flying in an airplane. One loses one's breath, equilibrium is momentarily lost, and then one proceeds smoothly until the next jolt. Stravinsky's rhythmic devices are compelling and exhilarating.

Stravinsky uses a wide variety of chords. He likes to add or substitute major or minor seconds to ordinary triads, giving the blurred, out-of-focus effect mentioned earlier. It has also been called the "wrong-note" technique—an inaccurate term, since there is nothing accidental in any of his writing. It must be admitted, however, that the chorales of *L'Histoire du soldat* sound as though they were willfully harmonized with wrong notes.

If Stravinsky can be said to have a favorite chord, it would be that which contains both a major and a minor third. Examples can be found at the beginning of the second movement of the Symphony in Three Movements, the postlude to Tom's aria, "Vary the song," opening the second act of *The Rake's Progress,* the "Devil's Dance" from *L'Histoire du soldat,* and the "Rondoletto" movement of the Serenade in A.

Frequently a complex structure can be analyzed as a polychord, the combination of two different chords. The unforgettable tom-tom chord of the "Auguries of Spring" in *Le Sacre* is an example (see Example 30). Another famous polychord is that found in *Petrouchka,* already mentioned. Stravinsky's polychords are not always complex. He often simply combines tonic and dominant. Other dissonant combinations result from polytonal writing or from the combination of two or more planes of harmony.

In spite of his extensive and freely treated dissonance, Stravinsky (up to the serial works) was essentially a tonal composer in that a basic tonality underlies all of his pieces. The term *pandiatonic* has been used to describe his harmonic practice; this is a useful, if somewhat loose, concept implying the use of the diatonic scale without functional harmony. Such music, of course, eludes analysis with Roman numerals, for the chords are not limited to structures built in thirds nor is there any predictable sequence of root progressions, except that the piece will ultimately end on the tonic.

Another of Stravinsky's major contributions was his revelation of a whole gamut of new sound potential in the conventional instruments. His musical ideas demanded an effect frequently described as "dry," obtained through precise articulation and the exploitation of ranges and combinations of instruments usually avoided. The bassoon solo at the beginning of *Le Sacre,* the spiky, percussive writing for the piano in the Concerto, the scratchy, multiple stops in the violin part of *L'Histoire du soldat* and innumerable other examples show the unusual demands he makes on the instrumentalists. The instrumental combinations are equally novel and tend to be different for each composition. It is seldom that Stravinsky wrote for the conventional symphony orchestra.

A wide variety of textures is found in Stravinsky's works, with a trend toward pure counterpoint becoming more and more apparent. While the earlier compositions were often conceived in planes, the lowest of which was an ostinato figure, later works show a greater interest in linear texture.

Suggested Readings

Stravinsky's own books are of prime importance. An English translation of Stravinsky's autobiography, *Chronique de ma vie,* was published in London in 1936 as *Chronicle of My Life* and in New York as *Stravinsky, an Autobiography.* The lectures given at Harvard in 1939 that formulate his aesthetic of music are published as *The Poetics of Music* (New York, 1956). *Conversations with Stravinsky* edited by Robert Craft (Garden City, N.Y., 1959) gives invaluable insights into the composer and man, as the conversations range over a wide variety of subjects. A second volume of conversations with Robert Craft, called *Memories and Commentaries* (Garden City, N.Y., 1960), contains more reminiscences and many photographs from all periods of his life. The series continued with *Expositions and Developments* (New York, 1962), *Dialogues and a Diary* (1963), *Themes and Episodes* (1966), and *Retrospectives and Conclusions* (New York, 1969). A useful *Complete Catalogue of the Published Works of Stravinsky* was published by Boosey and Hawkes in 1957.

Among numerous biographies and studies of his works, Tansman's *Igor Stravinsky, The Man and His Music* (New York, 1949), containing a lengthy analysis of his style elements, Eric White's *Stravinsky* (London, 1947), and Roman Vlad's *Stravinsky* (New York, 2nd ed., 1967), are recommended. Eric White's *Stravinsky: The Composer and His Works* (Berkeley, 1966) discusses each composition and contains much valuable information. Also see

Benjamin Boretz and Edward Cone: *Perspectives on Schoenberg and Stravinsky* (New York, 1968), a collection of essays originally appearing in *Perspectives of New Music*. *Stravinsky in the Theater* edited by Minna Lederman (New York, 1949) and *Stravinsky* edited by Edwin Corle (New York, 1949) contain essays written by a wide variety of critics and acquaintances as well as photographs of the composer and his friends, ballet sets, etc. Nicholas Nabakov's *Old Friends and New Music* (Boston, 1951) contains an interesting account of a visit to Stravinsky's home. An important collection of essays, first appearing as a special issue of the "Musical Quarterly" (Vol. XLVIII, No. 3, July, 1962) has been published in book form as *Stravinsky, A New Appraisal of His Works* (New York, 1963). This book contains a valuable bibliography. Later books are *Stravinsky* by Robert Siohan (London, 1965) containing many interesting pictures, and *Stravinsky* by Francis Routh (London, 1975).

After Stravinsky's death several books giving accounts of his last years were published. They include Lillian Libman's *And Music at the Close* (New York, 1972) and Paul Horgan's *Encounters with Stravinsky* (New York, 1972). Robert Craft's *Stravinsky: Chronicle of a Friendship 1948–1971* (New York, 1972) gives many insights into the man and his activities.

Schoenberg at U.C.L.A., c. 1940

Composition in twelve tones has no other aim than comprehensibility.

Arnold Schoenberg

Schoenberg
1874-1951

WHEN SCHOENBERG RETURNED TO CIVILIAN life in 1917, he found Austria impoverished, demoralized, and dismembered. Vienna, once the proud capital of a far-reaching empire, ornamented with opera houses, theaters, and universities, was now reduced to the shabby center of a small, unimportant country. Runaway inflation that completely wiped out savings and inheritances contributed to the confusion and desperation of the people.

In spite of this, Schoenberg entered what were probably the happiest years of his life. He received no official appointment, the musical taste of Vienna being far too conservative for that, but he resumed the roles he had played before the war—those of composer, teacher, and theorist. A group of enthusiastic and brilliant young musicians gathered around him, among them Alban Berg and Anton von Webern, who had been with him before the war. There were also younger men such as Paul Pisk and Egon Wellesz, pianists Rudolph Serkin and Edward Steuerman, violinist Rudolf Kolisch, and others.

Schoenberg's disciples regarded him with awe and devotion usually reserved for religious leaders. As he developed a new "gospel" of music, they became convinced he was revealing the path they must follow; they were fanatical in their devotion and firm in the belief that here they had found musical salvation. Some of them wrote commentaries on his compositions, while others busied themselves performing them. Some were to spend the rest of their lives in this service—even after Schoenberg left Europe, and even after his death when a new generation of disciples, commentators and, finally, apostates appeared.

This parallel with the career of a religious leader is not suggested satirically. There was something about the man and his ideas that inspired devotion and enthusiasm. His complete earnestness and dedication; his courage and persistence in spite of official neglect; the apparent chasm that separated his musical doctrine from that of the past (although one of the disciples' favorite occupations was to "prove" that the chasm did not exist*); and the tremendous difficulty and complexity of his music—all of these elements were conducive to forming a cult. The laudatory commemorative volumes published in 1924 and 1934 on the occasion of Schoenberg's fiftieth and sixtieth birthdays are important documents of the group. This statement of von Webern is typical:

> For truly, it is more than rules for art that you learn under Schoenberg. Whoever has an open heart is here shown the path of good.[1]

In 1925 Schoenberg accepted an invitation to become professor of composition at the Prussian Academy of Fine Arts in Berlin. Germany's recovery from defeat and inflation had been quicker than Austria's, and the years of the Weimar Republic (1919–33) witnessed tremendous activity in all of the arts. It is not surprising then, that Schoenberg, the most radical German-speaking composer, was invited to teach at the State music school. This long overdue public recognition and financial security came to an abrupt end in 1933, however, with the election of Hitler as Chancellor. Immediately thereafter all advanced art was branded "bolshevik" and banned, and Jews were removed from civil-service positions. This was, of course, the mildest act perpetrated against persons of Jewish faith, but it was the beginning of the great exodus of European Jews to other parts of the world. One result of this purely political action was the profound enrichment of the cultural and scientific atmosphere of the United States where so many distinguished artists, scholars, and musicians emigrated.

Schoenberg left Europe never to return again, and fled to the United States. En route, stopping in Paris, he reembraced Judaism, having become a Catholic earlier in his life. He arrived in New York on October 31, 1933, at the age of fifty-nine, and started to build a new life. He spent a year in Boston, teaching at the Malkin Conservatory, but the effects of the severe winter convinced him he should live in the more temperate climate of Los Angeles. He arrived there in 1934, where he lived until his death at the age of seventy-six in 1951.

* See, for example, the translation of a speech given by Alban Berg in 1930 on the Vienna radio entitled "What Is Atonality?" in Slonimsky's *Music Since 1900.*

As a person, he did not mellow or become the benign old master. Aware of the contributions he had made to the art of music, he was bitter that his compositions were not played. He was sarcastic and extremely critical of other living composers and depressed at the horrible fate of fellow Jews in Hitler's Europe. His greatest satisfaction was his family—the youngest son was born when Schoenberg was sixty-seven—and his home was a hospitable center for Americans as well as for fellow refugees.

If anyone had predicted in the 1920s that the two great European composers, the cosmopolite Stravinsky and the Austrian Schoenberg, would one day be neighbors in Southern California, the notion would have been dismissed as being too fantastic to consider. Nevertheless, the vagaries of the twentieth century brought this to pass. In spite of their proximity, however, the two composers did not associate with each other. Their totally different personalities, their diametrically opposed ideas as to the nature and function of music, the worldwide fame of the one and the relative obscurity of the other—all this made contact and communication impossible between them.

Twelve-Tone Music

It will be recalled that before World War I Schoenberg had already progressed through several style periods, from the chromatic idiom of the early works to the expressionist atonality of *Erwartung* and *Pierrot Lunaire.* It was after he returned to Vienna, following the war, that he developed an idiom that was to be among the most provocative and disturbing steps ever taken in the long history of music. This idiom, embodied in less than thirty compositions that are seldom performed, has nevertheless opened up musical horizons and musical space of staggering and bewildering proportions.

It is perhaps not too farfetched to make an analogy with developments in exploring outer space. There the problem is to become free and to exist outside of earth's gravity and atmosphere. In music, Schoenberg's problem was to learn how to exist outside the "gravitational" pull of tonality. His early solutions to the problem have already been described. Between 1915 and 1923 he worked on another:

> After many unsuccessful attempts during a period of approximately twelve years, I laid the foundations for a new procedure in musical construction which seemed fitted to replace those structural differentiations provided formerly by tonal harmonies. I call this procedure *Method of Composing with Twelve tones which are related only with one another.*[2]

In everyday language, various abbreviations or substitute expressions are employed. Some of these are *twelve-tone music, dodecaphonic music,* and *serial music.* It should be noted, however, that all serial music is not necessarily twelve-tone, because composers sometimes use a series of six, ten, or any other number of tones in their rows. Furthermore, other elements besides tones are sometimes used in series. This development will be treated in Part III.

It is important to remember that twelve-tone music resulted from the search for a "new procedure in musical construction . . . to replace those structural differentiations provided formerly by tonal harmonies." The *row* and its manipulation was the solution to musical composition without tonality in the conventional sense.

A twelve-tone composition is based on a series of notes chosen from the twelve tones of the chromatic scale. Such a series, or row as it is called, functions in some ways as a scale does in tonal music in that it serves as the raw material out of which the composition is made. There are, on the other hand, many differences between a row and a scale. There is no hierarchy in a row—no tonic, leading tone, or any functional tendencies. True democracy reigns; every tone is the equal of each of the others. Furthermore, the row is not simply the chromatic scale. It is a series of eleven intervals forming a melody with its own unique profile and character. For example, these are tone-rows on which compositions have been based:

EXAMPLE 70a, VARIATIONS FOR ORCHESTRA, OP. 31

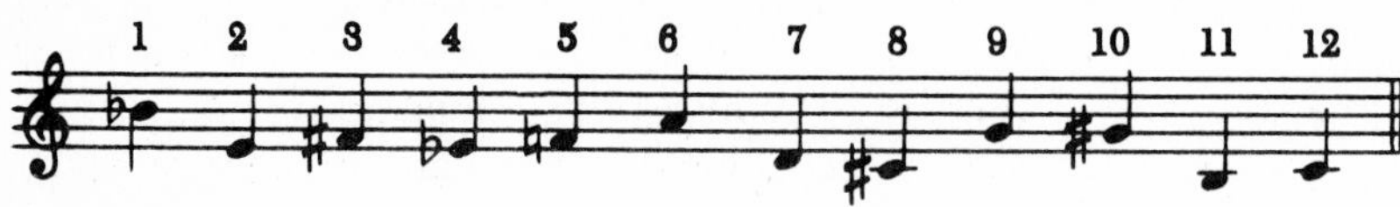

EXAMPLE 70b, SUITE, OP. 25

Mathematicians have calculated that there are 479,001,600 different tone-rows available.

Where does a row come from? Schoenberg assures us that it is as much a product of inspiration as the tonal themes of other composers. He admits that a row is sometimes edited and revised in the same manner that Beethoven and other composers reworked their themes until suitable for use in a composition.

A distinction must be made between the basic row (*grundreihe*) and the basic shape (*grundgestalt*). The row is simply a succession of tones without rhythmic differentiation. It is never used this way. It becomes a theme or shape only when the tones acquire rhythmic relationships. For example, the theme derived from the basic row of the *Variations for Orchestra* quoted above is as follows:

EXAMPLE 71*

How the Row Is Used

The principles of twelve-tone composition developed gradually from composition to composition. Schoenberg did not write a textbook of procedures or teach his students to compose in this manner, but in recent years several of his followers have attempted to describe his method of composition. Josef Rufer, one of the students, has provided one of the most thorough descriptions of the style in his book *Composition with Twelve Tones.* He gives a number of "rules" that will be paraphrased here and illustrated with examples from the *Variations for Orchestra,* which will be analyzed later in greater detail.

1. The row consists of the twelve different tones found in the chromatic scale, their order determined by the basic "shape." Once a tone is sounded it is not repeated until the series has been completed. (To repeat a tone would give it more prominence than another tone.) However, under certain conditions tones are repeated for reasons of sonority or rhythm (to sustain or articulate a tone), when used as a pedal point, or in trill or tremolo figures.

2. The row is used in four forms: Original (O), Retrograde (R), Inverted (I), and Retrograde Inversion (RI).

EXAMPLE 72

3. The series can be used both horizontally and vertically, as melody tones, as melody and accompaniment, or as chords. As a result, the notes of the row are not necessarily sounded in order, as can be seen in the following examples. The larger principle is that they all be sounded before the row is repeated.

4. The series may be used in any transposition, i.e. starting on any tone as long as the sequence of intervals is retained. (This means that with the four forms of the row there are forty-eight different series potentially available.)

5. Any tone of the row can be sounded in any octave. Endless variants of the basic row forms are possible because of this important principle.

6. Sometimes the row is subdivided into subgroups; for example, two groups of six tones each, or three of four tones, or four of three. This more complex concept, often exploited by Schoenberg, will be illustrated later in the discussion of the Piano Concerto.

From this summary of some of the basic procedures of twelve-tone music it must be apparent that instead of being a restricting, limiting procedure, it offers a tremendous number of possibilities to the composer. As Schoenberg has written, "the introduction of my method of composing with twelve tones does not facilitate composing; on the contrary, it makes it more difficult." In order to show how plastically a row may be treated, here are the beginnings of the movements making up the Suite, op. 25. In each case the row is the same, yet the profile and character of the pieces are entirely different:

EXAMPLE 73a, BASIC ROW

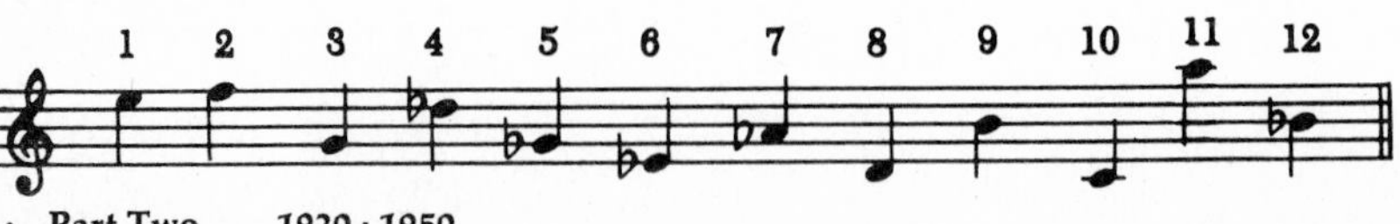

EXAMPLE 73b*

EXAMPLE 73c

EXAMPLE 73d

EXAMPLE 73e

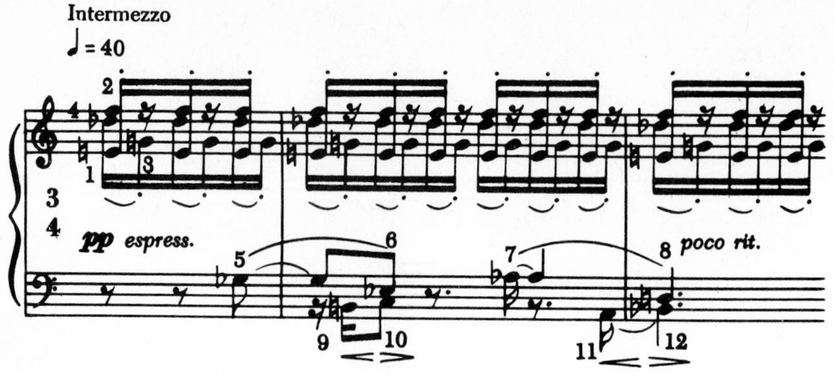

EXAMPLE 73f

EXAMPLE 73g

EXAMPLE 73h

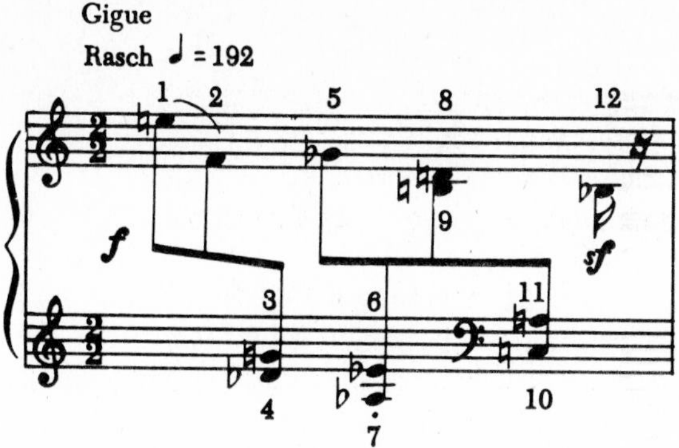

Schoenberg's Compositions

The mature works of Schoenberg may be divided into two groups (Periods 3 and 4): those written before and those written after his immigration to the United States. The "method" was developed while he was writing the former group of compositions, while the latter group shows modifications and relaxations of the doctrine; sometimes there is even a partial return to tonal principles.

PERIOD 3: TWELVE-TONE COMPOSITIONS

It was not until 1923 that the *Five Piano Pieces* (op. 23) were written.* The last piece in the set is his first twelve-tone composition. Other works are:

Op. 24	*Serenade* (for clarinet, bass clarinet, mandolin, guitar, violin, viola, cello, and bass voice; 1923)
Op. 25	Suite for Piano (1921–23)
Op. 26	Wind Quintet (1924)
Op. 27–28	Works for mixed chorus (1925)
Op. 29	Suite (for 2 clarinets, bass clarinet, violin, viola, cello, and piano; 1925)
Op. 30	String Quartet No. 3 (1927)
Op. 31	*Variations for Orchestra* (1927–28)
Op. 32	*Von Heute auf Morgen* (one-act opera; 1929)
Op. 33a,b	*Two Piano Pieces* (1927, 1932)

* Many of Schoenberg's opus numbers parallel or approximate the years in which works were written.

Several general observations can be made about these compositions, all key examples of twelve-tone writing. Schoenberg's preferences for piano music and chamber music may be noted. The only composition for orchestra is the *Variations* and in his entire output there are few works for orchestra alone. In the works listed above Schoenberg returns to conventional forms; Opus 25 and Opus 29 are organized as baroque suites, while the String Quartet and the Wind Quintet are sonatas. These works are no longer gloomy and heavy as were the prewar expressionist compositions. Instead, they are sprightly and precise, delicate in sound, and mercurial in expression.

The *Variations for Orchestra,* op. 31, is probably the most important work of the period. In it the twelve-tone principles of construction are employed with such richness of invention that it has become a source book of the manifold possibilities the idiom affords. But the *Variations* are much more than a textbook of procedures. A work of great expressiveness reflecting a wide gamut of contrasting emotions, beautifully sensuous sounds, and intense organization, it is one of the most significant compositions of the between-the-wars period.

Furthermore, it is important as the first twelve-tone work to be written for full orchestra. The idiom evokes a new manner of writing for orchestra because classic doublings and purely sonorous effects are foreign to the style. The orchestra used is the large, romantic assemblage: woodwinds by fours in this case, a large percussion section, harp, celesta, the usual strings, and a mandolin. However, as in the early orchestral pieces, Schoenberg uses mass sounds sparingly and the large orchestra is used for color and clarity of line rather than for volume.

The *Variations* are based on the row quoted in Example 71.

Introduction: The work starts pianissimo; harp harmonics over violin tremolos establish the nebulous atmosphere before woodwinds start a triplet vacillation between B-flat and E (the tritone), the first two tones of the row. The wide-ranging violin melodies, unusual flute flutter-tonguings, frequent meter changes, and polyrhythms are elements that build to an exciting climax.

When the music becomes quiet again, the solo flute plays a graceful passage, under which appears the first statement of the B-A-C-H (B-flat, A, C, B-natural) theme which becomes very important in the "Finale." The opening oscillating figure returns and a pizzicato chord completes the introduction; a surprisingly conventional device, it reminds one of the similar spot in the overture to *Der Freischütz.* The introduction is based on the row (as is the whole composition), but up to this point the row has not been heard *melodically* in a single voice.

Theme: The theme is presented by the cellos, the first twelve tones corresponding to the basic row. The next twelve are the Retrograde of the Inversion (RI) in the tenth transposition (nine semitones higher than the original pitch level). The next twelve tones are the Retrograde of the Original series (R), while the last twelve (in the violins) are the Inversion (I) of the tenth transposition. The theme, then, uses the row in all four versions:

EXAMPLE 74

The rhythm of the theme, in contrast to that of the introduction, is regular and waltzlike even though the phrases are asymmetrical. The orchestral accompaniment is thinly scored so that the theme may be easily heard. Leibowitz points out that a subtle relationship exists between the number of tones in these chords and the number of tones in the melodic phrases.[3] Thus the first phrase, consisting of five tones, is accompanied by a chord of five tones; the second phrase, consisting of four tones, is accompanied by a chord of four; and the third phrase of three tones, by a triad. Further, the chords are derived from a version of the row that is in a planned relationship with everything else in the section. For example, the first twelve tones under discussion are accompanied by chords derived from I^{10} (tenth transposition of the Inversion). Leibowitz shows the relationship in this chart:

MELODY	**(O) 1 2 3 4 5**	**6 7 8 9**	**10 11 12**
Accompaniment derived from	1	6	10
the tenth transposition	2	7	11
of the Inversion	3	8	12
(I^{10})	4	9	
	5		

The relationship of melody to accompaniment of the whole theme is as follows:

	PHRASE A	**PHRASE B**	**PHRASE C**	**PHRASE D**
Melody	O	RI^{10}	R	I^{10}
Harmony	I^{10}	R	RI^{10}	O

Variation I, Moderato, 24 measures, piano, cantabile: The theme is begun by the bass clarinet, bassoon, and contra bassoon in a straightforward version, but it soon passes to other instruments. Surrounding the theme, the other instruments play bright, nervous figures; the piccolo adds a shrill touch. There is continuous sixteenth-note motion gained through the superimposition of rhythm patterns. The sweet quality of this variation is achieved through the numerous doublings in thirds, sixths, and tenths (an unusual sound in this style of music) resulting from the simultaneous use of various transpositions.

Variation II, Langsam, 24 measures, pianissimo, dolce: In contrast to the first variation, Variation II is written for eighteen solo instruments. Muted violins present the theme followed by the first oboe in canon one beat later. There are other canons between various instruments, and the contrapuntal texture provides another contrast to Variation I. The solo instruments continue in fixed canonic relationships, but the remaining instruments (still in their serial order) enter from time to time to add color. Shortly before the end of the variation, the B-A-C-H theme is played by the trombone.

Variation III, Mässig, 24 measures, forte: This is a bustling, repeated-note variation, with continuous sixteenth-note motion. Superimposed over this busy figure is an energetic, jagged, rhythmic figure. The theme, played by two of the four horns, is in the middle register and remains there throughout the variation. The four phrases of the theme are punctuated by rests during which the other instruments continue their energetic conversations.

Variation IV, Walzer tempo, 48 measures, piano, grazioso: The notion of the "austere" Schoenberg writing musical puzzles without regard to their sound is completely belied by this variation. Scored for twelve solo instruments (others are added later), it is truly "delicious-sounding," as it has been described. The theme, transposed and manipulated, is heard in shimmering harp harmonics, celesta, and mandolin—but as an accompaniment to new counter-themes played by the flute, bassoon, and muted solo viola.

Variation V, Bewegt, 24 measures, fortissimo: The magic-garden atmosphere of Variation IV is brutally interrupted by Variation V. Here high-soaring melodies of opposing rhythmic patterns struggle against each other. The theme appears in the double basses but is scarcely heard because of the complications sounding above.

Variation VI, Andante, 36 measures, molto piano, dolce: Once again there is a marked contrast between this variation and the preceding. Variation VI is quiet in character with the theme played unobtrusively by the solo cello. The flute, English horn, and bassoon have important melodies derived from a transposition of the inversion of the original series.

Variation VII, Langsam, 24 measures, ppp: Here is an essay of the softest, most delicate sounds, the dynamics ranging from *p* to *ppp*. The theme is unobtrusive again, appearing high in the piccolo and glockenspiel in single notes, and in the solo violin in a short figure. A florid melody in the bassoon's high register pervades this section.

Variation VIII, Sehr rasch, 24 measures, forte: Variation VIII is another active, strident variation with an ostinatolike eighth-note motion in the bass, and above it an aggressive rhythmic pattern:

♪♩. ♫♫♩|♩

Strings and higher woodwinds punctuate in irregular groupings. Near the end, the theme is heard from the flute, clarinet, and violin.

Variation IX, L'istesso tempo, 24 measures, piano: The theme is played by the piccolo at the beginning. It is in original form but with a new rhythmic design entirely changing the mood. In the second half, the whole orchestra partakes in the treatment of the theme.

Finale: The Finale is an extended piece of 212 measures divided into definite sections, and permeated with the B-A-C-H theme. The first section, starting with flutter-tonguing by the flute and tremolos by the violin, recalls the beginning of the work. A *grazioso* central section follows. Next comes a breathless presto that is interrupted by a six-measure adagio. The presto resumes and the work comes to a close with a final statement of the B-A-C-H theme. The final chord contains all twelve tones.

Variations for Orchestra demonstrated that it was possible to compose an extended piece for full orchestra according to the rules of twelve-tone music. Previously Schoenberg and his followers had favored suitelike structures scored for small combinations of instruments, but the *Variations* showed that full-scale compositions were possible.

PERIOD 4: AMERICAN WORKS

These compositions were written after Schoenberg came to the United States. The principal works are:

Op. 36	Violin Concerto (1936)
Op. 37	String Quartet No. 4 (1936)
Op. 38	Chamber Symphony No. 2 (1906–39)
Op. 39	*Kol Nidre* (for speaker, chorus, and orchestra; 1938)
Op. 40	*Variations on a Recitative* for organ (1941)
Op. 41b	*Ode to Napoleon* (for speaker, string orchestra, and piano; 1942)
Op. 42	Piano Concerto (1942)
Op. 43a	*Theme and Variations* (for band; 1943)
Op. 45	String Trio (1946)
Op. 46	*A Survivor from Warsaw* (speaker, men's chorus, and orchestra; 1947)
Op. 47	*Fantasia* for violin and piano (1949)
Op. 50b	*Psalm CXXX* (for unaccompanied six-part chorus, sung and spoken in Hebrew; 1950)
	Moses und Aron (opera, started in 1930; incomplete)

Several of these works were the direct result of the composer's reactions to the Second World War. *The Ode to Napoleon* and *A Survivor from Warsaw* are examples. The texts reveal Schoenberg's hate for dictators and his deep concern for the fate of European Jews under Hitler.

The two concertos, string quartet, organ variations, string trio, and the *Fantasia* show a continuing interest in large-scale instrumental works. The Trio is of particular interest, because of its autobiographical elements. It was written after a serious illness during which the composer's heart actually stopped beating for a moment. Schoenberg almost never discussed his compositions, but in an uncharacteristic moment of candor he stated that the illness and convalescence are portrayed in the music, even the thrust of the hypodermic needle.

Characteristic of some of the last-period works is an apparent coming-to-terms between tonality and twelve-tone writing. The *Variations for Band* are unequivocally tonal. Other late compositions combine tonal and twelve-tonal practices resulting in a relaxed, autumnal mood quite different from the tenseness found earlier. The Piano Concerto is perhaps the best example of this phase of the composer's works.

The Piano Concerto, op. 42, is in four movements played without pause. The first, organized in sonata form, begins in an atmosphere of gentle melancholy with the following row-theme:

EXAMPLE 75*

The balanced regularity of the four-measure phrases and the lilt of a slow waltz give the movement an almost old-fashioned flavor.

At first the orchestra is subservient to the piano, but soon it takes over the main theme in a counterexposition. The fact that the violins start this section on a note a fifth higher than the opening suggests the tonic-dominant relationship of tonal music. Many similar relationships occur in this composition, since transpositions of the row and modulations from one to another are regular occurrences.

The development section starts with a trill-like passage in the middle register of the piano while the orchestra plays segments of the row. The piano is silent during the next section of the development, in which the basic rhythmic patterns of the whole composition are fragmented and heard in shorter and faster versions. The piano reenters with a cadenza leading to the recapitulation.

The main theme returns, starting on the same notes as in the exposition. The violins carry the soaring melody this time, while the piano adds figurations. The coda is marked by a *piu mosso* and contains raucous passages written for the trombones.

The second movement, based on transpositions of the basic row, is a scherzo in form and mood. There is a clear differentiation between the beginning section and the Trio, which reverts to a slow triple meter. The outer sections of the movement exploit the xylophone, snare drum, and the flutter-tongue flute effect so attractive to the composer.

The third movement is cast in the form of a theme with variations. The poignant adagio theme, derived from a transposition of the row, is divided between the oboe and bassoon:

EXAMPLE 76

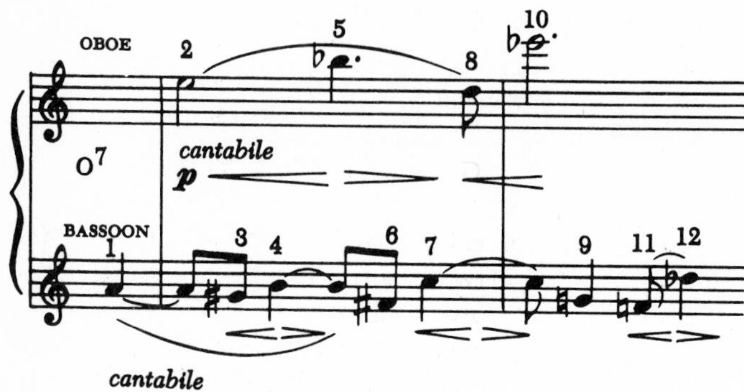

Five short variations and a coda follow. The latter is a cadenza for the piano, starting with a tremolo passage.

The last movement, a rondo, begins with an inverted version of the theme:

EXAMPLE 77

The form of the whole movement is A-B-A-C-A Transition D-A. The mood is that of the traditionally carefree last movement. There are occasional references to the original form of the theme. The work comes to an end after the original rows have been clearly established—another link with the practices of tonal music.

In this concerto Schoenberg makes extensive use of the subdivided row, resulting in a great increase in the number of serial possibilities. For example, the basic row (Example 75) is so constructed that the first six tones of O can be combined with the first six tones of R without repetition of tones. Thus, a hybrid row is formed, utilizing all the tones but altering their order from any of the "pure" forms. An example follows:

	1	2	3	4	5	6	7	8	9	10	11	12
O:	E♭	B♭	D	F	E	C	F♯	A♭	D♭	A	B	G
R:	G	B	A	D♭	A♭	F♯	C	E	F	D	B♭	E♭

combining O(1–6) and R(1–6)

E♭ B♭ D F E C G B A D♭ A♭ F♯

The same relationships and combinations exist between I and RI and between O and R with I and RI when the latter two are transposed a perfect fourth higher. Thus another whole group of row combinations is made available, providing a much greater flexibility than when only the "pure" row forms are used. Furthermore, a process similar to modulation in tonal music ensues, in that hexachords common to two versions of the row (with the order of the notes changed) can function in the way tetrachords common to two keys do in tonal music. This relationship between two rows is called *combinatoriality*.

The Piano Concerto is so expressive and its forms are so closely related to those of the classical concerto that the listener may have difficulty in realizing that it is completely built on a basic tone-row. The technique of twelve-tone composition is synthesized with many conventions of the classic and romantic piano concerto and negates the view that Schoenberg was an eccentric composer, completely removed from the mainstream of music history.

Another important work is the opera *Moses und Aron*, started in the 1930s but left incomplete with Schoenberg's death in 1951. The composer did not lose interest in it; in the year of his death he still hoped to write the music for the third act but added that it could "simply be spoken, in case I cannot complete the composition." *Moses und Aron* was first heard in a concert performance in Hamburg in 1954 and was staged in Zurich three years later. Since then it has received occasional European and American performances, sometimes with, sometimes without, the spoken third act. Actually, the last act is of little importance; it is very short and unessential to the plot.

This pageant-opera is concerned with the exodus of the Jews under Moses' guidance. As in *Boris Godounov*, the people, represented by the chorus, are the chief protagonists. They are on stage throughout most of the opera and express themselves through conventional singing, *Sprechstimme*, rhythmic speech, and various combinations of these techniques. The chief solo singing role is Aron's, a tenor. Moses speaks his lines except for one climactic sung phrase. The rest of the time he declaims, whispers, or uses *Sprechstimme.*

Most of the libretto is static dramatically and is given over to a theological discussion between Moses and Aron, but the long orgiastic scene before the Golden Calf is completely different. Here there is opportunity for spectacular and sensational staging.

If there is little dramatic unity in the opera there is a great deal of musical and textual unity. The whole of *Moses und Aron* is constructed on a single row, and the libretto, also written by the composer, is elaborately intricate. In addition to employing alliteration and onomatopeia, favorite devices of Wagner, Schoenberg organized each scene by using key words of opposite meaning but similar sound. Thus not only do the words tell a story but also their sounds, independent of meaning, are arranged in patterns at the same time. By associating such word-sounds with versions of the musical row, a close connection between words and music is achieved.

The ultimate place of *Moses und Aron* in Schoenberg's lifework is difficult to determine at this time. If the opera survives, it will not be because of the complexity of its text and music, but for the same reason that other operas have survived—the power to interest and move audiences.

An intriguing hypothesis has been put forward that Schoenberg possibly identified himself with Moses. There are certain parallels in the two lives because, like the religious leader, the composer led his followers to a new realm of music. Like Moses, he experienced bitter betrayals and abandonment for what were, to him, false gods who were worshiped while the true leader was ignored.

Style Characteristics

All the style traits of Schoenberg's mature works are determined by the twelve-tone idiom and many of the characteristics can be inferred from Rufer's codification of the practice, already summarized. There are problems in defining his style, for it is vastly different from one based on major-minor tonality, however modified and extended. Such concepts as modulation, dissonance, or chord have either no meaning or at least strikingly new connotations.

Because a tone in a row may be sounded in any octave, many of Schoenberg's melodies are characterized by wide leaps. He has a special fondness for sevenths, ninths, and compound intervals, as well as for diminished and augmented intervals. They are found in vocal lines as well as in instrumental, so that the distinction between vocal and instrumental style loses its former meaning.

As everything in his music is in a state of flux—of becoming—definite beginnings and endings are also avoided. The theme of the *Variations for Orchestra* is typical in that all of the phrases start after the beat (Example 74).

However, he occasionally wrote strongly accented themes, as in the beginning of the Quartet No. 4.

In keeping with his subjective and expressive attitude toward music, Schoenberg indicates a great many tempo modifications in his scores. In like manner, he was diametrically opposed to those composers of this century who wrote driving, machinelike rhythmic patterns.

When Schoenberg's harmonies are discussed, traditional terminology is strained, for we cannot talk about chords built in thirds or in fourths, or chord progressions, or even about consonance and dissonance. Vertical combinations are determined by the row of the piece, and may contain any number of tones, from two to twelve. As functional harmony is not used, there are no predictable root progressions. One can assess a chord as more complex than another, but such assessment is subjective.

The texture of his music is preponderantly contrapuntal, which is not to say that other textures are not employed. Schoenberg frequently writes melodies with accompaniment (for example, the beginning of the Piano Concerto) by extracting certain tones from the row for the melody and others for an accompaniment. Occasionally he writes a series of chords, as in the beginning of the first piano piece of Opus 33, where the twelve tones are presented in three four-note chords.

The twelve-tone idiom also has its effect on timbre, for many of the conventions of orchestration—sustained harmonies, repeated accompaniment figures, and a clear differentiation of function between the choirs of the orchestra—are foreign to this style.

Schoenberg has favorite instruments and instrumental effects that give his scores a personal sound. He is fond of the celesta, xylophone, and flutter-tonguing in the flute, and follows Mahler's lead in adding an unusual instrument to some of his most important works—the mandolin. Its nervous, tinkling sound often adds sheen to his music. When Schoenberg employs a large orchestra he almost never uses all of the instruments at once, for his style of writing is transparent and fragmentary, with constantly changing, fleeting sounds.

Schoenberg uses many of the forms of earlier music—sonatas, variations, and the stylized dances of the baroque suite. Regardless of the outer forms, the principle of developing variation underlies everything he wrote.

Suggested Readings

A thorough exposition of the technical aspects of Schoenberg's music is found in *Composition with 12 Notes, Related Only to One Another*, by Josef Rufer (New York, 1954). Another basic book that gives an exposition of this method of composition as well as valuable analyses of compositions is René Leibowitz's *Schoenberg and His School* (New York, 1949). However, both of these books are superseded by George Perle's *Serial Composition and Atonality, an Introduction to the Music of Schoenberg, Berg, and Webern* (Berkeley, 3rd edition, 1972), a study which proves that many of the generalizations about twelve-tone music are oversimplifications. Richard Hill's article, "Schoenberg's Tone-rows and the Tonal System of the Future," *Musical Quarterly*, Vol. XXII, No. 1 (January 1936) is still valuable. The collection of essays written by the composer called *Style and Idea* (New York, 1950) gives insights into his thinking and personality, as do the *Letters of Arnold Schoenberg* (London, 1964). "My Evolution," an autobiographical sketch published in the *Musical Quarterly*, Vol. XXXVIII, No. 4 (October 1952), tells of his early years. Walter Rubsamen's "Schoenberg in America," *Musical Quarterly*, Vol. XXXIX, No. 4 (October 1953), gives an account of Schoenberg's life in California. *Arnold Schoenberg* by H. H. Stuckenschmidt (New York, 1960) is a complete study of the man and his music. *Schoenberg*, by Anthony Payne (London, 1968), is also recommended, as is Boretz and Cone: *Perspectives on Schoenberg and Stravinsky* (New York, 1968). Willi Reich's *Schoenberg, a Critical Biography*, originally published in German in 1968, has been translated and published (New York, 1971). The booklet included in the recording of the String Quartets of Schoenberg, Berg, and Webern (DGG 272002d) contains a wealth of interesting material. Two other books are *Schoenberg Chamber Music* by Arnold Whittall (Seattle, 1972), and *Arnold Schoenberg* by Charles Rosen (New York, 1975).

Dika Newlin's *Bruckner, Mahler, Schoenberg* (New York, 1947) shows the continuity of the musical tradition in Vienna. Egon Wellesz's *Arnold Schoenberg* (London, 1925) is valuable for the early works. Among the analyses of particular works the accompanying booklet to the recording of *Moses und Aron* (Columbia K3L-241) by Milton Babbitt and Allen Forte and an article, "Schoenberg's Compositions for Piano" by T. Temple Tuttle, in *Music Review*, Vol. 18 (1957) are recommended. Karl Heinrich Worner discusses the operas in "Arnold Schoenberg and the Theater" in the *Musical Quarterly*, Vol. XLVIII, No. 4 (October 1962). See also his book *Moses and Aron* (London, 1963). Two valuable bibliographies are: *The Works of Arnold Schoenberg; A Catalogue of His Compositions, Writings and Paintings* by Josef Rufer (London, 1962), and *A Classified Bibliography of Writings on Twelve-Tone and Electronic Music* by Ann Basart (Berkeley, 1961).

A fascinating book by Alma Mahler Werfel, *And the Bridge Is Love* (New York, 1958), should be read by all students of the period. As the wife, successively, of Mahler, Gropius, and Werfel, the author was a leader of Vienna's cultural life and knew intimately many of its leading personalities.

Berg, with a portrait of himself by Schoenberg

12

How I would like to be able to write happy music like that!

Alban Berg, in Conversation With Paul Collaer, After Hearing a Composition by Milhaud

Berg and Webern

OF ALL THE SCHOENBERG DISCIPLES, Alban Berg and Anton Webern proved to be the most significant. Along with their teacher they have been called the second Viennese school—high praise indeed when one remembers that Haydn, Mozart, and Beethoven constitute the first.

As pointed out in Chapter 4, the young Berg and Webern adopted the style of their master and first wrote in a highly charged chromatic style; when he turned to atonality they too abandoned the major-minor system and wrote short expressionist pieces for orchestra and chamber groups. When Schoenberg worked out the principles of twelve-tone composition they were at his side, but at this point the similarities in their music ceased and the younger men developed strongly personal styles. Although they remained lifelong friends, their later careers and music followed diverging paths. Stravinsky comments on the contrast in their personalities and appearances in one of his "Conversations."

I have a photograph on my wall of Berg and Webern together dating from about the time of the composition of the *Three Pieces for Orchestra.* Berg is tall, loose-set, almost too beautiful; his look is outward. Webern is short, hard-set, myopic, down-looking. Berg reveals an image of himself in his flowing "artist's" cravat; Webern wears peasant-type shoes, and they are muddy—which to me reveals something profound.[1]

We will now discuss the careers and mature works of these "two great musicians, two pure-in-spirit, *herrliche Menschen,* . . . who made music by which our half-century will be remembered," to quote Stravinsky again.[2]

Berg, 1885–1935

Outwardly Berg's life was uneventful—as uneventful as possible for a Central European living in the first half of the twentieth century. Born in Vienna in 1885 and raised in a family of comfortable means and strong artistic interests, he was well educated and had so much interest in literature that during one period of youthful enthusiasm he planned to become a poet.

Berg's interest in music became evident in 1899, but he made no commitment to the art at this time. His father died in 1900, and soon thereafter Berg suffered his first attack of asthma and severe illness. For the rest of his life he was a semi-invalid, never enjoying complete physical well-being. After failing a general humanistic studies examination in 1903, he attempted suicide.

In 1904 he began studying with Schoenberg and for the next ten years this strong personality brought stability and confidence to Berg. As the result of a small legacy, he was able to devote himself entirely to composition. Had it not been for his ill health, his life would have been unusually free from the vicissitudes that have plagued many twentieth-century artistic creators. His opera *Wozzeck* enjoyed popular success, receiving more than 166 performances between 1927 and 1936, a record for a full-length, serious twentieth-century opera. However, the success disturbed the composer, for he felt that if it found an audience so readily it must be weak and contain concessions to popular taste.

During World War I Berg was on limited duty in Vienna, and after the armistice he taught composition there, making occasional trips to European music centers in connection with performances of *Wozzeck,* and spending as much time as possible at his summer home in the Austrian Alps. He died in 1935 at the age of fifty, from blood poisoning induced by an insect bite. One wonders what other mature works Berg would have written had he lived.

Berg's Compositions

The list of Berg's compositions is very short. Before meeting Schoenberg he wrote a great many songs, most of which are unpublished *juvenilia.* The prewar works have already been mentioned—the songs, the ultrachromatic Piano Sonata, and short atonal pieces.

The war interrupted his flow of composition (as it interrupted the work of all the composers under discussion). In 1921 *Wozzeck* was finished, followed by five other important works:

Chamber Concerto (for violin, piano, and thirteen instruments; 1923–25)
Lyric Suite (for string quartet; 1925–26)
Le Vin (a setting of a poem by Baudelaire, for soprano and orchestra; 1929)
Lulu (opera, incomplete; 1928–35)
Concerto for Violin (1935)

The reasons for the success of *Wozzeck* are not difficult to find. The music, although dissonant and at times apparently chaotic, expresses every nuance of a story that is human, timeless, and tragic. In performance its power to hold and move an audience is equalled by few operas, if any, old or new.

The libretto was put together from scenes of a play by Georg Büchner, a German writer of the early nineteenth century. The story is simple and sordid. Wozzeck is a poor soldier plagued by his superiors, poverty, the unfaithfulness of his common-law wife Marie, and his own unbalanced emotions. He lives in a world devoid of reason and order and filled with misery and oppression, fear and hopelessness.

There is little dramatic connection among the fifteen scenes grouped into the three acts that make up the opera. At the beginning Wozzeck is discovered shaving his captain. A realistic, but at the same time strange conversation follows, for the captain is completely erratic. Wozzeck stolidly accepts his taunts.

An orchestral interlude connects this scene with the second, which takes place in an open field. Wozzeck and another soldier are gathering wood, and at sunset when the sky is aflame, Wozzeck becomes hysterical with an irrational fear.

The next scene moves to the cottage in which Marie and her child live. A military band is playing and soldiers pass. Marie is attracted by a handsome drum major and flirts with him from the window until reminded by her friend Margaret that she already has a husband and child. Marie closes the window, takes her son on her lap, and sings a lullaby. Wozzeck appears, still incoherent from his experience in the fields.

Scene 4 takes place in a doctor's office. Wozzeck, in order to supplement his wages, has become a subject for the doctor's dietary experiments. The doctor, a sadist, is delighted that the experiment is causing Wozzeck to have aberrations and urges him to cultivate them.

The last scene of the first act is between Marie and the drum major, who is resplendent in black boots and red uniform and arrogantly aware of his appeal. It ends with the drum major sweeping Marie into his arms.

The five scenes in each of the two acts that follow carry the tragedy to its climax. Wozzeck becomes insanely jealous when he learns of Marie's unfaithfulness. He kills her and later goes mad and drowns himself. There are scenes in taverns, in the barracks filled with snoring soldiers, by a lake, and finally in a street before Marie's house where a group of children are playing. Among them is Marie's boy riding a hobbyhorse, unaware of the catastrophe. Some other children enter and announce that Marie's body has been found, but the child is too young to understand. He continues rocking and singing a nursery tune while the other children rush off leaving him alone. After a few moments he too runs off, leaving the stage totally bare.

The problem of building extended musical structures without the foundation of major-minor tonality has already been discussed. How can a full-length atonal but not twelve-tone opera be written? Berg's solution was surprising, and surprisingly effective.

In order to give musical structure to the opera, Berg employs instrumental forms familiar through centuries of use. Thus, the five scenes of Act I are organized as follows: a *suite,* consisting of a prelude, sarabande, gigue, air, and gavotte; a *rhapsody* based on three chords; a *military march;* a *passacaglia* with twenty-one variations; and an *andante.* Act II is organized as a *sonata;* the first scene is in sonata-allegro form, the second is a slow movement, the third is a scherzo with three trios, the fourth and fifth, an introduction and a rondo. Each scene of Act III is an *invention;* based on a theme, a tone, a rhythm, a chord, or on a key, in the tonal sense.

The use of instrumental forms and devices to organize scenes of an opera is not so arbitrary and willful as it first appears. By using these Berg not only achieved organization but also added to the dramatic impact of the scenes by choosing forms that had dramatic potentialities. For example, the murder scene in Act III is built on a note, B, used as a pedal throughout. It comes to a terrifying climax when Berg builds a gigantic crescendo by gradually bringing in the whole orchestra, instrument by instrument, on this note and its octaves. In this way, the brutality of murder is not only symbolized, but also bored into the consciousness of all who witness the scene.

The use of the structure of a passacaglia and a fugue in two different scenes gives the opportunity of stressing an important idea through repetition. The scenes organized on a march or dance rhythm have direct story connections. It is difficult to determine why the composer chose to accompany the opening scene between the irrational, cowardly officer and Wozzeck with the stylized niceties of the baroque suite. Perhaps this surprising juxtaposition ironically contrasts the meanness of the scene with the elegance suggested by the music.

There are many other musical riches in *Wozzeck* besides the forms the composer uses. The voices, for instance, are treated in several ways. In addition to the normal singing voice, *Sprechstimme* and everyday speech are used.

The neurotic and very excitable quality of some of the characters is expressed through the use of falsetto.

The orchestra is treated in the plastic, timbre-rich manner of Schoenberg's *Erwartung* and the *Five Pieces for Orchestra,* and reflects everything that happens or is mentioned on the stage. The sound of the wind, the rippling of water, even the fall of the curtain at the end of the scene—all of this is heard in the orchestral music.

Orchestral interludes are played while the curtains are closed for changes of scenes. These interludes contribute a great deal to the opera, for not only do they make entire acts musically continuous, but also they allow the music to expand freely, in contrast to the tautness prevalent during the drama's progress. They also give the audience an opportunity to relax from the opera's almost unbearable tension without breaking its spell during an entr'acte. The last interlude is particularly important, for it synthesizes the main musical ideas of the opera.

Wozzeck is one of the richest creations of the twentieth century. It is an all-inclusive work drawing upon idioms and forms of earlier music, as well as employing tonal combinations and instrumentation of startling originality. Some scenes are definitely tonal while others are twelve-tonal. The orchestra is often reduced to chamber proportions but occasionally it roars in ear-splitting tuttis. It is a successful opera, for all these devices and idioms are dramatically valid and are used to further characterization and mirror the stage action.

It is similar in many respects to James Joyce's *Ulysses,* a contemporary work. *Ulysses* is a novel that can be approached on many levels, though essentially it is the story of one day in the life of a little man lost in our contemporary world. Told with the utmost artificiality of manner, Joyce draws upon the forms and idioms of past literature whenever such early styles are appropriate. Both *Ulysses* and *Wozzeck* are encyclopedic, complex, and contrived. Both are great works of art—not for these reasons, but because their elaborate forms successfully organize and project a deeply felt compassion for man.

It is interesting to compare *Wozzeck* with *The Rake's Progress.* They are so different in music, drama, and aesthetic basis, that it is difficult to believe that they were created in the same quarter of the century. They represent, respectively, two principal poles of twentieth-century art—expressionism and neoclassicism. Only time will tell which is the greater opera, but it seems safe to predict, however, that more people will be moved by the Berg than by the Stravinsky.

The *Lyric Suite* is Berg's first extended composition in which he uses the twelve-tone idiom. Although it was written and published at the same time as Schoenberg's first compositions in this style, it is in no sense derivative.

The title *Lyric Suite* helps to classify this unique work; it is not a sonata (it has six movements) nor is it a baroque suite. "Lyric" is the key word—meaning "expressive of the poet's feelings." The adjectives modifying the tempo indications of the various movements emphasize their emotional content. The movements are:

Allegretto gioviale (twelve-tone)
Andante amoroso (not twelve-tone)
Allegro misterioso—(*trio estatico*) (twelve-tone, trio not)
Adagio appassionato (not twelve-tone)
Presto delirando—*Tenebroso* (only the trios twelve-tone)
Largo desolato (twelve-tone)

The unusual sequence of tempos should be noticed. Fast movements alternate with slow, the fast becoming faster and the slow becoming slower. The first movement is in baroque binary form as found in the Scarlatti sonatas and Bach suite movements. It is written on this row:

EXAMPLE 78

in this rhythmic configuration:

EXAMPLE 79*

The difference between the two forms clearly shows the relationship between basic row and basic shape.

The second theme, divided between the second violin and the viola, is derived from RI. At the same time the cello has a rhythmically augmented version of O. The second half of the movement starts with O by the second violin.

EXAMPLE 80

This is one of the most carefree of Berg's compositions. Lilting rhythms and long melodic lines recall the mood of Schoenberg's *Serenade.* While the movement is constructed according to twelve-tone practice, certain liberties are taken; for although every phrase is derived from the row so that there is continuous development, the sequence of tones in the row is not always slavishly followed.

The mood of the second movement is one of tender melancholy and nostalgia, much of it with a Viennese-waltz background. The frequent successions of chords that are almost, but not quite, parallel are surprising, as are the purely harmonic passages such as those which remind one of the pathetic parallel chords of Tchaikovsky's Sixth Symphony.

EXAMPLE 81

There is a reference to the first movement, establishing a pattern for the composition, as each movement is linked with the preceding.

The third movement is an amazing tour de force. The four instruments play the usual notes of the chromatic scale arranged in rows, but the effect is extremely bizarre, since Berg exploits so many special effects. The performers are directed to play on the bridge and on the fingerboard, as well as in the customary place; to hit the strings with a bouncing blow, or play the strings with the wooden back of the bow instead of with the hair; and to play harmonics, pizzicato, and flautando as well as in the usual manner. The startingly original and unique effect is enhanced by continual use of mutes, pianissimo dynamics, and very rapid tempos. There is a contrasting middle section (*trio estatico*) and then a condensed form of the first section is heard again, but this time backwards, or in mirror form.

The fourth movement is in some respects the heart of the entire piece. It is not in the twelve-tone idiom and is contrapuntal with prominent canons. Some of the principal themes of earlier movements appear, and the passionate intensity of the climaxes makes it one of the most eloquent of Berg's compositions.

The fifth movement rivals the third in fantastic, novel sounds. While the earlier scherzo was quiet in dynamics, this section sounds rude and shocking and is punctuated with glissandos. The twice-heard Trio, marked *tenebroso* (shadowy) is ghostlike in its scarcely heard, "breathy" chords, making the contrast of the return of the first section all the stronger.

The last movement is the slowest and most expressive. Wide-spanned, tension-filled melodies, typical of the period, are used. The chromatic texture prepares the way for the startling reference to the opening of the Prelude to *Tristan und Isolde*, which appears just before the end. The motive sneaks in, so to speak, divided among the four instruments so that no single performer can be held responsible for it (see Example 82).

This reference to Wagner's theme is perhaps the key to the whole work, for the *Lyric Suite* is best approached as music for an opera without singers or words, but still an opera in which love, mystery, ecstasy, passion, delirium, ghosts, and desolation—the words that Berg added to describe the movements—are the expressive content.

One by one the instruments stop playing. Finally only the viola remains, playing two notes in slow alternation, until they disappear into nothingness. This unusual ending (*Wozzeck* also ends in nothingness) seems to express the feeling of the concluding lines of T. S. Eliot's poem *The Hollow Men*, also written in 1926.

> This is the way the world ends
> This is the way the world ends
> This is the way the world ends
> Not with a bang but a whimper.[3]

EXAMPLE 82

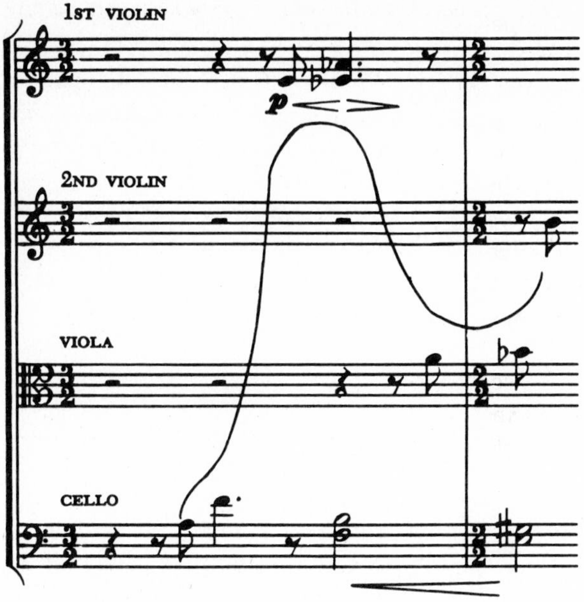

Berg's last composition, the Violin Concerto, is also a work of synthesis, combining elements and forms of the past with twentieth-century procedures. In 1935 Louis Krasner, the American violinist, asked the composer to write a violin concerto. Berg accepted the commission and decided to make the concerto a memorial to a young friend who had just died. The piece is not only dedicated to Manon Gropius (the daughter of Mahler's widow and Walter Gropius, the architect) but it is also her portrait.

It is cast in two large movements, each in two parts. The first movement, a prelude and a scherzo, is a characterization of Manon in life. The second movement, a cadenza and an adagio, depicts her death and transfiguration.

Musically, it consists of developments of three elements. The basic row:

EXAMPLE 83

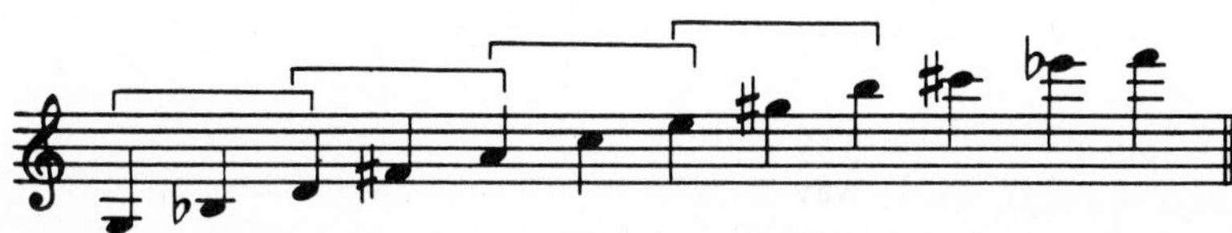

This row is unique in that it consists entirely of thirds, except for the four seconds at the end. It will be apparent at once that chords constructed from this row will resemble conventional chord structures, and indeed much of the concerto has a strong tonal feeling.

The second element is an Austrian folk melody:

EXAMPLE 84

The sweetness and sentimentality of the tune aptly characterize the girl. Because of the prominence of the thirds there are relationships with the basic row.

The third element is the chorale *"Es ist genug,"* the opening notes of which are implied in the last four notes of the row. It beautifully expresses the sorrow and resignation associated with death:

EXAMPLE 85

From these three elements Berg has created one of the most eloquent compositions of the century. As in *Wozzeck*, or as in Bach's music, intricacies of the structure completely serve the expressive content.

Style Characteristics

Schoenberg's music was at all times the most important formative influence on Berg's style. To support this we need only consider the many similarities between the two composers. First of all, their melodies are similar; both wrote wide, jagged lines that made extensive use of sevenths and ninths as well as augmented and diminished intervals. In their vocal music both composers employed *Sprechstimme* to increase the intensity of the words they set. Their harmonies, too, are alike in the several steps of development from a highly chromatic idiom through an atonal to the twelve-tone idiom. Strikingly similar is the sound of their orchestras, for Berg also uses the fragmentary style of orchestration and the unusual instruments and instrumental effects of his teacher. Because of *Wozzeck's* popularity, Berg's music became widely known before Schoenberg's and its originality was at first overestimated. Familiarity with such works as *Erwartung* and *Five Pieces for Orchestra* revealed Berg's debt to Schoenberg.

There is no question of Berg's debt to Schoenberg, but what of his original contributions? These lie in his free use of materials, for he is never a "systematic" composer, limited by a doctrine or theory. In *Wozzeck* there are scenes written in major-minor tonality, others without tonality, still others organized according to a serial technique. Sometimes he writes in strict twelve-tone style, and in other pieces he varies the order of the notes in the row. In addition to jagged melodies, he writes melodies as simple as folksongs. At times his orchestra is an "instrument" of weird, new sounds; at others it has the richness of Strauss.

In writing of Berg's opera, Norman Demuth said, "The technique of *Wozzeck* defies categorization because it falls into every category." [4] This sentence is equally applicable to all of Berg's works. His achievement was his ability to combine new and old in a completely personal language.

Webern, 1883–1945

The relationship between Schoenberg and his principal disciples, Berg and Webern, has been described by René Leibowitz:

> While the genius of Berg always strove to establish a connection between the discoveries of Schoenberg and the past—thus profiting by the retroactive elements in Schoenberg's work—the genius of Webern is concerned with the possibilities for the future inherent in his work, and thus succeeds in projecting the particularly novel and radical elements.[5]

During their lifetimes, Webern was the most obscure of the three, for neither did he have the crusading zeal of Schoenberg nor did he write a work that became as popular as *Wozzeck*. The few performances he heard of his music were at meetings of the International Society of Contemporary Music.

On the other hand, since his death his compositions have attracted a great deal of attention. His complete works have been recorded, an honor paid to few composers, and young composers all over the world have listened to his music for inspiration and guidance. Some critics have gone so far as to call the 1950s the "Age of Webern."

The son of a mining engineer, Anton Webern was born in Vienna. As a boy he lived there and in the mountain communities where his father worked. He entered the University of Vienna in 1902 to study under Guido Adler, the famous musicologist, and received his Ph.D. four years later. His dissertation was a study of Isaac's *Choralis Constantinus.* In 1904 he became Schoenberg's first pupil; this was the turning point of Webern's life, as it was to be for Berg several years later. For the next thirty years the three worked together, exploring the possibilities of the unknown territory, each making his own discoveries.

In 1911 Webern married and started a career as a conductor in several small cities in Germany and Austria. He joined the army in 1915, but after his release a year later because of weak eyes, he settled in a suburb of Vienna where he lived for the next twenty-seven years. In order to support his family he conducted amateur groups, which included both a chorus and an orchestra, and taught a few composition students. During the twenties he assisted Schoenberg in organizing and conducting a series of concerts devoted to contemporary music, and later served as advisor and reader for a music publisher and conducted the Austrian radio orchestra. In the thirties he began to be recognized as a conductor and was invited three times to conduct the BBC orchestra in London.

In spite of this activity, Webern and his family lived in near poverty through all of these years. His frequent letters to friends asking for their help in securing an appointment with an adequate stipend are pathetic, and remind one of similar letters written by Mozart to his friends in Vienna. "How I could work," Webern writes, "if I had a little financial security!"

He remained in Vienna during World War II until 1945, when the bombings reached their height. He then took his family to Mittersill, a mountain village not far from Salzburg. On the night of September 15th, 1945, he stepped out of the house to smoke a cigarette before going to bed. A strict curfew was in effect and a soldier, seeing the light, shot and killed the composer. This tragic act terminated the life of one of the most influential composers of the century.

When Europe's cultural life resumed after the war, it soon became apparent that Webern had a few disciples who had remained underground, so to speak, in the years when the totalitarian governments of Hitler and Mussolini had suppressed advanced art such as his. Once the war was over, articles and books appeared calling attention to him, and occasionally his music was performed. Interest in his style was widespread, from England, Italy, and even France, where the prevailing aesthetic had been strongly neoclassic, to Germany

Webern
Columbia Records Photo

and Austria. Looking for new ideas, young composers of all countries found them in Webern's works, and soon an international Webern "school" existed. The principles underlying his music became the starting place of a new avant-garde.

One of the most surprising champions of Webern's music was Igor Stravinsky, supposedly the leader of an ideal of music diametrically opposed to Webern's. In 1958 he wrote:

> Of the music of this century I am still most attracted by two periods of Webern: the later instrumental works and the songs he wrote after the first twelve opus numbers and before the Trio—music which escapes the preciosity of the earlier pieces and which is perhaps the richest Webern ever wrote. . . . Webern is for me the *juste de la musique* and I do not hesitate to shelter myself by the beneficent protection of the Muse of his not yet canonized art.[6]

This was not mere lip service; Stravinsky's compositions of the fifties were strongly influenced by Webern's.

Webern's Compositions

The lifework of this composer who has become such a force consists of thirty-one compositions (the longest lasts ten minutes), the prevailing dynamics of which are pianissimo, and whose scores consist of many more rests than notes. The complete works can be played in less than three hours.

The prewar compositions, including the first eleven opus numbers, have already been mentioned. These pieces have several characteristics that are constantly featured in all his works: they are extremely short; the melodies consist of wide, "dissonant" intervals; there are many rests; the predominant dynamic scale is the softest imaginable; they are pointillist in style, the musical line progressing note by note from solo instrument to instrument; the most subtle ranges and combinations of instruments are used; and effects such as mutes, harmonics, and flutter-tonguing are constantly employed.

For many listeners the first impression of these pieces is one of total chaos. The little islands of sound, appearing, disappearing, separated by pools of silence, seem to be signals sounded at random. It is only after repeated hearings, after painstaking analysis (or studying someone else's analysis) that total, meaningful impressions of the music are gained. What seemed to be complete chaos is now understood as an intensely organized pattern. The organization, the skeleton, as it were, is all that remains, for all the flesh—chords, sequences, bridge passages, and the sound of massed instruments—is eliminated.

The principle underlying all of Webern's music is economy. He starts with a few tones and builds a piece on them. It follows that these intensely concentrated pieces are most often contrapuntal. Some of Bach's fugues are also concentrated and economical, but in comparison with Webern's compositions they are loose and rambling structures.

This ideal of extreme purity, of reducing music to its absolute essentials (any further reduction would result in complete silence) was characteristic of one of the important trends that shaped a considerable amount of twentieth-century art. There was a school of painting for example, headed by a Russian named Malevitch who, according to Sheldon Cheney, "so purified painting that there was nothing left that the public recognized as art." [7] He painted a picture called *White on White* which consists of an almost white rectangle painted on a white background. This is perhaps a *reductio ad absurdum* of the movement but the serene nonobjective paintings of Mondrian approach the spirit of Webern's economical pieces. Twentieth-century architecture, perhaps the most characteristic art of the period, also is economical. Perret and Le Corbusier, Gropius and Mies van der Rohe, and Nervi—their works are as bereft of ornament and unessential detail as the compositions of Webern.

The compositions of Webern written after World War I are:

Op. 15 Five Sacred Songs (1923)
Op. 16 Five Canons for voice, clarinet, and bass clarinet (1924)
Op. 17 Three Sacred Folksongs (1924)
Op. 18 Three songs for voice, clarinet, and guitar (1925)
Op. 19 Two songs for chorus (1926)
Op. 20 Trio for violin, viola, cello (1927)
Op. 21 Symphony for small orchestra (1928)
Op. 22 Quartet for violin, clarinet, saxophone, and piano (1930)
Op. 23 Three songs (1934)
Op. 24 Concerto for nine instruments (1934)
Op. 25 Three songs (1934–5)
Op. 26 *Das Augenlicht* (*The Eye's Light*, cantata; 1935)
Op. 27 *Variations for Piano* (1936)
Op. 28 String Quartet (1938)
Op. 29 First Cantata (1939)
Op. 30 *Variations for Orchestra* (1940)
Op. 31 Second Cantata (1943)

Webern's interest in songs is obvious from this list of works. In them, the voice line gives a continuity absent in earlier instrumental works. These songs were probably influenced by *Pierrot Lunaire,* not only in timbre but also in the intricate contrapuntal relationships between the instruments and the voice. This tendency toward strict structural plans comes to a climax in Opus 16, the canons for soprano and clarinets. In the Five Canons, the first song begins:

EXAMPLE 86*

The clarinet and voice, it will be seen, are in canon at the distance of a measure and at the interval of a major second. At the same time, the bass clarinet is in inverted canonic relationship persisting without deviation to the end. The wide melodic line and prominence of sixths, major sevenths, and minor ninths are characteristic, while vertical combinations are often made up of these same intervals. Although there is no theme that unifies the piece as a whole, there is a rhythmic pattern 𝅗𝅥 𝅗𝅥|♩. ♪♩♩|𝅗𝅥 ♩ that recurs twice, giving additional organization to the composition.

The second canon, also inverted, is written for two parts: the soprano and one clarinet. The numerous precise dynamic indications should be noted, for they are imitated in the second voice along with the notes in many of Webern's pieces (see Example 87).

EXAMPLE 87

The third canon is a straightforward three-voice piece with a very subtle rhythmic relationship between the entrances of voices—another characteristic of the composer. (See Example 88.) The final two canons are similar in structure to those already described.

Interesting as they are, the question of the appropriateness of such complicated structures for songs can be raised. Are the words reflected in the music? Yes, in a general way. For instance, the rugged affirmation of the first, *Christus factus est pro nobis*, contrasts completely with the gentle lullaby *Dormi Jesu* that follows it.

Opus 16 is a useful introduction to Webern's style because we find here many of the traits that characterize all of his music. To be noted particularly is the tightness of structure resulting from an underlying plan that accounts for dynamics, articulation, and phrasing as well as the progress of the melodies. Other traits characteristic of the composer are the contrapuntal texture, the use of preferred intervals, and the uncompromising writing for the voices.

EXAMPLE 88

The canons were written in 1924. With his next composition Webern moved to the twelve-tone idiom along with Schoenberg and Berg, who took the crucial step at the same time. This did not result in any drastic change in style, for many characteristics of such writing—atonality, contrapuntal texture, and developing variations, for instance—were already prevalent in their music.

The Symphony, op. 21, was written four years after the canons and shows Webern's continuing interest in contrapuntal writing. The work is in two movements, the first a modified sonata form and the second a set of variations. The word "symphony" is misleading, since this is chamber music; the only instruments used are clarinet, bass clarinet, two horns, harp, and string quartet.

The opening of the first movement (Example 89) shows the extremely pointillistic manner in which the instruments are treated. They seldom play more than a few connected notes; often they emit single sounds separated by rests. The result is a thin web of sound of constantly changing color.

While this opening sounds as if the tones had no connection with each other, they are actually carefully plotted. Example 89 has been written in order to show the structure of the movement, which is in the form of a double canon. Canon 1 starts in the second horn (5 notes), proceeds to the clarinet (4 notes), and then to the cellos (4 notes). This is answered (in contrary motion) by the first horn, bass clarinet, and viola. While this proceeds, Canon 2 is given to the harp (1 note), cello (3 notes), second violin (1 note), and harp (2 notes); it is answered (again in contrary motion) by the harp, viola, first violin, harp, horn, and harp.

EXAMPLE 89*

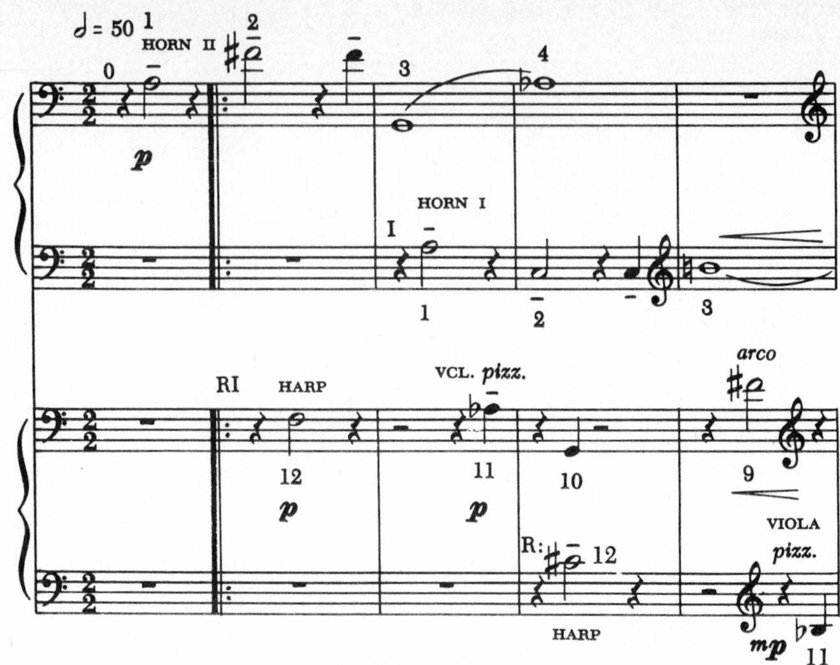

* Used by permission of Universal Edition.

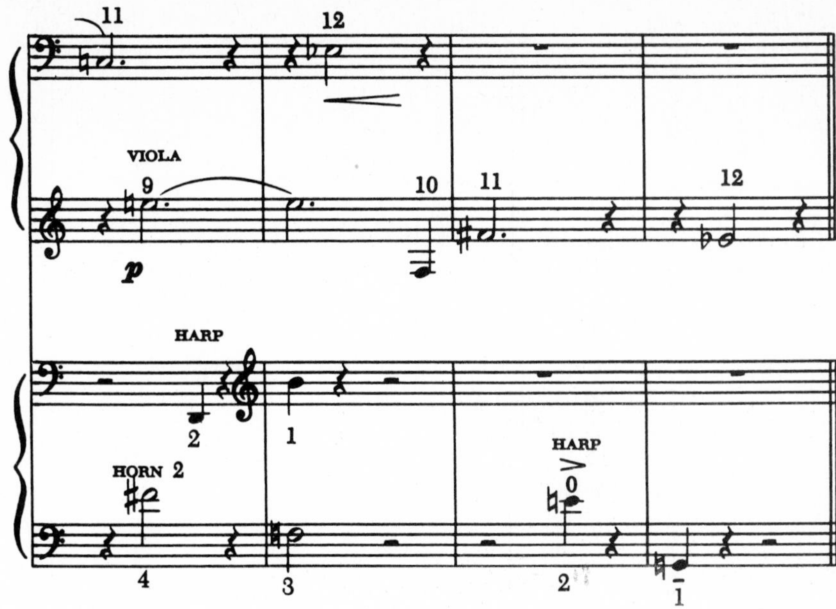

Another dimension is added to the complexity of the piece, in that these notes are also in twelve-tone relationships. Thus, the twelve notes in the upper score of Example 89 form the basic row (O) and the canon in contrary motion is an inversion (I). Canon 2 is a retrograde inversion (RI) while its answering voice is a transposition of the retrograde (R).

The opening measures of *Variations for Piano* (Example 90) show Webern's predilection for mirror forms (Retrograde-Inversions in twelve-tone terminology). The numbers indicate the relationships to the row and show that the second half is played in the left hand while the right hand plays the first half. These seven measures are followed by a three-measure phrase that in itself is a mirror, the first and last measures being reversed. The return of the opening material follows, except that the right hand now plays what the left hand played before. All of this is followed by a middle section that is a "variation" of the first section, and eventually figures similar to those of the opening return.

The second of the three movements is a strict canon in contrary motion. It is most difficult to play and it is difficult to hear, since the two melodies, consisting of leaps, are continually crossing. As in the Symphony, op. 21, the ear tends to follow the line as a unit instead of as two melodies.

Familiarity with the piece will reveal that instead of a spattering of random tones over the keyboard there is, rather, a most intricate structural pat-

EXAMPLE 90*

tern. At four points—Measures 1, 9, 13, and 19—the two voices arrive at the note A. While all the other notes go up and down by the same intervals, these measures form focal points on either side of which the elaborate structures are formed.

The third movement is the most extended, and at the same time the easiest to follow. It consists of a theme followed by five variations. The theme has three parts, the second of which reverses the relationship of the two hands. The third part is a retrograde of the first, so that it ends on the same tone with which it began. The variations are similar in structure, but differ greatly in expression. After repeated hearing of the *Piano Variations* some of the patterns become apparent to the listener. One hears the wonderful symmetry, the highs being answered by lows, and the foldings and unfoldings of tension and repose.

Among all of Webern's works the Concerto for Nine Instruments holds a special place, because in this nine-minute composition Schoenbergian principles are developed to a new level of refinement. This piece plays an important historic role, and the analyses and controversies it has inspired have profoundly influenced later composition.

The Concerto, written for flute, oboe, clarinet, violin, viola, trumpet, French horn, trombone, and piano, is based on the following row:

EXAMPLE 91

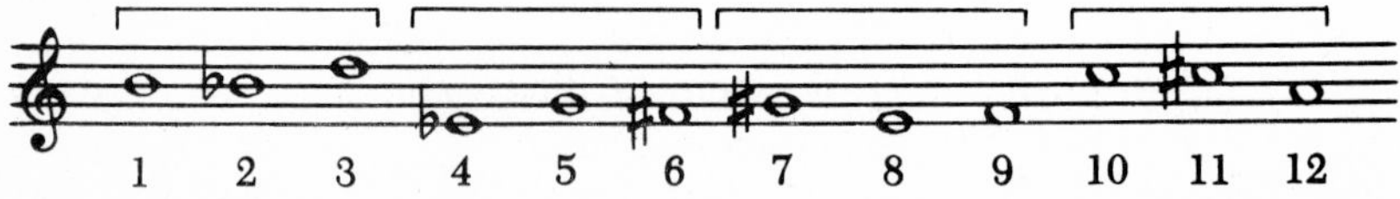

It will be noted that each three-note segment consists of a minor second and a major third. The first three notes can be considered a microrow followed by its retrograde inversion, retrograde, and inversion. The row itself, therefore, is more highly organized and controlled than the rows previously discussed.

The composition starts:

EXAMPLE 92a

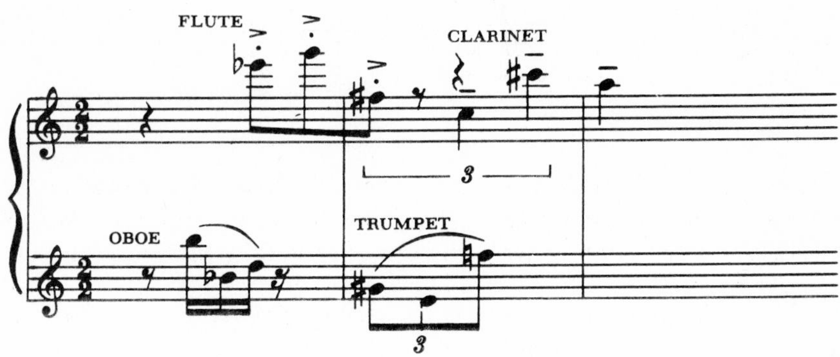

The following chart will clarify other aspects of the passage:

INTERVALS	TIMBRE	ARTICULATION	DURATION
Group 1 m9↓ M3↑	oboe	leggiero	
Group 2 M3↑ m9↓	flute	staccato	
Group 3 M3↓ m9↑	trumpet	legato	3
Group 4 m9↑ M3↓	clarinet	portato	

Each group is played by a different instrument, is differentiated by its articulation or attack, and by its duration. Only the dynamic level is shared.

In the measures that follow the original three-note groups reappear, but the internal sequence is varied, the time values and attacks are reversed, and the timbre sequence is altered.

EXAMPLE 92b

The movement continues with permutations and combinations of these three-note groups showing constantly changing relationships. Because the row itself is so highly organized, it is often possible to interpret a passage in more than one manner.

It will be obvious that this piece is based on principles considerably different from those found in Schoenberg. While the latter treats his rows as themes, that is, as melodic shapes, and therefore could use conventional forms such as sonata, rondo, and minuet and trio, Webern fragments the row into groups within which the interval order sometimes varies. As a result, this composition is without themes as such, and the permutations of the motives become the formal principle. One hears the same ingredients continuously but in ever-changing relationships. "It is always something different and yet always the same," said Webern. This concept, along with the "abstract" control of timbre (no longer does a particular instrument "fit" a particular melody), duration, and articulation, was to become of prime importance to the postwar composers to be discussed in Part Three.

Suggested Readings

Berg: *Alban Berg, the Man and His Music* by H. F. Redlich (New York, 1957), *Alban Berg* by Willi Reich (New York, 1965), and *Alban Berg, the Man and the Works* by Mosco Carner (London, 1975). An analysis of individual works will be found in Leibowitz (*op. cit.*) and Perle (*op. cit.*). The Violin Concerto is treated by Mosco Carner in *The Concerto,* edited by Ralph Hill (London, 1952). "*Wozzeck,* a Guide to the Words and Music" by Willi Reich in the *Musical Quarterly,* Vol. XXXVIII, No. 1 (January 1952) is recommended, as is the essay on the same work in Kerman's *Opera as Drama* (New York, 1956).

"The Symbolism in Berg's 'Lyric Suite' " is an interesting article by Brindle, in *Score,* No. 21 (October 1957).

Webern: *Anton Webern* by Friedrich Wildgans (London, 1965). *The Death of Anton Webern* (New York, 1961) by Hans Moldenhauer gives the whole story of the composer's tragic death. The second volume of *Die Reihe* (English edition, Theodore Presser, Philadelphia, 1958) is devoted to Webern and contains articles by eighteen European scholars. *Anton von Webern, Perspectives,* compiled by Hans Moldenhauer and edited by Demar Irvine (Seattle, 1966), is a collection of studies presented at the First International Webern Festival held in Seattle in 1962. The booklet published in conjunction with the recording of his complete works (Columbia K4L-232) by Robert Craft contains valuable material. Walter Kolneder's *Anton Webern* (Berkeley, 1968) includes an analysis of each work.

	FRANCE	GERMANY & AUSTRIA	OTHER COUNTRIES	OTHER ARTS, EVENTS
1930	Milhaud: *Maximilien* Roussel: *Bacchus et Ariane* Stravinsky: *Symphony of Psalms*	Hindemith: Concerto for Viola Webern: Quartet for Violin, Clarinet, Saxophone, and Piano	A. Hába: *The Mother* Shostakovich: *Golden Age*	Auden: *Poems* T. S. Eliot: *Ash Wednesday* Faulkner: *As I Lay Dying* T. Wolfe: *Look Homeward, Angel*
1931	Ravel: Piano Concerto in G Stravinsky: Violin Concerto		R. Thompson: Symphony No. 2 Bartók: Piano Concerto No. 2 Walton: *Belshazzar's Feast*	Calder: Mobiles
1932	Stravinsky: *Duo Concertant* for violin and piano	Hindemith: *Philharmonic Concerto*		Picasso: *The Mirror*
1933		Strauss: *Arabella*	Harris: Symphony 1933 Shostakovich: Piano Concerto	Adolf Hitler becomes Chancellor of Germany
1934		Webern: Concerto for 9 Instruments	Prokofiev: *Lieutenant Kije* Bartók: String Quartet No. 5	

	FRANCE	GERMANY & AUSTRIA	OTHER COUNTRIES	OTHER ARTS, EVENTS
1935	Stravinsky: Concerto for 2 Pianos Honegger: *Jeanne d'Arc au bûcher* Messiaen: *La Nativité*	Berg: Violin Concerto Hindemith: *Der Schwanendreher* Webern: *Das Augenlicht*	Prokofiev: Violin Concerto No. 2 Prokofiev: *Romeo and Juliet* Gershwin: *Porgy and Bess* Vaughan Williams: Symphony No. 4	
1936	Milhaud: *Suite provençale* Stravinsky: *Jeu de cartes* Poulenc: Mass	Schoenberg: Violin Concerto Schoenberg: String Quartet No. 4 Hindemith: Three Sonatas for Piano Orff: *Carmina Burana*	Harris: Symphony No. 2 Prokofiev: *Peter and the Wolf* Shostakovich: Symphony No. 4	Spanish Civil War begins
1937	Poulenc: *Tel jour, telle nuit*	Berg: *Lulu* (1st performance)	Bartók: *Music for Strings, Percussion, and Celesta* Shostakovich: Symphony No. 5 Piston: Symphony No. 1 Copland: *El Salón México* Barber: *Essay for Orchestra*	Picasso: *Guernica* Germany: Exhibition of Degenerate Art

	FRANCE	GERMANY & AUSTRIA	OTHER COUNTRIES	OTHER ARTS, EVENTS
1938	Stravinsky: *Dumbarton Oaks Concerto*	Orff: *Der Mond*	Copland: *Billy the Kid*	Sartre: *Nausea*
1939	Milhaud: Symphony No. 1	Webern: Cantata No. 1	Harris: Symphony No. 3 Walton: Violin Concerto Shostakovich: Symphony No. 6 Britten: *Les Illuminations* Dallapiccola: *Canti di Prigionia* Prokofiev: *Alexander Nevsky*	Outbreak of World War II
1940	Poulenc: *Banalités* Stravinsky: Symphony in C	Hindemith: Violin Concerto Webern: *Variations for Orchestra*	Harris: *Folksong Symphony* Piston: Violin Concerto Shostakovich: Piano Quintet	
1941		Hindemith: Symphony in E♭ Strauss: *Capriccio*	Copland: *Quiet City* Creston: Symphony No. 1 Schuman: Symphony No. 3 Copland: Piano Sonata Prokofiev: *War and Peace* Shostakovich: Symphony No. 7	United States and USSR enter World War II

	FRANCE	GERMANY & AUSTRIA	OTHER COUNTRIES	OTHER ARTS, EVENTS
1942	Messiaen: *Visions de l'amen*	Schoenberg: Piano Concerto	Schuman: Symphony No. 4 Copland: *Lincoln Portrait* Copland: *Rodeo* Prokofiev: Piano Sonata No. 7 Martinu: Symphony No. 1 Carter: Symphony No. 1	Camus: *The Stranger*
1943	Milhaud: *Bolivar*	Orff: *Catulli Carmina* Hindemith: *Ludus Tonalis*	Hanson: Symphony No. 4 Vaughan Williams: Symphony No. 5 Shostakovich: Symphony No. 8 Harris: Symphony No. 5 Bartók: Concerto for Orchestra Martinu: Symphony No. 2	Sartre: *The Flies*
1944	Poulenc: *Les Mamelles de Tirésias*	Hindemith: *Symphonic Metamorphoses*	Stravinsky: Sonata for two Pianos Piston: Symphony No. 2 Barber: *Capricorn Concerto* Copland: *Appalachian Spring* Prokofiev: Symphony No. 5	Brecht: *Mother Courage* Allied invasion of Europe

An Art Portfolio

A Look at Concurrent Styles in Art

1. Renoir: Bal à Bougival

Although the subject of these two paintings is the same–people dancing out of doors—the two are very different in effect, and clearly illustrate the difference between impressionism and expressionism in painting.

Renoir shows us a fleeting moment —almost a candid camera photograph—of a real event. We see people dancing, talking, smoking, and drinking, and we enjoy it all vicariously. We say, "What a pleasant day that must have been!"

Courtesy Museum of Fine Arts, Boston.

2. Munch: The Dance of Life

The Munch painting, on the other hand, is symbolic rather than realistic. These are not real people enjoying themselves, but dreamlike symbols. The girl on the left, dressed in white, symbolizes young innocence; the dancer in the middle, dressed in red, is the sensuously awakened woman; the one on the right, dressed in black, is the older woman who has renounced life. The painting does not celebrate the present; it expresses mysterious and disturbing psychological states. This could have been one of the visions of Schoenberg's protagonist in Erwartung.

Munch, Edvard: The Dance of Life. *1899–1900 Nasjonalgalleriet, Oslo, Norway.*

3. Picasso: Three Musicians

This well-known painting is a good example of Picasso's style of the 1920s. The three figures—a Pierrot, a Harlequin, and a monk—are commedia dell'arte **characters, showing the painter's interest in the Italian eighteenth century, an interest shared by Stravinsky in his** Pulcinella, **composed at about the same time. This combination of old and new, of presenting an old subject in a new manner, is heard in many of Stravinsky's neoclassic compositions of the time.**

The figures are flat and look as though they were superimposed cutouts of colored paper. This style of painting is called synthetic-cubism. **Picasso followed these conventions in the twenties, but soon thereafter he adopted radically different styles.**

Collection, The Museum of Modern Art, New York.
Mrs. Simon Guggenheim Fund.

4. Kandinsky: Picture with White Edge

Kandinsky is credited with being the first artist to create completely nonobjective paintings. These abstract paintings are like absolute music in that they depict nothing specific, and traditional perspective is not employed because there is no subject.

The abandonment of perspective is sometimes equated with the abandonment of tonality in music in which there is no modulation or traveling in musical space.

Kandinsky and Schoenberg were close friends, and the date of this painting coincides with Schoenberg's atonal compositions.

The Solomon R. Guggenheim Museum.

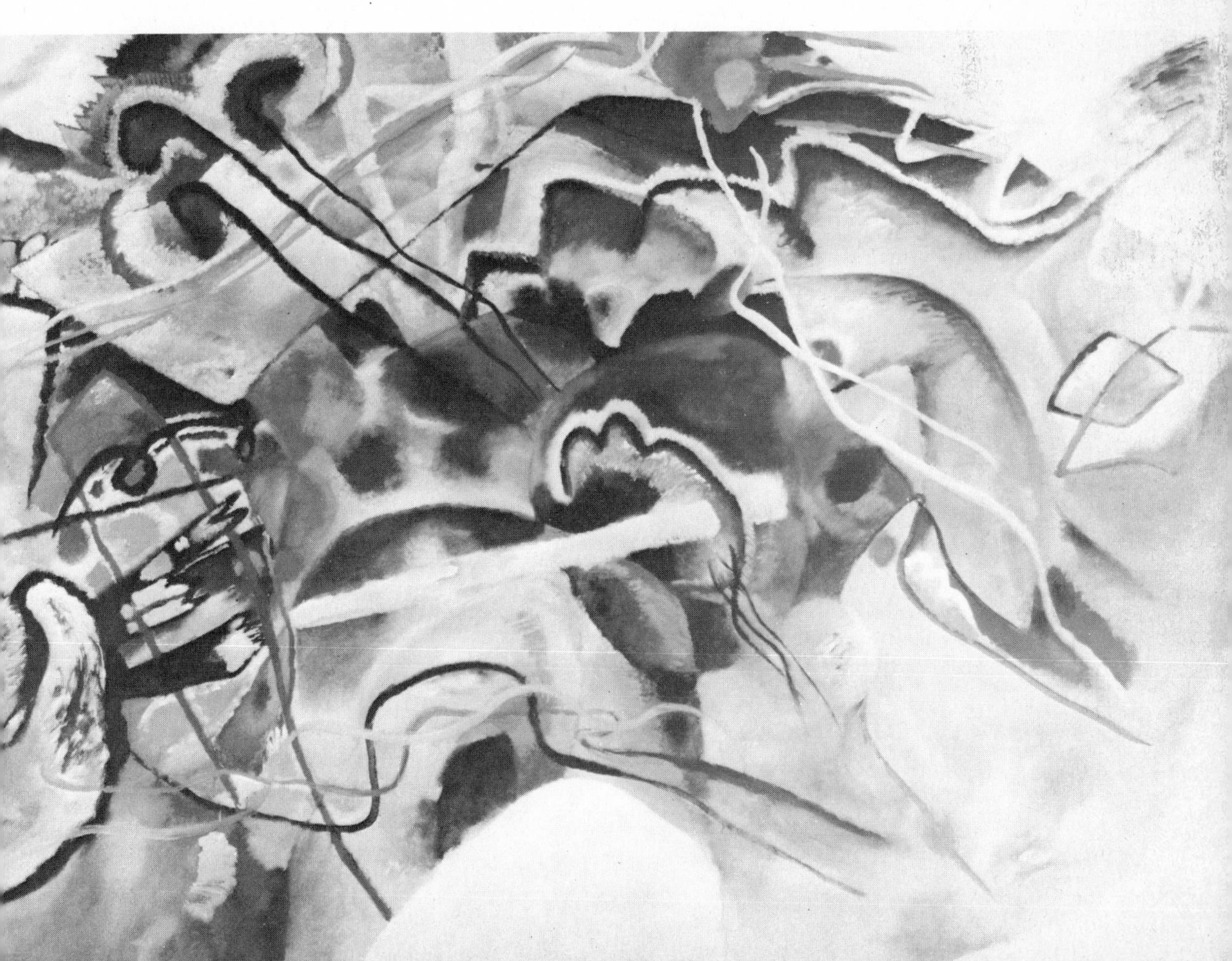

5. Mondrian: Composition No. 10

Mondrian was a purist in that he created paintings with greatly restricted resources. This picture is nothing more than an arrangement of asymmetrical crosses and lines, as minimal a motive as Webern's major third and minor second out of which he created the Concerto for Nine Instruments (see pages 212–214). While the arrangement of their slight materials might seem to be at random, both Mondrian and Webern were meticulous in the placing of their figures. Note that the crosses in the painting are denser—closer together—in some areas than in others, in the way that Webern sometimes overlaps his motive to create tension.

Rijksmuseum Kröller-Müller, Otterlo (G.) Copyright Holland.

6. Pollock: No. 10, 1949

Jackson Pollock did use random methods in his paintings, pouring or dripping paint directly on canvas without a preconceived plan. This untrammeled use of chance is similar in intent and effect to John Cage's indeterminate compositions.

Courtesy Museum of Fine Arts, Boston. Arthur C. Tompkins Fund and the Sophie M. Friedman Fund.

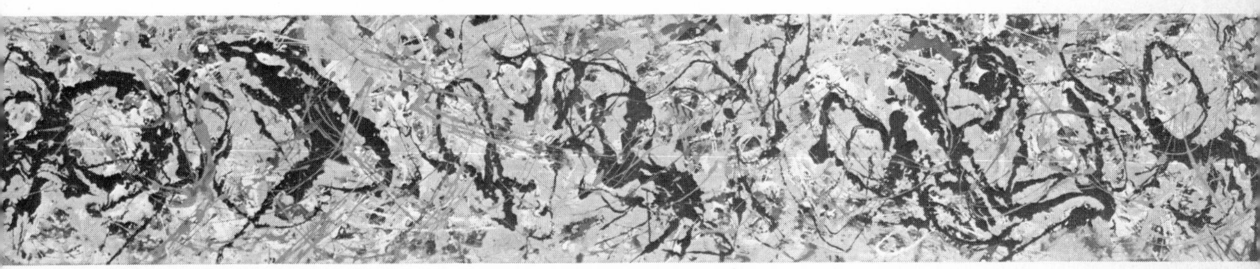

7. Robert Rauschenberg: Monogram
Artifacts such as Robert Rauschenberg's Monogram, **displayed in museums and reputable galleries, have raised fundamental questions about the nature and definition of a work of art, just as compositions by some avant-garde and experimental composers have raised questions about the nature of musical composition.**

The Commonwealth of Art, the life and the concurrence of all individual arts under a common law and fate, is not a vain, utopian wish, to be realized only in a distant future. It has been a reality, an inevitable fact from the very outset of civilization. From whatever different sensations the arts may derive, from touch or vision or hearing—on to whatever the artists may project their visions, on statues or murals or melodies—they are one in spirit and meaning. They are as different and as one as the parts of the body with which a man expresses his glee and grief, his hope and despair: the bright or saddened eyes, the speaking gesture of eloquent hands, the cheerful or listless sound of the voice. They all, though controlled by different physiological systems, obey one motor impulse under one will or reflex. The arts, like gesture and speech, are expressions of man: they confirm and corroborate, in their own individual ways, what their sister arts reflect: man's emotive reaction to stimuli from without and within.

Curt Sachs, *The Commonwealth of Art* (New York, W. W. Norton)

Bartók

13

(Debussy) restored a feeling for chords to all musicians. He was as important as Beethoven who revealed to us progressive form, and as Bach who introduced us to the transcendence of counterpoint. I always ask myself, could one make a synthesis of these three masters and create a vital contemporary style?

Béla Bartók, Speaking of Debussy

Bartók
1881-1945

ONE OF THE MOST ORIGINAL and influential voices of the twentieth century has been that of the Hungarian composer Béla Bartók. Although aware of and influenced by the current musical trends in Paris and Vienna, he was a follower of neither Stravinskian neoclassicism nor Schoenbergian expressionism. His musical language was his own, formed of indigenous elements, a thorough knowledge of the mainstream of music, past and present, and his own personality.

As with many composers, Bartók's gift for music was discovered when he was still a child. His mother, the widow of the director of a school of agriculture in a provincial Hungarian town, was his first piano teacher. Upon the death of her husband she became a school teacher, moving from town to town until 1893, when mother and son settled in Pressburg and Bartók began serious study of piano and composition. In 1899 he was accepted as a student at the Royal Conservatory in Budapest, receiving a thorough education as pianist and composer. The piano remained of greatest importance through all his life, for not only was he a virtuoso who gave concerts throughout Europe, but also piano teaching was his principal occupation, and the largest group of his compositions was for this instrument.

As early as 1904 he started collecting Hungarian folksongs, an interest that was to be lifelong and that was to have a strong influence on his compositions. His contributions and publications in the field of ethnomusicology, the science devoted to collecting and analyzing folk music and music of primitive cultures, are of major importance. He made countless trips to all the Hungarian provinces, recording songs and instrumental music. Later researches carried him further afield; in 1913 he went to Rumania and Arabia, in 1932 to Egypt, and in 1936 to Turkey. In the last years of life, when in the United States, he returned again to the publication of this material.

Among other things proven by this research was that the type of music commonly thought of as "Hungarian" was actually gypsy music as performed in restaurants and cafés of Central Europe. The *Hungarian Rhapsodies* by Liszt and the *Hungarian Dances* by Brahms are based on this type of gypsy music, for before Bartók, authentic Hungarian music was uncollected and unknown.

In 1907 Bartók became professor of piano at the Budapest Conservatory, and except for leaves of absence to give concerts or to collect folk music, he remained in the capital city for the next thirty years. During most of this time he received almost no recognition from his compatriots as a composer, and it was not until the late 1920s that some notice came from abroad. A ballet, *The Wooden Prince,* and an opera, *Duke Bluebeard's Castle,* were the first works to win any acclaim at home and in Germany.

In the years between the world wars, Bartók increased his activities as a concert pianist, playing in the United States as well as throughout Europe—most frequently performing one of his first two piano concertos. The Swiss conductor Paul Sacher became his particular champion and introduced several of the more important orchestral works.

The rise of Hitler and the collaboration of Hungary with Nazi Germany finally made it imperative that Bartók leave his native country, not on religious grounds, but because of his love of freedom and his outspoken hatred of Nazism. He came to the United States in 1940 and, except for a short return trip to Hungary to settle his affairs, remained here until his death in 1945.

The American years must have been bitter; after all, he was an exile from a fallen country, he was impoverished, and his health was precarious. He received an appointment from Columbia University to continue his folk-music research, he played concerts occasionally, and he worked on some commissioned compositions. Had it not been for illness, he probably would have been able to endure these years of exile and to resume his career. However, as his health grew worse his financial problems increased. A grant from ASCAP provided for medical care, but in spite of this he died of leukemia in 1945.

Since that time he has become recognized as one of the giants of twentieth-century music. His music has been performed more frequently than it ever was during his life. Biographies and studies of his musical idiom have been published, and elements of his style have entered into the vocabularies of younger composers. Practically all of his works have been recorded and many of them are frequently heard in concerts. It is most unfortunate that Bartók did not live another decade so that he might have enjoyed this recognition of his life's work.

Bartók's Compositions

Bartók's period of composition extended from 1903 to 1944. Because his style of writing underwent gradual changes, it is convenient to group his compositions into style periods. Throughout Bartók's entire career, the central, unifying core is his nationality, expressed musically by the use of elements of central European music—scales, rhythms, and melodies. While this feature is stronger in some works than in others, it is absent from none of them.

PERIOD 1: 1903–1908

The compositions of the first period are student works that show the formative influences and youthful ideals of a composer with great talent. *Kossuth* (1903), a long, patriotic symphonic poem, pays homage to Liszt and Strauss. Two Suites for Orchestra (1905 and 1907, rewritten in 1920 and 1943 respectively) show his admiration for Strauss and Debussy. This initial period is terminated by the first String Quartet (1908), which reveals the influence of Brahms as well as other mentors. The prevailing contrapuntal texture, including a motive that is heard in all the movements; the quasi-fugue of the opening movement; the recitative that opens the last—all these traits, as well as others, link Bartók with late nineteenth-century music.

PERIOD 2: 1908–1926

The most important works of this period are:

STAGE WORKS

Duke Bluebeard's Castle (1911)
The Wooden Prince (ballet; 1914–16)
The Miraculous Mandarin (1919)

CHAMBER MUSIC

String Quartet No. 2 (1915–17)
Sonata for Violin and Piano No. 1 (1921)
Sonata for Violin and Piano No. 2 (1922)

PIANO

Two Rumanian Dances (1909–10)
Allegro Barbaro (1911)
Suite, op. 14 (1916)

In the *Allegro Barbaro* Bartók made sounds as rude and startling as any other composer's in those brave years preceding World War I. In implication and influence it was as revolutionary as Stravinsky's *Le Sacre du Printemps* (1913) and Schoenberg's *Three Pieces for Piano* (1909). With it, all notions that music should be pretty, charming, or beautiful disappear, and brute force and angry vehemence take their place. Such expression is achieved by treating the piano as a percussion instrument to be struck and hammered instead of caressed or cajoled to "sing." The texture of the piece is chordal, and the chords consist of clusters of seconds, although the basic tonality is never lost.

This mood of intransigence and iconoclasm characterizes many second-period works. Examples are the opera *Bluebeard's Castle,* and the ballet *The Wooden Prince.* The two sonatas for violin and piano are important. They too are wild and rhapsodic, with wide leaps in the violin melodies, constantly shifting meters, and chords of strong dissonance in the piano.

Second-period works are not numerous, since Bartók, discouraged by the lack of interest in his music, stopped composing between 1915 and 1919. It was during these years that he devoted himself to the collection of folksongs.

PERIOD 3: 1926–1937

This is the richest and most important of Bartók's style periods, for it includes some undisputed masterpieces of twentieth-century music. Stylistically, the most important change over previous works is a new prevalence of contrapuntal texture. Key works of the period are:

Mikrokosmos (1926–37)
String Quartets 3–5 (1927, 1928, 1934)
Piano Concerto No. 2 (1930–31)
Music for Strings, Percussion, and Celesta (1937)
Sonata for Two Pianos and Percussion (1937)
Violin Concerto (1937–38)

Two of these works will be described.

String Quartet No. 4 (1927) has all the boldness and strength of the works immediately preceding, but at the same time the contrapuntal and formal aspects are developed in an entirely new manner. Among the five movements there are thematic connections as follows:

The form, then, extends to the work as a whole, beyond individual movements, in the manner of some of Beethoven's later quartets.

The first movement features Bartók's favorite interval, the minor second. It is used both melodically and harmonically, most of the melodies having a narrow compass resulting from a series of chromatic seconds, and most of the chords consisting of clusters of the same interval. Until one is accustomed to the effect, it is rather startling to hear such angry violence coming from the string quartet ensemble, for which so much literature has been written in more "polite" language.

After a bold introduction of a few measures, the principal motive of the movement is heard from the cello:

EXAMPLE 93*

A few measures later, the theme is presented in inversion against itself, ending in a characteristic cluster consisting of the following notes played *szforzando*, fortissimo—B-flat, B, C, C-sharp, D, D-sharp, E:

EXAMPLE 94

The viola begins a new figure making prominent use of harmonics. Under it, in the cello part, another conjunct, few-note theme centering on G-sharp is heard. Other voices imitate the cello's theme with characteristic rhythmic freedom, the figure starting on various parts of the measure and making an extraordinarily rich texture. The section ends with another explosive cluster. Example 93 appears in original and inversion simultaneously.

These are the chief elements making up the movement, which almost never lets down from its height of anguished expression. To add to the violence there are long glissandos by all the instruments introducing a shrieklike effect. In spite of this vehemence of expression the form of the movement is that of the classical sonata, with a clear-cut recapitulation and coda. The motto theme, in a Phrygian variant, is played again in the final measures by all the instruments in unison.

The second movement is a miracle of string writing, possibly influenced by a somewhat similar movement in Berg's *Lyric Suite*, already discussed. The tempo is breathlessly fast and the instruments are muted. The effect is unearthly, for one cannot hear individual tones but only "flashes" of sound.

Regardless of the effect, the movement is made up of individual tones arranged in patterns, the main theme a rising and falling chromatic figure. There is much contrapuntal ingenuity in the interplay of the themes, and the cluster chords that characterized the first movement are also strongly evident here. The form is A B A with a more static second theme:

EXAMPLE 95

Glissandos and other string effects, such as *ponticello* and alternations of pizzicato and bowed passages, add greatly to the bizarre sonorities.

The third movement is the keystone of this arch-form work. It is static and atmospheric in a Debussyan manner. An unusual effect is introduced at the beginning where the cluster chord played by the three upper strings is played nonvibrato. Throughout the movement there are indications from the composer to alternate nonvibrato and vibrato sounds.

Against this chord the cello plays a chromatic soliloquy, centered around a few notes, the phrases starting with the typical Hungarian rhythm: ♫. Later, the first violin takes over with birdlike, twittering sounds, an example of the "night-music"* mood so characteristic of the composer. The first melody returns to the cello, but this time the first violin answers in free canon.

* This is a special kind of Bartók piece that has aptly been called "night music" by Halsey Stevens, taking his cue from a piano piece so named by the composer.

The fourth movement corresponds to the second in its dependence on special string effects. Here the device is the pizzicato, the entire movement being played without bows. Again a special effect is indicated, a pizzicato so intense that a snap is heard as the string hits the fingerboard. The movement has a strong folk-dance flavor, derived from the syncopated triple meter and modal scales.

The first theme in the viola is in a modified Lydian mode:

EXAMPLE 96

Canons appear at various intervals and at irregular spacings. A little later there is strumming in the cello and viola, and a theme similar to the second theme of the second movement is heard. The scale passages recur and the movement ends in further canonic treatments.

The last movement is also dancelike. There are strong polytonal effects in this section. For example, the following accompanying cluster is based on C while the melody above it is based on F-sharp.

EXAMPLE 97

The Stravinsky-like rhythm, appearing first in the viola and later in the cello, adds to the vigor of the opening.

EXAMPLE 98

The middle section is introduced by raucous clusters in all the instruments, followed by a section that is light and graceful in mood—a mood, we might add, that is seldom found in the work. The melody of the first violin has a gypsy flavor with its ornamentation and prominent use of the augmented second:

EXAMPLE 99

Underneath, as an accompaniment figure, the rhythm of Example 93 from the first movement gradually asserts itself, clearly linking the last movement to the first. The material shown in Example 97 returns and the composition ends with ever-increasing vigor. At the climax, rasping twelve-note clusters are played fortissimo, *col legno* (with the back of the bow). The coda consists of various canonic treatments of material from the first section (see Example 97), but the final gesture of the whole quartet is again the principal motive of the first movement (see Example 93).

Bartók's Fourth String Quartet embodies many of his outstanding style characteristics. The boldness and audacity of dissonances, the unusual string effects, the rich treatment of contrapuntal devices, the narrow compass of the modal melodies—these are some of the elements of this important composition.

In this, the richest of Bartók's productive periods, there are several other compositions that should be known by every student of his works. Among them are the Violin Concerto, which has been called the most important work in the medium since Brahms's, the Sonata for Two Pianos and Percussion, and *Music for Strings, Percussion, and Celesta*—the latter two works showing Bartók's interest in writing for unusual combinations of instruments.

Music for Strings, Percussion, and Celesta is sensuously beautiful and deeply moving. At the same time, it is constructed with the most subtle skill, fulfilling Bartók's desire to combine the beauty of Debussy's sonorities with the formal structure of Beethoven and the counterpoint of Bach.

A fugue, based on a chromatic, narrow-ranged motive played pianissimo, is heard at the beginning of the first movement.

EXAMPLE 100*

Each voice enters, not in the usual tonic and dominant relationship, but according to the following diagram:

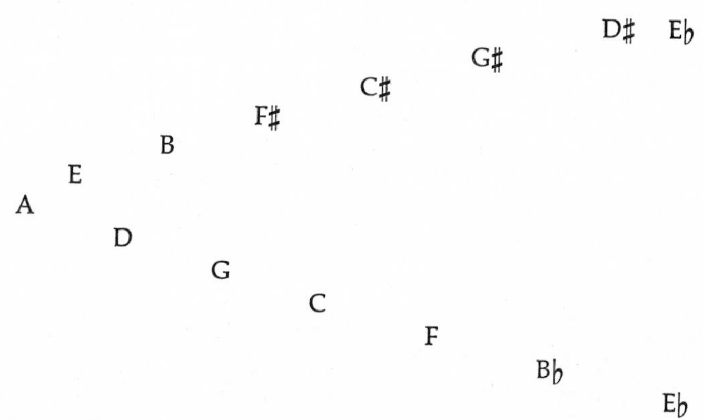

It will be noted that this double series of fifths reaches unanimity on E-flat, the climax of the movement. Afterward, the movement works back to simplicity and the central tonic A through an inverted form of the theme. At the end both forms appear simultaneously.

There is, of course, much freedom in imitation, since the theme is treated more as a characteristic shape than as an unchanging series of intervals. There are wonderful sonorities throughout—particularly at the end, when the shimmer of a celesta is added to the combination of the theme and its inversion.

The second movement with its strong rhythmic patterns and modal scales is rooted in the folk music that is the basis of so much of the composer's work. It is in sonata form, with definite cadence points separating the sections. The opening theme, with its many thirds, is related to the motto theme:

EXAMPLE 101

The strings are separated into two antiphonal groups throughout the movement. After a brief silence this dancelike theme is heard:

EXAMPLE 102

The relation of this theme to the germ theme of the whole becomes apparent if the first note is transposed an octave lower. A close, dissonant canon, a favorite device of the composer, leads to a pronounced cadence on a series of G-major chords.

The development falls into three large sections. The first is built on the theme shown in Example 101. It starts ominously in the lower strings, and soon the whole ensemble is busy with the motive except for the piano and the first group of strings, which play sharply syncopated chords. This is followed by a passage in which the pizzicato strings play modal scale fragments in a close canon. The final section is a fugue, whose subject is related to Example 100. Eventually, the material of the movement's opening is heard again in the original tonality. A free recapitulation and coda follow.

The third movement is a marvelous example of "night music" where hypnotic sound is the essence, and the xylophone, timpani, and celesta assume an importance rarely granted them. Although the movement seems amorphous and completely atmospheric, it is firmly tied to the whole work through references to the basic theme. An arch-form structure, A B C D C B A, gives it order.

The first section opens and closes with a rhythm tapped out on a high tone by the xylophone, while violas play a fragmentation of the basic theme in imitation. Section B has an eerie sound produced by the celesta and violins playing a derivative of the basic theme against glissandos in the other strings. These slides prepare the way for Section C where there is little besides glissandos for harp, piano, and celesta. The music grows in volume, reaching a shattering fortissimo that introduces Section D, consisting of another permutation of the basic theme. The bell-like motive is repeated in different rhythms, manners (*pizzicato* and *arco*), directions, and textures. This section returns to a pianissimo and then the movement reverses itself. Elements of Sections B and C are combined in the next section where tremolos take the place of glissandos and the violins play the version of the basic theme heard in Section B. The movement ends with the tapping on the xylophone.

EXAMPLE 103

The last movement is the simplest in structure and most direct in expression. A series of boisterous folk dances is heard in which the syncopations and modal scales of the main theme are typical. (See Example 103.) In form it is a rondo, with references to the motto theme becoming prominent toward the end.

In many ways *Music for Strings, Percussion, and Celesta* completely embodies the composer's ideals. In it he treats his cultural heritage—the scales and rhythms of Central Europe—with the sophistication and artistry of a master twentieth-century composer.

Piano Music

Bartók's piano works call for special attention. He was closely associated with the instrument at all periods of his life as a concert virtuoso, teacher, and editor of publications of classic composers. Furthermore, he composed for the piano from the beginning until the end of his career. Between 1897 and 1926 he wrote and published some thirty collections and individual works for piano. These vary from simple settings of Rumanian and Hungarian dances to a difficult sonata (1926). Between 1926 and 1937 Bartók worked on *Mikrokosmos*, a set of 157 piano pieces published in six volumes. The pieces are grouped according to their difficulty, from simple pieces for beginners to extremely difficult compositions for virtuosos. The complete work gives an insight into Bartók's particular musical world; not only is it an encyclopedia of pianistic figures but also it is just as much a catalog of his compositional devices, for many pieces seem to be sketches for more extended compositions.

The three piano concertos have entered into the repertoires of concert pianists and are counted among the most important written in the past fifty years. The chamber works with piano, such as the two violin and piano sonatas, and the Sonata for Two Pianos and Percussion, have also immensely enriched the literature.

PERIOD 4: c.1937–c.1945

In the compositions of Bartók's last years a marked stylistic change occurs. Much of the violence and complication of the earlier works disappear and are replaced by serenity and lyric charm. For this reason they have become the most popular of his works. Principal compositions of the time are:

String Quartet No. 6 (1939)
Divertimento for Strings (1939)
Concerto for Orchestra (1943)
Sonata for Violin Solo (1944)
Piano Concerto No. 3 (1945)
Viola Concerto (unfinished; 1945)

Because of their relative simplicity these compositions will offer no problem to anyone familiar with the earlier works.

Style Characteristics

Elements of Central European folk music impregnate much of Bartók's composition. Although this is primarily true of the earlier works, it nevertheless applies to the last period as well. Most obvious of these influences are the modal scales already mentioned. Free metric patterns, avoiding the symmetry of the four-bar phrase, are also to be traced to the same source. Melodies of narrow compass, with word-inspired rhythms, are also frequently heard (see examples previously given).

Bartók's music often sounds violent and angry because of the numerous harsh dissonances. This is particularly true in the works written before 1939, which certainly lack all trace of charm in the usual sense. He makes frequent use of clusters of minor seconds, for which he is said to have been inspired by the American composer Henry Cowell who toured Europe in the twenties, playing his own music. Melodies doubled in sevenths and played fortissimo gave Bartók the reputation of being one of the boldest of twentieth-century composers. For some time he was accused, along with Stravinsky, of writing "ugly" music. Toward the end of his life, Bartók wrote more ingratiating music, and the Concerto for Orchestra as well as the Third Piano Concerto are conservative in their use of dissonance.

While many works of the first and second period are predominantly harmonic and gain their effects from the harsh sounding chords, the texture of third- and fourth-period compositions is most frequently contrapuntal. This is particularly true in the string quartets, and Bartók's skill as a contrapuntist is shown in the inversions and rhythmic variants that characterize so many passages. He wrote counterpoint of highly dissonant character, of course, and the clashes between voices are uncompromising.

On the other hand, Bartók did not write in a consistently contrapuntal manner. That is to say, contrapuntal writing is alternated with passages or whole movements that are harmonically static in a Debussyan style—pieces in which sheer sound seems to be the most important element. Mysterious sonorities take the place of any kind of manipulation and involved relationships between voices.

While Bartók often used a highly chromatic idiom, he never entirely lost sight of tonality. His tonality is not based on cadence chords, but rather on the preferential use of certain tones, repeated often enough to give a feeling of a tonal center. An *ostinato* figure, rotating around a focal tone, for instance, sometimes gives tonal stability, even if the other voices are strongly centrifugal.

The extended works of Bartók show great variety in their formal structures. In the six quartets the number of movements varies from three to five and the sequence of tempi is unpredictable. The second and sixth quartets end with slow movements. The third, fourth, and fifth are in five movements with an arch structure. The sixth is unified by a motto theme first heard in the unaccompanied viola as an introduction to the first movement, and then in two- and three-voice texture introducing the second and third movements, and finally as the principal material of the last.

For this reason, and owing to the fact that his themes are often little more than strongly rhythmic motives, the similarity to the compositional techniques of Beethoven has often been mentioned. In his boldness and intransigence of expression he also reminds one of Beethoven.

In the realm of musical color, or timbre, Bartók is a great master in discovering the potentialities of individual instruments as well as their unusual combinations and groupings. His treatment of the piano and the string quartet in a harsh, percussive manner has been mentioned. He was fond of unusual string effects, including extensive use of harmonics, multiple stops, pizzicatos, and striking glissandos. The penchant for unusual combinations can be seen in his Sonata for Two Pianos and Percussion as well as in *Music for Strings, Percussion, and Celesta.* Timbre is so important for Bartók that he sometimes writes evocative compositions that are scarcely more than a fabric of sounds suggesting insect buzzings or bird calls. An example of such "night music" has been cited in the discussion of *Music for Strings, Percussion, and Celesta.*

The question raised by Bartók in the citation at the head of this chapter is answered by his works, for they do combine the color of Debussy, the all-pervading sense of form of Beethoven, and the contrapuntal texture of Bach. His style is original but not eccentric, for it is based on principles that have marked great music of all times. In general classification he is closer to the expressionists than he is to the neoclassicists, but at the same time, because of his strong roots in the folk idiom of his country, he does not approach Schoenberg's pinnacle of subjectivity.

Suggested Readings

The authoritative study is *The Life and Music of Béla Bartók* (New York, 1953; revised, 1964) by Halsey Stevens. A biographical study of the American years is Agatha Fassett's *The Naked Face of Genius* (Boston, 1958). The Autumn and Winter, 1949, issues of *Tempo* are devoted to Bartók and contain biographical and analytical material, as well as a comprehensive bibliography. John Vinton's article "Bartók on His Own Music," found in the *Journal of the American Musicological Society*, Vol. XIX, No. 2 (Summer 1966), is very illuminating.

Hindemith

14

A composer's horizon cannot be far-reaching enough: his desire to know, to comprehend, must incite, inspire, and drench every phase of his works.
Hindemith

Hindemith
1895-1963

PAUL HINDEMITH HAD AN EXTRAORDINARILY rich life in music, for there is scarcely a field he did not touch, from the most practical to the most theoretical. He performed on many instruments, ancient and modern, and played the viola with the mastery of a great artist. A prolific composer of music of all dimensions and for many media, he was also a conductor who led many of the world's orchestras. As an inspiring teacher he influenced a generation of composers, and his textbooks in basic musicianship and harmony are widely employed. Furthermore, he was a musical theorist in the true sense, in that his elaborately developed theory of tone relationship is one of the few that is comprehensive enough to include complex contemporary styles along with the music of the past.

Hindemith played many roles, and the public has thought of him successively as a brash young radical, a wild expressionist, an unfeeling neoclassicist, a mature, respected neoromantic master, and finally, as a reactionary. Each of these labels was appropriate at one time or another.

He was born in Hanau, central Germany, and attended the Frankfurt Conservatory. He was a spectacularly gifted student of the string instruments and composition and at the age of twenty was already concertmaster of the Frankfurt Opera and violist in a leading string quartet. After a year in the army in World War I, he plunged into the hectic musical life of postwar Germany.

This was an exciting time and place in which to come of age in the arts, for Germany's cultural life in the period after the war and before Hitler's time was unequaled anywhere. The country was torn with a cruel inflation and its very existence was threatened by one political crisis after another. Colonies were lost and industrial areas were expropriated, leaving thousands of Germans penniless, their life-savings dissipated by inflation. In spite of this general insecurity, the arts flourished. Opera houses and symphony orchestras were established by ephemeral governments in over a hundred different cities—this in spite of the fact that Germany is not as large, say, as Texas—and money was found to produce lavish new operas. It is characteristic, for instance, that Berlin and not Paris was the scene of the première of Milhaud's elaborate *Christophe Colomb* in 1930. Art and music schools were reestablished and theatrical production was revolutionized by the imagination and skill of Max Reinhardt and others.

A typical product of the time was the Bauhaus, a school of design and architecture whose aim was to strip away the vast accumulation of styles and ornaments from past ages, and return to basic, austere simplicity and honesty of expression. Disciples of the Bauhaus eventually changed the appearance of everything from packages to cities throughout much of the world.

The term *neue Sachlichkeit* (new objectivity) was used to designate this "no-nonsense" attitude that opposed the intense subjectivity of the expressionists. *Neue Sachlichkeit* found its expression in the bitter, satirical portraits of George Grosz; in the gaunt, cube-form, glass buildings of Gropius; and, for a time, in the music of Hindemith.

In 1927 Hindemith was called to Berlin to be a professor of composition at the Hochschule für Musik, and remained there until Hitler came to power and decreed that dissonant, "modern" music was degenerate and forbade any more performances. Hindemith and his music became openly involved in the struggle when Wilhelm Furtwängler, Berlin's distinguished conductor, insisted on playing his compositions after they had been condemned.

Seeing no future for himself in Germany, Hindemith left the country. He spent two years in Ankara, Turkey, organizing a state system of music education and toured widely as a conductor and violist, making several trips to the United States. In 1940 he became a professor of theory and composition at the School of Music at Yale University and remained there for thirteen years. In 1953 he returned to Europe, settled in Switzerland, and continued his busy life of composing, conducting, teaching, and writing about music until his death in 1963.

Hindemith's Compositions

Hindemith's main compositions include: three full-length operas—*Cardillac* (1926, revised 1952), *Mathis der Maler* (*Matthias, the Painter*, 1934), *Die*

Harmonie der Welt (*The Harmony of the World*, 1957); five short operas; three ballets, including *Nobilissima Visione* (1938) and *The Four Temperaments* (1944); large orchestral works, including the *Philharmonic Concerto* (1932), Symphony in E-flat (1941), and *Symphonic Metamorphoses of Themes by Weber* (1944); productions for amateurs; choral works with orchestra and *a cappella;* concertos for piano (two), cello (two), horn, and violin, and several for string instruments with chamber orchestra; six string quartets and other chamber music; sonatas for almost every orchestral instrument with piano; three sonatas for piano solo; *Ludus Tonalis,* a set of preludes and fugues for piano; and songs with piano and with instruments.

This is a long and comprehensive list of works including large and small, serious and casual, difficult and easy compositions. Hindemith resembles Milhaud in that there is no gradual evolution of style to be traced in his music after he achieved a personal style in the late twenties. Before that time he experimented widely and wrote in many of the idioms of the day; these compositions constitute his first style period.

PERIOD 1: 1917–1927

It is not at all surprising that Hindemith's rich gifts and vigorous curiosity led him to experiment in many different styles in his youthful works. The first compositions stem from the late romantic style of Reger and Strauss, and are characterized by rich, dissonant harmony, and thick contrapuntal textures. Typical early works include the string quartets and the sonatas for violin and piano, Opus 11. A very dissonant, expressionistic phase follows, examples of which are the song cycle *Die junge Magd* (*The Young Girl;* 1922) for contralto, flute, clarinet, and string quartet, and an opera, *Mörder, Hoffnung der Frauen* (*Murder, the Hope of Women;* 1921) whose libretto was written by Kokoschka, the expressionist painter. The piano suite *1922,* consisting of "March," "Shimmy," "Night Piece," and "Ragtime," shows the influence of jazz, but Hindemith's brutally dissonant and heavyhanded treatment of the popular idiom was very different from Milhaud's light-hearted approach. The directions that he wrote to the performer in the score are typical of his youthful iconoclasm:

> DIRECTIONS FOR USE
>
> Don't pay any attention to what you learned in your piano lessons!
>
> Don't spend any time considering if you should play D♯ with the fourth or sixth finger.
>
> Play this piece very savagely, but always rigidly in rhythm like a machine. Consider the piano as an interesting kind of percussion instrument and treat it accordingly.[1]

One of the most successful compositions of the period was *Eine kleine Kammermusik* (*Miniature Chamber Music;* 1922). Pert and irreverent, it is surprisingly close in spirit to the music then being written in Paris. The first movement opens with two planes of harmony and "slips" from one tonality to another—idioms typical of the twenties (see Example 104).

Succeeding movements continue this lighthearted mood; the second recalls a hurdy-gurdy, while the third is a nocturne with suggestions of the blues. The fourth movement is an acrid scherzo. There are many measures of irregular length in the final movement, and the strident dissonances in the coda are obtained by combining two disparate factors: a pedal in the bassoon and horn, and a series of parallel chords built in fourths played by the treble instruments. Modest as it is, *Eine kleine Kammermusik* is important in Hindemith's development, for it shows his emancipation from the overly serious, romantic style of the first works.

PERIOD 2: 1927–1963

By the time Hindemith left Frankfurt for Berlin in 1927 he had passed through his experimental phase and had arrived at a carefully worked out theory

EXAMPLE 104*

of composition as well as a philosophy of the function of music. He continued to write pieces of all dimensions, but his musical style remained essentially the same from then on.

Sensing that the complexity and dissonance of the early works had alienated many music lovers, he deliberately lightened the texture and simplified the expression of succeeding compositions. There was a strong socialist movement in Germany at the time, which led to the establishment of orchestras and choruses for working people. Hindemith wrote music for these amateur groups on down-to-earth, timely subjects. For example, one of his cantatas commemorated Lindbergh's flight.

These pieces are examples of *Gebrauchsmusik* (everyday music, useful music, functional music), a term that has become permanently attached to Hindemith in much the same way that the label "Les Six" was still applied to Milhaud and his friends long after they had changed orientation. Much later, in the United States, Hindemith explained the origin of the term. He tells of using it in a casual way in conversation with a group of choral conductors:

> Some busybody had written a report on that totally unimportant discussion, and when years later I came to this country, I felt like the sorcerer's apprentice who had become the victim of his own configurations: the slogan *Gebrauchsmusik* hit me wherever I went. It had grown abundant, useless, and disturbing as thousands of dandelions in a lawn. Apparently it met perfectly the common desire for a verbal label which classifies objects, persons, and problems, thus exempting anyone from opinions based on knowledge.[2]

Only a small number of Hindemith's compositions were "functional" in that sense. His general simplification of style and growing interest in contrapuntal textures rather than in dissonant chords, however, became a constant feature of his writing. The term *neoclassic*, or more appropriately, *neobaroque*, already encountered in the discussion of Stravinsky's music, is often applied to these compositions, as well as the phrase *back-to-Bach*. In form and texture many of his pieces of the late twenties and thirties resemble those of Bach.

The most Bach-like composition is *Ludus Tonalis* (*Musical Diversions*, 1943), a twentieth-century *Well-Tempered Clavier* that consists of a set of twelve fugues each in a different tonality and separated by interludes. The whole set is preceded by a prelude and terminated by a postlude, which is a retrograde version of the opening piece.

The sonatas for piano and various wind instruments are examples of *Gebrauchsmusik* in the best sense. Noting a lack of solo repertoire for the orchestral instruments, he wrote sonatas for most of them. These compositions filled a need, and have become popular.

Concurrent with these modest, "practical" compositions, Hindemith occasionally wrote large, serious works. The three operas make no concessions to popular taste or to amateur production. They have had few performances, but their "symphonic syntheses" (Hindemith's term) are often heard on symphony programs.

One of the best known of Hindemith's compositions is *Mathis der Maler*. Mathis, the hero of the opera, is Matthias Grünewald (born 1480), North German painter of the famous Isenheim Altar in Colmar, Alsace. Each of the three movements of the symphony represents a panel of the triptych.

The first movement is called "Engelkonzert" ("Concert of the Angels"). The picture that inspired the piece shows a group of angels playing instruments. In the foreground, before the Virgin and Child, is a smiling, blond angel playing the viola da gamba. The atmosphere is one of radiant happiness, reflected in the music through the prevailing consonance and dancelike rhythms.

The first movement is in a modified sonata form with a slow introduction. The modal themes establish a medieval atmosphere and the contrapuntal texture presents them in ever new lights.

The second movement is entitled "Grablegung" ("The Entombment") and is based on the central panel of the exterior of the triptych. It is a somber, realistic scene depicting the figure of Christ being laid in the grave, witnessed by the grieving figures of the two Marys and John.

This movement is quite short and is based on a slow, conjunct theme. The changing tonal centers are characteristic. A new theme, played by the oboe, starts with two leaps of a fourth, one of Hindemith's favorite melodic devices (Example 105).

EXAMPLE 105, *Mathis der Maler*: Grablegung

The last movement, "The Temptation of St. Anthony," is the most exciting. The picture itself is an amazing scene, full of fantastic birds, reptiles, and demons attacking the Saint. In the sky above, God is represented in the act of sending Michael to aid the suffering Anthony.

The music starts with a chromatic recitativelike passage in the strings interrupted by roaring dissonances played by full orchestra. The rhetorical introduction comes to an end; the movement proper starts with an eleven-note theme that is treated freely by the entire orchestra against a "panting" rhythmic motive in the background.

After a slow middle section, a strongly syncopated brass passage ushers in the concluding section. At the height of an exciting climax the main idea of the movement returns in its original tonality. Rhythmically altered and augmented, this time it is played by the trombones.

The coda begins with a *fugato* during which the deliverance of Anthony is suggested by the hymn "Lauda Sion Salvatore," discernible above all the hubbub. The piece ends impressively with a chorale-like alleluia played *mit aller Kraft* (with full strength) by the brass.

Style Characteristics

Hindemith has several prominent style characteristics that pervade his music. It has already been mentioned that he often wrote melodies that contain several intervals of the perfect fourth.

He also has a favorite metrical pattern, expressed by $\frac{6}{8}$ and $\frac{9}{8}$ signatures. The Violin Sonata in E is typical. Its first movement flows easily and quietly in $\frac{9}{8}$ with a constant eighth-note motion in either the violin or the piano, reminiscent of Bach. The last movement is a fast $\frac{6}{8}$ with frequent hemiolas and augmentations. This preference for compound meter is perhaps related to Hindemith's interest in medieval music. In other moods, he writes march and dance rhythms.

Hindemith's vocabulary and treatment of chords are consistent with his theory. He uses any combination of tones, no matter how dissonant, but always returns to simple consonance at cadences. Thus, his compositions are far removed from the constant dissonances that characterize Schoenberg's works. Tonal consonance is still the norm for Hindemith; dissonance is used for special effects.

He often writes in a contrapuntal texture; *Mathis,* for example, contains *fugatos* and other types of imitative writing. The many sonatas for orchestral instruments with piano resemble Bach's chamber sonatas in that they proceed in three lines, one in the solo instrument part and two in the piano part. Hindemith's counterpoint is often dissonant, but like his harmonies, the relationship of voices becomes consonant at the cadences.

Hindemith prefers chamber groups and ad hoc combinations to the conventional orchestra. His *Concert Music for Piano, Brass, and Harps* is typical, as are the variously scored compositions called *Kammermusik.*

Hindemith is very fond of baroque forms and textures, often writing canons and fugues, chamber sonatas, and sets of variations. His compositions called sonatas are more often than not built on the baroque rather than the classic plan.

At several points in this discussion comparisons have been made between the music of Hindemith and Bach, and there are also similarities in the careers of the two. Both were practical musicians, happy when performing on any of a number of instruments or when conducting student or professional groups. In the music of both men there is a good deal of what Germans call *Spielfreudigkeit*, or joy in sheer music-making. Both wrote incessantly without radical changes in style after they grew out of their first youthful exuberance. For that reason it is difficult to assign dates to their works on a stylistic basis. Both wrote simple compositions for instructional purposes as well as large, serious masterpieces. Both could be objective and casually expressive in their compositions, and both could on occasion write music of deep, symbolic meaning.

Suggested Readings

Ian Kemp's *Hindemith* (London, 1970) and Geoffrey Skelton's *Hindemith* (London, 1975) are two valuable books. There are numerous periodical articles of value. "Paul Hindemith as a Teacher" by Howard Boatwright in the *Musical Quarterly*, Vol. L, No. 3 (July 1964), describes the composer's teaching at Yale. Other valuable articles are: "Paul Hindemith and Neo-Classic Music" in *Music and Letters* (January 1932); William Hymanson's "Hindemith's Variations" in the *Music Review* (February 1952); and Rudolf Stephan's "Hindemith's *Marienleben*: an Assessment of Its Two Versions," *Music Review* (November 1954). Norman Cazden's "Hindemith and Nature" in *Music Review* (November 1954) and Richard Bobbitt's "Hindemith's Twelve-Tone Scale," *Music Review* (May 1965), are well worked-out rebuttals of Hindemith's theoretical views.

A catalog of Hindemith's works was published by Schott in London in 1954. This is particularly valuable because Hindemith stopped assigning opus numbers to his works after he reached Opus 50 in 1930.

Hindemith's lectures given at Harvard, published as *A Composer's World, Horizons and Limitations* (Cambridge, 1952), is recommended for the insights it gives into his thinking. His theory is expressed in *The Craft of Musical Composition* (English Ed., 1941). H. W. Heinsheimer's *Menagerie in F Sharp* (Garden City, N.Y., 1947) gives an accurate and amusing picture of the musical situation in Austria and Germany between the wars.

Shostakovich

15

The Soviet artist is an engineer of human souls.
Joseph Stalin

Soviet Russia

IN THE PRECEDING CHAPTERS THE main currents of twentieth-century music have been discussed and the two principal lines of development, the French and the German-Austro-Hungarian, have been defined. It is within this orbit that most of the important innovations and additions to the vocabulary of music have been made.

In this chapter the contributions of Russia—and in following chapters those of England and the United States—will be surveyed. It will be noted that composers of these countries have been influenced to greater or lesser degrees by Debussy, Stravinsky, or Schoenberg, depending on their contact and sympathy with them, and on the strength of the musical tradition of their respective countries.

The achievements of Russia are particularly interesting. Because of the physical isolation of this huge country, it was a late arrival to the European cultural scene, but by the middle of the nineteenth century it had made great contributions to the arts of music and literature. By that time Russian musicians had become thoroughly familiar with the music of Western Europe and were also becoming aware of the wealth of their indigenous folk material. Before the outbreak of the First World War, Russia rivaled the musical activity of other European countries with her composers, opera companies, orchestras, and the virtuoso performers trained at the great conservatories in Moscow and St. Petersburg. It has already been mentioned that composers of Western Europe were influenced by Moussorgsky, Rimsky-Korsakov, and Scriabin.

The Russian Revolution of 1917 ushered in a social upheaval

whose magnitude and consequences are still undetermined. Years of political chaos and of vast changes in the social order followed. Russia's participation in the Second World War threatened her existence, but her emergence after the war as a world power brought the once isolated nation into the center of the world arena.

Throughout all the tremendous changes experienced by Russia since the beginning of the century, the cultivation of music and musicians has never ceased. Whether under the czars or the Central Committee, the conservatories have continued to nurture musical talent; operas, ballets, and concerts have been given without interruption.

Russian artists have learned that their chief function is to glorify the State or to edify or amuse their fellow citizens. Edicts have been issued that prescribe the proper styles for music, painting, and literature. Individualistic artists who do not comply are cast aside—but those who follow the recommendations are handsomely rewarded.

In spite of these restrictions Russian composers have made contributions to twentieth-century music that cannot be ignored. Out of many, the two figures best known to the West are Serge Prokofiev and Dmitri Shostakovich, both of whom were in and out of official favor several times.

Prokofiev, 1891–1953

Prokofiev was a man of both East and West, for he spent many years in Western Europe before returning to his native country. He was born in the village of Sontsovka, where his father was the superintendent of a large estate. Because they were far removed from any cultural center, his well-educated parents personally supervised their son's schooling; his mother, an accomplished pianist, also provided his musical education. The boy's talent was unmistakable and he started composing little pieces when he was five. When eight, he was taken to the opera in Moscow and upon returning home he attempted to write an opera. When Serge outgrew his mother's teaching, the composer Glière was engaged to spend the summers of 1902 and 1903 with the family, to guide the boy in his compositions. In 1904 mother and son moved to St. Petersburg so that Serge could enter the Conservatory. The thirteen-year-old boy submitted four operas, two sonatas for piano, a symphony, and numerous piano pieces to the examining committee! For the next ten years he was a restive student, finding it difficult to accept the discipline of even such distinguished teachers as Lyadov and Rimsky-Korsakov. There was no question as to his ability as a pianist, for he quickly developed into a virtuoso.

During these years before World War I, St. Petersburg showed considerable interest in new Western music. Prokofiev was attracted to the new idioms and soon became known as a composer whose music rivaled Stravinsky's and Bartók's in its ruthless dissonance. He made a trip to London in 1914 to attend the opening of Diaghilev's season and to hear *Le Sacre*. Here he met the great impresario, who commissioned him to write a ballet. Hoping to obtain a production as sensational as Stravinsky's latest work, Diaghilev recommended another subject from Russia's savage past. The war prevented the production of the ballet, but the music Prokofiev wrote, the *Scythian Suite*, proved that Diaghilev had found a composer equal to the task.

Prokofiev had nothing to do with the Revolution of 1917 and left on a world tour as a pianist-composer before the year was over. He made his debut in New York in 1918 and for the next fourteen years lived the life of a touring virtuoso pianist, making seven tours of the United States. When not on tour he lived for several years in a mountain village in Bavaria, but in 1923 he settled in Paris and remained there for a decade.

At that time Stravinsky and neoclassicism ruled the music circles of

Prokofiev
Boosey and Hawkes

Paris. As Prokofiev's compositions were not in the same vein, they made little impression there. Only his two Diaghilev-commissioned ballets, *Le Pas d'acier* (*The Steel Leap*, 1924), which glorified the industrialization of new Russia, and *The Prodigal Son* (1929), were favorably received.

After a few visits to his native country where his concerts and music were greeted with great enthusiasm, Prokofiev returned in 1932 to the USSR to stay. He remained there for the rest of his life except for two more tours of the United States in 1937 and 1938. He apparently cooperated fully with the Soviet ideas of the role of the arts, and when necessary accepted his reprimands and apologized to the Central Committee for musical transgressions. He wrote a number of propaganda works; in one of them, a cantata, he used excerpts from the writings of Marx, Lenin, and Stalin for the text. It is interesting to note that this work was not a success with either critics or the public.

In spite of occasional reprimands by the State, the last two decades of Prokofiev's life were highly productive and filled with honors. He won several Stalin prizes, the highest accolade that Russia bestows, and generous financial rewards for his operas, ballets, and film music. His last symphonies, concertos, and piano sonatas are among the important achievements of our time, in spite of the fact that they came out of an environment in which most composers of the West would find it impossible to work.

Prokofiev's Compositions

A summary of Prokofiev's principal works includes eight operas (one unpublished), seven ballets, incidental music for plays and films, nine cantatas, seven symphonies, five piano concertos, two violin concertos, one cello concerto, a small amount of chamber music, and a long list of compositions for the piano that includes nine sonatas and many songs. The three phases of Prokofiev's life, his student days, his years abroad, and those after his return to Russia, constitute the three style periods in which these compositions will be discussed.

PERIOD 1: 1908–1918

During the first period Prokofiev's music was dominated by his strong iconoclasm and dislike of late-romantic chromaticism and overrefinement. Many of his early pieces are for piano, of which the well-known *Suggestion diabolique* (1908) is a characteristic example. It reveals an area of expression that will often be met in his later works—a penchant for grotesque, sardonic, "dark" emotions. Also characteristic is his treatment of the piano as an instrument to be pounded instead of caressed. The driving rhythms and blatant melodies doubled in minor ninths howl defiance at delicate sensitivity as thoroughly as any composition written at this early date. Other important piano works of the time are *Sarcasms, Fugitive Visions,* and the brilliant *Toccata.* These early piano pieces reveal many of the characteristics of Prokofiev's style of writing for the instrument, and they call for performers of stamina and dexterity to execute the flying leaps, repeated chords, and brilliant passage work.

The attitude expressed in these piano pieces—that of a bad boy delighting in making rude noises and poking fun at his elders—can also be recognized in the ballet music entitled *Chout* (*The Buffoon*) and the opera based on Dostoevski's story *The Gambler.*

The best-known work of Prokofiev's early period is the *Classical Symphony* (1917), which shows quite another side of his musical personality. In this evocation of the eighteenth century, the savagery of the *Scythian Suite* is absent and delicacy and lyricism reign. These more ingratiating traits become increasingly prominent in the composer's later works.

PERIOD 2: 1918–1932

These are the years Prokofiev spent away from Russia. They were disappointing years, however, for he did not acquire a circle of enthusiastic pupils such as that enjoyed by Schoenberg, nor did the spotlight of publicity play upon him as it did upon Stravinsky. He was regarded primarily as a pianist rather than a composer. As a matter of fact, many of the compositions of the time are not very ingratiating, for the verve of the earlier pieces is lost and the pure lyricism of the later works has not yet been achieved. There are some notable exceptions, however, such as his delightful fantasy opera *The Love for Three Oranges,* first produced in Chicago in 1921. The two Diaghilev ballets and the Third Piano Concerto are also highly successful compositions.

This popular Third Piano Concerto is one of the composer's happiest inspirations and it brings together many of his most characteristic style elements. It starts with a solo clarinet singing a gentle melody of Russian tinge:

EXAMPLE 106*

* Copyright by Editions Gutheil; copyright assigned 1947 to Boosey & Hawkes, Inc.

Soon a bustling, busy C-major passage is heard in the strings leading to the entrance of the solo piano that presents the main theme:

EXAMPLE 107

Interest in this subject lies largely in its rhythm, although there is a characteristic harmonic "slip" to a distantly related key at its conclusion. The orchestra and soloist engage in brilliant interplay until the second theme enters. Here is Prokofiev in his mock-serious, tongue-in-cheek mood:

EXAMPLE 108

A chromatic closing theme leads to the development, which is concerned exclusively with the slow theme of the introduction, a rather unusual and original procedure.

With the recapitulation, the roles of the piano and orchestra are reversed. Now the soloist plays the scalelike passage—one of the most exciting pages of the whole concerto repertoire. The second theme receives a more pungent "wrong-note" harmonization, and brilliant passage work brings the movement to a close.

The quiet second movement is in complete contrast to the forthright opening movement. The flute and clarinet present the melody which is the basis for the variations that follow:

EXAMPLE 109

The first variation starts as a piano solo in a distant key with the melody harmonized by rich chromatic chords. The next variation begins with tempestuous scales in the piano while the trumpet plays fragments of the main theme in another key. This variation is quite free but the prim, plagal cadence at the end restores decorum. Three contrasting free variations follow, and then the theme returns in its original form in the flutes while the soloist plays staccato treble chords, forming a charming conclusion to the movement.

The third movement is rich in contrasts. The main theme, whose periodic return gives the movement a modified rondo form, has a characteristic rhythmic irregularity:

EXAMPLE 110

There is a contrasting slow middle section with a broad, singing melody, resembling an American Negro spiritual:

EXAMPLE 111

In contrast to this there is a new melody that, in its slides and general outlines, is in the "blues" tradition:

EXAMPLE 112

The vigorous opening material returns and the concerto comes to a crashing close with both orchestra and piano pounding C-major chords.

Throughout the movement, the utmost in virtuosity is demanded of the pianist. Prokofiev wrote it for himself, and his fingers and wrists of steel were legendary.

PERIOD 3: 1932–1953

The works of Prokofiev written after his return to Russia show a great variety of forms and genres. At one extreme there are the popular patriotic songs and marches written for special occasions, such as the *Cantata for the Twentieth Anniversary of the October Revolution.* Then there are simple works such as *Peter and the Wolf* that have endeared the composer to millions of people around the world. His music for a film, *Lieutenant Kijé,* and his ballets, *Romeo and Juliet* and *Cinderella,* have also met with wide approval. In these works the lyric elements assume an importance they did not enjoy in earlier works. The opera *War and Peace,* the Fifth and Sixth symphonies, and the later sonatas for piano and for piano and violin are the mature works of a master composer.

The Piano Concerto just discussed reveals Prokofiev the athlete, the extrovert, while the Second Violin Concerto, written in 1935 after his return to the Soviet Union, reveals him as a lyricist of the first order. This composition has become one of the most popular twentieth-century concertos because of its singing melodies and idiomatic writing for the violin.

Style Characteristics

As a young composer Prokofiev took a stand against the ultrachromatic style of Scriabin and the fragmentary suggestiveness of Debussy, writing music that was forthright, clear, and blunt. While his compositions mellowed somewhat as he matured, directness of expression has always been their chief characteristic. For example, he preferred the key of C major at a time when the music of other composers was black with accidentals.

Attention has already been called to the lyric, singing quality of many of his melodies, and such a work as his Fifth Symphony, starting with a beautiful flowing line, is permeated with melodies to a degree unusual in twentieth-century music. These melodies frequently consist of small intervals, with an occasional soaring to the upper octave. Prokofiev habitually writes balanced, four-bar phrases that he builds into symmetrical periods; such regularity helps to account for the directness of expression. Occasionally the regularity is disturbed when a melody is repeated but starts on another part of the measure. He often uses the modal scales familiar to all Russians, with a special preference for the Mixolydian.

Prokofiev prefers strong, obvious rhythms, and wrote many marches (the "March" from the *Love for Three Oranges* is an example) and dance-inspired compositions. In fast movements he frequently repeats a simple eighth-note ostinato figure to build huge climaxes. An exception to his usual habit of using regular rhythms is found in the last movement of his Seventh Sonata for piano where an exciting $\frac{7}{8}$ meter prevails.

Prokofiev's music is firmly tonal, and his chords are built in thirds. He is conservative in his attitude toward dissonances, for he uses them to establish points of tension and not as the normal harmonic climate. Occasionally he writes short polytonal passages and sometimes he uses the major and minor third simultaneously or in close connection. A striking example of the latter is at the beginning of the Sixth Sonata for piano:

EXAMPLE 113*

One particular harmonic device, used by Prokofiev so often that it became one of his most characteristic traits, is that of starting a passage in one key and then suddenly shifting to a distantly related key without any transition or preparation. Examples are ubiquitous. Two that come to mind are found in the introduction to *Peter and the Wolf* and in the opening theme of the Third Piano Concerto. Since Prokofiev's style is essentially harmonic and rhythmic, counterpoint plays but a small role.

His treatment of the piano as a percussion instrument has already been mentioned. This is not his only technique, of course, for he also writes beautifully delicate effects for the instrument. When scoring for orchestra he shows the mastery that one would expect from a pupil of Rimsky-Korsakov. Unlike many of his contemporaries, he usually uses the full symphony orchestra, showing particular sensitivity for the solo woodwind instruments. While he is not often interested in novel effects, the "Battle on the Ice" movement from *Alexander Nevsky* is striking in its unique coloring.

In the organization of his compositions Prokofiev is content to use the time-tested forms of the classical period. In an interview published in the *New York Times* in 1937, Prokofiev said:

> I strive for greater simplicity and more melody. Of course, I have used dissonance in my time, but there has been too much dissonance. . . . We want a simpler and more melodic style for music, a simpler, less complicated emotional state, and dissonance once again relegated to its proper place as one element in music, contingent principally upon the meeting of the melodic lines.
>
> Music, in other words, has definitely reached and passed the greatest degree of discord and of complexity that it is practicable for it to attain. . . .
>
> Therefore, I think the desire which I and many of my fellow composers feel, to attain a more simple and melodic expression, is the inevitable direction for the musical art of the future.[1]

Good composers can be bad prophets!

Shostakovich, 1906–1975

A more representative composer of the USSR was Dmitri Shostakovich, who, in contrast to Prokofiev, received all of his training in Russia after the Revolution of 1917. Furthermore, he spent little time outside of its borders after that. He was born in St. Petersburg in 1906, and as is so often the case with composers (Prokofiev, Bartók, and Poulenc, for example), his mother was a well-trained pianist who guided his first experiences in music. At the age of thirteen, two years after the Revolution of 1917, Shostakovich entered the conservatory in his native city, where he was a brilliant and cooperative student, graduating as a pianist four years later. He continued his studies in composition, working under Steinberg, a pupil of Rimsky-Korsakov.

During the 1920s, interest in the new music of Western Europe continued in St. Petersburg, and key works such as the ballets of Stravinsky, Berg's *Wozzeck*, the symphonies of Mahler, and works of Schoenberg and Milhaud were heard and discussed. These performances were of great interest to the composition students whose training for the most part was academic and conservative. Shostakovich's early pieces, such as his *Three Fantastic Dances* and the satirical ballet *The Golden Age* (the well-known "Polka" originated here), show his awareness of aggressively dissonant, but good-humored music.

In 1925 he completed his first symphony. It is a remarkable composition, and although it shows the influence of composers with such contrasting traits as those of Stravinsky and Mahler, it is much more than a mere student piece. It was performed immediately in Russia and soon after in Europe and the United States, bringing worldwide attention to the highly gifted young composer. It is little wonder that the symphony made such an impression, for in spite of its eclecticism it established a strong musical personality. Of note are the transparent treatment of the orchestra (it is rare that there are any mass effects); the sardonic first theme; the sudden, unprepared modulations; the biting sarcasm of the scherzo; the poignant, melancholy oboe solo of the slow movement; the threatening trumpet calls that clash polytonally; and the mood of anxiety and terror of the last movement later transformed into the grandiose, triumphant peroration of the final pages. These are all areas of expression and effects that became constant factors in Shostakovich's mature style. The First Piano Concerto and the preludes for piano also made very favorable impressions at home and abroad.

With such an auspicious start, one would think that Shostakovich's career would have been untroubled and secure, and in the long run this was true. He became one of Russia's most honored citizens, but he nevertheless was seriously criticized twice by the official spokesmen of the Communist Party. His opera *Lady Macbeth of the District of Mtzensk* (1934) brought on the first reprimand. Although well received by the public it was suddenly withdrawn and accused of the most heinous of musical crimes. It was deemed to be "formalistic"—the convenient word of condemnation used in Soviet Russia to imply that a work is either not sufficiently propagandistic or that it is too much influenced by the "decadent" music of the West. The sordidness of the story and the *Wozzeck*-influenced dissonant music did perhaps make *Lady Macbeth* something less than an inspirational work. Shostakovich publicly accepted the reprimand and promised to mend his musical ways. He continued teaching at the Moscow Conservatory, a position of the highest honor, and went on composing. With his Fifth Symphony (1937) he assumed the position of Russia's most highly respected composer.

Shostakovich's Compositions

Some of the important works of Shostakovich have been mentioned in the preceding pages. A summary by categories follows. That he is primarily a symphonist is attested by the fifteen symphonies (1926–72). The two piano concertos and the numerous works for piano solo show his interest in that instrument. He wrote no operas after *Lady Macbeth,* but his revised version of this work called *Katerina Ismailova* received many performances and created interest in an earlier opera, *The Nose.* The chamber music is important, especially the Piano Quintet (1940), the second Trio (1944), and twelve string quartets (1939–68).

Shostakovich wrote his Fifth Symphony in 1937 after his reprimand caused by *Lady Macbeth* and called it a "Soviet artist's reply to just criticism." It brought the composer back into favor, and in many ways is his most representative composition. A large-scale symphony, it begins with a brooding, slow-paced movement in sonata-form. Two elements make up the first thematic group—a jagged, tortuous melody, presented in canon, and an ominous four-note descending scale fragment:

EXAMPLE 114

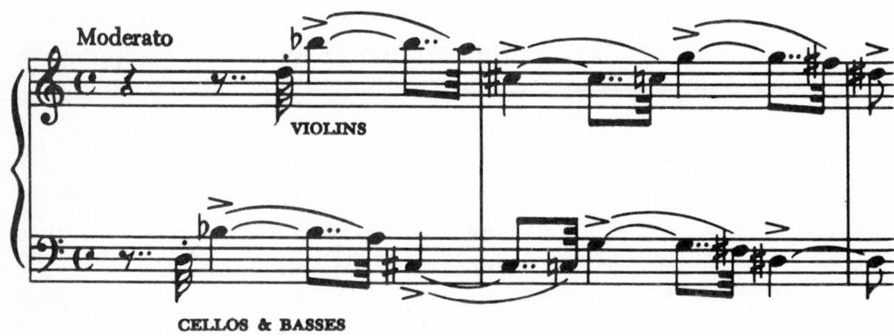

EXAMPLE 115

These two factors are the subject of a discourse carried out in the transparent orchestration already noted in the First Symphony.

The second theme is a widespread melody heard over a throbbing rhythmic figure. Except for its range, it has the effusiveness of a Puccini aria:

EXAMPLE 116

The four-note opening theme is again stated low in the brasses, as the development begins. It permeates this section and is heard in many guises and colors. Shostakovich treats his orchestra in planes, keeping each section busy with rhythmic figures or thematic derivatives, and often the groups create polytonal clashes. The turbulence resulting from this opposition of forces comes to a climax with a simultaneous presentation of the rhythmic figure of the opening bars sounding against the second theme played by the brasses.

The greatly shortened recapitulation starts with a powerful unison treatment of the first theme-group material, followed by a magnificently expansive statement of the second theme, this time in the parallel major key. Its canonic treatment between the flute and horn is of particular interest. As the movement sinks to its close, the opening melody is heard, inverted, in the flute. Low trumpets and a tinkling celesta add a final touch of color.

The boisterous scherzo of the second movement is characteristic of the grotesque, satirical mood so often found in Russian music. It is achieved here through the shrill E-flat clarinet in the opening statement, the frequent shifting of tonalities so that a passage starting in one key ends in another, and parodies of popular styles. In form it follows the traditional minuet-and-trio pattern. The solo violin is featured in the trio in an atmosphere of old régime sentiment. The third movement is an impressive, deeply moving largo. The violins are divided into three sections and the violas and cellos into two sections each, providing the warm string sound that characterizes the opening. Several chant-like themes are used. The first is static,

EXAMPLE 117

while the second, although closely related, is more urgent:

EXAMPLE 118

A third theme, first heard in the flute, recalls the principal theme of the first movement. After this material is repeated in various orders, the oboe starts the central portion of the movement with this contrasting theme:

EXAMPLE 119

The woodwinds offer a relief from the predominantly string tone of the first section, but soon the first two themes recur, working up to a climax of high tension, again reminiscent of Puccini. An abbreviated return of the opening section, including Example 114 from the first movement, brings the movement to a close.

The last movement is a wild burst of energy. It is marchlike and the pounding, recurring rhythms give it a savage strength. The first theme is blared by the trumpets, trombones, and tuba:

EXAMPLE 120

This is followed immediately by a frenetic dance:

EXAMPLE 121

These themes are developed into tremendous outpourings of sound that are eventually interrupted by a hymnlike horn-call that ushers in the quiet middle portion. The vigorous opening theme recurs and the coda, consisting of a chorale version of Example 120 in major, played in the horns, brings this heroic symphony to a close.

The Fifth Symphony closely links Shostakovich with his Russian heritage, for Rimsky-Korsakov and Tchaikovsky are the ancestors of music like this. Revolutions and radical changes in government apparently are not strong enough to destroy continuity of cultural patterns.

Style Characteristics

Since there are many similarities between the styles of Shostakovich and Prokofiev, a detailed exposition of the younger composer's music will not be given. This does not mean that the music of the two composers is indistinguishable. Each has his own style, but both share a common background of experience and general orientation to music.

Particularly in his early works, Shostakovich, like Prokofiev, showed his scorn of the past by writing satirical, grotesque caricatures of nineteenth-century popular music. The "Polka" from his ballet *The Golden Age* and the waltz in the third movement of his First Symphony are examples, characterized by the dissonant harmonizations and trite accompaniment figures.

The younger composer also shared Prokofiev's fondness for music of large dimensions and effects. His symphonies contain widespanned, exalted melodies, insistent rhythmic figures (♩ ♫ ♩ ♫ is a favorite pattern), elegiac slow movements, rough but good-humored scherzos, and vigorous finales. In his later works Shostakovich went beyond Prokofiev in expansiveness.

Shostakovich was the greater colorist in orchestral writing. One thinks of special effects such as a blatant trumpet at the end of the First Piano Concerto, the glissandos for the violins in the Fifth Symphony, and the many witty instrumental characterizations in the operas. One important difference in their styles was the result of Shostakovich's interest in counterpoint. Prokofiev did not write any formal fugues, but his younger colleague wrote a set of preludes and fugues for piano and the opening movement of the Piano Quintet is an extended fugue. The canonic beginning of the Fifth Symphony also shows his interest in contrapuntal textures.

In spite of the fact that he spent most of his life in his own country, the music of the younger composer is more eclectic, more influenced by Western composers such as Mahler, Stravinsky, and Berg, than is Prokofiev's. Nevertheless, the strongest influence on both of these composers and their lesser-known compatriots is their rich heritage of nineteenth-century Russian music. Perhaps because its composers were forbidden to use experimental idioms, perhaps because they were by nature conservative—for whatever reason—the music that has come out of the country that has experienced the most radical social changes in the early twentieth century has been the least experimental.

Suggested Readings

On Prokofiev, Israel V. Nestyev's *Serge Prokofiev, His Musical Life* (New York, 1946) is a Soviet-slanted, but thorough, study. The chapter "SRG SRGVTCH PRKFV" in Nicolas Nabakov's *Old Friends and New Music* (Boston, 1951) gives interesting insights into the personality of the composer. See also Victor Seroff: *Sergei Prokofiev: A Soviet Tragedy* (New York, 1968).

On Shostakovich, two biographies are: Ivan Martynov's *Dmitri Shostakovich: The Man and His Work* (New York, 1947), and Victor Seroff's *Dmitri Shostakovich: The Life and Background of a Soviet Composer* (New York, 1943). The article "Dmitri Shostakovich" by Nicolas Slonimsky in the *Musical Quarterly*, Vol. XXVIII (1942), and another by Hugh Ottaway, "Shostakovich: Some Later Works" in *Tempo* (Winter 1959), cover early and recent works.

There are several books covering a wider field of modern Russian music. Among them are *Eight Soviet Composers* by Gerald Abraham (London, 1944), *Realist Music: 25 Soviet Composers* by Rena Moisenko (London, 1949), and *Handbook of Soviet Musicians* by Igor Boelza (London, 1943). Also to be mentioned is Nicolas Slonimsky's article "The Changing Style of Soviet Music," in the *Journal of the American Musicological Society*, Vol. 3, No. 3 (1951), and his translations of various official decrees on music in *Music Since 1900* (op. cit.). *Musical Uproar in Moscow* by Alexander Werth (London, 1949) gives an account and translation of the speeches at the important World Congress of Intellectuals in 1948.

Two later books have superseded most of the foregoing. They are Stanley Krebs: *Soviet Composers and the Development of Soviet Music* (New York, 1970); and Boris Schwarz: *Music and Musical Life in Soviet Russia, 1917–1970* (New York, 1972).

Vaughan Williams

16

I usually feel content to provide good plain cooking and hope that the proof of the cooking is in the eating.

Ralph Vaughan Williams

England

DURING THE FIRST HALF OF the twentieth century, England once again became a producer of significant music after two hundred years of subservience to German and Italian music and musicians. While her musical achievements had been of prime importance in the late Middle Ages and the Renaissance, after the death of Purcell in 1695 there were no other outstanding native composers. From that time on foreign composers dominated the scene: Handel in the eighteenth century, and German symphonists from Mendelssohn to Brahms, and Italian opera composers from Bellini to Verdi, in the nineteenth.

However, because of a unique feature in English music—the great interest in choral singing—English composers throughout these years wrote countless cantatas and oratorios on Handelian or Mendelssohnian models for the numerous regional and national choir festivals.

In the Edwardian era, a respectable if not highly original group of composers emerged. Like their contemporaries in the United States (discussed in Chapter 6), they tended to follow either the conservative ideals of Brahms or the progressive directions of Wagner and Strauss. However, the most important English composer of this generation, Edward Elgar (1857–1934), was virtually self-trained. His *Enigma Variations* for orchestra (1899), the massive oratorio *The Dream of Gerontius* (1900), and the Violin Concerto (1910) have proved to be late romantic works of lasting value that are still performed, even outside England.

With the composers of the next generation, England entered the twentieth century. These men were aware of the new continental musical currents (many of them studied in France), but there were two indigenous activities, the results of which gave their music a unique "English" quality. The first was the founding of the English Folk Song Society in 1898. This was a group dedicated to collecting and publishing the treasure of native melodies that up to this time had gone unnoticed, and that, had they been noticed, would have been beneath the interest of serious composers. The young composers of the opening decades of the century were profoundly influenced by the modal melodies they found here, so unlike the tension-filled, chromatic melodies they had been taught to admire and write, and they were also attracted to the gentle $\frac{6}{8}$ meter that underlay many of the tunes. Both of these elements became prominent in many of their compositions.

The other noncreative activity that affected the music of this generation of English composers was the editing and publishing of another forgotten national treasure, sixteenth-century vocal polyphony. The madrigals of Weelkes and Morley as well as the masses and motets of Byrd and Taverner, now made available, opened the eyes and ears of the young English composers to rhythmic subtleties and harmonic practices that were also far removed from the textbook rules they had studied. Thus the English composer of the early twentieth century had a heritage far different from that of his colleagues across the Channel—a heritage often apparent in his music.

Vaughan Williams, 1872–1958

Among the large number of English composers active in the first half of the century, none is more important than Ralph Vaughan Williams. In the extent and variety of his compositions, in his slowly formed, highly personal style (based on the English tradition, but not reactionary), in his teaching activities—no contemporaneous English composer approached his stature.

There was nothing spectacular about his career; although he studied the piano, violin, and harmony as a child, he was never a professional performer. Upon graduation from Charterhouse, a public school, he entered the Royal College of Music and studied composition with Sir Hubert Parry, whose advice to his students was, "Write choral music as befits an Englishman and a democrat." [1] Although he went to Munich to hear the *Ring,* the young composer was "painfully illiterate" as far as the general literature of music was concerned. In his autobiographical sketch he tells of the amazement he felt when, at the age of twenty, he heard Beethoven's *Appassionata Sonata* for the first time.[2]

Vaughan Williams's years of apprenticeship were many. After graduating from the Royal College of Music, he took degrees at Cambridge, and following this he settled in London as a church organist and choirmaster. In 1896 he went to Berlin to study with Max Bruch. After his return to England, he joined the Folk Song Society and came to know the music that was to leave such a strong mark on his own. He started teaching composition at the Royal College after serving in World War I, and except for a few months of study with Ravel in Paris and three trips to the United States in 1923, 1932, and 1956, he remained there for the rest of his life. Vaughan Williams composed constantly and modestly, relying on the advice and counsel of a few colleagues, frequently rewriting his compositions on the basis of their criticism. In his autobiography he singles out and pays special tribute to his friend and fellow composer, Gustav Holst, who for many years acted as his mentor. Such acknowledgments are rare in the world of composers.

His works were performed occasionally at choir festivals, and in 1914, when he was over forty, his sprightly *London Symphony* made a favorable impression. Over the next forty years the musical world gradually came to realize that he was a composer who grew in maturity from year to year, that he did not follow changing continental styles, and that he did not repeat himself. Throughout his sixties, seventies, and eighties, he continued to compose works of ever-increasing power and unpredictability, and when he died at the age of eighty-six, he left an impressive list of compositions of all dimensions.

Vaughan Williams's Compositions

Among his works are the operas *Hugh the Drover* (1911–1914) and *Sir John in Love* (1929) (the composer's setting of the Elizabethan tune *Greensleeves* in this opera has become well-known), a chamber opera *Riders to the Sea* (1937), and the ballet *Job* (1931). There is also incidental music to plays and films, a wealth of sacred choral music of which the *Mass in G Minor* is the most extensive, choral works with orchestra, and part songs. He wrote nine large symphonies, shorter orchestral pieces, concertos, a small amount of chamber music, and nearly one hundred songs.

The *Fantasia on a Theme by Thomas Tallis* (1908, revised in 1913 and 1919), scored for string quartet and double string orchestra, is an example of his "English" style. The first decade of the century saw the creation of much feverish music on the continent–such works as *The Firebird, Erwartung,* and *Elektra*—but this contemporaneous English piece breathes an air of timeless calm and dignity. It is neither dissonant nor complex. Instead, it is rich in many-voiced string sonorities with antiphonal effects that resemble vocal writing.

With the *Tallis Fantasia,* English music shook off two centuries of German domination and tapped a rich source of native musical beauty. If he had done nothing more than write mellifluous fantasias on Elizabethan melodies, Vaughan Williams's place in twentieth-century music would have been important, though modest. Instead, he developed a musical style that was not only national and personal, but of international significance.

The nine symphonies, spaced throughout his life, mark various stages in the development of his style. The first three have descriptive subtitles. The first, with chorus, is the *Sea Symphony,* written in 1912. In 1914 the *London Symphony,* a wonderful evocation of the city in all its moods, was performed; this was followed in 1922 by the *Pastoral.* The Fourth (1935), Fifth (1943), and Sixth (1948) symphonies do not have titles, but their stormy dissonances and somewhat forbidding nature reveal a constantly developing musical style. The seventh symphony, called *Sinfonia Antartica* (1952), is an extension of music the composer wrote for a film, *Scott of the Antarctic.* The Eighth (1956) and Ninth (1958) symphonies are not programmatic and their fresh vitality gives no hint that they are the works of an octogenarian.

The Sixth Symphony is a far cry from the composer's early "English" style. This is a mid-twentieth century statement, complex and dissonant in harmony, strong in rhythm, rich in melody and orchestral effects, and equivocal and disturbing in expression.

The symphony is in three connected movements with an epilogue. A headlong, impetuous, bitonal introduction leads to a restless first theme:

EXAMPLE 122*

The rushing figures of the introduction continue as accompaniment after the theme enters. Following the seriousness of the opening, the second theme is a complete surprise, for it is a bouncy jazz tune played over an "oompah" base. A series of syncopated, "swinging" melodies follows until this warmly lyrical closing theme is heard:

EXAMPLE 123

It is obvious that the composer is fond of this material. He lingers over it, repeating it in ever-richer versions. He seems to leave it reluctantly for the short development and recapitulation and then returns to it as soon as he can.

A timpani roll and a note held in the double basses join the first and second movements—an ominous march with many military overtones, suggested by prominent trumpets and drums. The chromatic principal theme seems scarcely able to raise itself out of the gloom:

EXAMPLE 124

The theme eventually rises to more sonorous altitudes, and then parallel-chord harmonizations, reminiscent of the early Tallis piece, appear. Timpani and muffled snare drum add to the funereal solemnity. In the contrasting middle section, a hollow-sounding fanfare alternates with unison string passages. Gradually the rhythmic figure of the opening section becomes prominent and the muted opening material returns.

The third movement is entitled "Scherzo" but it is no lighthearted frolic. It is a piece of diabolical energy, resulting from strong rhythms and dissonant counterpoint, but most of all from the extreme exploitation of the *diabolus in musica,* the augmented fourth. Here is the opening:

EXAMPLE 125

The trio features the tenor saxophone in a rather maudlin melody.

The Epilogue is an eerie, disturbing piece of music, resembling the opening of Bartók's *Music for Strings, Percussion, and Celesta* in its fugal texture, involuted chromatic theme, and muted-string color.

EXAMPLE 126

Unlike the Bartók opening, however, which develops to a climax in volume and then subsides, this movement has but one dynamic—pianissimo—and continual warnings: *senza crescendo* (without crescendo). The canons, inversions, and augmentations progress in this dim atmosphere, and after the demonic energy of the earlier movements this quiet, mysterious close produces a profound effect.

The Sixth Symphony was by no means the last work of this grand old man of English music. The three symphonies that followed are warm, genial works which sum up the lifework of one of the major composers of the period.

Britten, 1913–1976

During the long years of Ralph Vaughan Williams's career, a number of younger English composers came into prominence, among them Gustav Holst

Britten
Boosey and Hawkes

(1874–1934), John Ireland (1879–1962), Sir Arnold Bax (1883–1953), Arthur Benjamin (1893–1960), Edmund Rubbra (1901), Sir William Walton (1902), Lennox Berkeley (1903), and Alan Rawsthorne (1905). The most spectacularly gifted composer of the younger generation, however, and the most widely performed, was Benjamin Britten. All musical prodigies are compared to Mozart, but the parallels in careers and similarities in creative personalities between Britten and Mozart are striking. Like Mozart, Britten started to compose while still very young; he continued without pause. He, too, composed with tremendous facility, working out compositions in his mind and then transferring his thoughts to notation no matter where he was—backstage or in airplanes. He wrote operas as well as instrumental music, sacred as well as secular choral works, pieces for children and pieces for sophisticates. Britten's style was eclectic and one can hear in his compositions traces of composers as disparate in style as Purcell and Berg. He seems to sum up, and to have at his disposal, all of the musical techniques and idioms of his time just as Mozart made thorough use of the ideals and vocabulary of his age.[3]

There are few important biographical details apart from the dates and events related to the performances of his compositions. Britten was born in the village of Lowestoft in Suffolk, where his father was a dentist and his mother was an enthusiastic choir singer and secretary of the local choral society. He studied piano and viola as a child and worked in composition with Frank Bridge. When he was sixteen he won a scholarship at the Royal College of Music where he continued his work in composition with John Ireland and in piano with Arthur Benjamin. After graduation he started to write music for documentary films and plays, an occupation for which his facility and ability to reflect situations in music eminently suited him. His work for the theater brought him in contact with W. H. Auden, the poet and dramatist, and when the latter left England for the United States shortly before the war, the young composer followed. Britten remained for three years, but then gave up his idea of becoming an American citizen and returned to wartime England. After some years he settled in the fishing village of Aldeburgh where he lived (when not on tour), composed, and directed a summer music festival until shortly before his death in December 1976.

Britten's Compositions

Britten's operas form an impressive group of works and they can be counted among the most successful of their time. They have all survived their premières and are performed regularly in the opera houses of the world. They are *Peter Grimes* (1945), *The Rape of Lucretia* (1946), *Albert Herring* (1947), *Let's Make an Opera* (1948), *Billy Budd* (1951), *Gloriana* (1953), *The Turn of the Screw* (1954), *Noye's Fludde (Noah's Flood,* 1957), *A Midsummer Night's Dream* (1960), *Owen Wingrave* (1970), and *Death in Venice* (1973). He has also written a number of song cycles for solo voice and instruments, such as *Les Illuminations* for high voice and strings (1939); *Serenade* for tenor, horn, and strings (1943); *Nocturne* for tenor and small orchestra (1958); and *Songs from the Chinese* for voice and guitar (1959). *A Ceremony of Carols* for boys' voices and harp (1942) and *The Young Person's Guide to the Orchestra* (1946) have achieved worldwide popularity. He has also written the *Sinfonia da Requiem* (1940), concertos for violin and for piano, and numerous works for chamber music combinations.

The première of *Peter Grimes* on June 7th, 1945, was a momentous day in England's musical life; critics and the public alike felt that after two hundred years an English opera had been written that would hold its own, not only at home, but on operatic stages anywhere. They were not mistaken; *Peter Grimes* has become one of the most successful twentieth-century operas, despite its lack of easy charm and light entertainment value.

The libretto, based on a poem by George Crabbe (1754–1832), offers no opportunity for glamorous costumes or elaborate settings. It is a psychological drama, the tragedy of a "little man," an unimportant, harassed fisherman, played against the background of sea and village. Peter Grimes is an "outsider" and recluse; poor, friendless, suspected of maltreating the apprentice boy who works for him. When the boy dies at sea, Grimes is brought to trial. He is exonerated, but the village still does not accept the solitary Grimes, with the exception of Ellen Orford, a widow. Grimes is driven with the ambition to make enough money to win the respect of the village and to marry Ellen. He takes on another apprentice. There is evidence that he is cruel to the boy and when Ellen remonstrates, he strikes her. Forced by Grimes to go fishing in the midst of a storm, the second boy falls off a cliff and is killed. The men of the village are aroused and seek Grimes, but he becomes insane and drowns as he sinks his boat.

In setting this grim story to music Britten has chosen a form of opera that, while showing the influence of many composers and styles, is perhaps closest to Verdi's *Otello*. This means that it is neither consistently through-composed in the manner of *Tristan* or *Pelléas,* nor is it divided into recitatives and arias as is *Figaro* or *Rake's Progress.* As in Verdi's later operas, Britten's opera proceeds primarily in arioso-recitative passages with the action pausing occasionally for freely formed arias. There are also occasional "set pieces" such as the round sung in the pub on the stormy night and the village dance. The choruses and ensembles are especially important, another feature that removes *Peter Grimes* from late Wagnerian ideals.

The orchestra is treated with great flexibility; accompanying the singers, characterizing the people in the story, and depicting what is happening on stage. In the interludes that separate the scenes, it takes over completely, providing compositions of great power and beauty. The "Four Sea Interludes," frequently heard in concerts, will be discussed, showing their significance in the opera.

The first interlude is played immediately following the Prologue (the trial of Peter), and serves to introduce the scene of the first act, the village beach and street "on a cold gray morning." The bleakness of the scene is portrayed in an unaccompanied melody, high in violins and flutes, interrupted from time to time with clarinet, harp, and viola arpeggios, like gusts of wind:

EXAMPLE 127*

Below, major chords played by the brass are heard, contradicting the mode of the melody:

EXAMPLE 128

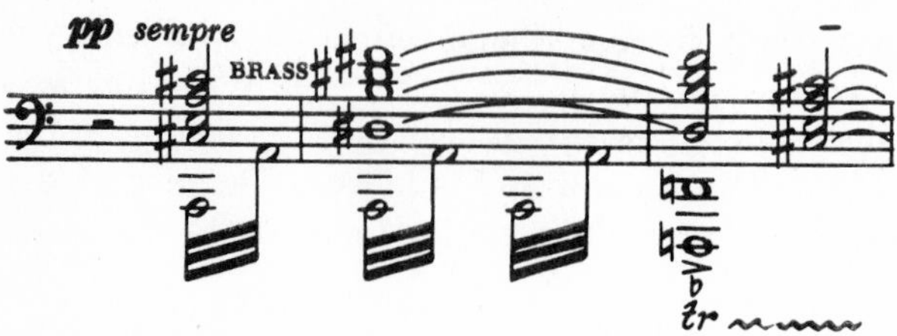

These three factors continue as the villagers come onstage and the chords thus become associated with the people. With these basic elements—melody, arpeggio, and chord—the sea and man, the theme of the opera, is established.

The second interlude, "Sunday Morning," occurs in the opera as a prelude to Act II. The scene is the same as before, but now it is "a fine sunny morning with church bells ringing." It must be difficult for a composer to write festive outdoor music with bells and not think of the Coronation scene from *Boris Godounov.* Britten does not resist the association. This interlude starts with overlapping thirds played *fp* (loud attack and then immediately soft) by the horns. The effect is bell-like, and the bright syncopated woodwind figures sound like overtones:

EXAMPLE 129

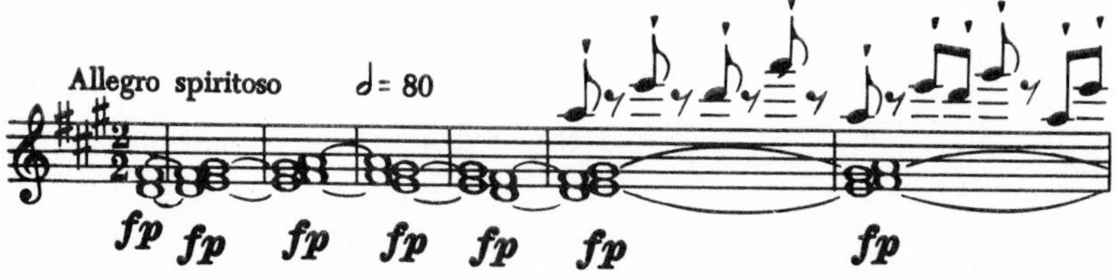

A *cantabile* melody, later the theme of the Sunday morning aria sung by Ellen, interrupts the tone-painting.

The third interlude is a nocturne, serving as a welcome relief after the tense scene that precedes it. Once again, the musical means are extremely economical. They consist of diatonic chords in the bassoons and lower strings, and a halting melody in the cellos. In the opera, this quiet interlude is followed immediately by a barn dance, and the raucous village music that breaks into it makes a vivid contrast, not unlike the village-inn scene in *Wozzeck* in which the out-of-tune piano breaks into the high tension of the preceding interlude.

The last section of the orchestral suite depicts a storm at sea. Here is a blustering, savage piece, strong in irregular rhythms and timpani accents, interspersed with progressions in parallel seconds and fifths for trumpets and trombones. Near the end an expansive phrase, associated with Grimes's hope for salvation through his love for Ellen, is heard:

EXAMPLE 130

This interlude is integrated directly into the scene that follows, as are all the others.

The most important interlude (not included in the concert suite) is a *passacaglia,* the basis of which is a theme sung by Grimes after he strikes Ellen. When he realizes the enormity of his act he sings:

EXAMPLE 131

Once again a similarity to *Wozzeck* comes to mind, as Berg's hero sings a passage expressing his misery:

EXAMPLE 132

The similarities to Berg's masterpiece do not end here. The central character in both operas represents the underdog, the underprivileged member of society who, through lack of opportunity, has no control over his fate. Wozzeck's ironic remark that it is difficult for the poor to be virtuous is echoed many times by Grimes. In both works tremendous compassion is raised for these unfortunate, timeless people. An interesting sidelight is the fact that the authors of the two librettos, Crabbe and Büchner, were contemporaries of the early nineteenth century.

Besides these similarities in the basic stories and in the impact of the two operas, there are also similarities in the overall musical structures as well as in details. Both composers achieve continuity by writing important orchestral interludes that connect the scenes. As Kerman points out, in speaking of *Wozzeck*, these sections give opportunity for the music to expand after the terseness demanded by a realistic setting of the words.[4] The use of "abstract" forms, such as the passacaglia, to provide a structural framework for dramatic scenes is also found in the two operas, but of course, much more consistently in Berg's. Both composers have the ability to characterize personages and situations with few notes (the Captain in *Wozzeck* and the lawyer Swallow in *Peter Grimes*), and both move from low life (the scenes in the pub and the beer hall, each with its appropriate music) to high pathos. Britten as well as Berg achieves tremendous, shattering musical effects with the simplest musical means, as shown by the terrifying drum beat that accompanies the villagers' search for Grimes and the mournful fog horn (tuba) that accompanies his last soliloquy.

Emphasis upon similarities does not mean that *Peter Grimes* is derivative from *Wozzeck*, and therefore a second-rate opera. Knowledge of such points of contact helps to classify Britten as a creative type. He is not a composer who holds originality to be of prime importance. He is reported to have said, "I do not see why I should lock myself inside a narrow personal idiom" [5]—an attitude completely at odds with that of many of his contemporaries who sought a highly personal style.

Britten's later compositions are discussed in Part Three.

Suggested Readings

A general survey of the period can be found in *British Music of Our Time*, edited by A. L. Bacharach (London, 1946), as well as in Norman Demuth's *Musical Trends in the Twentieth Century* (London, 1951). Two books devoted to Ralph Vaughan Williams and his music are: *Ralph Vaughan Williams* by Hubert

Foss (contains short autobiography by the composer; New York, 1950), and *The Music of Ralph Vaughan Williams* by Frank Howes (London, 1954).

Valuable books on Britten are: *Benjamin Britten, A Commentary on his Works from a Group of Specialists,* edited by Donald Mitchell and Hans Keller (New York, 1953), *Benjamin Britten, a Sketch of His Life and Work* by Eric Walter White (London, 1954), and *The Operas of Benjamin Britten* by Patricia Howard (London, 1969).

Young American composers during their stay at Paris in 1926

17

The way to write American music is simple. All you have to do is to be an American and then write any kind of music you wish.

Virgil Thomson

Music in The United States

THE MOST IMPORTANT FACT ABOUT American music between the two world wars was its diversity and vigor. In contrast to the situation in the early 1900s, when interest in and performance of music was largely limited to metropolitan centers and an American composer was a *rara avis,* by 1950 music was being written, played, and listened to across the land by ever-increasing numbers of people. This is not to say that our composers immediately found audiences and fame, but their chances for recognition and performances were as favorable here as in any other place. The growth of music departments in colleges and universities, with their composers-in-residence and festival concerts, helped to establish the American composer as a valuable and respected member of his community.

This chapter will be devoted to six American composers born close to the turn of the century. These men still went to Europe in the twenties for advanced study and stimulation, and each reacted in his own way to what he experienced. After their return they all (with one exception) became teachers and were extremely influential in forming the next generation of American composers. Each had a long, productive life and each had to meet the crisis of post-World War II music. Only their compositions of 1920 to 1950 will be discussed here.

Copland (born 1900)

Aaron Copland is one of the most prominent American composers of the twentieth century. He was born in Brooklyn to immigrant Russian parents, attended public schools, worked on Saturdays in his father's department store, and took his first piano lessons from his older sister. When his interest in music became predominant and he decided to become a composer, his parents were surprised, but they did not hinder his ambition.

After graduating from high school, Copland studied piano and harmony in New York, but he was more interested in the Strauss, Wolf, Debussy, and Ravel scores he found in the public library. During the summer of 1921 he went to France to attend the newly opened American School of Music at Fontainebleau. After overcoming his misgivings about studying with a young woman, he enrolled in the classes of Mlle. Nadia Boulanger, and became the first of a long series of Americans to work under this remarkable teacher. Finding the musical life of France stimulating (this was during the early twenties, it

Copland
Photo by Paul Moor, courtesy of Boosey and Hawkes

must be remembered), and encouraged by the acceptance of a piano piece by Durand, Debussy's and Ravel's publisher, he remained in Paris for the next two years.

The young composer returned to New York in 1924, and Mlle. Boulanger introduced his Symphony for Organ and Orchestra with the New York Symphony Orchestra early in 1925. It was after this performance that Walter Damrosch, the conductor, said to the audience, "Ladies and gentlemen! If a young man at the age of twenty-three can write a symphony like that, in five years he will be ready to commit murder." [1] This remark shows the total lack of sympathy for, and understanding of, new music on the part of New York's most prominent musician.

However, Copland received a Guggenheim Fellowship, the first to be awarded to a composer, and he returned to France for another stay. With this move the pattern of his life became established—residence in or near New York interspersed with frequent sojourns in Europe, Mexico, Hollywood, South America, and the Far East. Copland is typically American in his cosmopolitanism, in his restless energy, and in his wide-ranging interests. He has been an untiring promoter of new music: organizing concerts (Copland-Sessions concerts, 1928–1931); composers' societies (American Composers Alliance); festivals (Yaddo); and schools of music (Tanglewood). Although he has not held a full-time appointment at a college or university, he lectured for several years at the New School for Social Research in New York and filled guest appointments at Harvard and other universities. He has composed music for Hollywood movies, traveled as a cultural ambassador, written books and articles, conducted, and performed as a pianist.

Copland's Compositions

Since Copland, along with many other twentieth-century artists, has progressed through clearly defined style periods, it will be helpful in discussing his compositions to place them in the groups defined and named by Julia Smith in her study of the composer.[2]

Among the works written while he was still a student of Boulanger, the Passacaglia for piano (1922) is the most significant. Built on an expressive chromatic theme, this composition shows the disciplined workmanship he acquired from his teacher. (See Example 133.) Other early works are the Symphony for Organ and Orchestra (rewritten in 1928 without the organ, as the First Symphony), and a ballet *Grohg,* which later was incorporated in his *Dance Symphony.*

The principal works of Copland's first period (1925–1929), called "French-Jazz" by Julia Smith, are: *Music for the Theater* (1925), Concerto for

EXAMPLE 133*

Piano (1926), *Vitebsk* (1928), and *Symphonic Ode* (1929). These compositions were written after his return to New York and during the second European sojourn. Outstanding musical traits are the use of jazz idioms and rhythms, aggressive dissonances, and Jewish melodies in *Vitebsk*, for piano, violin, and cello.

Music for the Theater is a vital composition that clearly reveals Copland's background—that of a young American who knew authentic jazz as well as the sophisticated jazz stylizations of Milhaud and Stravinsky. The piece was not written for any particular production; it is "theatrical" in a general way. It opens with the trumpet playing a nervous, free-ranging melody with frequent repeated notes—an example of what Arthur Berger has called Copland's "declamatory" style.[3] Resembling wordless recitative, synagogue cantillation, or the wandering improvisation of a jazz musician, this type of melody is frequently encountered in Copland's works. A theme consisting of three descending notes (3-2-1 of the major scale) is introduced; it is used again by the composer in later compositions. A strongly syncopated middle section follows, and then the movement closes with references to the opening soliloquy.

The second movement, "Dance," recalls a jam session as one instrument after another comes into prominence. The rhythm is convulsive, and a distorted version of "East Side, West Side" is heard. This movement is close to real jazz—much closer than anything written by Milhaud, Stravinsky, or Hindemith. "Interlude" is in blues style, opening with an English horn solo. "Burlesque," which follows, reminds one of the music of Les Six with its music-hall flavor, and "Epilogue" returns to the mood and musical material of the opening.

There is no lighthearted gaiety in the compositions of the second or "Abstract" period (1929–1935). The principal compositions are: *Piano Variations* (1930), *Statements for Orchestra* (1932–1935), *Hear Ye! Hear Ye!*, a ballet (1934), and *Short Symphony* (1932–1933), later rewritten as a sextet (1937). These are difficult, austere works in which the working out of musical ideas to their logical conclusions seems to be the main concern of the composer.

The composition that most completely embodies this trend is the *Piano*

Variations, an uncompromising statement of a serious young composer. The piece abounds in accented fortissimos in the piano's most percussive registers. Among twentieth-century compositions exploiting the "spiky" aspects of the instrument, none is more severe. The theme is:

EXAMPLE 134*

The conflict between C-sharp, the tonic, and C-natural—both melodically and harmonically (Measure 2)—is an example of the Stravinskyan type of dissonance often used in this piece. Further influence of Stravinsky is expressed in the frequent octave transpositions of melody notes, the unrelenting doublings in major sevenths and minor ninths, as well as in the theme itself, which shows similarities to the theme of his Octet (Example 60).

The variations are skillfully tied together so that their effect is cumulative. In early sections the piece moves in a steady quarter-note motion (in measures of constantly changing length), but later on, notes of shorter time value add momentum. The moods vary from the granitic sonorities of the beginning to a playful scherzo; from brilliant toccatas to solemn hymns. Throughout the piece there is neither figuration nor accompaniment figures; everything is essential and sparse.

The *Variations* are highly expressive, moving, harshly dissonant, and rigorously constructed. They are an example of what the distinguished critic Paul Rosenfeld meant when he said that Copland's music "resembles nothing so much as steel cranes, bridges, and the frames of skyscrapers." [4]

In the mid-thirties, Copland made one of those abrupt shifts in style that have marked the careers of many present-day artists and composers. This about-face was caused in part by his growing social consciousness resulting from the economic depression of the thirties. Copland was not alone in this development; many artists, writers, and musicians of the time felt that they should leave their ivory towers and communicate more directly with "the people." He turned away from the forbidding austerities of his recent compositions and wrote music that was easy to perform and to listen to.

His operetta for children, *The Second Hurricane* (1937), and *An Outdoor Overture* (1938), for high school orchestras, are true examples of the *Gebrauchsmusik* ideal. *A Lincoln Portrait* (1942), for narrator and orchestra, is perhaps the composition most obviously aimed at mass appeal. Another piece that found an immediate audience was *El Salón México* (1937), a rhapsody on Mexican folk and street tunes. Unlike similar pieces of the romantic era (for example, Enesco's *Rumanian Rhapsody*), in which folk tunes were made glamorous by their colorful orchestral dress, in Copland's composition the vulgarity and humor of the tunes are emphasized by the brashness of the orchestration. Twentieth-century devices such as measures of varying lengths, dissonance, and polytonality add to its attractiveness.

Next, Copland wrote a series of ballets on American themes, in which he exploited popular and folk music of his own country. Among these are: *Billy the Kid* (1938), *Rodeo* (1942), and *Appalachian Spring* (1943–1944). In the first two he employed authentic cowboy and Western tunes, but in pieces such as *El Salón México* the simple melodies are presented with all the sophistication of an urbane contemporary composer. Jazz and ragtime rhythms, "vamps," unexpected silences—all contribute to the boisterous high spirits of these popular compositions. *Appalachian Spring* is another matter. To express the courtship and wedding of a Shaker couple in rural Pennsylvania in the early nineteenth century, Copland employs simple, old hymn tunes, triadic harmonizations, and a modest orchestra, resulting in a score of quiet beauty. Among his excellent film scores are those for *The Heiress, Of Mice and Men, The Red Pony,* and *Our Town.*

Having learned that he could write music that had wide appeal did not cause Copland to renounce his original orientation completely. After 1940 he occasionally wrote compositions that were neither functional nor "travel souvenirs." In these mature compositions, such as the Piano Sonata (1941), the Third Symphony (1946), Clarinet Concerto (1948), the songs *Twelve Poems by Emily Dickinson* (1950), and a Piano Quartet (1950), he reverted to a more austere idiom, but these later compositions are never as stark as the *Variations.* One frequently hears traces of the cowboy tunes and hymns he came to know when he wrote the ballets.

The Third Symphony is a full-scale work. Written without the external conditioning provided by a ballet or movie scenario, it is one of Copland's most personal statements.

The first movement is calm and hymnlike, showing the influence of the Shaker hymns Copland discovered while preparing to write *Appalachian Spring.* It starts with a disjunct, unharmonized melody in the violins, flutes, and clarinets, which immediately establishes a quiet, early-morning feeling:

EXAMPLE 135*

At first there is a steady march of quarter notes, but the pace becomes more animated with the addition of eighth notes. A four-square, contrasting second theme is introduced by the trombones:

EXAMPLE 136

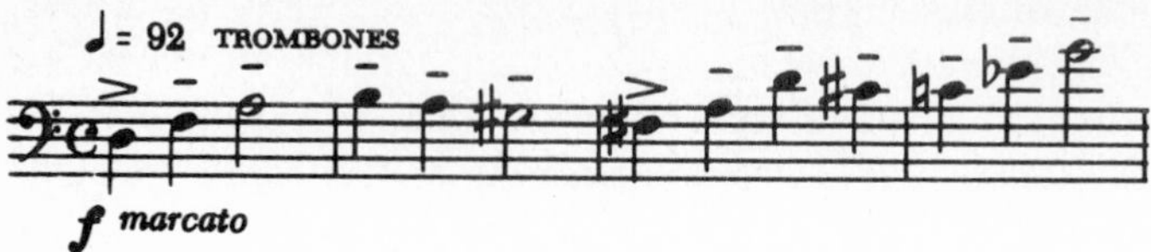

This theme is heard in various choirs of the orchestra with ever-increasing dynamics and busier accompaniment figures, until a noisy climax is reached and the quiet opening melody returns.

The second movement reminds one of the cowboy music of Copland's western ballets. After some introductory fanfares related to Example 135, the main theme appears:

EXAMPLE 137

This is a "perky" (the composer's word) scherzo, with a contrasting middle section. At the end, the main theme is presented again in octave doublings throughout the whole orchestra with noisy punctuation in the timpani.

The third movement also starts with a variant of Example 135 in the strings, after which the principal theme is heard in the flute:

EXAMPLE 138

This theme permeates the movement.

The last movement starts with a fanfare the composer had written during World War II, which serves as an introduction to a sonata-form movement. The main theme, presented by the oboe, is strongly rhythmic and reminds one of bird twitterings when it is presented contrapuntally in the high woodwinds:

EXAMPLE 139

This is a gay movement, bright with syncopation and rushing figures. The development section begins with a reference to the opening fanfare, but soon the busy figuration resumes. A new theme (Copland calls it his second theme, although its introduction in a development section is unusual) has a strong Latin American rhythmic feeling:

EXAMPLE 140

After a recapitulation of the opening theme there is an extended coda in which allusions are made to various elements of the whole symphony. At the end there is a blazing statement of the hymnlike melody heard at the beginning.

During the 1950s Copland, along with many other composers of his generation, showed his interest in serial music by writing some compositions organized according to twelve-tone principles. These later pieces will be discussed in Part Three in the context of post-World War II music.

Copland is considered by many the most interesting and significant American composer of his generation. He has achieved a genuinely personal musical style, not by exclusion, but by including European as well as American elements. His activities as teacher, writer, and entrepreneur have been extensive and his leadership unquestioned.

Harris (born 1898)

During the period under discussion many believed that Roy Harris was the most important American composer. In contrast to Aaron Copland, the New Yorker and cosmopolite, Harris was born in Oklahoma, grew up in rural California, and has spent most of his life on college campuses. Furthermore, while Copland was a dedicated musician and began to compose while still in his teens, Harris did not discover music until after he was discharged from service in World War I.

He was in Los Angeles at the time, and began his studies with Arthur Farwell, a composer and energetic champion of American music who recognized the unusual talent of his student and encouraged him to submit one of his first compositions, the *Andante* for orchestra, to the Eastman School of Music's 1926 Festival of American Music. The piece was selected to be played; Harris went East and recognition rapidly followed. A Guggenheim Fellowship took him to Paris where he worked for a short time with Nadia Boulanger. After returning to the United States, he started a long career of teaching, serving for various lengths of time at Colorado College, Cornell University, Peabody (Nashville), Pennsylvania State College for Women, Indiana University, the University of Puerto Rico, the University of the Pacific, and the University of California at Los Angeles.

During all of these years he composed constantly, and in the thirties his music was frequently performed both at home and abroad. A sign of his prestige is the fact that at this time when there were few recordings of "serious"

Harris
Roy Harris

American music, he was well represented in the catalogs. Always an admirer of Russia, Harris during World War II dedicated his Fifth Symphony to our then ally; it was performed with great success in Moscow.

Harris's Compositions

Roy Harris is primarily a composer of instrumental music. He has written eleven symphonies (1933–1968), a concerto for two pianos (1946), and a violin concerto (1950). Chamber works include three string quartets (1930–1939), a piano quintet (1937), a sonata for violin and piano, and three sonatas for piano. Perhaps his best known composition is his arrangement of the Civil War song "When Johnny Comes Marching Home."

Harris's Third Symphony (1939) did much to establish him as an important American composer. A short work, taking about seventeen minutes to perform, it is built on an original structural plan consisting of five sections played without pause.

The first section, described by the composer as "tragic, low string sonorities," starts with a long-spanned melody suggesting a Gregorian chant by its modal flavor and steady movement in quarter notes arranged in asymmetrical groups:

EXAMPLE 141*

The intervals become larger and other voices are added, at first in parallel, organumlike chords. Eventually, as other choirs of the orchestra enter, the texture becomes polyphonic until a climax in volume is reached.

Without any pause, the second section, described as "Lyric, strings, horns, and woodwinds," begins with a change in timbre when the solo flute enters above sustained strings. Its melody outlines the notes of an augmented triad, F–A–C-sharp–F, previously heard at the climax of the first section. This linking of one section to the next through a common theme is characteristic of the symphony. In this section the music continues to move in steady quarter notes in antiphonal passages between the woodwinds and strings with occasional punctuation by the horns. Once again a climax of volume is reached.

The mood changes completely in the third movement, described as "Pastoral—woodwinds with a polytonal string background." Over a shimmering, impressionistic figuration in the strings, this English horn melody is heard:

EXAMPLE 142

The figuration continues for 200 measures while individual woodwinds, brass, and then combinations of wind instruments are heard in answering phrases. Toward the end of the section these melodic entries become closer, the note values are shortened, and the dynamics increased.

At the height of the climax, a new theme, angular and brusque, is heard in the strings. This is the principal theme of the fourth movement, described as "Fugue—dramatic":

EXAMPLE 143

Later, the theme of the third movement (Example 142) is added to the lively syncopated polyphony.

Long melodies reminiscent of the opening announce the last section, described as "Dramatic, tragic." The coda is marked by a pedal in the timpani and a somber slowing of pace. The symphony ends on a somewhat theatrical note.

One of the reasons for Harris's quick acceptance by a relatively large audience lies in the basic simplicity of his music. There is none of the sophisticated, tongue-in-cheek quality prevalent in the music of some of his contemporaries; instead, sincerity and earnestness are felt in everything he writes. The long melodies, mild dissonances, clear differentiation between the choirs of the orchestra, strong, asymmetrical rhythms—above all, the adherence to a basic tonality—give a heartening "American" sound to his music. Furthermore, the America suggested is not that of nervous, neurotic cities, but an America of the plains and wide-open spaces. A decade that was attracted to the paintings by Grant Wood and John Steuart Curry found similar qualities to admire in the music of Roy Harris.

Since Harris has not sustained the prominent position he held in the thirties and forties, his final position in American music of the first half of the twentieth century is impossible to gauge. Nevertheless, it is safe to say that his has been one of the most individual and "American" voices of the time.

Piston, 1894–1976

Roy Harris can be classified as the rugged individualist, the sometimes rough, but sincere American who created his own musical language with a minimum of contact with the long heritage of music. Walter Piston was a completely different type of composer. He can be classified as a neoclassicist in that his music is conservative in form and restrained in expression, and shows a predominance of baroque textures and the skilled control of a master craftsman.

Piston's roots and home were in New England. His grandfather, an immigrant from Italy who settled in Maine, was named Pistone. The composer was born in Rockland, Maine, in 1894 and moved with his family to Boston in 1905. Throughout his high school days he showed casual interest and talent in music, but he did not decide to become a composer until after he had worked as a draftsman and spent a year studying painting. During that time he played the violin in dance and theater orchestras. Later, during World War I, he was a saxophonist in an army band stationed at the Massachusetts Institute of Technology.

Upon his release from the army in 1920, he entered Harvard as a music student. Graduating four years later, at the age of thirty, he went to Paris to study with Nadia Boulanger. He stayed there for two years and upon his re-

Piston
Boosey and Hawkes

turn started to teach in the music department at Harvard University, remaining there until his retirement from teaching in 1960. Throughout these years he taught a large number of young composers, and his textbooks on harmony, counterpoint, orchestration, and analysis have been widely used.

One of the most respected of American composers, Piston was honored with a Pulitzer Prize, a Guggenheim Fellowship, a New York Music Critics Circle Award, and several honorary doctorates.

Piston's Compositions

Piston was primarily a composer of absolute orchestral and chamber music. He wrote but few vocal compositions, no operas, and except for one ballet, no works for the theater.

The catalog of his works includes eight symphonies (1937–1965), a piano concerto (1937), two violin concertos (1940 and 1959), and a viola concerto (1958). Among the many chamber works are: sonatas for violin and piano, violin and harpsichord, flute and piano; a quintet for piano and strings; a woodwind quintet; a *Divertimento* for nine instruments; five string quartets (1962); a string sextet (1964), and a piano quartet (1964).

Piston's Fourth Symphony, written on a commission from the University of Minnesota in 1951, is a good example of the composer's mature style. It is lyrical and suggests that the austerity felt in the early works disappeared as the composer grew older. This symphony is neither dramatic nor heroic in expression; words such as "amiable," "economical," "restrained," or "witty" might well be applied to it.

The first movement, marked *piacevole* (peacefully), starts with a long, graceful melody in the violins soaring over a compass of more than two octaves. The interval of the fourth is prominent and occasional unexpected dissonances add bite:

EXAMPLE 144*

The flowing motion is interrupted by chords in the brass. Eventually a narrow-compassed chromatic theme is heard in the clarinets:

EXAMPLE 145

The first theme appears again, followed by the second, as the form reveals itself to be baroque binary (A B A B).

The second movement is marked *ballando* and is a vigorous, gay rondo with an overall structural pattern A B A C A B A. All sections are dancelike.

The first, in spite of its irregular measure lengths $\left(\frac{3}{4}\ \frac{7}{8}\ \frac{5}{8}\right)$, has a Spanish fandango character:

EXAMPLE 146

The next begins with a waltzlike accompaniment to an old-fashioned, sentimental melody:

EXAMPLE 147

The next digression sounds like a reel or a hoedown, with swirling violin figures over syncopated chords in the bass. The earlier sections all reappear and the movement ends with brilliance and *éclat*.

The slow movement, marked *contemplativo,* is less obvious because the main theme, presented by the clarinets, is not based on a clear tonality as are the themes of the previous movements. This theme contains ten different tones:

EXAMPLE 148

The two additional tones, G-flat and D, are heard immediately afterward from cellos and clarinets. However, this is not a twelve-tone composition, since there are underlying tonal centers in most of the sections. A contrasting middle part starts with a flute solo. An ever-increasing number of imitative entries build to a climax. At the height of volume and dissonance the original theme returns in the horns with octave transpositions of some of the notes. The last movement returns to the noisy brilliance of the second. The syncopated main theme exploits the interval of the augmented fourth:

EXAMPLE 149

By way of contrast the second theme, presented in canon, is diatonic and smoothly flowing:

EXAMPLE 150

Piston's Fourth Symphony is characteristic of the composer in the way it combines old and new elements. Classical sonata form provides the framework, and baroque polyphony the texture, while harmony, key relationships, and rhythm are of the twentieth century. The whole is welded together with the sure hand of a master craftsman. Herein lies the neoclassical quality of Piston's music.

Sessions (born 1898)

Roger Sessions stands in the same relationship to expressionism as Piston to neoclassicism. This statement is meant to be more suggestive than precise, but it does point to a difference in approach on the part of these two important composers. For Sessions, music is a medium for the expression of highly serious musical thoughts and convictions in compositions that are necessarily difficult and challenging to perform and listen to.

Sessions was born in Brooklyn, but his ancestors had lived in New England since Colonial days. His mother, a pianist who had studied in Leipzig, guided his first musical experiences. After she took her fourteen-year-old son to a performance of *Die Meistersinger,* he resolved to become a composer. A brilliant youth, he entered Harvard the same year. After his graduation the outbreak of World War I prevented a projected trip to France for study with Ravel.

Unable to go abroad, Sessions went to the Yale School of Music for graduate study. This was followed by his teaching at Smith College where he

Sessions
Edward B. Marks Music Corporation

remained from 1917 until 1921. The major musical influence on him during those years was the Swiss composer Ernest Bloch, with whom he studied. When Bloch went to Cleveland to head the Institute of Music, Sessions followed, and later joined the faculty.

In 1925 he made his first trip to Europe and remained until 1933, with occasional visits to the United States. Subsidized by his family and various fellowships during these eight years, Sessions showed his independence of thought by avoiding Paris and the Boulanger circle and, instead, spent his time in Italy and Germany. Returning home in 1933, he resumed his activity as a teacher, working in Boston, in New York, at Princeton University, at the University of California, again at Princeton, and then at the Juilliard School of Music.

Sessions's Compositions

Sessions has never been a prolific composer and the list of his works is not long, but there are no insignificant or "little" works among them. Among the orchestral music is the suite arranged from music he wrote for a college production of Andreyev's play *The Black Maskers;* eight symphonies (1927–1964); a violin concerto (1935); and a piano concerto (1956). There is a one-act opera, *The Trial of Lucullus* (1947), and the full-length opera *Montezuma* (1947), produced in Berlin in 1964. Among the chamber music are two string quartets (1936, 1950), a duo for violin and piano (1942), and a string quintet (1957). In addition, there is a sonata for violin solo (1953), two sonatas for piano (1930 and 1946), a collection of piano pieces called *From My Diary,* and a set of chorale preludes for organ.

Sessions's Second Symphony (1946) is a good example of his chromatic style. Compared to a symphony by Copland or Harris of this period, it is a complex work closer to Schoenberg or Berg than to his American contemporaries. Its rushing strings, angular chromatic melodies, muted trumpets, and strident xylophone make for a highly charged atmosphere not unlike that of the *Five Pieces for Orchestra.*

Sessions has defined his aims in the following statement:

> I reject any kind of dogma or platform. I am not trying to write "modern," "American," or "neo-classic" music. I am seeking always and only the coherent and living expression of my musical ideas. . . . I dislike rhetoric, overemphasis, vulgarity, but at the same time believe that perfection in art is a sort of equilibrium which can be neither defined nor counterfeited. . . . I have no sympathy with consciously sought originality. I accept my musical ideas without theorizing.[5]

Hanson (born 1896)

Howard Hanson is America's neoromantic composer. He was born in Wahoo, Nebraska, to Swedish-American parents. After graduating from a local Lutheran college, he studied composition with Percy Goetschius at the Institute of Musical Art in New York, and in 1916 accepted a position in the music department of the College of the Pacific in California. Three years later, the twenty-three-year-old instructor was made Dean, and when twenty-five he was awarded the Prix de Rome. During the three years he lived in Italy, he composed his first symphony, the *Nordic,* a work more expressive of Scandinavia's gray clouds than of the azure skies of Rome. This independence from surroundings and outer influences gives insight into Hanson's creative personality. In contrast to those composers who have responded to every new current and every whim of fashion, he has been undeviating in his goal—to write highly romantic music.

He returned to the United States in 1924 to become director of the recently established Eastman School of Music and in the following decades gradually assumed a position of leadership in American musical life. An untiring champion of American music, Hanson started the annual festivals of contemporary music in Rochester that have given performance opportunities to hundreds of composers representing all schools of musical thought. As a teacher he has influenced scores of students, many of whom have become composers of stature. His activities in national and international musical organizations—often as president—have further spread his influence.

Hanson's Compositions

During the years he devoted to creating a school of music and working for the cause of American music, Hanson composed a large number of works. These include: six symphonies, the *Nordic* (1923), the *Romantic* (1930), the Third (1938), *Sinfonia da Requiem* (1943), *Sinfonia Sacra* (1955), and the Sixth (1969); and a number of symphonic poems, among them *Pan and the Priest* (1926), *Lux Aeterna* (1926), and *Mosaics* (1958). He has also written a piano concerto (1948), an organ concerto (1926), and numerous works for chorus and orchestra, including *The Lament for Beowulf* (1926), *Three Songs from Drum Taps* (1935), *The Cherubic Hymn* (1949), and *The Song of Democracy* (1957). His opera *Merry Mount* (1933) was commissioned and performed by the Metropolitan Opera.

In his compositions Hanson reveals a consistent point of view. He is loyal to the principles of tonality and uses dissonances to build climaxes. His

Hanson
Eastman School of Music, photographed by Louis Ouzer

melodies have immediate appeal and his orchestrations are rich and colorful. That these are "old-fashioned" traits has never disturbed him.

The Second Symphony, subtitled *Romantic,* is Hanson's most popular and characteristic work. It was written in the 1930s, when Stravinsky was simultaneously working on the *Symphony of Psalms,* Schoenberg on *Moses und Aron,* and Copland on the *Piano Variations.* It has little to do with such music and suggests rather the symphonies of Sibelius. The first movement opens with an adagio introduction in which the basic theme of the symphony is immediately presented:

EXAMPLE 151*

This motive (and its inversion) is used throughout the introduction as an ostinato. Trumpets and an imperious horn call usher in the principal theme of the movement, played by the horns against brilliant accompaniment figures:

EXAMPLE 152

This is presented in canon, works up to a climax, and leads directly to a contrasting second theme in the oboes:

EXAMPLE 153

Another quiet melody, which serves as the closing theme, follows. The restrained development is primarily concerned with the principal theme, with one section exploiting the two fourths of Example 152 in an impressionistic manner. A full recapitulation, including all three themes, follows.

The second movement, *andante con tenerezza,* presents a simple melody that is related to the themes of the first movement in the prominence of the interval of the third:

EXAMPLE 154

No other composer discussed in this chapter would claim paternity to such a theme. Hanson develops it lovingly, including a setting for strings *divisi.* The contrasting middle section refers to the motto theme as well as to the closing theme of the first movement.

Most of the material of the last movement is related to themes already presented. It is a brilliantly orchestrated piece with a middle section recalling *The Rite of Spring* in its irregular rhythmic patterns:

EXAMPLE 155

Hanson is fond of such patterns and they are frequently found in other compositions, showing that even he could not resist Stravinsky's rhythms. There is a brilliant coda with polychordal dissonances, finally resolving into a blazing D-flat chord.

Hanson's position in twentieth-century American music can be accurately ascertained from the *Romantic Symphony*. It shows how far removed he is from neoclassic austerity or daring experimentation. Instead of reducing his orchestra to a thin, unblending group of instruments, his motto seems to be "the more the better," and some of his most successful compositions are for full orchestra, chorus, and soloists, culminating in shattering climaxes.

It has been said of Brahms that he composed "as if Liszt and Wagner never existed." Perhaps Hanson is a twentieth-century parallel; the music of many of his contemporaries has not existed for him.

Thomson (born 1896)

If Howard Hanson represents the conservative, neoromantic, twentieth-century American composer, Virgil Thomson is his complete antithesis. The former's music is serious, expressive, and highly personal; the latter's witty, sophisticated, and highly objective.

Virgil Thomson was born in Kansas City in 1896. He studied music and played the organ while still a schoolboy and, after brief, noncombatant service in World War I, continued his studies at Harvard. He made his first trip to Europe in 1921 with the Harvard Glee Club, but instead of returning with the group, remained in Paris to study with Nadia Boulanger. He returned to graduate from Harvard in 1923 and spent the next two years in New York where he continued his studies in composition and began his career as a church organist, choirmaster, and critic.

In 1925 he went back to France and remained there until 1940 when the imminent German occupation forced his return to the United States. He then became music editor of the *New York Herald Tribune*, and a powerful force in raising musical standards and shaping musical taste. Like Schumann, Berlioz, and Debussy—other composer-critics—he combined high musical standards, based on a thorough technical knowledge of music and performance, with an urbane and witty prose style. His critiques are among the few that make good reading in book form. He left this position in 1954 to devote all of his time to composition and lecturing.[6]

Thomson's Compositions

A list of Thomson's compositions would give little indication of their style and content; their generally noncommittal titles give little indication of their originality. For instance, who would expect to hear a tango in a *sonata da chiesa* or gospel hymns in a symphony? There are a great many piano works, including four sonatas, numerous etudes, and over fifty "portraits"—character sketches of friends and acquaintances who "sat" for their piece in the same way they would sit for a painted portrait. The composer's interest in the organ accounts for the numerous works for that instrument; of these the best known is *Variations on Sunday School Tunes* (1926). There are two symphonies (although what Thomson calls a sonata or symphony is likely to have little in common with what the term usually connotes). He has written two string quartets and two sonatas for violin and piano; two operas on librettos of Gertrude Stein, *Four Saints in Three Acts* (1928) and *The Mother of Us All* (1947); a ballet, *The Filling Station* (1937); music for documentary films; and incidental music for plays.

Anyone familiar with the critical writings of Virgil Thomson will recognize similar qualities in his music: urbanity and sophistication, lack of reverence, and a refusal to be proper and dull. He shares these attributes with Les Six and Erik Satie, and if a pigeonhole classification is required, he can be considered their American equivalent.

Suggested Readings

Copland. Two full-length studies have been written: Julia Smith, *Aaron Copland: His Work and Contribution to American Music* (New York, 1955) and Arthur Berger, *Aaron Copland* (New York, 1953). There are numerous periodical articles and the Autumn 1948 issue of *Tempo* is devoted to his works. Among Copland's own writings, *Music and Imagination* (Cambridge, 1952) and the autobiographical sketch in *Our Modern Composers* (New York, 1941) are of interest. See also "Conversation with Aaron Copland," *Perspectives of New Music,* Vol. 6, No. 2 (Spring-Summer 1968).

Harris. No comprehensive study of Harris's style has been published. Among periodical articles, the following are recommended: Arthur Farwell, "Roy Harris," *Musical Quarterly,* XVIII, No. 1 (January 1932); Walter Piston, "Roy Harris," *Modern Music* (January-February 1934); and Nicolas Slonimsky, "Roy Harris," *Musical Quarterly,* XXXIII, No. 1 (January 1947). The last article is particularly recommended for the analysis of style elements it contains. Harris's own views on his compositions can be found in *American Composers on American Music,* edited by Henry Cowell (Palo Alto, 1933).

Piston. "Walter Piston" by Elliott Carter, in *Musical Quarterly,* XXXII, No. 3 (July 1946); "Piston's Fourth Symphony" by W. Austin, in *Music Review* (May 1955). See also "Walter Piston: For His Seventieth Birthday," *Perspectives of New Music,* Vol. 3, No. 1 (Fall-Winter 1964).

Sessions. Mark A. Schubart, "Roger Sessions: Portrait of an American Composer," *Musical Quarterly,* XXXII, No. 2 (April 1946); various reviews of compositions in *Musical Quarterly.* See also "Roger Sessions: In Honor of His Sixty-fifth Birthday," *Perspectives of New Music,* Vol. 1, No. 1 (Fall-Winter 1962). Writings by Sessions: *The Musical Experience of Composer, Performer, Listener* (Princeton, 1950); *Reflections on the Music Life in the United States* (New York, 1956); *The Intent of the Artist,* edited by Augusta Centano (Princeton, 1941); *Questions about Music* (Cambridge, 1970). A useful bibliography of Sessions's compositions and critical writing about them can be found in *Current Musicology,* No. 15 (1973).

Thomson. Virgil Thomson, His Life and Music by Kathleen Hoover and John Cage (New York, 1959); an autobiography, *Virgil Thomson* (New York, 1966).

Books useful as references are *American Composers on American Music,* a symposium edited by Henry Cowell (Palo Alto, 1933), *Our Contemporary Composers* by John Tasker Howard (New York, 1941), *Composers in America* by Claire Reis (New York, 1947), *American Composers Today* by David Ewen (New York, 1949), *Modern Music-Makers* by Madeleine Goss (New York, 1952), *America's Music,* 2nd ed., by Gilbert Chase (New York, 1966), and the entries in *Baker's Biographical Dictionary of Musicians,* 5th ed. (New York, 1958; 1971 supplement included).

American Music Since 1910 by Virgil Thomson (New York, 1970) contains valuable essays on American music and composers as well as thumbnail sketches of 106 American composers.

The American Composer Speaks, edited by Gilbert Chase (Baton Rouge, 1966), is an interesting collection of statements by American composers from the earliest times to the avant-gardists.

For bibliography, see *Some Twentieth Century American Composers; A Selective Bibliography* by John Edmunds and Gordon Boelzner (New York Public Library, New York, Vol. I, 1959; Vol. II, 1960).

Edgard Varèse and Karlheinz Stockhausen at Hamburg in 1954

18

I dream of instruments obedient to my thought and which with their contribution of a whole new world of unsuspected sounds, will lend themselves to the exigencies of my inner rhythm.

Edgard Varèse

Edgard Varèse 1883-1965 and Harry Partch 1901-1974

THE SIX COMPOSERS JUST DISCUSSED—Copland, Harris, Piston, Sessions, Hanson, and Thomson—were chosen as representatives of their generation, and to show the diversity of styles found in American music during the first half of the century. They are also important because most of them devoted much of their time and energy to teaching. Among their pupils are scores of composers, most of them teachers themselves, who are the creators of mid-century American music in all its variety.

Three composers, Edgard Varèse, Harry Partch, and John Cage, stand apart. They were the products of no "school"; they were not concerned with teaching. They were original thinkers and explorers who had an incalculable influence on later twentieth-century music in the United States and abroad. Varèse and Partch will be discussed here, and Cage in Part Three.

Edgard Varèse, 1883–1965

Strictly speaking, Varèse is not American, because he was born in Paris to a Corsican family and his youth was spent in Italy, where he received an engineer's training and degree. In 1900 he was studying harmony and counterpoint at Turin Conservatory, and two years later he was in Paris studying with d'Indy, Roussel, and Bordes at the

Schola Cantorum and with Widor at the Conservatoire. He was an outstanding student even for Paris, where talent and originality are expected, and he won a composition prize sponsored by the city. Debussy heard some of his compositions and was enthusiastic about the future of the young composer.

In 1907 Varèse was in Berlin where he became acquainted with Richard Strauss and Ferruccio Busoni. He conducted a chorus and wrote an opera, *Oedipus und die Sphinx,* on a libretto by Hofmannsthal, the Viennese poet and favorite librettist of Strauss. He also wrote a symphony that was performed, but all of his early compositions were destroyed in a fire.

With the outbreak of World War I, Varèse came to the United States, where he remained until his death in 1965. During the twenties he was active as a propagandist for new music and founded the International Composers' Guild. In the following years he quietly composed a series of very noisy compositions of great originality, and at the end of his life he was acknowledged as a prophet and leader by many of the young avant-gardists.

Varèse wrote only a small number of compositions but in them he made great strides in expanding the sound material of music. In the twenties he wrote six pieces: *Amériques, Offrandes, Octandre, Hyperprism, Intégrales,* and *Arcana. Octandre,* written in 1924, is a good example of his unconventional use of instruments and his new concept of musical form. It is written for seven wind instruments and double bass, and at times suggests the opening of *Le Sacre du printemps* in timbre. Its blocklike, static structure shows a different concept of form, however, as the strident and extremely dissonant blocks of sound, almost resembling factory whistles, form the content of the piece without the rhythmic or tonal developments normally used by composers. *Intégrales* (1925), for wind instruments and percussion, also suggests big city sounds. The first section consists of two unchanging chord structures around which a melodic pattern oscillates. It is one of the first of those "crystal" musical forms that were to be used so much in the following years. This term implies that the basic sound material is unchanging and that the shifting relationships between its elements is the only thing that "happens." The phrase "ever the same yet ever different," which Webern used to describe his Concerto, is appropriate here.

In the thirties Varèse wrote four additional compositions: *Ionisation, Métal, Density 21.5,* and *Equatorial.* Of these, *Ionisation* (1931) is the best known. Written entirely for percussion instruments plus a siren, it is one of the first of the many all-percussion pieces that were to follow. *Equatorial* calls for two theramins, showing the composer's interest in new sound sources.

In 1937 Varèse stopped composing because he was no longer interested in seeking new sounds in conventional instruments; it was not until the tape recorder became available that he finally gained the vast new sound resource he had been seeking. His mature works, utilizing noises and electronically produced sounds, are *Déserts* (1954), for woodwinds, brass, percussion, and piano plus taped sound, and the *Poème électronique* (1958). These two pieces are landmarks in the development of electronic music. They will be discussed in Chapter 20 (Part Three).

It is a tragedy that Varèse did not live longer in the electronic music era he so keenly anticipated. He broadened the concept of music to include all sound, not just musical sound, and the space he opened to music, beyond tempered scales, beyond octaves divided into twelve equal half-steps, beyond conventional instruments, is the space that was so avidly explored by many composers of the second half of the century.

John Cage, the leader of the avant-garde composers, said of Varèse:

> . . . more clearly and actively than anyone else of his generation, he established the present nature of music. This nature does not arise from pitch relations (consonance-dissonance), but arises from an acceptance of all audible phenomena as material proper to music. While others were still discriminating "musical" tones from noises, Varèse moved into the field of sound itself, not splitting it into two by introducing into the perception of it a mental prejudice. That he fathered forth noise—that is to say, into twentieth-century music—makes him more relative to present musical necessity than even the Viennese masters, whose notion of the number 12 was some time ago dropped and their notion of the series will be seen as no longer urgently necessary.[1]

Speaking of himself, Varèse said, "Don't call me a composer. Call me an engineer of rhythms, resonances, and timbres."

Harry Partch, 1901–1974

Harry Partch is another composer who felt that there was need for new sound material but his solution was more radical than Varèse's. Having decided that "the door to further musical investigation and insight has been slammed shut by the inelastic and doctrinaire quality of our one system and its inelastic forms," he devised his own tonal system in which the octave was divided into 43 unequal tones. This meant that new instruments had to be constructed, and Partch spent a good part of his life inventing and making them.

Many of his instruments are percussion, both pitched and unpitched. There are huge marimbas made of planks with wooden resonators, seven-foot high kitharas (Greek lyres), bellshapes made of glass, and ceramic gourds. The size of these instruments, each one-of-a-kind and cumbersome, was a great impediment to performance of his works as was the necessity of the performers to learn the special notation and for the singers to learn to sing unfamiliar intervals. Performances were usually limited to the universities at which Partch held occasional appointments, and fortunately some of them have been recorded.

Most of Partch's compositions are theater pieces in which dancing, chanting, singing, and shouting are combined in a kind of ritualistic ceremony suggesting Greek drama. Two of them, *Oedipus* (1951) and *Revelation in the Courthouse Park* (1960), are actually based on classical tragedies.

While Partch and his music can be considered eccentric, and without strong influence, he is significant because of his firm belief—and he devoted his whole life to furthering it—that an enriched tonal resource must be found for music. He belongs, then, with Busoni, with the Futurists, and with Varèse in holding this view. This belief has never died, and in fact, one of the chief aims of Pierre Boulez's newly established *Institut de recherche et de coordination acoustique-musical* in Paris is to pursue the matter.

Suggested Readings

Following Varèse's death, several of his pupils and friends wrote articles about him. Among the most important are: Chou, Wen-chung: "Varèse: A Sketch of the Man and His Music," *Musical Quarterly*, Vol. L, No. 2 (April 1966), and Gunther Schuller, "Conversation with Varèse," *Perspectives of New Music*, Vol. 3, No. 2 (1965). The Spring-Summer issue of the same periodical included tributes by several of Varèse's friends and an article by Milton Babbitt, "Edgard Varèse: A Few Observations of His Music." In the Fall-Winter 1966 issue there is an article by Chou, Wen-chung, "Open Rather than Bounded," a chronology of Varèse's life and works, and an article written by the composer, "The Liberation of Sound." A book devoted to the composer is Fernand Ouellette's *Edgard Varèse* (New York, 1968). Varèse's widow Louise has published the first volume of a biography called *Varèse: A Looking-Glass Diary* (New York, 1972).

Harry Partch's views are expressed in his *Genesis of a Music* (Madison, Wisconsin, 1949).

Benny Goodman Band

19

We have a language that goes beyond music, that goes into the language of life itself.

Dizzie Gillespie

JAZZ AND POPULAR MUSIC

JAZZ BECAME SO IMPORTANT IN the between-the-wars period that the whole era—particularly the twenties—is known as the Jazz Age. No longer confined to New Orleans, jazz spread throughout the world first through recordings, and later through the radio.

Chicago Style

Chicago became a new center, at first through the efforts of New Orleans players who went there, but soon with important contributions made by white musicians from the Midwest. Perhaps the most important figure in this dissemination of jazz was Louis Armstrong, whose trumpet playing and "scat" singing (vocal imitations of trumpet sounds) added a new exuberance. Although he still played in Dixieland groups, his sensational solos made him one of the first important jazz soloists. Armstrong soon had a white counterpart in Bix Beiderbecke.

Big-Band Style

After Chicago, Kansas City became an important jazz center, but eventually New York took precedence. Jazz in the late twenties turned away from the small, improvising Dixieland groups in favor of large groups playing arrangements that had been written by well-schooled musicians. Improvisation was limited to the soloists.

Fletcher Henderson was one of the first exponents of the new style. In his recording of *Wrappin' It Up* (1934), the chorus is played four times, each with a different instrumentation drawn from three trumpets, two trombones, three clarinets (one doubling alto saxophone), tenor saxophone, piano, guitar, double bass, and drums. In the first chorus the saxophones play the melody with brass responses. In the next there is also a saxophone solo, with a soft, sustained brass accompaniment. The third chorus features a trumpet solo with saxophone accompaniment, while the last is similar to the first, except that a clarinet solo is included. This planned, balanced orchestration is very different from early Dixieland.

The thirties and forties saw the development of this big-band style as well as Swing. The big bands had about fifteen players in organized sections—three or four trumpets, three trombones, four saxophones, and four rhythm instruments—piano, guitar, bass, and drums, playing carefully rehearsed written arrangements with improvisation limited to the interpolated solos. Harmonies became very rich, and the massed effects of the different timbre groups suggested symphonic orchestration.

Swing was a special kind of big-band music, noted for its danceable tempo and rhythm. Swing reached its peak in the Tommy Dorsey, Glenn Miller, and Benny Goodman bands in a time in which dancing became an international craze. The most creative figure of the era was Duke Ellington, whose band included more fine soloists than any other. Ellington, a brilliant composer, developed a unique orchestral style that featured reed chords in close harmony and a rich variety of muted brass sounds. In addition to playing arrangements of popular tunes in a freer, more venturesome harmonic idiom, the band also played Ellington's extended original compositions.

Bebop

In the 1940s there was a reaction against the smooth big-band sound, resulting in a return to small groups in which individual performers were again given opportunity to improvise. These improvisations differed from those in

Dixieland jazz in that they were much freer, i.e., they strayed further from the original melodies. In some cases there was no original melody at all, but simply a chord progression over which wide-ranging melodies were improvised. Performers such as Charlie Parker, Dizzie Gillespie, and Thelonius Monk became famous for their ability to improvise in this way, and their audiences listened carefully and enjoyed their skill. This kind of jazz was not dance music; people listened to it with the attention they gave to concert music. As it was no longer dance music, the strong, driving beat disappeared. The drummer became a soloist, playing polyrhythmic patterns between cymbals, bass, and snare drum. The pianist was relieved of his rhythmic function and played fast-moving arabesques.

The most influential figure of the period, and perhaps the most important of post-World War II jazz figures, was Charlie Parker. He was noted for his extraordinary technical ability, his exploration of complex harmonies, and the ease with which he employed a wide variety of rhythmic nuances that were contrary to the underlying structure of the piece.

Many of his performances were based on the blues form, to which he gave such titles as *Now's the Time, Billie's Bounce,* and *Cheryl,* but Parker is also known for his free improvisations on such standard songs as Gershwin's *Embraceable You.*

1950·1975

Part Three

Alberto Ginastera

20

The astonishing thing is that these composers all exist at the same time, and the inference to be drawn from this fact is that none of the revolutions has been definitive.

Winthrop Sargeant

Settlers and Explorers

TO ATTEMPT TO SUMMARIZE THE state of music since World War II is almost as complicated as to try to summarize the socioeconomic-political situation during that time. One can enumerate the important events that have taken place since 1950—the explorations of space and the moon landings, the demoralizing wars, the changing mores—but it is difficult, if not impossible, to define a unified pattern that encompasses everything. One can only be sure that the "good old days," no matter when they were, or what values they represent, will not return. The conclusion must be that ours is a pluralistic world in which widely divergent philosophies exist, side by side.

The same pluralism exists in the world of the arts. In painting, for instance, a new style called abstract expressionism appeared in the 1950s. It was primarily an American style, but it soon spread around the world, and galleries everywhere were filled with large canvases, heavy with paint that had been poured, or slashed on with large, partially unplanned motions. This "action painting" was subjective, "romantic," and completely devoid of images. Its dominance was so complete that many believed that this style would characterize the second half of the century as cubism and expressionism had characterized the first.

By the 1960s, however, abstract expressionism was already considered to be old-fashioned. In 1967, when there were large retrospective showings of the paintings of Jackson Pollock, Willem de Kooning, and Franz Kline, the acknowledged masters of the style, there was wide interest and critical appreciation for their achievement, but the style was considered representative of the past, and not of the present. Young painters found nothing to emulate.

Other ideals, seemingly diametrically opposed, came to the fore. In "Pop art" subject matter returned with a vengeance, but it was a new kind of subject—banal, everyday objects from everyday life, such as Campbell soup cans and mechanically reproduced multi-images of movie stars. A few years later, abstraction returned with "Op" art (optical) characterized by hard-edged stripes and geometrical figures in primary colors, only to be followed by the Minimal and Conceptual schools a few years later.

In the midst of these changing styles, an exhibition of the meticulously realistic paintings of Andrew Wyeth was held in New York in 1967. The public response was enormous, showing that the newer trends, even though they had received great publicity, had not caused older values to disappear.

"Flux" and "pluralism" are the words that characterize the world of painting since 1945.

The same words describe the world of music. Masterworks of the eighteenth and nineteenth centuries continue to be the main concern for concertgoers, record collectors, and performers, many of whom show little interest in any music later than Debussy's. In smaller circles there is a growing interest in renaissance and baroque music, and in non-Western music as well. In still smaller circles there has been great activity in creating and performing new music, and a succession of new styles and idioms has appeared and, in some cases, soon disappeared.

A unified twentieth-century musical style, a synthesis of new trends, has often been announced, but it has not been achieved in music any more than it has in painting. Diversity, rather than uniformity, characterizes the scene, and the gulf separating conservative and progressive composers is as wide as that separating totalitarian and democratic governments. It is necessary to emphasize this coexistence of divergent styles because one is often subjected to strongly partisan and one-sided propaganda.

Disappearance of National Schools

One significant change in the post-World War II world of the arts is the virtual disappearance of national styles. This is the result of rapid communication through the news media, and the increased mobility of people through air travel. New tendencies in the arts (like new fashions in women's clothing) are frequently unveiled with publicity and fanfare, and are widely disseminated within days after the openings. The international style of architecture, making it difficult to know if one is in Tokyo, New Delhi, Athens, or Paris, is reflected in the international styles in music. The Chronological Charts found on pages 416–427 reflect this change. No longer will compositions be listed by countries, as they were in earlier charts, but by the tendencies they represent.

Influence of Phonograph Records

Developments in the recording industry have also helped to change the music situation. The long-playing record was perfected by 1950 and refinements in stereo recording and speakers continue to be made. Vast segments of music literature, including recent twentieth-century compositions, are now available everywhere. While young people take this situation for granted, they should be reminded that before World War II there were virtually no recordings of recent music. This meant that in order to hear new music one had to attend the annual meetings of the International Society for Contemporary Music or live in one of the larger musical centers where new music was occasionally performed. Very few people, even professional musicians, were acquainted with the main styles of twentieth-century music.

Acquaintance with Twentieth-Century Music

One can learn something of the state of awareness of twentieth-century music immediately following the war by reading the music journals of the time. The *Musical Quarterly* started a new section devoted to contemporary music in 1948, after the demise of *Modern Music,* an American magazine devoted to new music. In the January 1949 issue, one can read of the first performance in over twenty years in New York (and hence in the United States) of Schoenberg's *Five Pieces for Orchestra.* This was, therefore, the first hearing of the 1909 masterpiece for virtually everyone in Carnegie Hall, including the orchestra. The April 1949 issue reports a performance of Bartók's *Music for Strings, Percussion, and Celesta* as a newsworthy event calling for a descriptive analysis.

A clue to the international musical atmosphere of the immediate postwar years can be found in the report of the 1950 Salzburg Seminar, a conference of young European and American intellectuals and creative artists, by John Amis, an English critic. He wrote in the Winter 1950–1951 issue of *Tempo:*

> What sort of music are they writing? Well, prettiness is out; politics seem to be out too. The taste is for the classics, the pre-classics, not too much 19th-century music, and Berg, Stravinsky, Bartók, and Hindemith (hereinafter referred to as the modern masters). Twelve-tone music aroused tremendous storms and arguments—but apart from a general admiration for the genius of Berg, and to a lesser extent Schoenberg, a young German critic was the only one to have much to say in favor of it. It seems that in countries where twelve-tone music was forbidden, like Germany and Italy, it is mainly the older generation, those who would have attended I.S.C.M. festivals before the war, who are using the technique. American music was little liked. . . . Of the recent French composers, Messiaen was universally disliked and so was the latest French craze, "*musique concrète.*" *Musique concrète* was invented by a radio engineer and it is possible only in recordings. The sounds are concrete as opposed to abstract sounds: coughs, casserole lids twirled onto a resonant slab, train noises and certain freak musical noises such as the sound of a piano recorded after being struck. . . . The painters at Salzburg were angry with the musicians for not recognizing the genius of this art form of the future! A parallel was reached when the musicians, but few of the painters, were much impressed by Alexander Caldwell's (*sic*) "mobiles," fascinating structures of wire and other materials which vibrate when you touch them.[1]

Because of Europe's highly charged and chauvinistic atmosphere in the years between the wars, the generation of composers who grew up then did not share a common background. This fact is important to realize, because the one-world cultural atmosphere of mid-century did not prevail before the war. The young German composers of this generation, too young to have experienced the stimulation of the Weimar Republic years (1919–1933), grew up while National Socialism was clamping a rigid censorship on all advanced idioms or art of Jewish origin. This meant that the music of Schoenberg, Webern, or Berg was as unknown to them as was that of Stravinsky or the French composers. The young French musicians were somewhat better off because they had had the opportunity of knowing the works of Stravinsky and Les Six, but they were almost totally ignorant of the second Viennese School or of Bartók. Young Russians knew little of the contemporary music of other countries.

Perhaps the young musicians of the United States had had more contact with the main trends of twentieth-century music than their European contemporaries, even if there was a strong pro-French, neoclassic influence to be noted here. Leonard Burkat, summarizing the musical climate of the United States in 1948, wrote, "Most of our younger men who are performed take or make their styles in Stravinskyisms by way of Copland." [2] Many of our university music departments were staffed by composers who had been trained by Boulanger, Hindemith, or Piston.

Because of the war a large number of European composers were living in the United States and their presence and activities added tremendously to the musical ambiance. Stravinsky was living in Hollywood and wrote his *Ebony Concerto* and the Symphony in Three Movements during the war years. Schoenberg, also in California, completed his Piano Concerto and "returned" to tonality in his Theme and Variations for Band. Bartók, dying in New York, completed his Concerto for Orchestra and two movements of his Viola Concerto, and almost completed his Third Piano Concerto. Hindemith was teaching at Yale and wrote his tribute to Bach in his *Ludus Tonalis.* Milhaud was at Mills College, writing one work after another.

Perhaps a clearer picture of the state of music in the postwar period can be gained if one thinks of the whole of twentieth-century music as a vast continent in the process of being explored and settled. The achievements and discoveries of the first generations of pioneers have been described in earlier chapters of this book. Each composer chose his route and went as far into the unknown as he desired. Some were content to penetrate only a short distance before they settled and established a colony within sight of the familiar world. Others returned to safety after a brief sortie. Still others went further before they settled; some refused to settle anywhere and tirelessly explored the new territory.

The explorations go on. Once the achievements of the earlier composers were known, the younger generation continued the quest, free to stay in any of the already acquired territories or to take off for still unknown destinations. Their paths and accomplishments will be discussed in the remaining chapters.

The "Schools" of Music, 1950–1975

The composers of the 1950–1975 period will be presented in the following groups:

Conservative composers
Serial composers
Aleatoric composers
Electronic composers
"Sound," Minimal, Environmental, and Conceptual composers

These groupings should not be thought of as being water-tight compartments, or necessarily following one another successively. The same composers will be found in more than one category as their interests have changed. Furthermore, it will be pointed out that electronic music is a medium that reflects all of the other style tendencies, and in turn has influenced nonelectronic music. These categories are perhaps best thought of as paths that are being established in the third quarter of twentieth-century music, leading we know not where.

Conservative Composers

Conservative twentieth-century composers can be defined as those who write tonal music for the usual instruments and instrumental combinations and who use traditional forms. Such composers are frequently ignored by critics who find novelty more interesting, but they have not been ignored by the general public.

Benjamin Britten

Benjamin Britten can be considered the archetypal figure. His *War Requiem* (1962) has little in common with many other compositions of the time, but his treatment of a universal theme has found wide acceptance all over the world. Written for the consecration of St. Michael's Cathedral, Coventry, which had been destroyed during World War II, this is a large work, calling for chorus, boys' choir, soloists, orchestra, and chamber orchestra.

This Requiem is not meant for liturgical use because, in addition to the traditional Latin prayers for the dead, Britten has interspersed nine wryly bitter war poems by Wilfred Owen, an English poet killed in World War I. The poems, sung by the tenor and baritone soloists, form an ironic commentary on the formalized statements of the Mass, and the juxtaposition of these poignant protests against war with the ageless acceptance of death expressed in the Catholic rite gives rise to many dramatic, even theatrical, contrasts.

For example, the calm opening chorus, *Requiem aeternam* (*Rest eternal*), in which actual bells and bell-tolling effects are prominent, is interrupted by the tenor soloist singing the first Owen poem, that starts:

> What passing bells for these who died as cattle?
> Only the monstrous anger of the guns.

The portentous fanfares of the *Dies irae,* summoning the dead to arise on Judgment Day, are echoed in the baritone solo that follows, with these words:

Bugles sang, sadd'ning the evening air
And bugles answered, sorrowful to hear.

This is a human-dimensioned poem about men asleep on the eve of battle and the contrast with the cosmic bugles of Judgment Day is striking.

The final poem, a conversation between two enemy soldiers who have killed each other in battle:

I am the enemy you killed, my friend
I knew you in the dark.

is followed immediately by the boys' choir (angelic) singing *In paradisum* (*Into paradise may the angels lead thee*).

The musical idioms used by the composer reflect the all-inclusive quality of the text, for they also draw upon a wide variety of musical styles. When he feels it appropriate, Britten draws upon plainchant (*Domine Jesu; Te decet hymnus*), Bach (the high trumpets in the D major *Hosannah*), Verdi (*Lacrimosa*),

EXAMPLE 156

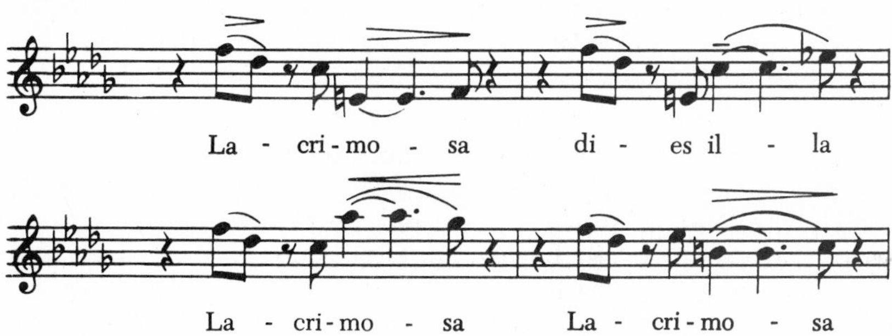

and twentieth-century idioms such as irregular meter and rhythmic patterns (*Dies irae, Quam olim Abrahae, Agnus Dei*), dissonant counterpoint (*Pleni sunt coeli*), polytonality (*Bugles sang*), and dissonant pedal effects (*Dies irae, Liber scriptus, Libera me*).

The interval of the augmented fourth gives unity to the entire work. It is heard in the opening section, where the chorus chants antiphonally on C and F-sharp. In the *Sanctus* the same interval alternates in the accompaniment to the soprano's jubilant melody. Other prominent appearances of the tritone are in *Pie Jesu, Pleni sunt coeli, Agnus Dei,* and in the final section, *In paradisum.*

After the *Requiem*, Britten continued to write works that confirm his role in twentieth-century music. He moved freely within his self-imposed limits and used any idiom he found appropriate for the task at hand. He experimented with new musical-theatrical forms in his *Curlew River*, a stylized short opera based on the conventions and sounds of the Japanese No drama. His biblical "parables," *The Burning Fiery Furnace* (1966), *The Prodigal Son* (1968), *The Children's Crusade* (1969), and *The Journey of the Magi* (1971), are cast in the mold of medieval mystery plays. They are meant to be performed in churches with the singer-actors portraying monks who perform the play in their church.

Conservative composers tend to be practical and compose when they are commissioned to do so, or when they have need for a particular piece. Britten's friendship with Mstislav Rostropovich, the Russian cellist, and his wife, soprano Galina Vishnevskaya, resulted in the Symphony for Violoncello and Orchestra (1964), a Suite for Cello Solo (1964), and the Pushkin song cycle (1966). There are two important late operas: *Owen Wingrave* (1970) and *Death in Venice* (1973), that were soon produced in many parts of the world.

Michael Tippett (born 1908)

England has another important conservative (in this sense) composer in Sir Michael Tippett. Although he is eight years older than Britten, he was a late starter as a composer and did not receive wide recognition until the 1950s. Among his early works frequently performed is a Double Concerto for String Orchestra (1939), noted for its intricate rhythms, described by the composer as being madrigal-like in the independence of the individual parts, its astringent though tonal harmonies, and its rich string sonorities.

Much of Tippett's music is vocal, and in the words he uses (usually his own) he expresses his concern about the human condition. The oratorio *A Child of Our Time* (1953) is a strong and moving protest against Nazi atrocities of World War II. Tippett uses Negro spirituals in this piece in the manner Bach used chorales in his choral works.

There are three operas: *A Midsummer Marriage* (1952), *King Priam* (1962), and *The Knot Garden* (1970), but because of his concern about his "message" they are static on stage rather than dramatic. In the last movement of his Third Symphony, Tippett quotes the dissonant chord heard at the beginning of the last movement of Beethoven's Ninth Symphony and then a soprano soloist sings four long songs in blues style.

Dmitri Shostakovich

Dmitri Shostakovich was another composer who continued to write operas, symphonies, concertos, and string quartets. In his case, of course, a conservative style was ordered by his government, but this did not stop the flow of his compositions or their performance in Russia and abroad.

His Cello Concerto in E-flat, Opus 107 (1959), is a concerto in the nineteenth-century sense in that it is a vehicle to show off the prowess of the soloist. The first movement, a sprightly allegro, starts with a theme that is firmly anchored to E-flat even though it is teased with many nonharmonic tones:

EXAMPLE 157

This movement is in sonata form and the following slow movement is an extended binary form, memorable for its songlike modal theme. The last movement, a vigorous dance, is introduced by an extended cadenza that serves as a development. Before the end of the last movement, the first-movement theme reappears, establishing an overall unity to the piece.

Shostakovich's Symphony No. 14 is unusual in that it is a setting of eleven poems by various poets for soprano and baritone. The subject of all the poems is death, and the music is appropriately serious. The Symphony No. 15 is jovial again, and it contains quotations from Rossini's *William Tell Overture* and from the Wagner *Ring*.

Samuel Barber (born 1910)

Samuel Barber is a typical American conservative composer. His two operas, *Vanessa* (1950) and *Anthony and Cleopatra* (1966), the latter written for the opening of the new Metropolitan Opera House in New York, are not similar, since one is intimate and quiet and the other is grand and noisy, but they are alike in that they are "singers' " operas and give ample opportunity for the soloists to show their singing and acting ability. Contrary to many mid-century operas, these works contain ensembles and arias, and the old-fashioned emotions of love and sorrow form the content of the librettos.

Barber's Piano Concerto (1962) is a brilliant piece in the tradition of the Liszt and Prokofiev concertos, calling for expert, athletic playing. It is dissonant and chromatic, but the tonal basis is always clear. In its harmonic and rhythmic idioms it is undeniably a twentieth-century work of conservative cast.

Among many American composers who could be classified as conservatives are Gian Carlo Menotti, Howard Hanson, Ned Rorem, Virgil Thomson, and Roy Harris.

Serial Composers

The discovery and dissemination of the music of Schoenberg, Webern, and Berg created the predominant musical language of the 1950s. It has already been pointed out that this music was virtually unknown during the lifetimes of the composers. After Schoenberg moved to California in 1934 his music continued to be ignored outside the small circle of his students, and even they did not hear live performances of the larger works. Webern lived in semi-retirement after the outbreak of the war in 1939. He too had a few students, but his scores, largely unpublished, remained on his closet shelves, neatly wrapped and tied with ribbon. Berg's *Wozzeck,* of course, had received many performances before the war, but his other works were as unknown as those of his colleagues. Berg died in 1935, Webern in 1945, and Schoenberg in 1951. Each must have felt that he had failed to make any lasting impression on the music of his time.

Within a few years, however, there was worldwide recognition of their achievement. Their music was played in concerts and recorded, analyses of their compositions were published, and many composers, young and old, became "twelve-tone" composers. That the time was right for a change in direction was dramatically revealed as early as 1945 in Paris, the traditional home of neoclassicism, where a series of concerts devoted to Stravinsky's orchestral music was given to celebrate the end of the war. Most of the audience was delighted to hear the music again (it had been banned during the occupation) but at the third concert in the series there was an unexpected, if typically French, demonstration in the gallery. The hisses and catcalls came from a group of Conservatoire students, pupils of Olivier Messiaen. Their leader was an unknown student named Pierre Boulez. The protest was against *Jeu de cartes* and the *Norwegian Sketches,* and the aesthetic doctrine these compositions represented.

Reaction against neoclassicism was the negative bond; an espousal of serial music was the positive, and acquaintance with and extension of its principles became the most important musical development of the decade. The steps can be traced with some accuracy because most of them took place at the International Summer Course for New Music held in Darmstadt, Germany, which had started in 1946 while the city was still in ruins. Young Germans, such as Hans Werner Henze and Karlheinz Stockhausen; Frenchmen, such as Pierre Boulez and Gilbert Amy; Italians, such as Luigi Nono and Bruno Maderna, and many others, gathered there to hear, analyze, and perform serial music.

The idea of serial music stimulated many young composers, but when Stravinsky, the guiding spirit of tonal neoclassicism, espoused the technique the musical world was amazed at what seemed to be another of his changes of style. For forty years he had been the unchallenged leader of an ideal of composition held to be the antithesis of Schoenberg's, and their differences were so great that it extended to their social life; there was no communication or friendship between the two composers when they lived in Southern California. Nevertheless, all of Stravinsky's compositions after 1952 were serial and he often expressed his admiration, sometimes in extravagant terms and gestures, for Webern's music.

STRAVINSKY'S SERIAL WORKS

Stravinsky's last neoclassic work, *The Rake's Progress,* was written in 1951, the year of Schoenberg's death. His later works are:

Cantata (on old English texts; 1952)
Septet (for violin, viola, cello, clarinet, horn, bassoon, and piano; 1953)
3 Songs from William Shakespeare (for mezzo-soprano, flute, clarinet, and viola; 1953)
In Memoriam Dylan Thomas (for tenor, string quartet, and four trombones; 1954)
Canticum sacrum (1956)
Agon (ballet; 1957)
Threni (a setting of the Lamentations of Jeremiah; 1958)
Movements for Piano and Orchestra (1959)
A Sermon, a Narrative and a Prayer (for chorus and orchestra; 1960)
Monumentum pro Gesualdo (madrigals recomposed for instruments; 1960)
The Flood (written for television performance for narrator, vocal soloists, chorus, orchestra, and dancers; 1962)
Eight Instrumental Miniatures (for fifteen instrumentalists; 1921–1962)
The Dove Descending Breaks the Air (for chorus, a cappella; 1962)
Abraham and Isaac (sacred ballad for baritone and orchestra; 1963)
Elegy for J.F.K. (mezzo-soprano and nine instrumentalists; 1963)
Variations in Memory of Aldous Huxley (for orchestra; 1964)
Introitus: T. S. Eliot in Memoriam (for small male chorus, 10 timpani, 2 tam-tams, piano, harp, contrabass, and violas; 1965)
Requiem Canticles (for small choir and orchestra; 1967)

All of these works are written according to the tenets of serial music, albeit with certain modifications. Twelve of them are for voice, ranging from large-scale works for chorus and soloists, such as *Canticum sacrum* and *Threni,* to chamber-sized pieces for solo voice and a few instruments, such as the

Shakespeare and Dylan Thomas songs. Several of the works are religious and others are based on biblical texts. Still others are memorials written on the death of friends or acquaintances.

Agon is a ballet of about twenty minutes' duration for twelve dancers. It is completely abstract, having neither a story nor personifications, and unlike the earlier ballets *Orpheus* and *Apollon Musagète,* it is performed in rehearsal attire. *Agon* is simply a series of seventeenth-century dances written for various combinations of the four male and eight female dancers.

The orchestra consists of three flutes, two oboes, English horn, two clarinets and bass clarinet, two bassoons and contrabassoon, four horns, four trumpets, two tenor trombones and bass trombone, harp, mandolin, piano, percussion, and strings. Although it is a large group, Stravinsky never uses it in tuttis. Each dance calls for a different chamber group, and the composer's imagination for new combinations is unflagging. Thus, a male solo dance is accompanied by a solo violin, xylophone, and tenor and bass trombones. The *Gaillarde* for two female dancers is for strings (without violins), harp, mandolin, and three flutes. The ever-different timbres are one of the fascinations of the piece. Much of *Agon* is based on three tone-rows:

EXAMPLE 158

The prevalence of seconds makes it possible for Stravinsky to write melodies of typically narrow range. (See Example 159.)

Stravinsky's attraction to the music of Webern is clearly shown in certain sections of the score where the aerated, one-note-to-an-instrument style is employed. An example is the adagio *Pas de Deux with Variations.*

EXAMPLE 159*

But even when Stravinsky writes in what seems to be a pure Viennese manner his music is always his own. His melodies, dry timbres, and above all, his sinewy rhythms give an individual profile to a style that can be amorphous and merely sound "like Webern" when used by composers of less personality. *Agon* is lithe, athletic, and healthy—qualities that we almost always associate with Stravinsky's music, whether it be an early ballet, a neoclassic sonata, a piece for jazz band, or a setting of the Mass.

Movements shows the influence of Webern more clearly than any of the other late compositions. It is almost completely athematic and the sparseness of the writing as well as the disjunct melodies point to the Viennese composer. The piece is based on this row:

EXAMPLE 160

The opening measure of the piano part employs the series in its O form.

EXAMPLE 161*

Although *Movements* takes only ten minutes to perform, it is divided into five sections of contrasting tempos. A fairly conventional orchestra is used, except that there are no horns, timpani, or percussion; there are no tuttis. Each section has its own instrumentation, reminding one again of Webern's early orchestral pieces.

The most striking features of Stravinsky's late serial works are their brevity and self-imposed limitations. At a time when many younger composers were writing ear-shattering, massive pieces in which details could not possibly be heard, the old master was writing pieces lasting about ten minutes, for a few voices and instruments in which every detail was important and apparent. No longer interested in big effects, he made each note necessary and essential.

Stravinsky once defined music as "controlled time and tone." It is no wonder that the octogenarian turned to serial methods of organization, because through them he retained and even increased his control over these elements.

Luigi Dallapiccola, 1904–1975

Any survey of dodecaphonic music must include mention of the works of Luigi Dallapicolla, the first Italian composer to use the method. In his compositions he demonstrated again that twelve-tone music does not imply a style; his music is uniformly expressive and songlike, and resembles neither the Viennese composers nor Stravinsky. From the beginning, he wrote primarily for voice and his choice of words shows not only his highly developed literary taste but also his concern for the human condition. He was a serious and religious

* From *Movements for Piano and Orchestra,* Copyright 1960 by Hawkes & Son (London) Ltd. Reprinted by Boosey & Hawkes, Inc.

man who lived through the Fascist regime in Italy, and he was deeply concerned with the problem of freedom in an increasingly mechanized world.

His works include three operas, *Volo di notte* (1937–39) (based on St. Exupery's *Night Flight*), *Il Prigioniero* (1949), and *Odysseus* (1968); several choral works, *Six Choruses from Michelangelo* (1933–36), *Canti di Prigionia* (1938–41), and *Canti di Liberazione* (1955); and several song cycles, mostly for voice and a small group of instruments. Among these are *Five Fragments from Sappho,* for soprano and 15 instruments (1942–1945), his first twelve-tone composition, Five Songs for baritone and 8 instruments (1956), and the *Goethe Lieder* (1953). For piano he wrote a Sonatina Canonica (1943) and *Quaderno Musicale di Annalibera* (1952), which he later orchestrated and called *Variazioni per Orchestra* (1954).

Dallapiccola, in explaining why he adopted serial methods, said, "What interested me above all in the dodecaphonic system were its expressive and melodic possibilities, a principle, moreover, which I have never abandoned in the works that followed in later years, no matter how much more complex they may have been." [3]

In Example 162 the row on which he wrote his Goethe songs is given. Example 163 shows the highly expressive melody he constructed. The first phrase consists of the O form of the row, while the second is a transposed version of the I form.

EXAMPLE 162

EXAMPLE 163*

* By permission of Edizioni Suvini Zerboni—Milano.

This small example illustrates Dallapiccola's lyric treatment of the row. In all of his works one is aware of his concern for beautiful, suave sound. To quote the composer again, "It seemed to me that twelve tones would enable me to articulate a melody better than seven—to write a richer and (as far as my capacities would allow) more expressive melody."

Other Twelve-Tone Composers

Many composers, both old and young, experienced or tyros, turned to serial composition in the 1950s. Those who had established their personal musical styles, such as Stravinsky or Aaron Copland, continued to sound like "themselves" after they adopted the twelve-tone mthod. Copland's *Fantasy* for piano (1957) is built on the following ten-note row: E-flat, B-flat, F, D-flat, B, F-sharp, A, G, D, and C. At the opening of the piece the first four notes are spread over four octaves, each played fortissimo, achieving Copland's characteristic "spiky" sound.

Two later compositions for orchestra, *Connotations* (1962) and *Inscape* (1967), are also freely serial, without losing the characteristic Copland "sound." The composer has explained why he adopted the idiom. "The attraction of the method for me was that I began to hear chords that I wouldn't have heard otherwise. Heretofore I had been thinking tonally, but this was a new way of moving tones about. It freshened up one's technique and one's approach. To this very day that remains its main attraction for me." [4]

Roger Sessions is another American composer whose works since the 1950s have been serial. The first was his Violin Sonata of 1953, to be followed by his Third Piano Sonata and the Symphonies Nos. 3 through 8.

Reference to the Chronological Charts will show the names of many familiar composers who adopted the dodecaphonic technique at this time.

In spite of its popularity and the feeling held by many that dodecaphony would be a prevailing idiom for many decades, it did not retain its importance in the following years. In an interview reported by the *New York Times* on December 6, 1964, Igor Stravinsky declared that "Card-carrying 12-toners are practically extinct." A critic writing about a first performance of a string quartet in the October 1965 *Musical Quarterly* described it as being "almost old-fashioned in its Webernian atmosphere." [5]

The "Age of Webern" proved to be a short one. It is more appropriate to speak of the "Decade of Webern."

Toward Total Control

While the music of the second Viennese School was the first great discovery of the post-World War II musical world, many of the younger composers were not content to stay within Schoenberg's practice. After Schoenberg's death, Pierre Boulez published an obituary entitled *Schoenberg Is Dead,*[6] paralleling the French proclamations, "le Roi est mort . . . vive le Roi." This was not the usual laudatory obituary. It was critical of the founding father of serial music, claiming that he was reactionary in using themes, differentiating between melody and accompaniments, and organizing his compositions by using conventional forms. Webern (the new "roi"), on the other hand, had abandoned these vestiges of the past and his sparse scores seemed to be nothing more than the logical playing out of a pattern that had been worked out before the composition had been written. Furthermore, and most important, in some of his compositions such as the Concerto for Nine Instruments (discussed in Chapter 12) there were indications that Webern was approaching an ideal in which elements besides pitch, such as durations, timbres, attacks, and dynamics, were divorced from their traditional subservience to melody and were being treated serially.

Several composers had already devised new rhythmic and durational patterns. Boris Blacher, the German composer, devised and used "variable meters" in many of his compositions—a systematic employment of measures of varying lengths. For instance, in a piano sonata (1951) the measures contain eighth notes in the following quantities:

EXAMPLE 164

etc.

Eventually the pattern is reversed and the measures shorten. Other sequences are built of progressing series such as 2-3-4, 3-4-5, 4-5-6, and reverse; symmetrical series, 2-3-5-8-13; and cyclical variations, 2-3-4-5, 5-3-2-4, 3-2-4-5. Blacher's melodic phrases coincide with these varying measure-lengths, resulting in a highly personal style.

The French composer Olivier Messiaen (born 1909) has also made use of new rhythmic concepts. Basing his music on models as heterogeneous as Hindu music, the songs of birds, and Gregorian chant, he employs augmentations and diminutions of rhythmic patterns, not by the usual doublings and halvings, but by the addition or subtraction of fractional values. Here is an example of augmentation by quarter value:

becomes

A diminution by two-thirds means that

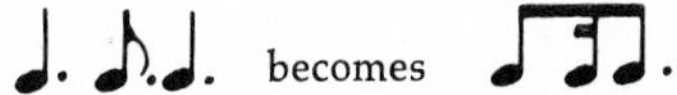

Credit for having written the first totally controlled piece is usually given to Olivier Messiaen, but Milton Babbitt, the American composer, also wrote some compositions before 1950 that serialize elements other than notes. These are *Three Compositions for Piano, Compositions for Four Instruments,* and *Compositions for Twelve Instruments.* When Messiaen played his *Mode de valeurs et d'intensités* at Darmstadt in 1949, the young musicians who heard it were tremendously excited by the possibilities it revealed. This piece is built on a plan consisting of thirty-six notes (in three twelve-note series), a rhythmic series of twenty-four durations, a dynamic series of seven intensities, and a "timbre" series of seven modes of attack. In the opening measures, shown in Example 165, each note has its own dynamic, duration, and attack. These ex-

EXAMPLE 165

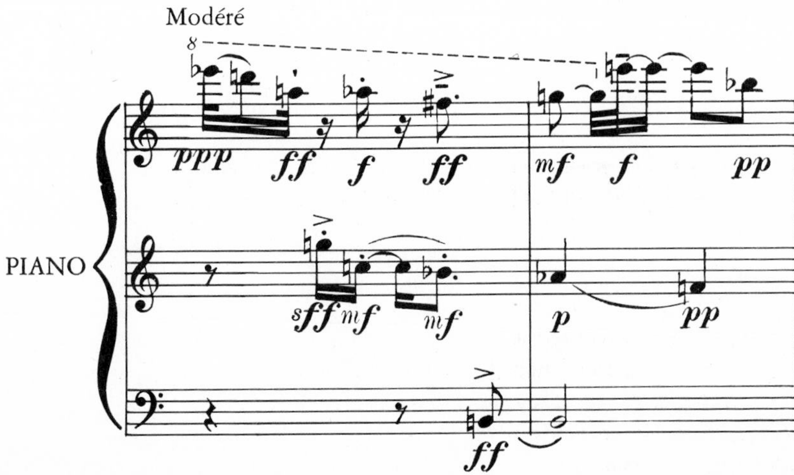

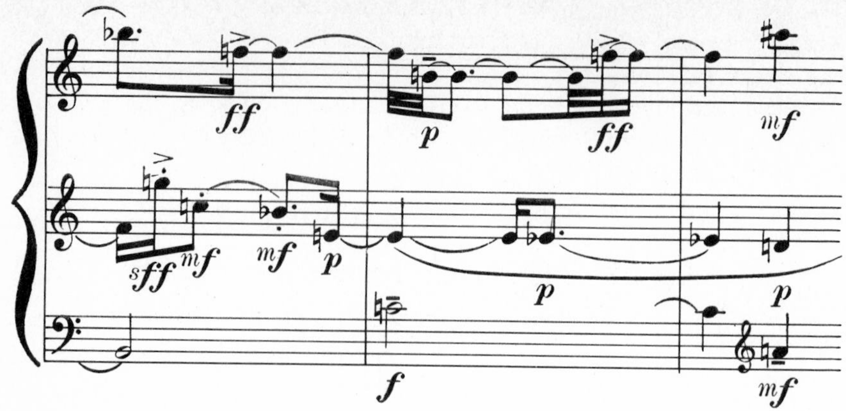

plicit specifications call for almost superhuman control by the performer. In most earlier music, dynamics and attacks work together to enhance the melody and rhythm of the piece, and performers are trained to follow the directions of the composer. In Messiaen's piece, however, rhythmic values, attacks, and dynamics have a life of their own. Each follows its own pattern, and the performer is obliged to follow several sets of directions at once.

The logical, mathematically trained Pierre Boulez lost no time in composing in the totally controlled manner. His *Structures* for two pianos (1952) applied serial structure to notes, octave pitches, durations, and dynamics. He described his piece as being "freed from all melody, all harmony, and all counterpoint since serial structure has caused all these essentially modal and tonal notions to disappear."

In his Second Piano Sonata he used Messiaen's series of durations, attacks, and dynamics:

EXAMPLE 166

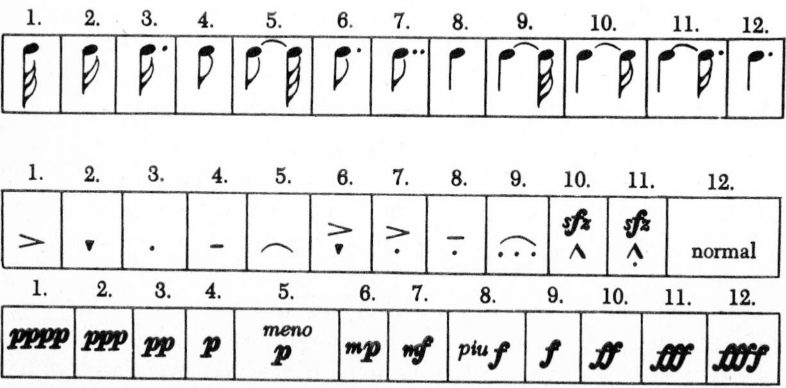

Luciano Berio's *Nones* (1954), an orchestral piece inspired by a poem of Auden, is another example of a musical composition based on tremendously complex precompositional decisions. The pitches used derive from the following row:

EXAMPLE 167

It will be noted that there are thirteen notes in this row, so that it can be treated as two seven-note segments. The row itself is completely structured, as was that of Webern's Concerto. Each three-note segment contains a major and a minor third and the retrograde inversion of the form is the same as the original in one transposition.

The duration of each note is derived from a series of seven basic duration values, and there are seven dynamic values and five modes of articulation.

This approach to music has been described by Reginald Smith Brindle as "a mathematical method that allows a composer to compute a musical edifice in its entirety. A chain of permutations of a series of notes gives the note order throughout the music. Similarly, chains of permutations determine the exact place in time for each sound, the coincidence of sounds (chords), the duration of silences, and so on."

Music written according to such elaborate plans offers great problems to both performers and listeners. The intricacy of the rhythmic patterns, often including fractional values never encountered before, the quick changes of dynamic levels without any relation to "natural" dynamics, the frequent leaps from one note to the next, the precision called for in the manner in which notes are to be attacked—all of these matters confront the performer with formidable problems. Example 168, the opening of Stockhausen's *Klavierstücke No. 2,* I, is typical.

For the listener there are also problems. Music that is so highly organized should be easy to listen to, but the intricacy and multiplicity of the simultaneous patterns make for the opposite effect, and instead of seeming planned such music often sounds chaotic or capricious. Each of the parameters is equal in interest, so there is no prime character, be it melody, or rhythm, or harmony, as there was in older music.

Stockhausen's *Kontra-Punkte* (1953) is typical of its time in the elaborate "plan" that determines its structure. The composer described his intent as follows: "Six different tone-color groups are used: flute-bassoon; clarinet-bass-

EXAMPLE 168, *Klavierstücke No. 2*, I (KARLHEINZ STOCKHAUSEN)*

clarinet; trumpet-trombone; piano, harp, violin-cello (three pairs of wind instruments blown differently and three kinds of stringed instruments struck, plucked, and bowed, respectively). These different tone colors merge into a single one: the struck strings of the piano. There are six degrees of dynamic intensity (from *ppp* to *sfz*), and one after the other they fall away to *pp*. Large differences between very long and very short notes are avoided; only closely related, medium-length notes remain (sixteenth notes, sixteenth-note quintuplets, etc.). Through the opposition of vertical and horizontal sound relations a homogenous two-part counterpoint is obtained. These external countersigns are clearly audible. By following these clues, and guided by his musical taste, the listener can decide whether I have discovered the right relations and the necessary degree of sensitivity for the profound structural material which lies at the basis of the construction." [7]

As a matter of fact, it is impossible to hear the details of this carefully planned construction in sound. Perhaps for this reason, the ideal of total control was eventually dropped by most of the composers who were most involved with it. Edward Helm, the distinguished American composer and critic, in reviewing the 1959 Darmstadt Festival, wrote: "The fact is, however, that the period of utter determinacy in which every element of music is calculated and treated serially is on its way out in most advanced circles." [8]

Aleatoric Music

The same decade that saw the development of totally controlled music also witnessed the birth of another kind of music that was very different in intent. Perhaps repelled by the mechanization of extreme control, or perhaps discouraged because the intricate compositional plans could not possibly be heard, some composers investigated the effects of partially unplanned happenings in musical composition and performance. This kind of music was called *aleatoric* (from the Latin *alea,* or dice), or *chance music.*

How can music, the purest of the arts in that it has less relationship with the objective world than the other arts, exist without a content that will be the same every time the piece is repeated? How can a composer turn over his prerogatives and responsibilities to other persons? How can musical notation, the purpose of which is to give precise directions to the performer, give unprecise and equivocal directions so as to produce uncertain results?

John Cage, the American composer, has repeatedly shown how this can be done. For instance, he has written a piece for piano printed on several different sheets of paper. He instructs the performer to drop the pages and then play the music in the random order in which it is picked up. In another series of pieces the order of the notes is determined by the "pointal imperfections" in a sheet of transparent paper, but the durations and clefs are determined by coin throws (heads, treble; tails, bass). The I-Ching, a Chinese device consisting of a box from which marked sticks are shaken, determines the manner in which the notes should be sounded on the piano—normally, muted, or plucked on the strings. His most extreme "composition" involves twenty-four radios. They are switched on or off by twelve "performers" who follow their directions with stopwatches. The sound montage that results is determined by the type of programs being broadcast at the moment.

While John Cage was the pioneer and perhaps the most extreme of the aleatoric composers, he was by no means alone.

Karlheinz Stockhausen, the German composer previously cited, wrote a piece called *Piano Piece XI,* printed on a long roll, which when opened on a special wooden stand (supplied with the piece) measures 37 × 21 inches. On it are printed nineteen fragments that can be played in any order, with any of six different speeds, dynamics, and articulations. The performer is instructed to look at random at the sheet of music and begin with any fragment that catches his eye. At the end of each group of notes he reads the tempo, dynamic, and attack indications that follow and then looks at random at another group, which he then plays in accordance with the latter indications. When a group is arrived at for the third time one possible realization of the piece will be completed. In any performance some sections of the piece may be omitted and no two performances are ever likely to be the same.

Henri Pousseur's *caractères* for piano solo consists of six double pages, each containing several groupings of notes. Four single sheets are also supplied, on which there are groups of notes as well as three "cutouts" or "windows." The sheets with "windows" are placed at random among the printed sheets and the performer plays what accidentally appears before his eyes, which can be that which appears on the printed sheet or that which appears through the "window." Again, the piece will probably never be played twice in the same manner.

Sometimes one of the parameters is left to chance while the others are more or less specified by the composer. Here is a description of Morton Feldman's *Straits of Magellan:*

> It is a graph piece with unspecified notes, but specified durations. The score is written on coordinated paper, with each box equal to MM 88. The player enters on or within the duration of each box (unless the box is empty, in which case he is silent). The number of sounds to be played within each box is given. Register and choices of notes are for the most part free, with occasional indications that high or low register be used within a specific box. The color (flutter-tongue, harmonics, etc.) is given, as well as the dynamics (very low throughout).[9]

The same composer, in another composition for a group of wind instruments, directs that each instrument should enter as the others begin to fade. In other words, the time sequence or tempo of the piece is not ordered, but is determined by the breath power of the performers.

Earle Brown, an American composer who has written compositions that offer the performer choices like these, has likened the process to the mobile sculptures of Alexander Calder. In these suspended structures, the elements created by the artist are constant, but their relationships are ever changing because of the extreme flexibility with which they are joined. Even the slightest breeze changes the overall shape, which is "ever the same but ever different." A photograph of a mobile would be comparable to a recording of one of Brown's compositions. It would be a record of one possible shaping of a rich and malleable basic material.

NOTATION PROBLEMS IN ALEATORIC MUSIC

It is easy to see why conventional notation is no longer serviceable for music in which the performer has several possibilities from which to choose. Musical notation, for all its inadequacies, tells the performer what notes to play and establishes the rhythmic relationships between them. If these matters are left undetermined until the moment of performance the composer must devise a new system of signals for the performer.

As a result, the scores of aleatoric compositions bear little resemblance to conventional scores, and each piece contains elaborate directions for the symbols chosen by the composer. For example, Berio's *Tempi Concertanti* uses proportional notation. In this kind of notation, the space separating the notes indicates their separation in time. Thus, notes further apart on the page are separated by a longer time interval than notes close together. This separation is relative and unmeasured, of course, because pulse in the sense of an underlying beat does not exist. In the same piece the composer uses this notational device to ensure a chance performance:

The directions read: this figure "can be read starting from any point whatsoever and going left to right or vice versa. The pattern may be repeated several times—always as fast as possible and within the limits of proportionally indicated duration." In this score the notes without stems are played legato and notes with stem and flag (♪) are played "freely." Small notes (like old-fashioned grace-notes) are played as "fast as possible."

In *caractères,* by Henri Pousseur, notes without stems "take up the entire duration of the metric subdivision in which they occur. If they are to be played staccato, the rest of the duration is held out as silence. Groups of notes designated in this way [symbol] correspond to an accelerando up to 'as fast

EXAMPLE 169, *Liaisons* (ROMAN HAUBENSTOCK-RAMATI)*

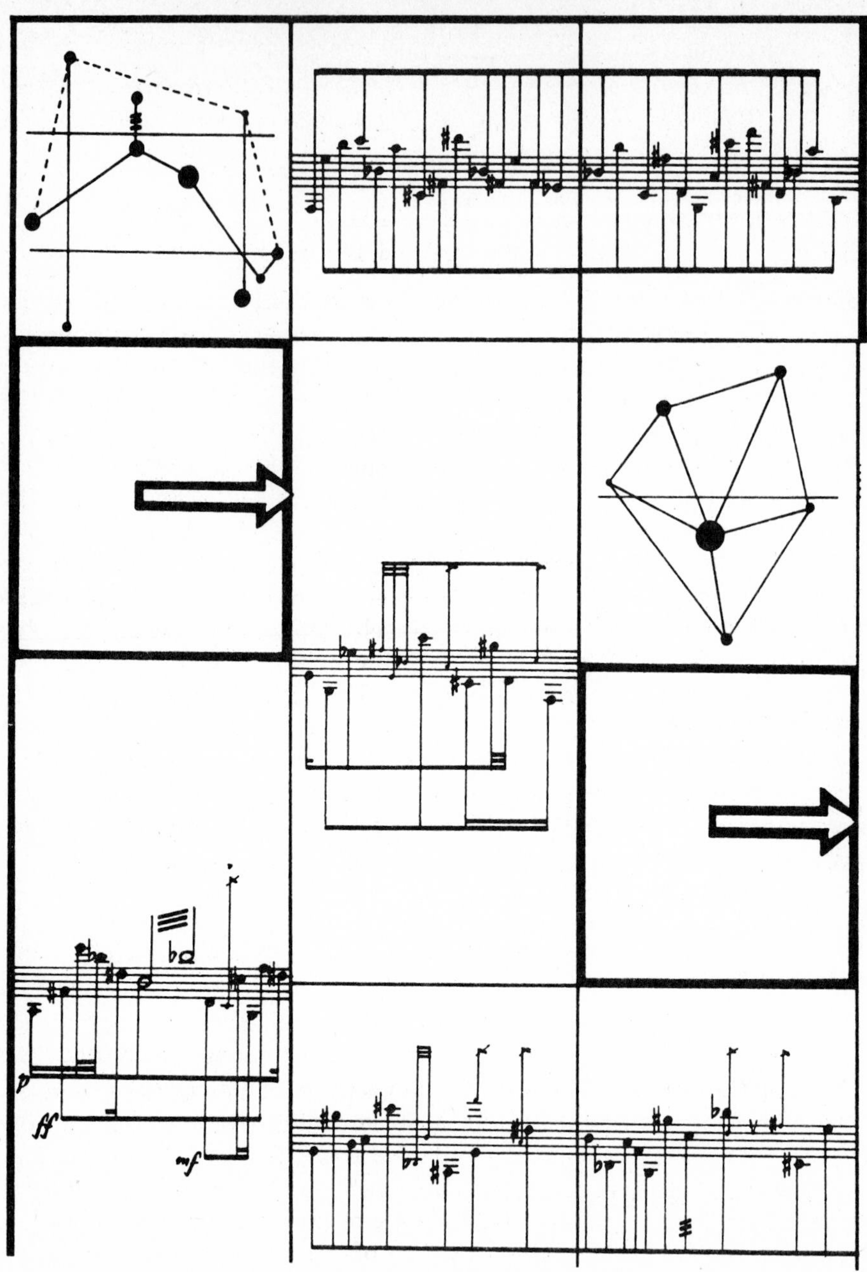

as possible.' Those designated in this way correspond to a rallentando beginning from 'as fast as possible.' signifies: a little shorter than the other notes of the group. signifies: much shorter than the other notes." In Stockhausen's *Refrain* "loudness is indicated by the thickness of the dots (notes) in 6 degrees ; the largest corresponds to mf. The sign indicates sound duration: the duration is dependent on the loudness: play on only when the tone has reached the dynamic level indicated by the narrowing of the line. means hold to extinction, then play on. written in red is the sign for a velar click: the player, simultaneously with a sound on his instrument, should produce a loud and very short click with the tip of his tongue on his (upper inside) gums."

Shown in Example 169 is a small section of *Liaisons*, by Roman Haubenstock-Ramati. It is written for vibraphone, or for vibraphone coupled with marimbaphone, but it can also be played as a duet or with a previously prepared tape recording. In this case, the recording is started from six to ten seconds after the performer begins. Traditional notation alternates with proportional. In the latter, the distance between the round dots and the horizontal line shows relative pitch, size indicates relative loudness, and the space separating them relative duration. The piece can be played from the left to the right, or vice versa, or up and down. The arrows suggest possibilities of changing directions.

While totally controlled music seems to have run its course, the aleatoric idea continues to attract some composers as a resource for bringing variety into their compositions. In many recent pieces there are sections in which the performers are freed from precise notes or rhythms alternating with sections in which the composer is in control in the traditional manner.

Electronic Music

While all of the preceding developments were taking place, another path to the music of the future was being explored—electronic music. After years of anticipation by impatient composers and theorists who felt that familiar tonal resources had been exhausted, the way was found to eliminate conventional instruments and conventional sounds. Some of the earlier moves in this direction have already been mentioned—the desire of the Futurists in the early years of the century to include noise in their music, and the experiments using microtones. As early as 1907, Busoni predicted the use of electrically produced sound, as did Leopold Stokowski in 1932 and Carlos Chávez in 1937. John Cage and

Edgard Varèse avoided pitched instruments and wrote pieces for percussion. *Ionisation* (1931), by the latter, is a classic of preelectronic "noise" music. Among the unusual electric instruments the Theremin, which is "played" by moving the hands toward or away from a steel rod, was invented in 1924, and the Ondes Martenot, which utilizes a keyboard, in 1928.

With the invention and perfection of the tape recorder the way was found to capture, store, and transform all kinds of sounds for use in musical compositions. The door opened on a vast new sound world and the dimensions of the art expanded so tremendously that the very concept of Western music, which has always been limited to sounds with definite pitches, was widened to include any sound, musical or otherwise. The musicalization of noise made possible through the tape recorder opened a new style period in music that made all previous revolutions seem insignificant. It is impossible to predict what the final consequences will be, because electronic music is less than a quarter-century old. Everything that has been accomplished to date must be regarded as exploratory, but it has already changed the world of music as explorations in outer space have changed the basic concepts concerning our planet.

THE BEGINNING OF ELECTRONIC MUSIC

The first steps were taken almost simultaneously in France and in Germany. Pierre Schaeffer, a radio engineer employed by the French National Radio, was the pioneer in France. Through his work in broadcasting, he was familiar with recorded "sound effects"—locomotive sounds, wind and thunder, bird calls, etc.—and his first compositions were made by arranging such pre-existing sounds and making a collage-recording of them. A group of these pieces was broadcast in Paris in October 1948, a historic date, in that it was the first public performance of music that was not played by humans. Schaeffer called his kind of music *musique concrète*, because the sounds were concrete, sonorous objects that could be plastically manipulated, and not "abstract."

The perfection of the tape recorder a few years later made it possible to change pitch by altering the speed of the tape, to play the tapes backward, so that the normal attack-release pattern is reversed, to add reverberation and echo effects, to filter out overtones, and to add various kinds of noises. Little of the early French music is still available on recordings, but Pierre Henry's *Veil of Orpheus* (1952) is typical. This piece is made of weird, rather frightening sounds combined with a distorted, echoed reading of a Greek text. It is programmatic and theatrical, characteristics of many of the early French pieces.

Electronic music in Germany started with the establishment of the Studio for Electronic Music by the West German Radio in Cologne in 1951 under the direction of Herbert Eimert and Werner Meyer-Eppler. From the beginning, German electronic composers differed from the French. They were not so much concerned with creating atmospheric "mood" compositions as they were in conducting scientific experiments. They also differed from the French in that they used only studio-created sounds, at first a simple sine tone, free from overtones, produced by an electric oscillator, instead of sounds collected from the outside world.

Karlheinz Stockhausen returned to Cologne, his native city, after a year's stay in Paris where he had worked with Schaeffer in the French studio. His first compositions, *Elektronische Studien I and II* (1953–1954) are early landmarks of this more intellectual approach. Example 170 is the first page of the published score of the second Study. The upper section, calibrated from 100 to 17,200, refers to pitch and timbre. The individual pitches used in this composition are chosen from a scale of 81 steps with a constant interval ratio of $\sqrt[25]{5}$ (the tempered scale is based on a ratio of $\sqrt[12]{2}$) and 193 mixtures constructed from them. The heavy horizontal lines indicate the high and low frequencies of the first sound mixture, to which another overlapping mixture is added. The two horizontal lines in the middle of the page indicate the duration of the sounds in terms of centimeters of tape moving at a specified speed. The triangular shapes at the bottom indicate volume in decibels.

In order to "realize" the composition, i.e., "perform" it, a tape recording would first be made of the 193 tone mixtures that serve as its basic material. This is the "keyboard," the gamut of sounds from which selections would be chosen and recorded following the instructions of the diagrams. Most electronic compositions are not notated and exist solely on tape.

TAPE-RECORDER MUSIC

It was not long before the distinction between *musique concrète* and electronic music disappeared as composers started to combine both kinds of sounds in the same composition. American composers soon entered the field. As early as 1952 Vladimir Ussachevsky of Columbia University wrote a piece called *Sonic Contours* for tape and instruments. In his *Piece for Tape Recorder* he used the following nonelectronic sounds: a gong, a piano, a single stroke of a cymbal, a single note on a kettledrum, the noise of a jet plane, a few chords on an organ, and combined these with electronic sounds: four pure tones produced on an oscillator and a tremolo produced by the stabilized reverberation of a click from a switch on a tape recorder.

EXAMPLE 170, *Elektronische Studien II* (STOCKHAUSEN)*

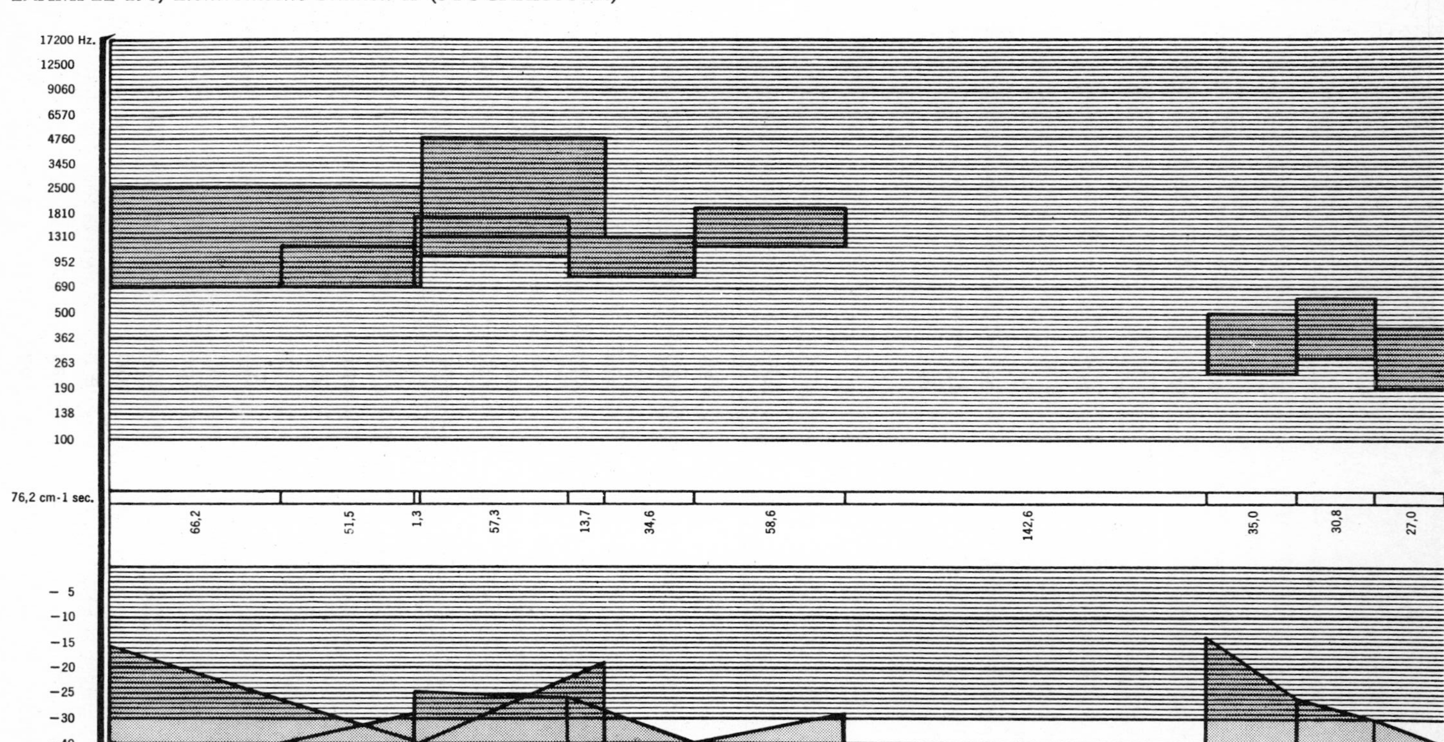

A MEDIUM—NOT A STYLE

It must be emphasized that electronic music does not connote a style, but simply a medium. Taped sounds, regardless of their source, can be used to form any kind of piece, serious or trivial, large or small. Electronic compositions can consist solely of definite pitches of the tempered scale, or of any pitch, or of any noise, or of any combination. Any degree of loudness at either end of the soft-loud continuum is available. Because no human performers are used, any melodic leap, no matter how wide, or sudden dynamic change is possible. Electronic music can move faster or slower than instrumental music. As a result, composers using the medium have more possibilities and more choices to make than composers who are limited by human performers.

In the following pages a few of the many thousands of pieces of electronic music that have been composed will be described. They will serve as a survey of the principal styles that have developed in the first twenty years of its history.

THE FIRST DECADE OF ELECTRONIC MUSIC

As mentioned previously, Edgard Varèse stopped composing in 1937 because he was no longer interested in seeking new sounds in conventional instruments. Electronic music was the answer to his lifelong desire to work with all kinds of sounds and he lost no time in using the new idiom. *Déserts* (1954) was written at the Paris studio. A twenty-five-minute piece, it has two distinct sound groups: instruments—woodwinds, brass, percussion, and piano—alternating with electronic noise-sounds. According to the composer, the instrumental parts produce a sense of movement in space, associated with the element within which the human operates. The tape section is associated with distance and the nonhuman elements of the universe. There are three interpolations of the taped material and a gradual mixing of the two elements. In fact, one must listen carefully to distinguish the instrumental sections from the taped sounds, showing the influence of electronic sounds on conventional instrumental writing, even at this early date.

The next important landmark is Stockhausen's *Gesang der Jünglinge* (1955–1956). This composition is important for two reasons: the use of the human voice as a sound source to be manipulated, and the use of four-channel tape and four loudspeakers in performance, introducing space into composition. Both of these features were to become important and often-used devices in later compositions. The principal sound source here is the voice of a boy soprano. The original recording is manipulated, fragmented, and transposed to other pitches, subjected to reverberation and combined in canon with itself. The presence of the human voice, no matter how distorted, gives the piece an unusual expressiveness.

During the 1950s many electronic music studios, large and small, were established in the United States, Canada, and Europe. The two pieces described next are examples of the many unpretentious pieces that were written at the time when the medium was being explored.

While not an "important" piece, Hugh le Caine's *Dripsody* (1955) is an example of the tape-splice technique of its time. This is pure *musique concrète*, in that the sound source was the sound of a single drop of water. This sound was recorded and then reproduced at various speeds, from a low of 45 vibrations per second (close to the lowest note on the piano) to 8,000 vibrations (over an octave above the top note). The tape lengths of these sounds were then spliced together to form an amusing piece suggesting xylophone sounds, but unmistakably sounding like water dripping from a faucet. This is a simple piece because only one kind of sound is used, and all the sounds have definite pitches.

Pinball, by Jean Ivey, is a more complex piece found on the same recording. Here all the sounds originate in a pinball machine. They are much more complex than the sounds of a single drop of water, because not only is there the clang of the bell, but there are numerous noises caused by the levers and the ball as it hits obstacles. The piece is in no sense simply a recording of a pinball machine in operation; its sounds are made the material of the piece. There is a much larger noise component in this piece than in the first.

In 1958 two vastly different electronic pieces were written showing the wide range of possibilities offered by the medium. The first is Varèse's *Poème électronique*, written for the Phillips Pavillion for the 1958 World's Fair in Brussels. The building was designed by Le Corbusier, the distinguished French architect, and the music was written to be heard as the visitors walked through it. Here is a description of the setting:

> This music was heard from over 400 loudspeakers as the auditors walked through the building seeing at the same time a series of projected images some of them photographs, others montages, paintings, printed or written script. No synchronization between sight and sound was attempted by the two artists; part of the effect achieved was the result of a discordance between aural and visual impressions and part the result of their not infrequent accidental concordance. The audience, some fifteen or sixteen thousand people daily for six months, evinced reactions almost as kaleidoscopic as the sounds and images they encountered—terror, anger, stunned awe, amusement, wild enthusiasm.[10]

Varèse uses a variety of bell and noise sounds, including clicks, sirens, and occasional moans. The piece is not meant to be listened to in the usual attentive manner, where the auditor tries to hear connections between the parts. There is little continuity here. This lack of "causality," of one section leading logically to another, was also to characterize much of the later electronic music.

In the same year that Varèse wrote *Poème électronique,* John Cage wrote an outrageous piece called *Fontana Mix.* This was not his first electronic piece. In fact, he had been one of the pioneers, in pieces such as *Imaginary Landscape No. 5* (1952), made by fragmenting the sounds of forty-three jazz records and recording the fragments on tape, following a score written according to chance methods. *Fontana Mix* consists entirely of noises. It sounds as though one were turning a shortwave radio dial and tuning in on one program after another, the whole being surrounded by horrendous static. Occasionally one hears laughter and a dog barking. The piece was written while Cage was living in Italy. Senora Fontana was his landlady. The piece must somehow be the composer's impressions of his stay in Milan. It is an example of electronic music that is as far removed as possible from older music.

In *Trois visages de Liège* (1961) Henri Pousseur, a Belgian composer, created a sophisticated and poetic evocation of the Belgian city. It is a three-movement symphonic poem similar in concept to Debussy's *La Mer* or *Ibéria.* The first movement is called "Air and Water"; the title and music reveal indebtedness to the impressionist ideal. It employs gentle swishing sounds suggesting the surf, sirenlike glissandos, and bell sounds. The second movement, "Voices of the City," employs instrumental sounds: strings pizzicato playing a dissonant chord as the primary sound source, to which the sounds of children's voices are added, in the manner of Stockhausen's *Gesang der Jünglinge.* The third movement is called "Forges," and it pictures the industrial activities of the city. This section uses rougher sounds than the earlier sections and mixtures of slow, organlike sounds with voices, noises, and some pitches. *Trois visages de Liège* is a highly successful, if somewhat conservative, use of the medium.

THE SECOND DECADE OF ELECTRONIC MUSIC

Originally, electronic music was stored on tape, and sometimes transferred to a disc, and listened to as it emanated from a loudspeaker. This made for an unsatisfactory concert experience, because there was nothing but loudspeakers for the audience to watch while listening. To enrich the situation some composers and entrepreneurs flashed lights, projected slides, or showed moving pictures simultaneously with the sounds to form a multimedia performance.

Other composers experimented with "live performance" electronic music. In this type, the sounds are produced and manipulated in full view of the audience. Stockhausen, in *Mixtur* (1964), wrote for five groups of instruments that are played in normal fashion before the audience. Each group has its own microphone supplying sounds to manipulators who alter timbres and dynamics.

The audience sees the total operation and hears the mixture of live and manipulated sounds. In his *Mikrophonie I* (1965), the sounds come from a huge tam-tam. One performer produces a wide variety of sounds on it, another moves a contact microphone on its surface, while still another transforms the sounds through filters and voltage dividers. This composition is very "loose" in structure and unpredictable in sound, because everyone involved improvises.

Sometimes the sound sources used were novel and startling. John Cage once attached contact microphones to his throat and then drank a glass of water. The amplified modified resultant sounds were Niagara-like. Robert Ashley attached electrodes to the "performer's" scalp. Contact microphones and amplification revealed the sound of brain waves.

Among the most interesting uses of electronic sound has been that used in combination with conventional instruments. Mario Davidovsky has written a number of pieces called *Synchronisms* for solo players or groups of instruments, performed simultaneously with a tape. The contrast in timbres is most attractive. Milton Babbitt's *Philomel*, for soprano and taped sounds, is another example of the genre.

SYNTHESIZERS AND COMPUTERS

The "classic" electronic studio had several drawbacks. The method was very complex and time-consuming when the composer had to create the sounds he wished to use, modify them, and then make the innumerable splices necessary to form his piece. A typical studio looked like a satirical cartoon of a mad scientist's laboratory with its numerous generators and modifiers, tape-decks and speakers, tape loops, and patch cords.

The development of synthesizers made the process simpler, and gave the composer more freedom than the original system allowed. A synthesizer has been described as "a unit combining sound generators and modifiers in one package with a unified control system." The mammoth and expensive RCA synthesizer installed in the Columbia-Princeton New York laboratory became the center for this development. It is now considered to be obsolete, and much smaller and cheaper portable models are being widely adopted. The best known system is that devised by Dr. Robert Moog. Others are the Buchla, developed by Donald Buchla and composer Morton Subotnik, and the Syn-Ket, developed by an Italian engineer, Paul Ketoff. Still another is the ARP synthesizer, which offers further simplifications. Sounds are produced on the Moog and Syn-Ket by playing a conventional keyboard, while the Buchla is "played" by depressing a sensitized metal strip. These instruments are primarily monophonic; that is, single melodies are played and recorded, and complex textures are obtained by combining recordings of several different melodic or rhythmic lines. One of the

Moog Synthesizer
Courtesy of Robert Moog

best-known pieces "written" on the Buchla instrument is Subotnik's *Silver Apples of the Moon* (1967). In the second half of this piece, commissioned by the Nonesuch Record Company, a montage of ten different melodic and rhythmic lines is superimposed, creating an exciting and jazzy ostinato. New developments in synthesizers are occurring every day. We can expect them to play an increasing, and perhaps revolutionary, role in the future.

Computers can be used both in the creation of sound and in the construction of compositions. Computers, of course, only carry out orders, and they do only what they have been "told" to do. Up to the present their use has been limited in musical situations because the process is extremely complicated and costly. Among others, Lejaren Hiller and Milton Babbitt have investigated their possibilities.

We should be reminded that electronic music is only twenty-five years old and regardless of what has been accomplished, it is still in its infancy. The extreme versatility of the medium has been demonstrated and "schools" and styles have already defined themselves, from the austerity of the first Stockhausen studies to the baroque profusion of Subotnik; from the humor of *Dripsody* to the planned monotony of *Déserts*; from the poetic, evocative quality of Pousseur to the rude noises of John Cage.

Out of all this working with sound, a new concept of the nature of music seems to be developing. Music for some has come to be an art in which sound, any kind of sound, is the whole *raison d'être,* instead of being an art that operates somewhat in the nature of a language, with its syntax and grammar; statements, developments, and recapitulations of themes; patterns of tension and relaxation; consonances and dissonances, and its underlying pulse and organizing rhythms. The source of the sound doesn't matter; the sound doesn't have to "do" anything, it doesn't have to "mean" anything, it simply has to "be."

This is, of course, an extreme view, and it is not held by all electronic music composers. However, all have been affected by the freedoms offered by the medium: freedom from performers, from metrical patterns, from the limitations of instruments, from any kind of a pitch grid, from any preconceived sound. These freedoms have been infectious, and have inspired a whole group of composers who, even when they write for conventional instruments, compose with the sounds of electronic music in their consciousness. Such composers can be called "postelectronic," not necessarily meaning that they have superseded the electronic composers, but that their music has been influenced by the freedom of electronic music.

"Sound" Composers

This obsession with sound can be heard in the compositions of György Ligeti, the Hungarian composer. His *Atmosphères* is well-known because it was appropriately used to accompany the outer-space scenes in the film *2001.* Written for a large orchestra without timpani, each instrument plays a separate part, making for an extremely rich texture. The piece starts very softly, with a widely-spaced complex chord that seems to be hanging in the air because there is no meter or pulse. Almost imperceptibly there are minute changes in timbre as some of the instruments drop out and others take their place. In the next section there are trills instead of single notes, enriching the sound. The woodwinds gradually rise in overlapping chromatic scales to a high, shrill climax. Next, the instruments center around a common note, buzzing like flies, followed by a section in which the wind players blow through their instruments without sounding tones, making an eerie sound. The piece disappears into silence at the end, the last sounds created by brushing the strings of a piano.

Ligeti's *Volumina* for organ and *Continuum* for harpsichord are similar in style. "In these pieces," the composer has said, "my main goal was to build up an art form in which the tone color is more important than melody, harmony, and rhythm . . . which have been reduced and woven together in a heavy dense texture." [11] This static music was anticipated in Schoenberg's "Summer Morning by the Lake" from the *Five Pieces for Orchestra,* discussed earlier, as well as by Varèse's sound-block pieces.

Minimal Music

Another kind of music being written and performed in the early 1970s can be called Minimal, because of its similarities with a parallel movement in the art world, characterized by its drastic limitation to the basic visual elements. Ad Reinhardt, one of the principal painters of the group, recommended that there be "no texture, no brushwork or calligraphy, no sketching or drawing, no light, no space, no time, no movement, no object, subject, or matter." [12] What is left? Reinhardt's paintings are large canvasses painted solid black. Other painters of this persuasion sometimes painted two or three stripes on a canvas and the sculptors constructed boxes and other geometrical figures.

Terry Riley has written a composition called *In C* that shares some of these attributes. It consists of fifty-three melodic fragments that can be played in any order and repeated as often as desired by as many instruments as possible. Because of a preponderance of certain notes, a basic chord progression could result, but if in any performance the chords did not appear, it would not matter.

Steve Reich's music is somewhat similar in effect except that its rhythmic structure is controlled. His piece *Four Organs* is written for four electronic organs and a pair of maracas that beat a steady beat while the organs play the same chord progression for twenty-four minutes but with varying lengths of silence between the chords. In *Come Out* Reich uses electronically controlled sound. Here the sound source is a spoken sentence repeated from start to finish. It was recorded on two channels, first in unison, and then with the second channel slowly beginning to move ahead. Eventually the two voices divide into four and eight, resulting in an interesting, almost hypnotic sound composition.

Pauline Oliveros's *I of IV* consists of a very complex sound, more noise than pitched, sustained for almost twenty minutes. Occasionally new sounds are added, some subtle, some obvious, but the basic drone persists. In these pieces the ideal of theme-oriented music that prevailed for so many centuries is replaced by a sound-oriented ideal.

Karlheinz Stockhausen has written a piece called *Stimmung* for eight singers, each equipped with a microphone, who sit on the floor as though around a campfire. They intone the notes of the B-flat–major chord for about twenty minutes, occasionally calling out the name of a deity.

Environmental Music

Stimmung has to be seen as well as heard. It is a theater piece, and many composers of this genre combine their sounds with lights or with dance. LaMonte Young, one of the leaders, presents continuous sound and light "environments" that might last as long as a week, that can be visited from time to time, like a phenomenon of nature such as a waterfall or a panorama. In *Music for the Beethovenhalle* (1970) (a concert hall in Bonn) Stockhausen planned and composed music to be played continuously and simultaneously in three different halls and three lobbies of the building. The public walked through the building, hearing now one, and now another, and now the overlapping of more than one group. Mattresses were provided on the floors for those who wished to rest; poetry was read, and films were shown on the walls.

Max Neuhaus has written true environmental music in his *Walkthrough*. This piece is made up of electronic sounds that are heard when one passes in front of a building in New York City. The pitch and direction from which the sounds come are controlled by changes in the weather. He has also created *Drive-in Music* consisting of a number of radio transmitters lining a piece of highway. Passing motorists can tune into the channel and listen to the sounds.

Conceptual Music

Even further removed from the conventional idea of music is Conceptual music, again paralleling an art movement in which visual concepts are conceived and described but not necessarily carried out. Here there is no sound at all, but simply the imagining of one. For instance, Stockhausen's score for *Aus den sieben Tagen* is a verbal one:

Play a note
Play it until
You feel
that you should stop.

Christian Wolff's composition *Stones* (1968) has the following content: "Make sounds with stones, draw sounds out of stones, using a number of sizes and kinds (and colours); for the most part discreetly; sometimes in rapid sequences. For the most part striking stones with stones, but also stones on other surfaces (inside the open head of a drum, for instance) or other than struck (bowed, for instance, or amplified). Do not break anything." [13]

In spite of the novelty of much of this music, it is not entirely new. Here are some of the predecessors:

Schoenberg's concept of *Klangfarbenmelodie* as found in his "*Summer Morning by a Lake*" (page 68);

Varèse's concept of sound structures as found in his *Octandre* and *Intégrales* (page 318);

Satie's concept of music not-to-be-listened-to as found in his wallpaper music (page 114);

Satie's concept of "endless" repetition of simple units. (In 1890 he wrote a piece called *Vexations* consisting of a series of dissonant chords with the direction that they be repeated 840 times. The piece was played in New York and other places in 1970, taking over twenty-four hours to perform and wearing out several sets of pianists and several audiences.)

The oriental concept of repetitive music as a part of religious ritual to induce contemplation or mystical states. (Several of the American composers of Minimal music are students of African, Indian, and Far Eastern music.)

The biggest influence of all, however, is John Cage, whose concepts will be discussed in the next chapter.

Suggested Readings

For further discussion of recent developments in music, the following books are recommended: Hans Stuckenschmidt, *Twentieth-Century Music* (New York, 1969); Peter Yates, *Twentieth-Century Music* (New York, 1967); John Cage, *Silence* (Middletown, Conn., 1961), *A Year from Monday* (Middletown, Conn., 1963), and *Notations* (New York, 1969). The latter contains many examples of new notation. Schwartz and Childs, *Contemporary Composers on Contemporary Music* (New York, 1967) contains many interesting statements, including Babbitt's "Who Cares If You Listen?" The September 1968 issue of *High Fidelity Magazine* is devoted to "New Music" and contains an excellent overview. Among journals, *Perspectives of New Music, The Musical Quarterly* (Current Chronicle), *Tempo,* and frequently *High Fidelity* are indispensable. *Source, Music of the Avant Garde* contains scores and "directions" for performing avant-garde music but it also contains essays by the composers, and sometimes recordings as well. It is published twice a year in Davis, California. Another periodical devoted to recent music is *Numus West,* published three times a year at Mercer Island, Washington.

David Cope's *New Directions in Music* (Dubuque, Iowa, 1971) surveys many of the trends discussed in this chapter, as does Reginald Smith Brindle's *The New Music: The Avant-garde since 1945* (London, 1975).

Minimal and Conceptual music are discussed in Michael Nyman's *Experimental Music* (New York, 1975). John Vinton's *Dictionary of Contemporary Music* (New York, 1974) contains many articles about the composers and movements discussed in this chapter.

Recent books on electronic music include: Walter Sear, *The New World of Electronic Music* (New York, 1972); Elliott Schwartz, *Electronic Music: a Listener's Guide*, 2nd ed. (New York, 1975); Allen Strange, *Electronic Music: Systems, Techniques, and Controls* (Dubuque, 1972); and Gilbert Trythall, *Principles and Practice of Electronic Music* (New York, 1973).

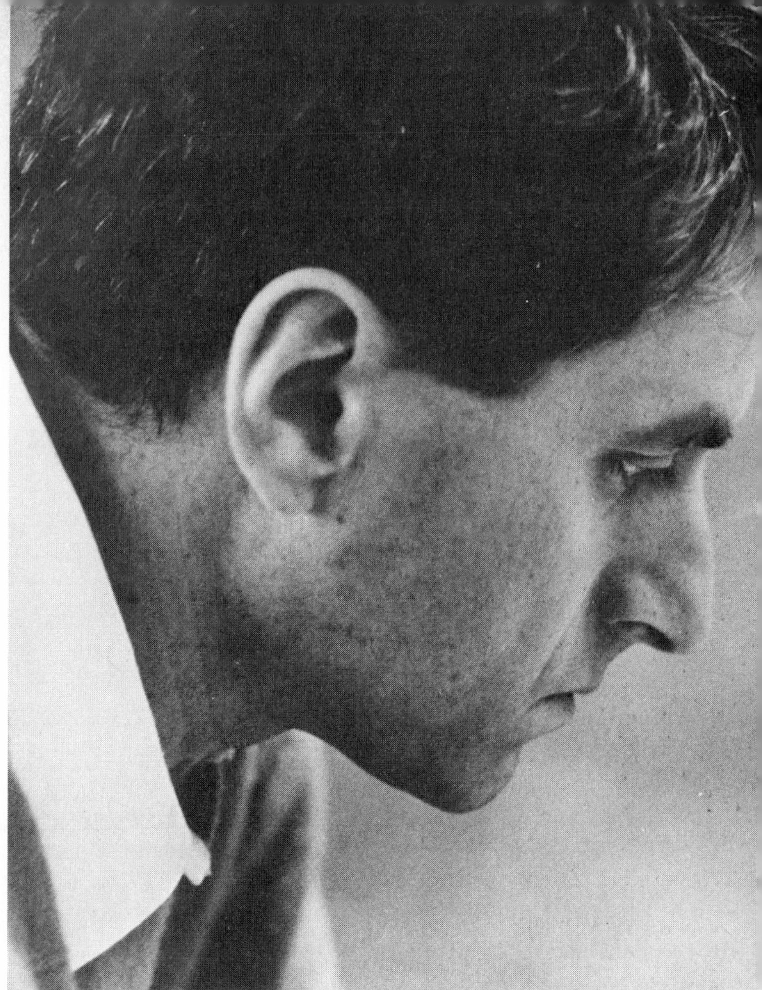

Yannis Xenakis

21

How can you make a revolution when the revolution before last has already said anything goes?
Charles Wuorinen

Representative Composers, 1950-1975

In the preceding chapters, the main musical developments of the third quarter of the century have been defined and described. Such movements, of course, are not spontaneous—they are the products of the creative imaginations of individual composers who themselves are the products of their backgrounds and musical experiences.

In this chapter, the paths followed by some of the most prominent younger composers will be traced. Born for the most part in the 1920s and 1930s, their starting point was the music of the masters of the first half of the century: Stravinsky, Schoenberg, Bartók, and Hindemith. Each has acted either as a settler developing territory already discovered, or as an explorer searching for the new. Some of the composers discussed in previous sections will be met again in the following pages, but this time they will be presented as individuals in order to show the continuity of their development and the extent of their contribution.

John Cage (born 1912)

It might seem out of place to introduce a composer born in 1912 at the beginning of a chapter devoted to younger composers, but John Cage has been such a powerful force in postwar music that he belongs here rather than with his contemporaries. Peter Yates calls him "the most influential composer, world wide, of his generation." [1] This is a broad statement, and can be understood only by reviewing his activities.

He was born in Los Angeles in 1912 and spent most of his early life in southern California. Piano lessons did not reveal extraordinary talent, and it was only after two years of college and several years in Europe and his return to Los Angeles that he decided to devote himself wholeheartedly to music. In 1933 he went to New York to study harmony and composition with Adolf Weiss, a former Schoenberg pupil, and a year and a half later he returned to Los Angeles to study with Schoenberg. "He is more of an inventor than a composer," Schoenberg is reported to have said, and from the beginning Cage was more interested in devising new ways of composing than in mastering already existing idioms.

Working with modern dance groups, his first compositions were for percussion players. He next wrote pieces with elaborate precompositional plans, similar but not identical to serial devices. These were followed by compositions that had intricate rhythmic structures replacing the tonal structures of earlier music. For example, a percussion piece called *First Construction* (*in Metal*) contains sixteen parts each containing sixteen measures. Each of the sixteen measures is divided into five phrases of four measures, three measures, two measures, three measures, and four measures, and the sixteen parts of the whole are grouped in large sections in the same proportion: 4, 3, 2, 3, 4.

Cage's next interest was in discovering new sounds in the piano, of converting the instrument into a new kind of percussion instrument by inserting metal screws, bolts, little pieces of rubber, and wood at prescribed places between the strings of the piano and thereby completely changing its sound. The prepared piano becomes a one-man percussion orchestra of great charm and surprise.

The next stage in Cage's development came as a result of his study of Indian music and Zen philosophy. From the former he gained the concept of a music that was improvised but based on prescribed scales and rhythmic formulae. From the latter he gained an attitude toward life totally different from that which has dominated Western civilization since the Renaissance. Zen is essentially mystical, antilogical, and seeks no "purpose" in life. It accepts life in all of its diversity and does not attempt to "make sense." Adapting such an attitude to music, Cage concluded that the purpose of music was not to communicate or to entertain. In his book called *Silence* he explains:

> And what is the purpose of writing music? One is, of course, not dealing with purposes but dealing with sounds. Or the answer must take the form of paradox: purposeful purposelessness or a purposeless play. This play, however, is an affirmation of life—not an attempt to bring order out of

chaos or to suggest improvements in creation, but simply a way of waking up to the very life we're living, which is so excellent once one gets one's mind and one's desires out of its way and lets it act of its own accord.[2]

The compositions that follow are a result of this philosophy that attacks the foundations of Western music. Chance operations play an increasing role and Cage developed many ingenious devices for achieving unpredictable results. The use of I-Ching sticks (similar in effect to rolling dice), as well as the audacious montage of the radios, have already been mentioned. *Music for Piano* (1952) is written entirely in whole notes and their length is determined by the

John Cage
Photograph by James Klosty

performer. The notes themselves correspond to the imperfections in the paper upon which the piece was first written. In *Music for Piano* (1953) the tempo and dynamics are undetermined. Tone production is determined by chance operations, the tones themselves by paper imperfections. "The sixteen pages may be played as separate pieces or continuously as one piece, or." The *Concert for Piano and Orchestra* (1958) has a sixty-three–page piano part containing eighty-four different aggregates to be played in whole or part in any sequence. In the words of Wilfrid Mellers: "Indeed since each player in the *Concert* is instructed to play all, any, or none of the notes allotted to him, it is theoretically possible, if improbable, that a performance could result in complete silence." [3] This state of affairs was achieved in 4′ 33″ (four minutes, thirty-three seconds), a piece for piano "performed" in utter silence as the pianist sits immobile before the keyboard for that length of time, marking the divisions of the three sections by closing and opening the fall-board of the piano at the prescribed moments.

The "point" of this piece is that during the silence the audience becomes aware of the random and accidental sounds that occur. Perhaps they are nothing more than the sound of a cough, of shuffling feet, or even of the ringing in one's ears—sounds that are normally ignored. Cage wants us to "simply wake up to the life we're living."

"What he is proposing is, essentially, the complete, revolutionary overthrow of the most basic assumptions of Western art since the Renaissance. The power of art to communicate ideas and emotions, to organize life into meaningful patterns, and to realize universal truths through the self-expressed individuality of the artist are only three of the assumptions that Cage challenges," according to Calvin Tomkins in his study of the composer. He continues, "In place of a self-expressive art created by the imagination, tastes, and desires of the individual artist, Cage proposes an art born of chance and indeterminacy, in which every effort is made to extinguish the artist's own personality; instead of the accumulation of masterpieces, he urges a perpetual process of artistic discovery in our daily life." [4]

Cage's influence has gone beyond music. In fact, his music has gone beyond music in the direction of multimedia happenings in which the senses are bombarded with sights and sounds, and possibly smells and tactile sensations as well, in unstructured sequences. The 1969 production of Cage's and Lejaren Hiller's *HPSCHD* in the 16,000-seat assembly hall at the University of Illinois was probably one of the most elaborate of such occasions. Experienced were seven harpsichords, fifty-two amplified, computer-generated sound tapes, six motion-picture projectors showing technological films, computer programs, foreign-language instructions, and multicolored "psychedelic" slides. The performance lasted for hours, during which time the audience walked around the huge area, coming and going as they wished. The joining of "art" and "life" was accomplished.

We cannot know what Cage's ultimate importance in the history of music will be. That he anticipated many of the innovations of the second half of the century, of "emancipating music from the notes," cannot be denied. Whether he is a prophet of the future or a good-natured prankster remains to be seen.

Karlheinz Stockhausen (born 1928)

Karlheinz Stockhausen is the most prominent German composer of the post-World War II generation. His compositions reflect, and in some cases have created, some of the style trends defined in the last chapters. He has been fortunate in having the resources of the West German Radio in Cologne to perform and publicize his works, and as a charter member and later a teacher at the Darmstadt Summer Course, he has had an international center at which to bring his name and music before a large public. His career is a phenomenon rarely encountered before this time—that of an extremely difficult and uncompromising composer becoming highly successful. He travels widely, and is as much at home on American college campuses, where he frequently teaches and lectures, as he is in Cologne, Darmstadt, or Tokyo. Each of his new compositions is awaited with interest, reviewed by critics, and recorded.

He was born in a suburb of Cologne, where his father was a schoolteacher. He studied several musical instruments as a child, but it was not until after his demobilization from the German army in 1945 that he decided to become a musician. He entered the Musik Hochschule in Cologne in 1947 and started musicological studies at the University, supporting himself by playing in dance bands and improvising background music for a vaudeville hypnotist.

His first compositions date from 1950; they were strongly influenced by Schoenberg and Webern, and have complex serial plans and pointillistic texture. *Kreuzspiel* (1951) is a good example. Written for oboe, bass clarinet, piano, and percussion, it is in three parts. In the first, each instrument has its own "region" to play in—the piano at the high and low extremes, and winds in the middle four octaves. Durations, tones, and dynamics are serialized and gradually the instruments "cross" and invade the other's territory. The second part of the piece reverses the directions and order of events, and the third part plays both versions together.

In 1951 Stockhausen attended the summer course at Darmstadt where he became acquainted with Messiaen and Boulez. He found these French composers so stimulating that he spent the next year in Paris and attended Messiaen's classes at the Conservatoire. He also worked in Pierre Schaeffer's newly-established *musique-concrète* laboratory.

When he returned to Cologne, he joined the newly-established electronic music studio and wrote his *Elektronische Studien* I and II (1953), and *Gesang der Jünglinge* (1955), already described.

In the mid-fifties he became interested in aleatoric possibilities. *Zeitmasse* (1956), for woodwind quintet, employs various kinds of "time." Some are metronomic (twelve specified tempi), while others are relative. These are "as fast as possible" (dependent on the technique of the players); "as slow as possible" (dependent on the breath of the players); from "very slow to approximately four times faster" and from "very fast to approximately four times slower." Because most of these designations call for relative tempi, traditional rhythmic notation is abandoned and proportional notation is used in which the distance between the notes on the score is equated with their distance in time. The rhythmic relationships between the instruments are so complex that the traditional score and parts are also abandoned. Each player must play from a full score in order to see what his colleagues are playing. Because several different "levels" are often employed simultaneously, a common barring is impossible. These two new ways of notating rhythms that cannot be notated by traditional means were adopted by many composers in the next decade.

Aleatoric principles also govern *Klavierstücke XI,* already described, *Zyklus for One Percussionist* (1959), and *Refrain for Three Players* (1959).

In the following years Stockhausen's interests turned toward compositions calling for large groups of instruments, sometimes combined with electronic sounds, in which spatial effects play a role. *Gruppen* (1955–1958) calls for 109 instrumentalists arranged in three groups, seated in front of, and at the left and right of, the audience. They play alone and in various combinations in a texture that is so thick that it is impossible to distinguish individual sounds. The next large piece, *Carré* (1960), was written for four orchestras of twenty pieces, each with a small chorus. When this piece is performed, the orchestras are located against the four walls of the room; the audience sits in the middle, so as to hear the sounds from all sides.

Momente (1961, revised 1965) is another huge sound conglomerate calling for soprano, four choral groups, and thirteen instruments. "In this piece," the composer said, "the distinction between sound and music disappears." It starts with the sounds of hand clapping, and then words, grunts, whispers, and shouts are added, giving the impression that one is listening to a political meeting. Gradually the voice of a soprano is heard in a variety of trills, chirps, "double-tonguings" and ululations, vocal sounds of a preverbal nature. The piece lasts about fifty minutes and has been described as containing "everything: parody, persiflage, wit, childlikeness, psalmody, and electronic, yet manmade sounds." It offers many problems to the listener because of its length, its lack of direction, and the strangeness of its sounds.

Another vast montage is *Hymnen* (1966) based on the national anthems of many countries. This intention should not lead anyone to believe that the piece is a medley of recognizable melodies. On the contrary, it sounds as if one were listening to the random noises one would hear by twisting the dials of a shortwave radio. Snatches of words, static, sustained organ chords, cries, and whistles follow each other in no apparent order. Occasionally a distorted version of an anthem can be recognized. At one point there are several minutes in which nothing is heard except a low, unchanging hum that sounds like an amplifier in need of repair.

What to make of all this? Stockhausen has said that there is no causality in these works. "Although one moment may suggest the one which follows it, the connection is in no way causal, and it would be equally possible for a different moment to follow." As a result, he does not expect his listeners to listen in the usual attentive way. "One can ignore a moment if one no longer wishes, or no longer is able to listen." "The musical events do not take a determined course from a fixed beginning to an inevitable end. A moment is not merely the result of what has happened or the cause of what is about to occur. Rather, it is a concentration on the here and now."

This is a remarkable statement, showing a totally new concept of the nature of music and of the manner of listening to it.

After writing these large works, Stockhausen's incessant explorations followed other paths. One new path led to "live" electronic music in which soloists or ensembles perform in view of the audience while sound technicians, also in view, electronically alter and distort the sounds being made. The auditors hear the combined original sounds and their transformations. Examples are *Solo* (1969) for an unspecified solo instrument and four electronic technicians, and *Mikrophonie I* (1965), already described.

In some later works Stockhausen seems to be trying to reflect the diversity of the world through quotations of music from a wide variety of cultures. In describing his *Telemusik* he said, "I am sure you will hear it all—the gagaku player, that mysterious familiar of the Japanese Imperial court, music from the happy island of Bali, from the southern Sahara, from a Spanish village festival, from Hungary, the Shipibos of the Amazon River, the Omizutori ceremony of Nara, in which I took part for three whole days and nights, the fantastic virtuosity of the Chinese, music of the Kosason temple, or the highland dwellers of Viet Nam . . . music from the No drama and from goodness knows where." [5]

In another composition, *Musik für ein Haus* (1968), for fourteen instrumentalists, simultaneous free improvisation alternates with the reading of short "meditative" texts. In this, and in some other late compositions, the composer is influenced by certain elements of Japanese and other Far Eastern music.

Stockhausen is the perfect example of the composer as explorer. Each of his works is written for a different combination of instruments and each explores a new sound world. "I am a product of many influences," he has said, "naturally I draw upon them freely and sometimes unconsciously. My music makes sense to me. I can't ever understand why it poses difficulties for others."

Pierre Boulez (born 1925)

Pierre Boulez is among the most important French composers of the post-war generation. He graduated from the Paris Conservatoire in 1945, where he had studied with Messiaen, and he was of that generation who received the full impact of serial music at Darmstadt. His activities in protesting against neo-classic music and in leading the movement away from Schoenberg to Webern, and eventually to the ideal of total control, have already been mentioned. From that time on he has been in the vanguard of musical tendencies, and his activities

Pierre Boulez
Universal Edition Archive, Vienna

as conductor, essayist, and teacher, as well as composer, have made him one of the pace- and taste-setters of recent years.

Two of his intensely organized compositions, the Piano Sonata No. 2 (1952) and *Structures* (1952), for two pianos, have already been discussed. Other works in this style are *Polyphonie X* (1951), for seventeen solo instruments, and his Etudes I and II (1951), for *musique-concrète* sounds.

Le Marteau sans maître (1952–1954) marks a turning away from these ascetic structural forms. This piece is a setting of three poems by the surrealist poet René Char, for alto voice and six instruments—flute, viola, vibraphone, marimba, guitar, and a large group of percussion instruments—a combination recalling *Pierrot Lunaire,* which without doubt was a strong influence. It consists of nine sections alternating purely instrumental pieces with songs, each section exploiting its own group of instruments.

Although structural devices associated with serial music are used in the piece, its outstanding characteristic is its luscious sound. The low register of the flute and the viola carry many of the melodies, surrounded by the ever-present shimmer of the vibraphone, xylorimba, and guitar—suggesting the music of the Far East. The voice sings long melismatic lines with sudden changes of register and frequent distortion of the normal accentuation of the words.

Boulez has written two other works for voice and a small group of instruments that also show his respect for the Debussyan sound ideal. These are *Le Soleil des eaux* (revised, 1959) and *Improvisations sur Mallarmé* (1958), works that are permeated with the "magical" sounds of harp, vibraphone, bells, and a large group of percussion instruments.

In his Piano Sonata No. 3 (1957) Boulez employs aleatoric principles. This is a large work, consisting of five sections: *Antiphonie, Trope, Constellation, Strophe,* and *Sequence;* but they are not necessarily played in that order. The only requirement is that the longest section, *Constellation,* remain in the center.

The third movement is the longest and most complex It is an extended piece, through which two designated "routes" can lead. In order to make the routes clear one is printed with red ink and the other with green. Within each "route" the performer has a choice of durations, dynamics, and attacks, and the possibility of "switching" from one route to another. Thus, there are many different ways of playing the piece and a strong likelihood that each performance will differ from other performances.[6]

Subsequent compositions by Boulez exploit the stereophonic effects gained through the use of spatially divided orchestral groups. His *Poésie pour pouvoir* (1958) calls for three orchestras and two conductors, a tape recording of a poem that has been treated with all possible manners of distortion so that it becomes incomprehensible sound, and recorded electronic sounds. There are loudspeakers at the center of each wall and a rotating speaker at the center of the ceiling moving at variable speeds.

Pli selon pli (1964) is Boulez's most important later composition. The title, translated as "fold by fold," comes from a poem by Mallarmé describing the Belgian city of Bruges emerging from the mist. This impressionist concept is reflected in the music (although the poem is not used) in its delicate and relaxed sound. Lasting almost an hour, the piece is in five sections, the middle three being scored for soprano and chamber orchestra (previously published as *Improvisations sur Mallarmé*) and the outer movements for full orchestra.

Because of the many reverberating instruments, such as bells, vibraphone, piano, celesta, harp, and numerous nonpitched percussion instruments, the piece frequently suggests the sound of a gamelan. In the first and last movements the orchestra is divided into three groups that merge, separate, and overlap like layers of mist.

In his next piece Boulez returned to electronically altered sound. It is called *explosant/fixe* and is written for eight performers, each of whom has his own microphone that feeds into a mixing box where an operator can alter or transmit unaltered the sounds to the loudspeakers placed throughout the hall. Thus it is similar to some of Stockhausen's pieces.

Boulez's increasing activities as a conductor have limited his composing since 1965. He has been in demand by the leading orchestras of the world, climaxed by his acceptance of the musical directorship of the New York Philharmonic Orchestra in 1970, as Leonard Bernstein's successor. This phase terminated in 1975 when he resigned to become head of the *Institut de recherche et de coordination acoustic-musicale,* a newly established research institute for music and acoustics in Paris.

Luciano Berio (born 1925)

Luciano Berio, Italy's leading mid-century composer, is a close contemporary of Stockhausen and Boulez; his music and career show many parallels with theirs. Having become friends at Darmstadt in the early 1950s, all three wrote compositions of the same general type at about the same time. They are internationalists who spend as much time in the United States as they do in Europe. All have taught at American universities, have expressed their views on the state of music and the state of the world in books and articles, and have conducted orchestras and music festivals in various parts of the world. Together, they form the image of the young, mid-century composer, who is a far cry from the introverted, "ivory-towered artist" stereotype.

Berio was born in Oneglia, a small town in northern Italy, where both his father and grandfather were church organists and composers. After prelim-

Luciano Berio
Broadcast Music Inc. (B.M.I.) Archives

inary study with them he entered the Milan Conservatory, specializing in piano, conducting, and composition. In 1951 a scholarship took him to the Berkshire Music Center at Tanglewood, in Lenox, Massachusetts, where he studied with Luigi Dallapiccola, who taught there that summer. In 1953 he attended the Darmstadt Summer School and met Stockhausen and Boulez, and learned about their musical interests. His totally-controlled *Nones* (1955), already described, reflects this trend.

Back in Milan, he established the first electronic music studio in Italy, and in 1955 wrote *Mutazione*, his first electronic piece. His most important piece for the medium is *Ommagio a Joyce* (1958), the sound content of which is a reading of the opening section of the "Sirens" chapter of James Joyce's *Ulysses*. In Berio's piece, the words are not presented for their meaning, but for their sound, because through electronic manipulation the words become unintelligible. This interest in the expressive potential of words was a lasting one and was expressed in many of his later works.

Visages (1960), originally written for radio performance, for voice and electronic sounds, is a study of all kinds of vocal sounds—laughs, cries, whispers, shrieks, gasps, sobs—a wordless drama. This piece was written for Berio's first wife, the American singer, Cathy Berberian, who has developed an amazing vocal technique. *Circles* (1961), for voice, harp, and percussion, is another piece that treats words in an unusual manner. They are "fractured," that is, vowels and consonants are separated in a highly unorthodox manner that reflects the typography of the e. e. cummings poems. The composer finds new connections between the sounds of instruments and voice, for example in the hissing of "s" sounds and the wire-brushed cymbals, and "ing" sounds with sharp harp chords.

In the 1960s, Berio wrote a series of solo pieces for flute, harp, solo voice, piano, and trombone called *Sequenza.* In each selection he discovers and exploits new sounds from the instruments. The *Sequenza* for trombone is particularly interesting in its absolutely new sounds, some a combination of the trombonist's singing or humming while he plays, some a result of blowing through the instrument without embouchure, others by tapping the side of the instrument. The *Sequenza* for voice also calls for sounds that have never been heard emanating from the human throat. These pieces show Berio's interest in enriching timbral resources. They call for a new kind of virtuosity that goes far beyond conventional demands.

The most ambitious and successful of Berio's works to date is *Sinfonia* (1968), written for eight voices (the Swingle Singers) and orchestra, combined in that close connection—voices sounding like instruments, and instruments sounding like voices—already found in *Circles.* In no sense a conventional symphony, the word *Sinfonia* is used in its original meaning of "sounding together." *Sinfonia* is in four movements. The first is dominated by voices, speaking and humming, occasionally punctuated by crashing orchestral sonorities. The texts, spoken in a stuttering manner, are from *Le Cru et le cuit,* a study of Brazilian folklore by Claude Levi-Strauss, the French anthropologist. It is slow moving, and carefully articulated between the vocal and instrumental sections. It is obviously planned and purposeful, and is therefore unlike Stockhausen's *Hymnen,* where there is little if any causal relationship between the parts. The second movement is a tribute to the memory of Martin Luther King; the vocal parts consist of nothing more than the chanting of his name. The movement is elegiac and bell-like in timbre and melodic outline. Instruments and voices are so interwoven in long, sustained unisons that it is difficult to distinguish between them. The third movement is the longest and most original. It is based on the third movement of Mahler's Second Symphony, which is played as a more or less constant "background" but there are also references to Bach, Schoenberg, Debussy, Strauss, Ravel, Brahms, Boulez, Stockhausen, and others. In the "foreground" one hears snatches of a Beckett play, and student slogans from recent confrontations. It is an amazing, dreamlike jumbling together of sound images from the past and present, reminding one of the free associations of James Joyce's *Ulysses* or *Finnegans Wake,* where different languages and dictions are brought together in a time-destroying present. Berio speaks of the movement as a "documentary on an *object trouvé* (the Mahler movement), recorded in the mind of the listener. As a structural point of reference, Mahler is to the totality of the music of this section what Beckett is to the text." [7]

The fourth movement can only be described as a "work in progress" because it has been performed in several versions.

Sinfonia is one of the most significant works of the late 1960s. It is a tremendous omnibus, carrying past and present, voices and instruments, and popular and sophisticated styles. Above all, it is "relevant." Music, for Berio, is a social art, a medium of communication between composer and audience. He is a man of deep convictions about the human condition and his all-embracing musical style is his statement.

Yannis Xenakis (born 1922)

Yannis Xenakis is a Greek composer who lives in Paris and the United States as a naturalized French citizen. He was educated as an engineer at the Institute of Technology in Athens, and during World War II he was a member of the Greek resistance. He was jailed several times and his life was often in danger. These experiences, along with more peaceful memories, have conditioned his compositions.

Having decided to abandon engineering and become a composer, Xenakis went to Paris in 1947. He studied with Honegger, Milhaud, and most important with Olivier Messiaen. In order to support himself he worked as an architect-engineer for Le Corbusier, the famous French architect, and designed, among other buildings, the Phillips Pavillion for the 1958 Brussels World's Fair, the building for which Varèse wrote his *Poème électronique.* Since then, Xenakis has continued to be both architect and composer. In 1967 he accepted an appointment as Professor of Mathematical and Automated Music at the University of Indiana, where he spends part of every year.

Early in his career, Xenakis wrote a few pieces of electronic music, but since then he has written primarily for conventional instruments. The sounds he favors, however, are not conventional. He employs a tremendous variety of string effects—harmonics, pizzicatos, glissandos—and the other instruments are frequently called upon to play in unusual ranges. The resultant texture is always extremely complex. The composer organizes his scores not by serial methods, but by following what he calls "stochastic" laws, which have to do with probability. In some of his pieces he has used a computer to define all the sounds, not only their pitches, but their moment of occurrence, class of timbre, duration, and dynamic. He then transcribes the computed result to conventional notation.

Xenakis has attempted to explain the workings of the abstruse formulas that condition his compositions but they are so complex that only mathematicians understand them. More helpful in the understanding of his music are the biographical clues he has given. "In my music there is all the agony of my youth, of the Resistance, and the aesthetic problems they posed with the huge street demonstrations, or even more the occasional mysterious deathly sounds of those cold nights of December 1944 in Athens. From this was born my conception of the massing of sound events, and therefore, of stochastic music." At another time he wrote, "As a boy in Greece I used to go camping, and I remember hearing the locusts at night—thousands of disconnected sounds coming from all directions."

Pithoprakta (1956), meaning "actions of probabilities," is one of his most characteristic pieces. It is written for forty-six strings (usually divisi), two trombones, one xylophone, and one woodblock. The opening section consists of soft, unpitched knocks, made by the string players hitting their instruments with their knuckles and bows. The pattern is too complex to analyze; it sounds like summer-night crickets, or rain and hail on a roof. This is followed by a section consisting of fragmentary string pitches, bowed and pizzicato, which in turn is succeeded by a section in which all the instruments play glissandos. *Pithoprakta* is striking in its new sounds, all made on conventional instruments.

Other important pieces by Xenakis are *Achorripsis* (1957) (*Jets of Sound*), and *Eonta* (1964), for piano and five brass instruments. In *Terretiktorh* (1966), for large orchestra, the members of the orchestra are seated individually throughout the audience. Besides their instruments, each of the players has several noisemakers, such as maracas and siren whistles. The sounds come from all over the room; the effect has been described as "a shower of hail or even a murmuring of pine forests."

In each of his pieces, Xenakis has created a new sound world. He has proven that the sounds of the familiar instruments have not been exhausted and that there are still innumerable possibilities.

Witold Lutoslawski (born 1913) and Krzysztof Penderecki (born 1933)

One of the unexpected events of the postwar musical world was the emergence of a vigorous and adventurous group of Polish composers, because music in the Iron Curtain countries was traditionally ultraconservative. After the

Stalinist regime was overthrown in 1956, however, the succeeding Polish government encouraged free expression in the arts and, once the lid was off, there was a great deal of healthy experimental activity in the Polish theater, films, painting, and music. The Warsaw Fall Festivals of Contemporary Music, founded in 1956, became important international cultural events. During the first years, music from all of Europe was played, but soon it became the showplace for the exciting music being written by young and hitherto unknown Polish composers.

The first major composer to emerge was Witold Lutoslawski (1913). His earliest works, *Symphonic Variations on a Theme by Paganini* (1938) for two pianos, and a Symphony, show the influence of Stravinsky. His *Concerto for Orchestra* (1954) is closer to Bartók, an influence he acknowledged in *Trauermusik* (1958), written in memory of the Hungarian composer. In this piece he used a modified twelve-tone technique, showing his awareness of Schoenberg, but this was not to be a permanent influence. "My music," he said, "has no direct relationship to the traditions of the Viennese school. I am much more strongly tied to Debussy, Stravinsky, Bartók, and Varèse."

In his later compositions, *Venetian Games* (1961), *Three Poems by Henri Michaux* (1963), and a Second Symphony (1969), he uses controlled aleatoric effects, leaving the individual orchestral members free to choose their own notes and rhythms in some passages. In the *Poems*, written for a choir of twenty individual parts and twenty-three instruments, he asks the singers to speak, whisper, moan, and shout, as well as sing, thus exploiting some of the new vocal sounds that Stockhausen, Berio, and others were using at this time.

Lutoslawski's use of such devices is always for expressive purposes. Kurt Stone, writing in the *Musical Quarterly*, has said, "No matter how experimental his latest works may be, his musical vitality, combined with the discipline of traditional craftsmanship, lends even to these probing, advanced works a commanding dignity, seriousness, and unerring power of communication found only rarely among today's composers." [8]

Krzysztof Penderecki (1933) is without question the most prominent of the younger Polish composers. A large percentage of his numerous compositions has been recorded, and performances of his works are events of wide interest, even for general audiences.

Penderecki came into prominence in 1959 when he submitted three compositions under different pseudonyms to a competition organized by the Polish Composers' Union. To everyone's surprise, each piece received one of the first three prizes; one of them, *Strophes*, was performed at the 1959 Warsaw Festival and brought early recognition to the young composer.

Penderecki was born in Debica, a provincial town in southern Poland. During World War II, when he was still a child, he witnessed some of the worst of the Nazi atrocities against Poland's Jewish population. "The problem of that great Apocalypse (Auschwitz), that great war crime, has undoubtedly been in my subconscious mind since the war, when, as a child, I saw the destruction of the ghetto in my small native town of Debica." This traumatic experience had an undeniable influence on many of his later compositions.

Penderecki started his musical studies early and graduated from the Cracow Conservatory in 1958. He was discovered soon afterward, and since then he has composed a large number of works for orchestra, choir, and an opera, *The Devils of Loudun.* In each work he has exploited new sounds and performing techniques, proving himself to be one of the most imaginative and expressive composers of this generation.

Each of the early prize-winning works showed traits that were to mark subsequent works. *Strophen* shows the influence of Webernian athematicism. *Emanations* is written for two string orchestras tuned a quarter tone apart. The *Psalms of David* (1958) for *a cappella* choir is in four parts. Two of the parts utilize serial techniques with very conjunct rows, suggesting dodecaphonic Gregorian melodies. Another part is for double chorus; one speaks while the other sings, and the last shows a strong Stravinskian influence in its additive rhythms and jazzy ostinatos. These are the works of a talented young composer, showing his assimilation of the principal styles of earlier twentieth-century music.

In *Threnody for the Victims of Hiroshima* (1961), he achieved a highly original style. Written for fifty-two strings and lasting eight-and-a-half minutes, it does not contain a single "normal" sound. Most of the pages of the score are filled with graphs and symbols invented by the composer to convey his wishes. The opening page, shown in Example 171, for instance, calls for the strings, divided into ten groups, to play "the highest note possible" on their instruments. The entrances are staggered, played *fortissimo,* and held for fifteen seconds. The sound is a shrill, frightening whistle. Next, the large wavy line directs the players to play "with a very slow vibrato, with a quarter-tone difference produced by sliding the fingers," causing sounds that remind one of jet engines. The small wavy lines indicate "molto vibrato," another sound effect. In the course of the piece the players are directed to raise or lower written notes by a quarter or three quarters of a tone, to play between the bridge and tailpiece, to tap the body of the instrument with fingers or bows, and to play with a wide variety of timbral effects. There are frequent huge clusters of massed half-steps, and glissandos of such clusters, a sound that also resembles airplane takeoffs. There is no meter. At the bottom of each page of the score there is a wide line with a designation in seconds indicating how long the section should be played. The conductor indicates the beginning of new time blocks, but there are no beats or subdivisions of them.

Example 172 is the last page of the score. The large black bands represent clusters, the exact notes being indicated in the string players' parts.

EXAMPLE 171*

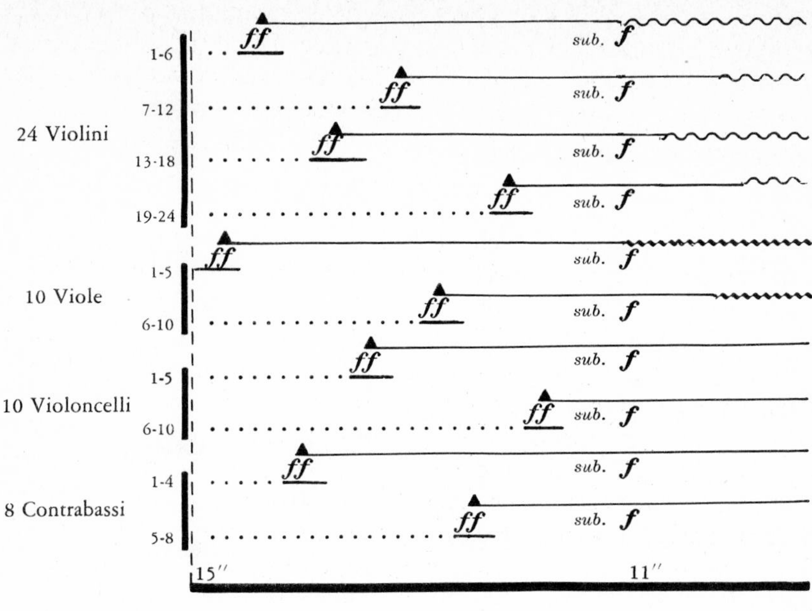

24 Violini
1-6
7-12
13-18
19-24
10 Viole
1-5
6-10
10 Violoncelli
1-5
6-10
8 Contrabassi
1-4
5-8
ff
sub. f
15″
11″

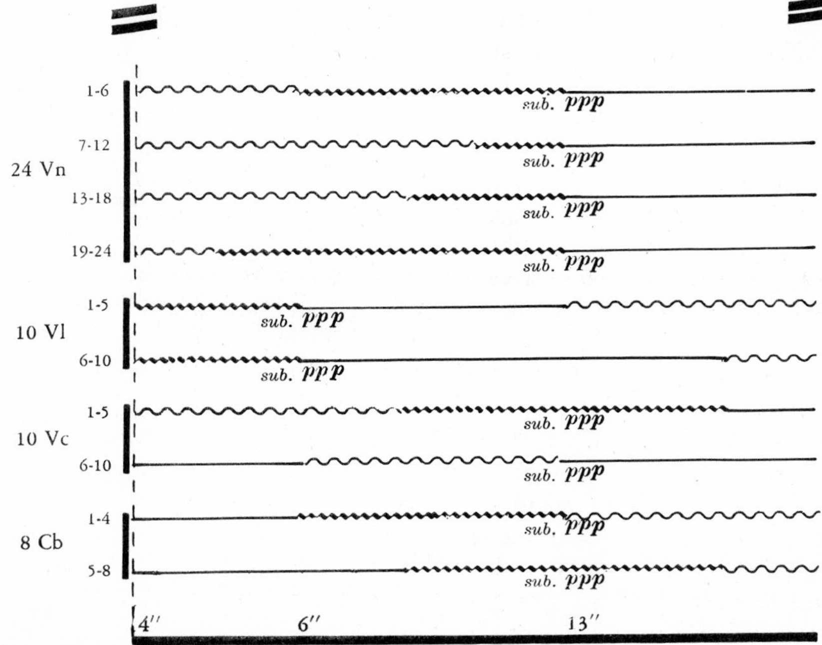

24 Vn
1-6
7-12
13-18
19-24
10 Vl
1-5
6-10
10 Vc
1-5
6-10
8 Cb
1-4
5-8
sub. ppp
4″
6″
13″

EXAMPLE 172*

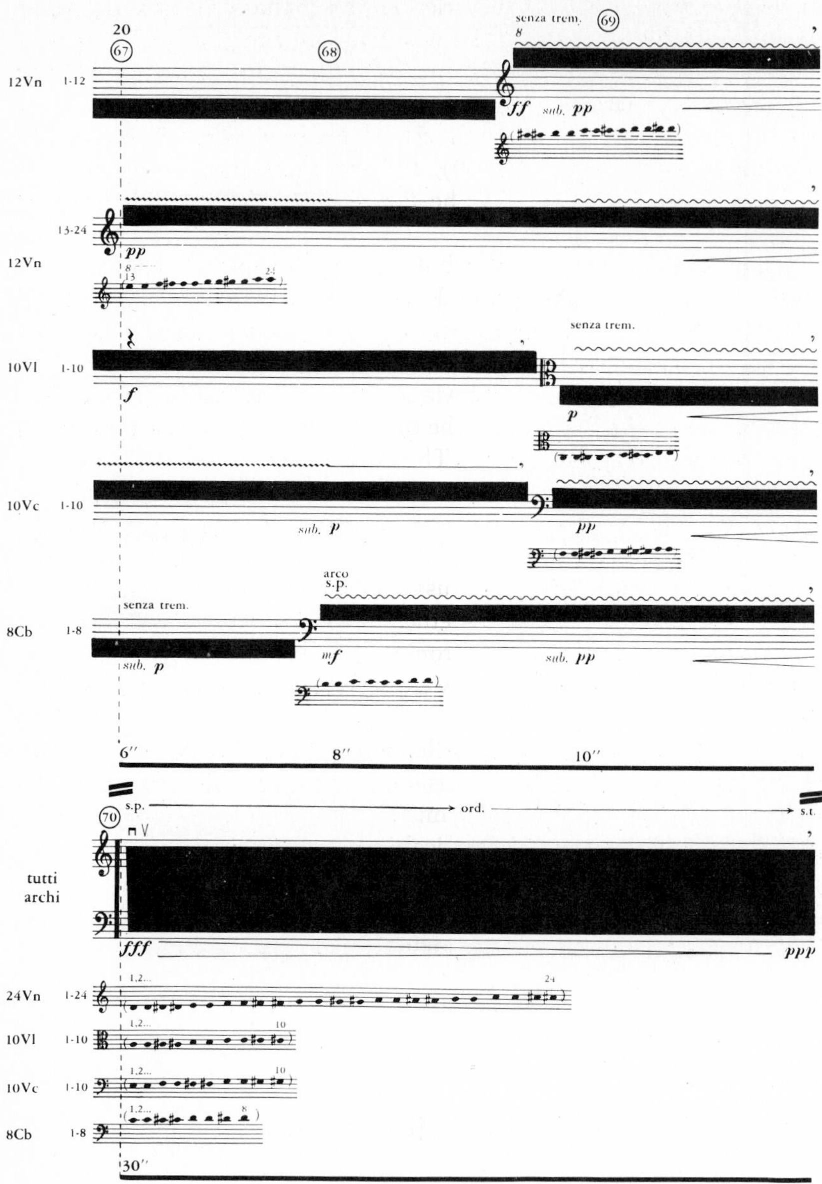
20
67
68
senza trem.
69
12Vn 1-12
ff sub. pp
13-24
12Vn
pp
10Vl 1-10
f
senza trem.
p
10Vc 1-10
sub. p
pp
arco
s.p.
senza trem.
8Cb 1-8
sub. p
mf
sub. pp
6″
8″
10″
s.p.
ord.
s.t.
70
tutti
archi
fff
ppp
24Vn 1-24
10Vl 1-10
10Vc 1-10
8Cb 1-8
30″

Hiroshima is a piece for conventional instruments but it could not have been written if the composer had not experienced the sounds of electronic music. The whole concept of the timbres and the way they are superimposed is that of electronic music. The score, in fact, resembles that of Stockhausen's *Studien* (Example 170) more than it does a conventional score.

Other instrumental pieces of Penderecki that exploit new and expressive instrumental sounds are *Anaklasis* (1960), *Polymorphia* (1961), *Fluorescences* (1961), *De natura sonoris* (1966), and the *Capriccio* for violin and orchestra (1968).

He has also made important contributions to contemporary choral literature, in works that call for new vocal sounds as exacting as those he draws from the orchestra. The important choral works are: *Stabat Mater* (1963), for three *a cappella* choirs, the *St. Luke Passion* (1966), a *Dies Irae* (1967) to the memory of the victims of Auschwitz, and a Slavic Mass (1969). The *Passion* is the best-known of these choral works. It follows the baroque pattern and has a narrator, as well as a singer personifying Christ. The chorus acts as commentator and participant when it sings the part of the mob. In the work great use is made of a twelve-tone row that consists largely of seconds and thirds, including the familiar "Bach" motive (B-flat, A, C, B). Both orchestra and choir make use of clusters and glissandos, and the choir hisses, shouts, laughs, whispers, and chants. The *St. Luke Passion* brings together a wide variety of styles; it is a sincere amalgamation of tonal resources from the Gregorian chant to the latest experimental sounds. The result is highly successful; the work has been performed widely.

Unlike some composers of the so-called *avant-garde,* Penderecki does not believe that the fundamental nature of music has changed. He has said, "The general principle at the root of a work's musical style, the logic and economy of development, and the integrity of a musical experience embodied in the notes the composer is setting down on paper, never changes. The idea of good music means today exactly what it meant always. Music should speak for itself, going straight to the heart and mind of the listener." [9]

Alberto Ginastera (born 1916)

Alberto Ginastera is South America's most prominent mid-century composer. He is an eclectic who has successfully absorbed many of the stylistic innovations of his time, giving them a personal imprint in highly successful compositions.

He was born in Buenos Aires to a Spanish-Italian family. He received his musical training at the National Conservatory, and by the time he graduated in 1938, he was already known to be a gifted composer. A Guggenheim Fellowship brought him to New York in 1945, and since then many of his commissions and first performances have taken place in the United States. He has been active as a teacher and administrator, and heads the Latin American Center for Advanced Musical Studies, an international graduate school of composition in Buenos Aires.

Ginastera's first compositions had a strong folk music flavor, not unlike the music of Villa-Lobos or Carlos Chávez. Two early ballets, *Panambi* (1937) and *Estancia* (1941), as well as some piano music and songs, represent this phase. By 1950 he was no longer a conscious folklorist, although he continued to use rhythmic patterns associated with the folk and popular music of his country. His Piano Sonata (1952) is an example of the next stage in his development. Stravinsky and Copland can be heard in the stark first movement, Bartók in the eerie scherzo, and Prokofiev in the noisy toccata last movement.

The *Cantata para America Magica* (1960) for soprano, fifty-three percussion instruments, and two pianos is one of his most striking and original compositions. In this setting of four ancient South American Indian poems, the soprano sings wide-ranging melodies while piano, celesta, xylophone, and percussion instruments of all kinds provide an exciting accompaniment. It is sophisticated and primitive-sounding at the same time.

Three full-scale operas, *Don Rodrigo* (1964), *Bomarzo* (1967), and *Beatrix Cenci* (1970), are important later compositions. The first has an elaborate structure, similar in plan to the one Berg used in *Wozzeck*. Each act is divided into scenes, each one of which has its own absolute form. *Bomarzo*, written to a wildly extravagant libretto concerning a highly neurotic Italian nobleman (an antihero), employs serial structures, tone clusters, special effects, and all varieties of speech, *Sprechstimme*, recitative, and singing. It is a thoroughly contemporary work bringing together many of the innovative sounds and manners of its time.

Ginastera is a good example of the composer as settler rather than explorer.

Hans Werner Henze (born 1926)

Hans Werner Henze is a German composer who also can be considered more of a settler than explorer. He was exposed to all of the influences that all of his European contemporaries experienced, but he achieved a highly personal, if somewhat eclectic, style.

As a child he studied at the State School of Music in Brunswick. He was drafted in 1944 but fortunately was soon captured and made a prisoner of war by the British. As soon as he was released, he became a coach and accompanist at the opera house in Bielefeld, a small German city, and studied composition with Wolfgang Fortner, a progressive German composer. Fortner introduced him to the music of Stravinsky, Hindemith, and Bartók, and then took him to the Darmstadt Summer School, where the young composer became acquainted with the music of Schoenberg and Webern. His response to serial music was so enthusiastic that he went to Paris in 1948 to study with René Leibowitz.

All of these formative influences can be heard in his early compositions. These include his first three symphonies, *Boulevard Solitude* (1951), an opera based on an updated version of the Manon story, as well as a piano and a violin concerto.

In 1953 Henze left Germany to live in Italy, a turning point in his life and music. He left behind the avant-garde Darmstadt "establishment" and found his own style. This has been expressed primarily in operas: *King Stag* (1952–1955), *Der Prinz von Homburg* (1958), *Elegy for Young Lovers* (1959–1961), *The Young Lord* (1964), and *The Bassarids* (1965). All of these operas have

Hans Werner Henze
Broadcast Music Inc. (B.M.I.) Archives

been successfully produced in Germany and elsewhere, making him and Britten the most successful opera composers of their time.

Any composer who writes successful operas has to have a sense of theater, of poetry, and the conviction that music is above all an expressive art. In a *New York Times* interview Henze said, "Music can carry this message of a human condition: of love, for example, or forgiveness. I am aware that it is a little dangerous to talk like this. Some regard it as foolish and old-fashioned, but I believe it wholeheartedly."

Henze is a prolific composer. Besides the operas he has written six symphonies, several ballets, concertos, choral and chamber works. In the late 1960s his crystallizing political views strongly influenced his music. He spent considerable time in Cuba and his subsequent compositions are frankly propagandistic. An oratorio, the *Raft of the Frigate Medusa* (1968), is dedicated to Che Guevara. Its first performance in Hamburg turned into a political demonstration. His *Essay on Pigs* (1969) is a theater piece for reciter-singer using a wide variety of musical resources, including tape and a jazz orchestra. Another politically oriented work is *El Cimmarón* (*The Runaway Slave*) (1970). For baritone and a small group of instruments, it lasts for an hour and a half and employs a great diversity of musical styles.

Peter Maxwell Davies (born 1934) and Harrison Birtwistle (born 1934)

Peter Maxwell Davies is one of the most interesting English composers of his generation. Born in 1934 in Manchester, he studied there until 1957 when a scholarship took him to Rome to work with Goffredo Petrassi. In 1962 another scholarship took him to Princeton University. Since then he has devoted himself to composition and the direction of a small group of instrumentalists called the Pierrot Players (they frequently performed *Pierrot Lunaire*) and later another group called the Fires of London. One of the high points of his career to date was the production of his full-scale opera *Taverner* at Covent Garden in 1972. Since then many of his compositions are "theater pieces" calling for a singer or dancer as well as costumes and a stage setting.

In his compositions Davies frequently incorporates previously written music chosen from the most diverse sources. For example, his *Antichrist* is based on a thirteenth-century motet, while his *L'Homme Armé* starts with a fifteenth-century version of the mass. Purcell, Taverner, 1920s jazz, and Victorian ballads are freely quoted or parodied. In *St. Thomas' Wake*, in the words of the composer, "I had worked with three levels of musical experience—that of the original sixteenth-century pavanne played on the harp; the level of the foxtrots derived from this, played by a foxtrot band, and the level of my 'real' music, also derived from the pavanne, played by the symphony orchestra. These three levels interacted on each other." In another context he said, "I became interested in this sort of musical ambiguity, where, because the music contains disparate, opposed elements, the total effect of these elements can be interpreted by the listener on different levels, according to his means." [10]

His *Vesali Icones* (1969) is a good example of this multilevel concept. The title refers to the anatomical drawings found in a book by Andreas Vesalius, the sixteenth-century Flemish anatomist. These drawings are mimed by a male dancer, who is accompanied by a solo cellist, and an ensemble consisting of viola, basset clarinet, flute, piano, and percussion. Another level of "meaning" is added by associating the fourteen Stations of the Cross with the gestures of the drawings. The music, based on Gregorian chant, foxtrots of the twenties, and a great diversity of other styles, at times reflects the pathos of Christ's suffering, while at others it is wildly satirical, as in the final dance, which represents the Resurrection, and is accompanied by banal, old-fashioned jazz tunes.

Another highly original work is *Eight Songs for a Mad King* for male singer and a small group of instrumentalists. The protagonist is the pathetic George III, who after his mental derangement was incarcerated and lived many

Peter Maxwell Davies, 1976
Courtesy of Boosey and Hawkes

years of semimadness. The singer portrays the king, and expresses his many moods—of anger, of pleading, of trying to teach his caged birds how to sing. In performance, the instrumentalists sit in cages dispersed around the stage, while the king sings to them, in moans, shouts, squeals, and falsetto. In spite of its strangeness, it is a very moving piece.

Later works include *Runes from a House of the Dead* (1973), a set of four songs preceded and separated by orchestral interludes, described as being in "neo-Webern" texture, a suite arranged from incidental music to *The Devils*, a Ken Russell film, and *Miss Donnithorne's Maggott* (1973), another theater piece, this one about a madwoman.

Another English composer associated with Davies is Harrison Birtwistle (1934) because his early musical training was also received in Manchester. He is best known for two unusual operas, *Punch and Judy* (1968) and *Down by the Greenwood Side* (1969). Both are based on traditional English folk theater but they are violent in action and highly stylized. In his instrumental music, such as *Chorales for Orchestra* (1963) and *Nomos* for orchestra without violins (1968), elaborate compositional devices are used.

Elliott Carter (born 1908)

By general agreement Elliott Carter is the most distinguished American composer of the mid-seventies. He has received most of the prestigious foundation prizes and fellowships and the first performances of his compositions have become newsworthy events reviewed in all the music journals and even in the news magazines. This recognition has been achieved in spite of the extreme difficulty of his music, making it a genuine challenge for performers as well as listeners. Carter's sincerity, his courage in developing his own style, and his refusal to follow fashionable "trends" have gained him the highest respect.

Although somewhat older than the other composers presented in this chapter, his music warrants discussion here rather than in earlier sections of the book because it did not come into prominence until the 1950s.

Carter is a native New Yorker who graduated from Harvard with an A.B. in English and an M.A. in Music. After this, he studied with Nadia Boulanger in Paris for several years and then returned to New York. A private income made it possible for him to devote himself exclusively to composition, although he has accepted teaching appointments from time to time. At present he is on the faculty of the Juilliard School. His mature compositions are:

Elliott Carter
Broadcast Music Inc. (B.M.I.) Archives

Piano Sonata (1946)
Sonata for Violoncello and Piano (1948)
Three String Quartets (1951, 1959, 1971)
Sonata for Flute, Oboe, Cello, and Harpsichord (1952)
Variations for Orchestra (1951)
Double Concerto for Harpsichord and Piano with Two Chamber Orchestras (1961)
Piano Concerto (1965)
Concerto for Orchestra (1969)
Quintet for Brass Instruments (1974)
Duo for Violin and Piano (1975)
A Mirror on Which to Dwell (1975) for Soprano and Nine Instruments

The outstanding characteristic of these pieces is the complexity of their predominantly polyphonic texture. Individual instruments are strikingly independent and share neither themes nor rhythms. "I regard my scores as scenarios, auditory scenarios for performers to act out with their instruments, dramatizing the players as individuals and as participants in the ensemble," he has stated. In the Second Quartet "each instrument is like a character in an opera made up primarily of quartets." The individual components of his compositions are "typecast" and consistent. Thus in the Piano Concerto, there is a "dramatic idea of a conflict between the pianist, whose part emphasizes sensitivity, and the orchestra, which progressively dissociates itself from the piano part, becoming increasingly insensitive, unvaried, and brutal—in terms of which all the specific local events and details were subsequently determined." [11]

In some of the later pieces this independence is emphasized spatially as well. In the Duo for Violin and Piano the two performers are placed at opposite ends of the platform, each playing his own music. In the Third Quartet the composer recommends that the two duos—violin and cello and the violin and viola, each duo having its own characteristic music—should perform as separated from each other as is conveniently possible, so that the listener can not only perceive them as two separate sound sources, but also be aware of the combinations they form with each other." [12] Example 173, the opening page of the Quartet, shows the contrasting material played by the two duos. Duo I plays major sevenths, Furioso (quasi rubato sempre) at ♩. = 70, in $\frac{12}{8}$ meter, while Duo II plays perfect fifths, Maestoso (giusto sempre) at ♩ = 105 in $\frac{6}{4}$ meter. The whole quartet consists of such divergencies, resulting in a most complex texture.

Along with these textural complexities there are also rhythmic ones. Not only does each instrument have its own rhythmic patterns, but the basic pulse changes constantly through a process known as *metrical modulation*. Here is an example from the First Quartet:

In this example, the sixteenth notes do not change in speed. Therefore in the second measure, where there are seven sixteenths to the unit rather than four, the pulse almost doubles in length. As a result, in the last measure quarter notes take on the new, slower value, and the tempo has "changed smoothly and accurately from one absolute metronomic speed to another by lengthening the value of the basic note unit."

Unlike many of his younger contemporaries, Carter carefully notates his intricate rhythms, and as a result his scores are dotted with metronome marks and meter signatures.

EXAMPLE 173*

STRING QUARTET No.3

Elliott Carter
(1971)

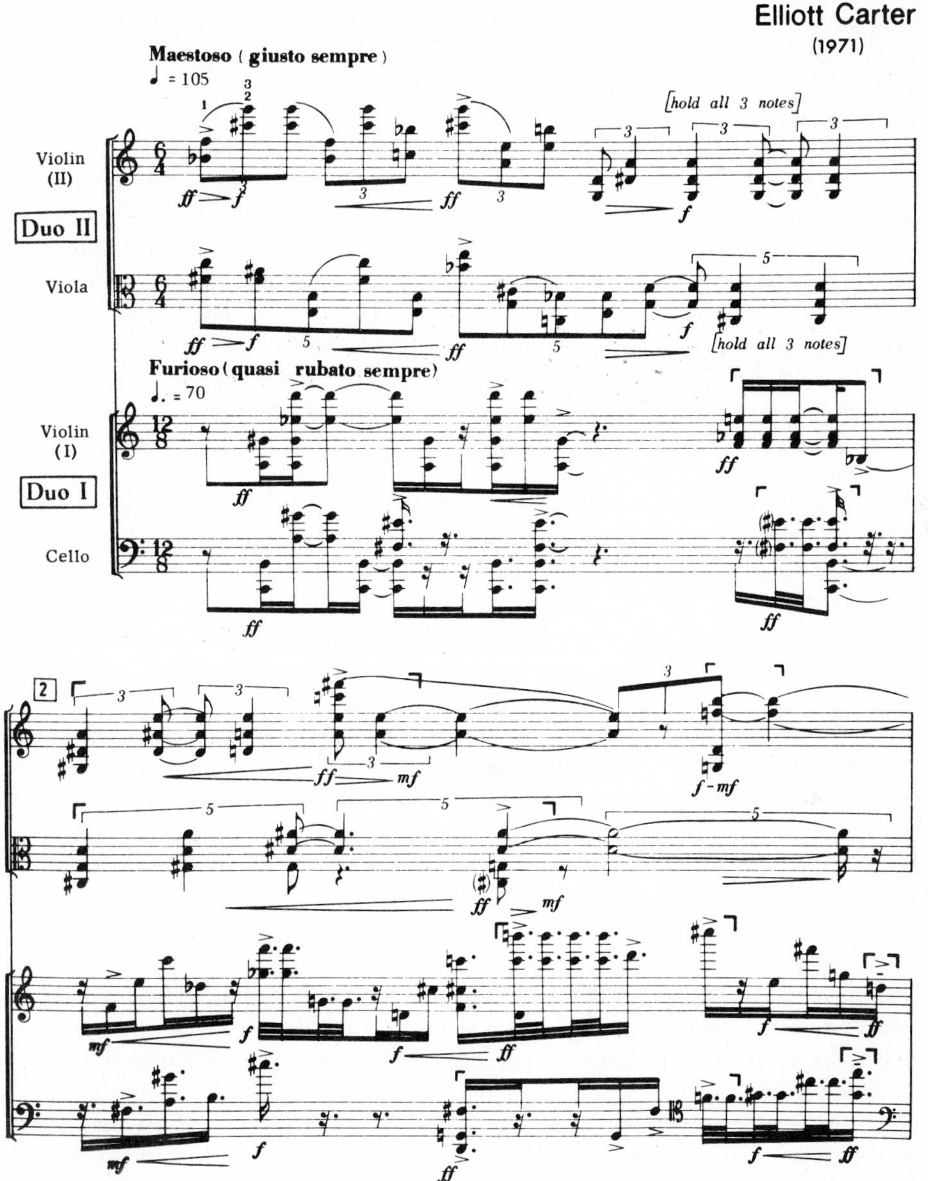

Elliott Carter: String Quartet No. 3.
* © Copyright 1973 by Associated Music Publishers, Inc. Used by permission.

Here is the notation of an accelerando of subsequent measures from the Second Quartet†:

♩ = 90 | ♩ = 127 | 𝅗𝅥. = ♩. = 60 | ♩. = 67 | ♩. = 76 | ♩. = 90 | ♩. = 107 | ♩. = 127 | ♩. = 151 | etc.

Meter in the usual sense does not exist in Carter's music any more than major-minor tonality. How then, does he organize his compositions?

Each of the mature works is organized through the use of select groups of notes used both melodically and harmonically. The basic material of the Piano Concerto is formed of twelve different groups of triads—six assigned to the soloist, six to the orchestra. Each of the twelve triads is related to one or more speeds and characters. The Third String Quartet is based on four-note chords, while the Concerto for Orchestra is based on five seven-note chords.

Carter's music, then, is not serial but it is organized in a way that somewhat resembles the processes found in the atonal works of Schoenberg, Berg, and Webern in their pre-twelve–tone music of 1908–1911 in which there was also a unity between melodic and harmonic structures.

Carter not only gives the various components of his compositions their own material, but he usually presents all of the strands together, resulting in an almost Ivesian multilayered simultaneity. The composer's description of his Concerto for Orchestra illustrates his practice. The piece is in four continuous movements each with its own character and featured instruments, but all are presented simultaneously, with now this, and now that component foremost.

The first movement "features the cello section (sometimes divided into as many as seven different soloists, as are all the strings), piano, harp, marimba, xylophone, and wooden percussion. It centers around the lower middle register and is in a moderately fast speed throughout." The second movement "features high strings, high winds, and metallic percussion and starts very fast and lightly, and bit by bit becomes slower." The third movement "features the double basses, tuba, horn, timpani, and other low-pitched instruments and keeps to its recitativelike character." The fourth movement "features violas, oboes, trumpets, snare drum, and other medium-high instruments and starts with slow fragments that become faster as the work progresses, until it expands into a rapid conclusion. As with all my works, the primary intention is expressive and the entire musical vocabulary, instrumentation, and form have been to further this." [13]

The problem for the listener is that material from more than one movement is presented simultaneously so that it is extremely difficult to distinguish one from the other. A further difficulty arises from Carter's practice of not using themes and their development but instead "groupings of sound material out of which textures, linear patterns, and figurations are invented." Each type of music has its own identifying sound and expression, usually combining instrumental color with some "behavioral pattern that relies on speed, rhythm, and musical intervals. There is no repetition, but a constant invention of new things —some closely related to each other, others remotely." [14]

Like "difficult" books and poems that call for work and concentration, Carter's music calls for repeated hearings. "I write for records," he once said. "My last three pieces run about twenty-five minutes—the length of an LP side. They should be so rich that they can be played many times." He could have said, "They *must* be played many times."

Milton Babbitt (born 1916)

Milton Babbitt's contribution to mid-century American music is very different from Carter's. Educated as a mathematician as well as a musician, his approach has always been analytical and experimental rather than expressive.

Milton Babbitt
Broadcast Music Inc. (B.M.I.) Archives

This problem-solving approach is seen as early as 1948, when he wrote some totally-controlled pieces, anticipating Messiaen's moves in this direction. His analyses and insights into Schoenberg's dodecaphonic music revealed structural principles and potentialities unnoticed before. He created a vocabulary for describing twelve-tone music that is widely used.

In 1958 Babbitt published an article, "Who Cares if You Listen?" in which he argued that composers should have the same intellectual freedom that abstract scientists, mathematicians, and philosophers enjoy. Abstract thinkers such as these create for a very small audience of experts; no one but a specialist can understand their thoughts. Babbitt believes that a composer should not be concerned if he does not reach a wide audience, but should accept his isolation as a fact of modern life.

In 1948 Babbitt started teaching at Princeton University and shortly thereafter he became interested in the production of sound through the use of synthesizers. He helped to design the huge Mark II synthesizer installed at the Princeton-Columbia Electronic Music Center in New York, and since then has been one of the leaders of this kind of music in the United States. He has not composed a great deal, his best-known pieces being *Vision and Prayer* (1961), *Philomel* (1963) for soprano, recorded soprano, and synthesized sound, and *Relata I* and *II* (1968) for orchestra. As a professor at Princeton he has been a highly influential teacher, and his pupils form a so-called "Princeton School."

George Crumb (born 1929)

Although his music is entirely different from Carter's or Babbitt's, George Crumb also achieved wide acclaim in the 1970s. Interested in music since childhood, he earned an M.M. from the University of Illinois and later a D.M.A. from the University of Michigan where he was a student of Ross Lee Finney. After teaching at the University of Colorado for several years he went to the University of Pennsylvania as professor of composition.

This essentially academic career might suggest an academic composer. Nothing could be further from the truth. In fact, Crumb is one of the most imaginative and inventive composers of his generation.

The titles of some of his compositions show his interest in expressing poetic ideas. Some of them are: *Eleven Echoes of Autumn* (1965), *Echoes of Time and the River* (Pulitzer Prize, 1968), *Songs, Drones and Refrains of Death* (1968), *Night of the Four Moons* (1969), *Voice of the Whale* (1969), and *Ancient Voices of Children* (1970). Most of these pieces have literary connections, the chief being the poetry of Federico García Lorca.

Crumb does not write for the usual combinations of instruments. Each of his pieces has its own sound, many of them his own discoveries. Some of

George Crumb
Courtesy of C. F. Peters Corp.

his characteristic sounds are: piano strings vibrating sympathetically by singing into or playing instruments close to them, by rubbing them with the fingers or various objects, striking them with mallets, or stopping them to produce harmonics; the "windy" sound produced by blowing through wind instruments without making tones; the tinkle of small percussion instruments such as antique cymbals or a gong immersed in a pail of water. All of these sounds are soft and discreet, and indeed much of Crumb's music is extremely soft.

Echoes of Time and the River is written for a conventional orchestra with the addition of two pianos, mandolin, and a huge percussion section including vibraphones, xylophone, bamboo wind-chimes, Indian temple bells, and thirty-five pairs of antique cymbals. In addition, the orchestra members whisper or shout cryptic words from time to time and forty of them whistle a plaintive, notated melody at the end. Another unusual feature are the "processions" that various members of the orchestra make when they march across the stage while playing. According to Crumb, the processions are "conceived as both visual and sonic events."

There are Ivesian quotations from Sunday school hymns, quarter-tone "bending," and aleatoric passages—a unique combination that expresses mysterious, wistful, tender feelings.

Ancient Voices of Children, probably the best known of Crumb's compositions, is written for soprano, boy soprano, oboe, mandolin, musical saw, harp, electric piano, toy piano, and three percussionists playing a wide variety of unusual instruments. The words are by Lorca.

In this piece the singer is asked to vocalize on changing vowel sounds, to flutter-tongue, make "bright nasal sounds," whisper, shout, sing through a megaphone, and sing onto the strings of a grand piano to make them vibrate sympathetically. Obviously, Crumb is writing for an unusual singer, just as Schoenberg did in *Pierrot Lunaire*.

The first song, "The little boy was looking for his voice," is a bravura cadenza for the singer with minimal accompaniment by the harp, electric piano, and "cricket sounds" whispered by the percussionists. An instrumental interlude follows, featuring an oriental-sounding melismatic oboe solo with percussion accompaniment including clicks made by hitting Tibetan prayer stones together. The oboe and mandolin "bend" their tones, i.e. play quarter tones.

In the second song, "I have lost myself in the sea," the singer whispers the words through a speaking tube. The most striking sound is that of the musical saw, whining its notated melodies to the accompaniment of sounds produced by moving a chisel along a piano string.

The third song, "From where do you come, my love, my child?" starts with another vocal cadenza followed by an exciting spoken dialogue between the soloist and the offstage boy soprano. While this ensues there is a strong bolero rhythm in the drums, the only obvious rhythmic passage in the work, forming the dynamic climax of the piece.

The soloist sings in a normal, expressive manner in the next song, "Each afternoon in Granada." The unique sound is the constant soft major-third trill played on the marimbas, the major chord sung by the percussionists, and the toy piano tinkling "Bist du bei mir," from the *Notebook of Anna Magdalen Bach*—a surrealist bringing together of incongruous elements that creates a dreamlike, musty-attic feeling.

A short instrumental piece follows, featuring the mandolin played with a paper-clip plectrum while the strings are stopped with a glass rod. The unique sound of the last song, "My heart of silk is filled with lights," comes from tubular bells, sleigh bells, and vibraphone. The oboe quotes a poignant melody from Mahler's *Das Lied von der Erde*. The boy soprano, heretofore unseen, slowly walks onstage and the two sing into the piano strings.

Ancient Voices is a work of exquisite sound and deep expressiveness. The composer has said of the mixtures of styles and references, "In composing *Ancient Voices of Children* I was conscious of an urge to fuse various unrelated stylistic elements. I was intrigued with the idea of juxtaposing the seemingly incongruous—a suggestion of Flamenco with a Baroque quotation, or a reminiscence of Mahler with a breath of the Orient. It later occurred to me that both

EXAMPLE 174*

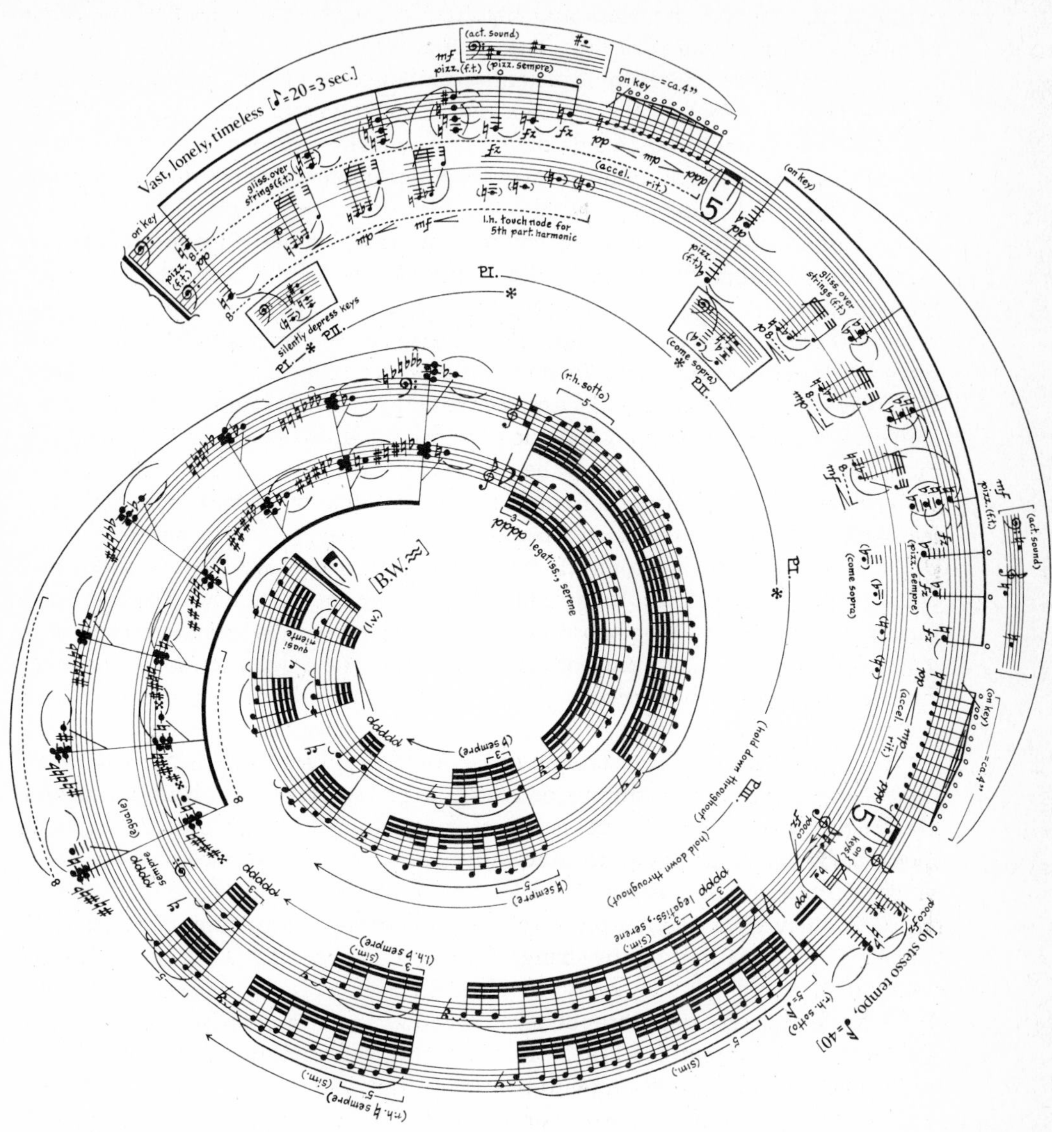

* No. 12, "Spiral Galaxy," from *Makrokosmos*, Vol. I by George Crumb. Copyright © 1974 by C. F. Peters Corporation, 373 Park Avenue South, New York, N.Y. 10016. Reprint permission granted by the publisher.

Bach and Mahler drew upon many disparate sources in their own music without sacrificing stylistic purity." [15]

Crumb's next compositions were for the piano. They are *Makrokosmos*, Vol. I (1972) and Vol. II (1973), each containing twelve pieces, and *Music for a Summer Evening* (1974) for two pianos and percussion. Bartók and Debussy are the obvious models of these pieces, but Crumb outstrips them in creating new sounds. The pianist plays inside the piano as much as on the keys, and in addition he is asked to shout, whistle, or moan from time to time.

All of these sounds function to express the moods suggested by the titles of the individual pieces in *Makrokosmos*, some of which are "Primeval Sounds," "Crucifixus," "Night Spell," "Magic Circle of the Infinite," "Dream Images," and "Spiral Galaxy."

There are a few quotations from other composers' compositions. Chopin's *Fantasie impromptu* is alluded to in "Dream Images," the pianist whistles *Will There Be Any Stars in My Crown?* in "Night Spell," and snatches of Beethoven's *Hammerklavier* Sonata and a Bach fugue are heard in the two-piano piece.

There are still other extramusical associations, in that each of the pieces is associated with a different sign of the zodiac and every fourth piece is printed in the shape of its title-subject. Thus, "Crucifixus" is printed in the shape of a cross, "The Magic Circle of the Infinite" is printed as a circle, and the "Spiral Galaxy" as a spiral. Of course, this is pure "eye-music" suggesting some of the artifices of Renaissance music printing, and cannot be detected by the listener. Example 174 is the opening of "Spiral Galaxy," printed in a manner to suggest the concept.

In these pieces Crumb has revealed himself to be an unashamed romantic. His medium is evocative sound, and his principal areas of expression are nostalgia, the dream world, and the mysteries of the universe. "I have always considered music to be a very strange substance," he has said, "a substance endowed with magical properties. Music is tangible, almost palpable, and yet unreal, illusive. Music is analyzable only on the most mechanistic level; the important elements —the spiritual impulse, the psychological curve, the metaphysical implications— are understandable only in terms of the music itself. I feel intuitively that music must have been the primitive cell from which language, science, and religion originated."

George Rochberg (born 1918)

George Rochberg is another American composer who became well-known in the 1970s. Although his music is highly personal, his career has paralleled that of many others of his generation in that he has reflected the principal style tendencies of his time. He has recounted some of the steps. After student days at the Curtis Institute of Music he "entered the world of atonality and serialism and came to terms with the musical *esperanto* that Arnold Schoenberg had conceived . . . I was convinced of the historical inevitability of the twelve-tone language. I felt I was living at the very edge of the musical frontier, of history itself."

The composition that best exemplifies this stage of Rochberg's development is his Symphony No. 2 (1956). This is an out-and-out twelve-tone work in four connected movements, full of tension and pathos.

"Webern's personal style began to have its impact on my works about 1957 and the result was an even more concentrated and refined use of serialism." His *Serenata d'estate* for chamber orchestra is an example of this more restrained and gentle music.

Next came the discovery of Ives, and in his Second Quartet Rochberg employed different simultaneous tempos. "I suspect that my fascination with the possibilities Ives opened was one of the factors that led me to recognize the severe, binding limitations in serialism. By the beginning of the sixties I had become completely dissatisfied with its inherently narrow terms. I found the palette of constant chromaticism increasingly constricting, nor could I accept any longer the limited range of gestures that always seemed to channel the music into some form or other of expressionism. The overintense manner of serialism and its tendency to inhibit physical pulse and rhythm led me to question a style which made it virtually impossible to express serenity, tranquility, grace, wit, energy. It became necessary to move on."

Rochberg now entered an interesting phase in which he rediscovered the musical past and incorporated it into his compositions. His *Music for a Magic Theater* includes long stretches of Mozart's Divertimentos and Serenades, as well as borrowings from Mahler, Beethoven, and Varèse. Another piece, *Contra Mortem et Tempus* for violin, flute, clarinet, and piano (1965), contains excerpts from no less than seven different composers. The composer has explained his motivation in including lengthy quotations from other composers as "my obsession with the many-layered density of human experience and the contradictory nature of all unitary systems of composing contemporary music."

The Quartet No. 3 (1972) "comes at the end of almost twenty-five years of a ceaseless search for the most potent and effective way to translate my musical energies into the clearest and most direct patterns of feelings and thought." In this tonal work there is an interesting mixture of personal style with music written in the style of other composers, but not through quotations. After a stormy opening in which both tonal and atonal elements are introduced, a variation movement follows that is unmistakably in late-Beethoven style. It uses the harmonic, melodic, and textural devices of Beethoven and suggests the sublime calm of the variation movements of the Quartet, Opus 131, or the Piano Sonatas,

Opus 109 and Opus 111. A later movement is thoroughly in the manner of Mahler, a folksy, charming Austrian dance. The quartet is an excellent example of the composer's desire to "abandon the notion of 'originality' in which the personal style of the artist and his ego are the supreme values." [16]

Rochberg's Violin Concerto, first performed in 1975, continues in this direction, combining style elements of baroque and late romantic music with atonality.

Charles Wuorinen (born 1938)

Wuorinen is both a product and an integral part of the New York music world. Growing up in New York City and attending Columbia University, where he studied with Vladimir Ussachevsky, Otto Luening, and Jack Beeson, he experienced all of the diverse musical activities of the fifties and sixties at first hand. He is a prolific composer whose music is performed and frequently recorded, and like Carter he has won practically all of the available prizes and honors. He performs frequently as a pianist and as a member of the Group for Contemporary Music that he cofounded, and he writes for the music journals. He is the typical successful composer of his generation.

His compositions reflect the musical interests of his time and place. He has written electronic music, using both the synthesizer and computer, the best-known piece being *Time's Encomium,* which won a Pulitzer Prize in 1970. Electronic sounds with orchestra are used in his Concerto for Amplified Violin (1971) and the Concerto for Amplified Piano (1973). Percussion music is also important. *Ringing Changes* (1970) is for a large percussion ensemble, including piano four-hands, vibraphone, chimes, and timpani. This piece is organized on a row of durations that determine individual sounds as well as the length of whole sections. Other percussion pieces are *Janissary Music* (1966) for twenty-six percussion instruments and one player, and *Orchestral and Electronic Exchanges* (1965) for percussion and taped music.

Wuorinen has also written a great deal of chamber music, usually for an *ad hoc* group, such as his *Chamber Concerto for Flute and Ten Players* (1963), another for *Cello and Ten Players* (1963), and still another for *Tuba, with Twelve Winds and Twelve Drums.* Many of these pieces were written for and performed by the Group for Contemporary Music.

Much of Wuorinen's music is highly dissonant, polyphonic, and organized according to intricate plans that are difficult to perceive, a characteristic he shares with many of his contemporaries. To return to our simile about explorers and settlers, Wuorinen is an explorer, but he is not traveling alone because many other composers of his generation are following similar paths.

Suggested Readings

The books and journals listed in the Suggested Readings of Chapter 19 also contain information about the composers discussed in this chapter. The main sources of information besides scores and recordings are magazine articles; they can be located by using the *Music Index*.

Extended accounts of John Cage are found in Peter Yates, *Twentieth Century Music* (New York, 1967); Calvin Tomkins, *The Bride and the Bachelors* (New York, 1965); and Wilfred Mellers, *Music in a New Found Land* (London, 1964). The book *John Cage*, edited by Richard Kostelanetz (New York, 1970), is a "collection of pieces both by and about the pioneer of the contemporary avant-garde."

Elliott Carter has discussed his compositions in various publications. He talks about the Concerto for Harpsichord, Piano, and Orchestra in Hines's *The Orchestral Composer's Point of View* (Norman, Oklahoma, 1970), and about other works in Allen Edwards's *Flawed Words and Stubborn Sounds: A Conversation with Elliott Carter* (New York, 1972). The catalogue prepared for an exhibition held in the New York Public Library in 1973–1974 contains much valuable bibliographical material (New York, 1973). Boretz and Cone's *Perspectives on American Composers* (New York, 1971) contains important articles on Carter, as well as on Ives, Varèse, Sessions, Copland, Piston, and others that originally appeared in various issues of *Perspectives of New Music*.

Stockhausen has written extensive analyses of his compositions in the liner notes accompanying his Deutsche Grammophon recordings. See also: Karl H. Worner, *Stockhausen: Life and Work* (Berkeley, 1973, translation from German of 1963); Jonathan Harvey, *Stockhausen* (Berkeley, 1975), containing analyses; and an article, "Stockhausen's Writings on Music," in the *Musical Quarterly* (January 1975). Robin Maconie's *Stockhausen* (London, 1975), an exhaustive study of the man and his music, was written with the cooperation of the composer.

Two valuable books edited by Gregory Battcock and containing essays on various phases of contemporary art are *The New Art*, rev. ed. (New York, 1973) and *Minimal Art* (New York, 1968). Leonard B. Meyer's *Music, the Arts, and Ideas* (Chicago, 1967) is a masterful presentation of the state of the arts since 1950.

The Voices of East Harlem

22

Elvis Presley ripped off Ike Eisenhower by turning our uptight young awakening bodies around. Hard animal rock energy beat surged hot through us, the driving rhythm arousing repressed passions.

Jerry Rubin

Jazz and Popular Music

One of the dominant styles of the 1950s was "cool" jazz, a more refined and controlled kind of bop. Like bop, it was played by a small group of soloists, and it was also a style to be listened to, rather than danced to. In contrast to the wild melodic improvisations of the former, "cool" artists paraphrased the original tunes, often paring them down to their essentials. Restraint was also to be noted in the gentle flutes, vibraphones, fluegelhorns, French horns, and even cellos and violins that were sometimes used. The Modern Jazz Quartet and the Dave Brubeck Quartet were the best-known exponents of this style. Brubeck had studied with Darius Milhaud and the Modern Jazz Quartet members were Juilliard-trained, so they were well aware of the mainstream of music as well as of the innovations of twentieth-century music. This background is reflected in the harmony, textures, and forms they used, including rondos, fugues, and even elements of the twelve-tone style.

Rock

Cool jazz, a kind of chamber music, appealed to a relatively small, sophisticated audience. The general public—worldwide—responded to an entirely different kind of popular music in Rock and Roll, or Rock. The origins of Rock are as difficult to define as those of jazz, but rhythm and blues (an underground, black, rural style), country-Western, and folk music all contributed to it. Rock songs are all accompanied by guitar, with a strong, unrelenting beat. Elvis Presley was the first famous exponent of the style, to be followed by the Beatles, whose music, persons, and life-styles enthralled millions throughout the world.

The Beatles were twentieth-century minstrels, telling stories and commenting on social conditions in the words of their songs. They developed their own sound in which the electric guitar, electric piano, and organ, amplified to earsplitting volume, were especially important. The audio equipment of a Rock group and the sound man are essential parts of the whole; in fact, the group could not perform without them. Later, the Beatles used a surprising variety of instruments as accompaniment, including the string quartet, harpsichord, baroque trumpet, and even the sitar and tambour. The other musical elements were very simple. The melodies were often modal and folklike and the harmonies triadic.

New Wave

In spite of the popularity of Rock, the true jazz tradition continued in the sixties in the strikingly original improvisations of saxophonists such as John Coltrane, Ornette Coleman, and Sonny Rollins. Called the New Wave, this was music for small solo-oriented groups. The improvisations were even freer than those of the Bebop style, and often amounted to spontaneous compositions in which the soaring melodic lines progressed with no relationship to a previous existing melody.

Third Stream

Yet another style was the Third Stream, a conscious attempt to combine jazz with concert music, of which Gunther Schuller is the chief proponent. The merger is made in various ways, either by joining a jazz group with a symphony orchestra, in a concerto grosso manner, or by a jazz group playing concert music idioms. Two examples of Third Stream music are Rolf Liebermann's *Concerto for Jazz Band and Orchestra* (1954) and Lukas Foss's *Concerto for Improvising Solo Instruments and Orchestra* (1960).

Krzysztof Penderecki

23

The trouble with our times is that the future is not what it used to be.

Paul Valéry

Where to Now?

IN THE PRECEDING THREE CHAPTERS, the author has attempted to summarize the state of music between 1950 and 1975. The principal developments have been described, as well as the accomplishments of composers who have been especially prominent during this time. Selections were made in the hope that no significant trend or composer would be neglected, although the author is aware that other choices could have been made.

It has been shown that a great diversity of musical styles exists side by side. There are composers who are still loyal to the principles of tonality, and others who organize their compositions through the serialization of one or several of the parameters. There are composers who are content to present general musical situations and to allow their performers considerable latitude in forming a unique sequence of tone and time. Still other composers have adopted the vast sound world created by electronics; but among these there is every point of view from those who use "musical" sounds, to those who prefer the infinite variety of noise. There are also composers who use conventional instruments in new ways, so that they sound as though they are electronic.

Some composers write music to be heard in opera houses and concert halls, but others believe that a new relationship must be found between performer and audience in new surroundings. Still others believe that music should be experienced along with other sensations in multimedia productions, not in a Wagnerian *Gesamtkunstwerk* sense, in which all the arts worked together to produce a planned emotional effect, but in more casual and accidental happenings.

The music of all past periods, as well as non-Western music, has been a source of inspiration for other composers. Medieval motets, 1920s jazz, Siamese gamelans, Indian talas, indeed, even the rich tonal harmonies of the late nineteenth century are being used either in direct quotations or as styles to be imitated or parodied. Past and present have merged; any and every style is available for use.

Still other composers sacrifice melody and meter and set up monolithic blocks of continuous sound, while others create sheer time intervals, alternating sound and silence. Others write pieces consisting of units without causal relationships that can be played in random order.

Many of the composers discussed take their compositions as seriously as Beethoven did, and in them have expressed their feelings about love and death, or war and peace, and other eternal concerns. Others worry little about the communicative power of their music because of their interest in abstract structure. Still others flatly state that there is no "purpose" to music other than "purposeless play."

Pierre Boulez has perhaps taken the most decisive step to give direction to the music of the future. He has little respect for avant-garde activities, and believes that little has been accomplished since the masterpieces produced by Schoenberg, Stravinsky, Berg, and Webern before World War I.

His solution was to bring together a team of acousticians, instrument makers, electronic and computer scientists, as well as composers, to work together to create an entirely new sound world. A research institute, called the "Institut de recherche et de coordination acoustique-musical" was established in Paris in 1975, and the musical world awaits its findings with great interest.[1]

Is there no direction to all this activity, no overall pattern? Isn't it all leading someplace? Will not some composer of genius bring it all together to form a unified style that will be the basis for music of the next century?

The chances are that this will not happen. Plurality is likely to remain the normal state. Leonard Meyer has expressed this point of view very clearly in his book *Music, the Arts and Ideas* and in subsequent writings and lectures. After surveying the current situation in the sciences, the arts, and philosophy, he concludes, "Our culture—cosmopolitan world culture—is, and will continue to be, diverse and pluralistic. A multiplicity of styles, techniques, and movements, ranging from the cautiously conservative to the rampantly experimental, will exist side by side." [2]

In another context Meyer likened the current situation in the arts to a "swarm of bees, where every individual bee is flying furiously first in one direction and then in another, while the swarm as a whole is either at rest or sails slowly through the air." Meyer does not deplore this situation. "If our time appears to be one of 'crisis' it does so largely because we have misunderstood the present situation and its possible consequence. The 'crisis' dissolves when the possibility of a continuing stylistic coexistence is recognized and the delights of diversity are admitted. The question then becomes, not is this style going to be *the* style, but is this particular work of art well-made, challenging, and enjoyable."[3]

Although this is a logical point of view, it might be difficult to accept because we have been brought up to believe that there has always been a dominant "best" style in the arts that automatically puts other styles in second or third place. However, if we accept the idea that all styles are valid it doesn't mean that we like everything equally well, but it will greatly increase the possibilities of our having enjoyable experiences in the arts.

	CONSERVATIVE	SERIAL AND TOTAL CONTROL	ALEATORIC
1945	Milhaud: *Suite francaise* Shostakovich: Symphony No. 9 Britten: *Peter Grimes*	Dallapiccola: *Cinque Frammenti di Saffo*	
1946	Honegger: Symphonies No. 3 and 4 Prokofiev: Symphony No. 6 Menotti: *The Medium*	Schoenberg: String Trio	
1947	Milhaud: Symphony No. 4 Poulenc: *Calligrammes* Hindemith: Piano Concerto	Schoenberg: *A Survivor from Warsaw*	
1948	Vaughan Williams: Symphony No. 6 Piston: Symphony No. 3 (Pulitzer Prize)	Dallapiccola: *Il Prigioniero*	
1949	Blitzstein: *Regina* Thomson: *Louisiana Story* (Pulitzer Prize)	Schoenberg: *Fantasia* for Violin and Piano Babbitt: Three Compositions for Piano Messiaen: *Modes de valeurs et d'intensités*	
1950	Poulenc: Piano Concerto Menotti: *The Consul* (Pulitzer Prize) Prokofiev: Symphony No. 7		

ELECTRONIC	OTHER STYLES	OTHER ARTS, EVENTS
	Bartók: Viola Concerto (unfinished)	Hiroshima: first atomic bomb World War II ends United Nations created Rossellini: *The Open City*
	Carter: Piano Sonata	Giradoux: *The Madwoman of Chaillot*
	Sessions: Symphony No. 2 Kirchner: Duo for violin and piano Carter: The *Minotaur*	Tennessee Williams: *A Streetcar Named Desire* Camus: *The Plague*
Schaeffer: Broadcast of *"Concert of Noises"* Schaeffer: *Etudes aux chemins de fer* Schaeffer: *Etudes aux tourniquets* Schaeffer: *Etudes aux casseroles*	Carter: Woodwind Quintet	Pound: *Pisan Cantos* Breton: *Poems* Sartre: *Dirty Hands* Pollock: Number 1
Henry and Schaeffer: *Symphony for a Man Alone*		Orwell: *1984* Miller: *Death of a Salesman* T. S. Eliot: *The Cocktail Party* de Sica: *The Bicycle Thief*
Cage: Cartridge Music		Korean War begins Riesman: *The Lonely Crowd* Wilder: *Sunset Boulevard* First microgroove recordings

	CONSERVATIVE	SERIAL AND TOTAL CONTROL	ALEATORIC
1951	Honegger: Symphony No. 5 Menotti: *Amahl . . .* Stravinsky: *The Rake's Progress* Britten: *Billy Budd*	Stockhausen: *Kreuzspiel* Boulez: *Polyphonie X* Henze: *Boulevard Solitude*	Feldman: *Projections* Cage: *Music of Changes* Cage: *Imaginary Landscape* No. 4 (for 12 radios) Cage: 4′ 33″
1952	Vaughan Williams: Symphony No. 7	Boulez: *Structures* Stravinsky: *Cantata* Messiaen: *Timbres-Durées* Nono: *Epitaffio per Garcia Lorca*	Cage: *Music for Carillon*
1953	Poulenc: Sonata for Two Pianos Shostakovich: Symphony No. 10	Stockhausen: *Kontra-Punkte* Stravinsky: Septet Britten: *The Turn of the Screw* Dallapiccola: *Goethe-Lieder*	Brown: *For Piano*
1954	Milhaud: *David* Barber: *Prayers of Kierkegaard* Copland: *The Tender Land*	Dallapiccola: Variations for Orchestra Stravinsky: *In Memoriam Dylan Thomas* Maderna: *Serenade* Berio: *Nones*	
1955	Henze: *Five Neapolitan Songs*	Dallapiccola: *Canti di Liberazione*	
1956		Stravinsky: *Canticum Sacrum* Rochberg: Symphony No. 2	Stockhausen: *Zeitmasse* Stockhausen: Piano Piece XI

ELECTRONIC	OTHER STYLES	OTHER ARTS, EVENTS
Henry, P.: *Le Microphone bien tempéré*	Carter: String Quartet No. 1	
Henri: *Veil of Orpheus* Ussachevsky: *Sonic Contours* Cage: *Imaginary Landscape* No. 5	Ginastera: Piano Sonata	Beckett: *Waiting for Godot* De Kooning: first of "Women" portraits
Stockhausen: *Electronic Studies*		Robbe-Grillet: *The Erasers*
Varèse: *Déserts* Leuning and Ussachevsky: *Poem of Cycles and Bells* for Tape and Orchestra	Bennett: Piano Sonata	Dylan Thomas: *Under Milk Wood* Hydrogen bomb perfected
Stockhausen: *Gesang der Jünglinge* le Caine: *Dripsody*	Carter: Variations for Orchestra	Rauschenberg: *Bed*
	Xenakis: *Pithoprakta*	Eugene O'Neill awarded Pulitzer Prize (posthumously) for *Long Day's Journey Into Night* Fellini: *La Strada*

	CONSERVATIVE	SERIAL AND TOTAL CONTROL	ALEATORIC
1957	Poulenc: *Dialogues des Carmélites*	Stravinsky: *Agon* Copland: *Fantasy* Dallapiccola: *Christmas Concert*	Boulez: Sonata No. 3 Stockhausen: *Klavierstück XI*
1958	Barber: *Vanessa*	Stravinsky: *Threni* Lutoslawski: *Trauermusik*	Cage: Concert for Piano and Orchestra Stockhausen: *Gruppen*
1959	Shostakovich: Cello Concerto in E♭ Britten: *Noye's Fludde*	Stravinsky: *Movements* Sessions: Violin Concerto Rochberg: Symphony No. 2	Cage: *Aria* Stockhausen: *Refrain* Bussotti: *Five Pieces for David Tudor*
1960	Milhaud: *Bar Mitzvah Cantata*	Stravinsky: *A Sermon, A Narrative and a Prayer* Babbitt: Composition for Tenor and Six Instruments	
1961	Shostakovich: Symphony No. 12 Britten: *A Midsummer Night's Dream* Henze: *Elegy for Young Lovers*		Wolff: *The Swallows of Salagan* Brown: *Available Forms* No. 1 Ashley: *Public Opinion Descends Upon the Demonstrators* Berio: *Circles*

ELECTRONIC	OTHER STYLES	OTHER ARTS, EVENTS
Ussachevsky: *Metamorphosis* Hiller: *Illiac Suite*	Xenakis: *Achorripsis*	Sputnik launched by USSR Camus awarded Nobel Prize for literature
Cage: *Fontana Mix* Varèse: *Poème électronique* Boulez: *Poésie pour pouvoir* Berio: *Ommagio a Joyce*	Penderecki: *Psalms of David*	MacLeish: *J. B.* Williams: *Sweet Bird of Youth* Bergman: *The Seventh Seal* Mies van der Rohe, Seagram Building, N.Y.
Kagel: *Transiçion*	Carter: String Quartet No. 2	Fidel Castro seizes power in Cuba Moon rocket successfully launched by USSR Frank Lloyd Wright: Guggenheim Museum, New York
Berio: *Visages* Stockhausen: *Kontakte*	Penderecki: *Anaklasis* Ginastera: *Cantata para America Magica*	The "pill" approved for use J. F. Kennedy elected President Albee: *The Zoo Story* Ionesco: *Rhinoceros*
Babbitt: *Vision and Prayer* Pousseur: *Les Perses*	Lutoslawski: *Venetian Games* Penderecki: *Threnody for the Victims of Hiroshima* Carter: Double Concerto	Major Gagarin, USSR cosmonaut, first man to orbit the earth Berlin Wall built Museum of Modern Art Assemblages Exhibition Resnais: *Last Year at Marienbad* Fellini: *La Dolce Vita*

	CONSERVATIVE	SERIAL AND TOTAL CONTROL	ALEATORIC
1962	Britten: *War Requiem* Barber: Piano Concerto	Stravinsky: *The Flood* Fine: Symphony	Brown: *Available Forms II* Mumma: *Gestures* No. 2
1963	Bennett: *The Mines of Sulphur*	Stravinsky: *Abraham and Isaac; Elegy for J.F.K.* Copland: *Connotations*	Feldman: *Vertical Thoughts* Xenakis: *Strategie*
1964	Henze: *Der Junge Lord*	Sessions: Symphony No. 5 Finney: *Divertissement*	Boulez: *Figures; Doubles Prismes* Wolff: Septet Riley: In C
1965	Hanson: Psalm 46 Britten: Symphony for Violoncello and Orchestra Henze: *The Bassarids*	de la Vega: *Exametron* Dallapicolla: *Parole di San Paolo*	Stockhausen: *Momente*
1966	Britten: *The Burning Fiery Furnace* Barber: *Anthony and Cleopatra*		Stockhausen: *Hymnen*
1967		Stravinsky: *Requiem Canticles* Copland: *Inscape* Wuorinen: Duo for Violin and Piano	Schwartz: *Elevator Music* Pousseur: *Votre Faust*

ELECTRONIC	OTHER STYLES	OTHER ARTS, EVENTS
Davidovsky: *Electronic Study* No. 2 Schaeffer: *Haiku*	Penderecki: *Fluorescences*	Cuban Crisis Albee: *Who's Afraid of Virginia Woolf?* Robert Rauschenberg: "Pop art"
Blacher: *Elektronische Studie* Amy: *La Femme sauvage*	Penderecki: *Stabat Mater* Lutoslawski: *Three Poems by Henri Michaux*	J. F. Kennedy assassinated Op art Robbe-Grillet: *le Chosisme* Fellini: 8½
Babbitt: *Philomel* for Voice and Electronic Sound Henry: Variations	Ginastera: *Don Rodrigo* Xenakis: *Eonta*	L. B. Johnson elected President Vietnam War Marcuse: *One Dimensional Man* MacLuhan: *Understanding Media*
Stockhausen: *Mikrophonie* Wuorinen: *Orchestral and Electronic Exchanges*	Carter: Piano Concerto Crumb: *Eleven Echoes*	L. B. Johnson inaugurated President Grissom and Young orbit earth three times Selma, Alabama, protest march
Reich: *Come Out* Oliveros: *I of IV*	Penderecki: *St. Luke Passion* Xenakis: *Terretiktohr* Rochberg: *Nach Bach*	Whitney Museum: exhibition of minimal sculpture New Metropolitan Opera House opens, N.Y.
Subotnik: *Silver Apples of the Moon* Stockhausen: *Prozession*	Ginastera: *Bomarzo* Penderecki: *Dies Irae* Musgrave: *Music for Orchestra*	First transplant of human heart Jackson Pollock: retrospective show Mike Nichols: *The Graduate*

	CONSERVATIVE	SERIAL AND TOTAL CONTROL	ALEATORIC
1968	Britten: *The Prodigal Son* Shostakovich: String Quartet No. 12	Dallapiccola: *Odysseus* Babbitt: *Relata*	Bussotti: *Passion According to Sade* Bussotti: *Instrumental Theater*
1969	Shostakovich: Symphony No. 14		Cage and Hiller: *HPSCHD*
1970	Ginastera: *Beatrix Cenci* Britten: *Owen Wingrave* Piston: Fantasia for Violin	Sessions: *Rhapsody*	Cardew: *The Great Learning*
1971	Bernstein: *Mass* Britten: *Journey of the Magi* von Einem: *Visit of the Old Lady* Ginastera: *Milena*	Sessions: Concerto for Violin, Cello and Orchestra	Cardew: *Composition for Scratch Orchestra* Feldman: *The Rothko Chapel*
1972	Shostakovich: Symphony No. 15 Tippett: Symphony No. 3	Sessions: Concertino for Chamber Orchestra	
1973	Britten: *Death in Venice*	Babbitt: Two Sonnets	Stockhausen: *Musik für ein Haus*

ELECTRONIC	OTHER STYLES	OTHER ARTS, EVENTS
Reich: *Pendulum Music*	Penderecki: *Capriccio* for Violin and Orchestra Ginastera: Cello Concerto Berio: *Sinfonia*	Robert Kennedy and Martin Luther King assassinated Nixon elected President Columbia University student revolt *Hair*
Stockhausen: *Telemusik*	Carter: Concerto for Orchestra Henze: *The Raft of Medusa* Lutoslawski: Symphony No. 2 Penderecki: *Slavic Mass*	First moon landing Harvard and Cornell student revolts Woodstock Festival draws crowd of 400,000 *Oh! Calcutta!*
Stockhausen: *Mantra* Wuorinen: *Times Encomium* (Pulitzer Prize)	Henze: *El Cimarron* Reich: *Four Organs* Crumb: *Ancient Voices of Children*	U.S. troops to Cambodia Kent State conflict Exhibition of Conceptual Art, N.Y.
Lucier: *The Duke of York* (voice and synthesizer) Wuorinen: Concerto for Amplified Violin Davidovsky: Synchronism No. 6 for Piano and Tape (Pulitzer Prize)	Ligeti: *Melodien* Berio: *Bewegung* Carter: String Quartet No. 3 Reich: *Drumming*	Moon explorations Exhibition of antiobject art, Boston
Stockhausen: *Momente* (completed)	Crumb: *Makrokosmos I* Druckman: *Windows* (Pulitzer Prize) Rochberg: Quartet No. 3	Richard Nixon renominated Christo: *Valley Curtain* hung in Rifle, Colo.
Wuorinen: Concerto for Amplified Piano Druckman: Woodwind Quintet and Tape	Crumb: *Makrokosmos II* Berio: Concerto for Two Pianos Davies: *Runes from a House of the Dead* Reich: *Music for Pieces of Wood*	Richard Nixon reelected

	CONSERVATIVE	SERIAL AND TOTAL CONTROL	ALEATORIC
1974	Rochberg: Violin Concerto Martino: *Notturno* (Pulitzer Prize)		
1975	Argento: *From the Diary of Virginia Woolf* (Pulitzer Prize)		Felciano: *The Angel of Turtle Island* Glass: *Einstein on the beach* Cage: *Renga*

ELECTRONIC	OTHER STYLES	OTHER ARTS, EVENTS
Felciano: *Background Music for Harp and Electronics* Berio: *Per la Dolce Memoria* (ballet)	Crumb: *Music for a Summer Evening* Wuorinen: *The W. of Babylon* Carter: Quintet for Brass Instruments	Watergate hearings Richard Nixon resigns Gerald Ford inaugurated President
	Wuorinen: *A Reliquary for I.S.* Ligeti: *San Francisco Polyphony* Carter: Duo for Violin and Piano Henze: *The River* (opera)	End of Vietnam war Energy crisis "New Realists" in painting

References

CHAPTER 2

1. Léon Vallas, *Claude Debussy, His Life and Works* (London: Oxford University Press, 1951), p. 86.
2. Oscar Thompson, *Debussy, Man and Artist* (Dodd, Mead & Co., 1937), p. 103.

CHAPTER 3

1. Ralph Vaughan Williams, "Musical Autobiography," in Hubert Foss, *Ralph Vaughan Williams* (New York: Oxford University Press, 1950), p. 35.
2. Igor Stravinsky and Robert Craft, *Expositions and Developments* (Garden City: Doubleday & Co., Inc., 1962), p. 161.

CHAPTER 4

1. Bruno Walter and Ernst Krenek, *Gustav Mahler* (New York: The Greystone Press, 1941), pp. 198–99.
2. Arnold Schoenberg, "My Evolution," *Musical Quarterly,* 38 (October 1952), p. 518.
3. Arnold Schoenberg, *Style and Idea* (New York: Philosophical Library, 1950), p. 8.
4. *Ibid.*, p. 13.

5. Schoenberg, "My Evolution," p. 518.
6. Schoenberg, *Style and Idea,* p. 5.
7. *Ibid.,* p. 105.
8. Arnold Schoenberg, *Die glückliche Hand* (Vienna: Universal Edition, 1923).
9. Mark Van Doren, ed., *An Anthology of World Poetry* (New York: Reynal & Hitchcock, 1928), p. 45.
10. James Huneker, *Ivory, Apes and Peacocks* (New York: Charles Scribner's Sons, 1925), p. 93.
11. Igor Stravinsky, *An Autobiography* (New York: Simon and Schuster, 1936), p. 67.

CHAPTER 5

1. Charles Ives, *Second Pianoforte Sonata, Concord, Mass., 1840–1860* (New York: Arrow Music Press, Inc., 1947), preface.
2. Charles Ives, Symphony No. 4 (New York, Associated Music Publishers, Inc., 1965), preface.
3. Charles Ives, *The Unanswered Question, a cosmic landscape* (New York: Southern Music Publishers, Inc., 1942), preface.
4. Charles Ives, *114 Songs* (privately printed, 1922), preface; new edition (New York: Associated Music Publishers; Peer International Corp.; Bryn Mawr, Pa.: Theodore Presser Co., 1975).

CHAPTER 7

1. Nicolas Slonimsky, *Music Since 1900* (Boston: Coleman-Ross Company, 1949), p. 642.

CHAPTER 8

1. Darius Milhaud, *Notes Without Music* (London: Dennis Dobson, Ltd., 1952), p. 85.
2. Jean Cocteau, *Cock and Harlequin,* Rollo Myers, trans. (London: The Egoist Press, 1921), pp. 4 ff.
3. Rollo H. Myers, *Erik Satie* (London: Dennis Dobson, Ltd., 1948), p. 60.
4. Cocteau, *op. cit.,* p. 6.
5. *Ibid.,* p. 8.
6. Paul Collaer, *La Musique moderne* (Paris: Elsevier, 1955), p. 156.
7. Milhaud, *op. cit.,* p. 82.
8. Milhaud, *op. cit.,* p. 87.

CHAPTER 9

1. Milhaud, *Notes Without Music,* p. 117.
2. Milhaud, *Les Choëphores* (Paris: Heugel & Cie., 1947), preface.
3. Milhaud, *Notes Without Music,* p. 127.
4. *Ibid.,* p. 130.
5. Arthur Honegger, *Je suis compositeur* (Paris: Editions du Conquistador, 1951), p. 32.
6. *Ibid.,* p. 15.
7. *Ibid.,* p. 25.
8. *Ibid.,* p. 117.

CHAPTER 10

1. Stravinsky, *The Poetics of Music* (Cambridge, Mass.: Harvard University Press, 1947), p. 83.
2. Alexandre Tansman, *Igor Stravinsky* (New York: G. P. Putnam's Sons, 1949), p. 9.
3. Stravinsky, *The Poetics of Music,* p. 52.
4. *Ibid.,* p. 54.
5. *Ibid.,* p. 67.
6. Eric White, *Stravinsky* (London: John Lehmann, 1947), p. 63.
7. Stravinsky, *An Autobiography,* p. 128.
8. Heinrich Strobel, "Igor Stravinsky," *Melos* 2 (January 1921), p. 40.

9. Stravinsky, *An Autobiography,* p. 162.
10. Walter Piston, "Stravinsky's Rediscoveries," in Minna Lederman, ed., *Stravinsky in the Theatre* (New York: Pellegrini & Cudahy, 1949), p. 130.

CHAPTER 11

1. Anton Webern, "Homage to Arnold Schoenberg," *Die Reihe,* 2 (1958), p. 9.
2. Schoenberg, *Style and Idea,* p. 107.
3. René Leibowitz, *Introduction à la musique de douze sons* (Paris: L'Arche, 1949), pp. 111 ff.

CHAPTER 12

1. Stravinsky and Craft, *Conversations with Igor Stravinsky,* p. 81.
2. *Ibid.,* p. 82.
3. T. S. Eliot, "The Hollow Men," *Collected Poems, 1909–1935* (New York: Harcourt, Brace & Co., Inc., 1934, 1936), p. 105.
4. Norman Demuth, *Musical Trends in the 20th Century* (London: Rockliff Publishing Corp., Ltd., 1952), p. 242.
5. René Leibowitz, *Schoenberg and His School* (New York: Philosophical Library, 1949), p. 190.
6. Stravinsky and Craft, *op. cit.,* p. 136.
7. Sheldon Cheney, *The Story of Modern Art* (New York: The Viking Press, 1941), p. 474.

CHAPTER 14

1. Paul Hindemith, *1922,* piano suite (Mainz: B. Schott's Sohne, 1922).
2. Hindemith, *A Composer's World* (Cambridge, Mass.: Harvard University Press, 1952), p. 120.

CHAPTER 15

1. *New York Times,* April 1, 1937, p. 20.

CHAPTER 16

1. Ralph Vaughan Williams, "Musical Autobiography," in Hubert Foss, *Ralph Vaughan Williams,* p. 24.
2. *Ibid.,* p. 23.
3. Hans Keller, "The Musical Character," in Donald Mitchell and Hans Keller, eds., *Benjamin Britten* (New York: Philosophical Library, 1953), p. 319.
4. Joseph Kerman, *Opera as Drama* (New York: Alfred A. Knopf, Inc., 1956), p. 230.
5. "Profile—Benjamin Britten," *Observer* (London), October 27, 1946. Quoted in Mitchell and Keller, p. 37.

CHAPTER 17

1. *New York Times,* January 12, 1925, p. 27. Quoted in Julia Smith, *Aaron Copland* (New York: E. P. Dutton & Co., Inc., 1955), p. 74.
2. Smith, *op. cit.*
3. Arthur Berger, *Aaron Copland* (New York: Oxford University Press, 1953), p. 52.
4. Paul Rosenfeld, *One Hour with American Music* (Philadelphia: J. B. Lippincott Co., 1929), p. 129.
5. "Roger Sessions," in Henry Cowell, ed., *American Composers On American Music* (Palo Alto, Calif.: Stanford University Press, 1933), p. 78.
6. Three volumes of Thomson's critiques have been published: *The Musical Scene* (New York: Alfred A. Knopf, Inc., 1945); *The Art of Judging Music* (New York: Alfred A. Knopf, Inc., 1948); *Music,*

Right and Left (New York: Henry Holt & Co., 1951).

CHAPTER 18

1. John Cage, "Edgard Varèse," *Nutida Musik* (Stockholm, Fall 1958), reprinted in John Cage, *Silence* (Middletown, Conn.: Wesleyan University Press, 1961), p. 83.
2. Harry Partch, *Genesis of a Music* (Madison, Wis.: University of Wisconsin Press, 1949), preface.

CHAPTER 20

1. John Amis, "The Salzburg Seminar," *Tempo*, Vol. 18 (Winter 1950–1951), p. 31.
2. Leonard Burkat, "Current Chronicle," *Musical Quarterly*, Vol. XXXIV, No. 2 (April 1948), p. 249.
3. Luigi Dallapiccola, "On the Twelve-Note Road," *Music Survey*, (October 1951).
4. Edward T. Cone, "Conversation with Aaron Copland," *Perspectives on American Composers* (New York: W. W. Norton and Co., Inc., 1971), p. 141.
5. Kurt Stone, "Current Chronicle," *Musical Quarterly*, Vol. LI, No. 4 (October 1965), p. 690.
6. Pierre Boulez, "Schoenberg Is Dead," *Score*, No. 6 (May 1952), p. 30.
7. Karlheinz Stockhausen, liner notes to RCA VICS-1239.
8. Edward Helm, "Report from Darmstadt, 1959," *Musical Quarterly*, Vol. XLVI, No. 1 (January 1959), p. 103.
9. H. Wiley Hitchcock, "Current Chronicle," *Musical Quarterly*, Vol. L, No. 1 (January 1964), p. 91.
10. Karl H. Worner, "Current Chronicle," *Musical Quarterly*, Vol. XLV (April 1959), p. 240.
11. Louis Christensen, "An Introduction to the Music of György Ligeti," *Numus West* (February 1972), p. 7.
12. Ad Reinhardt, "Writings," *The New Art* (New York: E. P. Dutton and Co., Inc., 1966), p. 200.
13. Christian Wolff, Copyright, 1968–1969.

CHAPTER 21

1. Peter Yates, *Twentieth Century Music* (New York: Pantheon Books, 1967), p. 310.
2. John Cage, *Silence* (Middletown, Conn.: Wesleyan University Press, 1961), p. 12.
3. Wilfred Mellers, *Music in a New Found Land* (London: Barrie and Rockliff, 1964), p. 187.
4. Calvin Tomkins, *The Bride and the Bachelors* (New York: The Viking Press, 1965), p. 73.
5. Karl Worner, *Stockhausen* (Berkeley: University of California Press, 1973), p. 58.
6. Antoine Golea, *Rencontres avec Pierre Boulez* (Paris: Julliard, 1958), pp. 241–245.
7. Luciano Berio, liner notes to Columbia record MS-7268.
8. Kurt Stone, "Current Chronicle," *Musical Quarterly*, Vol. L, No. 2 (April 1964), p. 265.
9. Ates Orga, "Penderecki, Composer of Martyrdom," *Music and Musicians*, Vol. 18, No. 1 (September 1969), p. 35.
10. Peter Maxwell Davies, in *Tempo*, 105 (June 1973), p. 36.
11. Elliott Carter, liner notes to RCA record LSC-3001.
12. Elliott Carter, directions to performers in the score.
13. Elliott Carter, liner notes to Columbia record M-30112.
14. Elliott Carter, liner notes to Nonesuch record H-71314.

15. George Crumb, liner notes to Nonesuch record H-71255.
16. George Rochberg, liner notes to Nonesuch record H-71283.

CHAPTER 23

1. For further information concerning the *Institut* see Peter Heyworth: "Boulez at Beaubourg" in *Saturday Review*, October 18, 1975, p. 65.
2. Leonard Meyer, *Music, the Arts, and Ideas* (Chicago: The University of Chicago Press, 1967), p. 156.
3. *Ibid.*, p. 172.

Composers*

* Listed by years of birth; capitalized composers are discussed in the text.

1860 Gustave Charpentier
Gustav Mahler

1861 Edward MacDowell

1862 CLAUDE DEBUSSY
Frederick Delius

1864 Richard Strauss

1865 Paul Dukas
Alexander Glazunov
Carl Nielsen
Jean Sibelius

1866 ERIK SATIE

1869 Hans Pfitzner
Albert Roussel

1872 Hugo Alfvén
Alexander Scriabin
RALPH VAUGHAN WILLIAMS

1873 Sergey Rachmaninoff

1874 Gustav Holst
CHARLES IVES
ARNOLD SCHOENBERG
Josef Suk

1875 Reinhold Glière
MAURICE RAVEL

1876 Franco Alfano
Manuel de Falla
Carl Ruggles

1879 John Ireland
Ottorino Respighi
Cyril Scott

1880 Idlebrando Pizzetti

1881 BÉLA BARTÓK
Sem Dresden
Nikolai Miaskovsky

1882 Zoltán Kodály
Gian Francesco Malipiero
IGOR STRAVINSKY
Karol Szymanowski
Joaquín Turina

1883 Arnold Bax
Alfredo Casella
ANTON VON WEBERN

1885 ALBAN BERG
Wallingford Riegger
EDGARD VARÈSE

1887 Heitor Villa-Lobos

1890 Jacques Ibert
Frank Martin
Bohuslav Martinu

1891 SERGE PROKOFIEV

1892 ARTHUR HONEGGER
DARIUS MILHAUD

1893 Douglas Moore
1894 Willem Pijper
WALTER PISTON
1895 PAUL HINDEMITH
Carl Orff
1896 HOWARD HANSON
ROGER SESSIONS
VIRGIL THOMSON
1897 Henry Cowell
1898 George Gershwin
ROY HARRIS
1899 Georges Auric
Carlos Chávez
FRANCIS POULENC
Silvestre Revueltas
Randall Thompson
1900 George Antheil
AARON COPLAND
Ernst Krenek
Otto Luening
Kurt Weill
1901 Conrad Beck
Raymond Chevreuille
HARRY PARTCH
Marcel Poot
Edmund Rubbra
Henri Sauguet
1902 William Walton
1903 Aram Khachaturian
1904 LUIGI DALLAPICCOLA
Dmitri Kabalevsky
Goffredo Petrassi
Nikos Skalkottas
1905 Alan Rawsthorne
MICHAEL TIPPETT
Dag Wirén
1906 Paul Creston
Ross Lee Finney
DMITRI SHOSTAKOVICH
1907 Henk Badings
Camargo Guarnieri
1908 ELLIOTT CARTER
OLIVIER MESSIAEN
1910 SAMUEL BARBER
Rolf Liebermann
Mario Peragallo
William Schuman
Heinrich Sutermeister
1911 Alan Hovhaness
Gian Carlo Menotti
1912 JOHN CAGE
Jean Françaix
1913 Henry Brant
BENJAMIN BRITTEN
Norman Dello Joio
WITOLD LUTOSLAWSKI
1915 Robert Palmer
Vincent Persichetti
Humphrey Searle
1916 MILTON BABBITT
ALBERTO GINASTERA
1917 Lou Harrison
1918 Leonard Bernstein
Gottfried von Einem
GEORGE ROCHBERG
1919 Leon Kirchner
1920 Paul Fetler
Peter Racine Fricker
Bruno Maderna
Harold Shapero
1921 William Bergsma
Andrew Imbrie
Ralph Shapey
1922 Robert Evett
Lukas Foss
YANNIS XENAKIS
1923 Chou Wen-Chung
GYÖRGY LIGETI
Peter Mennin
Ned Rorem
1924 Lejaren Hiller
Billy Jim Layton
Luigi Nono
Robert Parriss
1925 LUCIANO BERIO
PIERRE BOULEZ
Giselher Klebe
Gunther Schuller
1926 Earle Brown
Barney Childs
Morton Feldman
HANS WERNER HENZE
1927 Dominick Argento
Kenneth Gaburo
1928 Tadeusz Baird
Jacob Druckman
Robert Helps
Thea Musgrave
KARLHEINZ STOCKHAUSEN

1929 GEORGE CRUMB
Toshiro Mayuzumi
HENRI POUSSEUR

1930 Robert Ashley
Larry Austin
David Burge
Christobal Halffter
Gilbert Trythall

1931 Sylvano Bussotti
Mauricio Kagel
Donald Martino

1932 Michael Colgrass
Pauline Oliveros

1933 KRZYSZTOF PENDERECKI
Morton Subotnick

1934 HARRISON BIRTWISTLE
Mario Davidovsky
PETER MAXWELL DAVIES
Christian Wolff

1935 Gordon Mumma
Terry Riley

1936 Gilbert Amy
Richard Rodney Bennett
Cornelius Cardew
Steve Reich

1937 David Del Tredici

1938 William Bolcom
Jean-Claude Eloy
Yuji Takahashi
CHARLES WUORINEN

1939 Max Neuhaus

1942 Charles Dodge

Index